WEST COAST MAIN LINES
1957–1963

WEST COAST
MAIN LINES
1957–1963

JOHN PALMER

PEN & SWORD
TRANSPORT
AN IMPRINT OF PEN & SWORD BOOKS LTD.
YORKSHIRE · PHILADELPHIA

First published in Great Britain in 2022 by
Pen and Sword Transport
An imprint of
Pen & Sword Books Ltd.
Yorkshire - Philadelphia

ISBN 978 1 52679 182 5

Typeset in 10.5/12.5 pt Times New Roman
by SJmagic DESIGN SERVICES, India.
Printed and bound in India by Replika Press Pvt. Ltd.

Pen & Sword Books Ltd incorporates the imprints of Pen & Sword Books Archaeology, Atlas, Aviation, Battleground, Discovery, Family History, History, Maritime, Military, Naval, Politics, Railways, Select, Transport, True Crime, Fiction, Frontline Books, Leo Cooper, Praetorian Press, Seaforth Publishing, Wharncliffe and White Owl.

For a complete list of Pen & Sword titles please contact

PEN & SWORD BOOKS LIMITED
47 Church Street, Barnsley, South Yorkshire, S70 2AS, England
E-mail: enquiries@pen-and-sword.co.uk
Website: www.pen-and-sword.co.uk

Or

PEN AND SWORD BOOKS
1950 Lawrence Rd, Havertown, PA 19083, USA
E-mail: Uspen-and-sword@casematepublishers.com
Website: www.penandswordbooks.com

Contents

Acknowledgements

Much of the research for the content of this book was undertaken in the months just prior to the outbreak of the global pandemic. The availability of the outputs from that research then enabled a lengthy period of reflection and pleasurable writing while the world learned how to cope with a new danger. The research involved many visits to the Search Engine at the National Railway Museum, the National Archives at Kew and the British Newspaper Library; my thanks to the staff there for help and assistance.

An early interest in railways is often carried through life and, for me and many readers, the events as described in the book will recall many happy memories of the route of interest. Amongst those who have been absorbed by railways is Steve Leyland who has happily given up time to respond to my requests and his knowledge and help is appreciated. He spent some time working with the railways, as did another gentleman – Ron Herbert – who has provided a great deal of information about the difficult years of transition from steam to diesel in the north-west of England.

The written work is supported by the use of photographs and, in addition to the commercial providers, I would like to thank John Carter for further use of some of his collection and to Dick Manton for transferring John's work into modern technology format. Thanks also to David Coverley and Phil Waterfield who have supplied some images taken in more recent times. Thanks also to David Knapman who has helped with the process and provided images.

The photographs used in this book are credited as follows and with each provider retaining copyright:

Blenkinsop, Richard J.	12
BR	31, 41, 61
Carter, John	11, 21, 22, 34, 74-78
Coverley, David	85
Kidderminster Railway Museum	49
Knapman, David J.	15, 66, 86
Palmer, John	2, 19, 27, 30, 32, 35-38, 40, 42, 54, 60, 62-65, 67, 82, 83, 87, 88
Rail On-line	25, 29, 47, 73, 80
Rail On-line/Rail Archive Stephenson	4, 7-9, 13, 28, 33, 39, 43, 44, 46, 48, 50, 51, 58, 68-72
Rail Photoprints	1, 3, 5, 10, 16-18, 20, 23, 24, 26, 45, 52, 53, 55, 56, 59, 79, 81
Real Photographs Ltd*	14
Unknown	57
Waterfield, Philip	6, 84

Finally, I would like to thank Karen Proudler for taking on the typing of a third manuscript of mine and having the patience and skill to make it more readable.

---

* The author acknowledges that copyright is held by the company, but has been unable to identify the successors in title.

Glossary of Terms

ASLEF	Associated Society of Locomotive Engineers and Firemen
backhead	rear-most part of firebox with control fittings
balanced working	scheduled outward working with a scheduled return working
banker	locomotive to assist trains up adverse gradients
BR7	*Britannia* Class
BRB	British Railways Board
BTC	British Transport Commission
CHR	Chester and Holyhead Railway
CLC	Cheshire Lines Committee
CME	Chief Mechanical Engineer
CTCC	Central Transport Users Committee
CR	Caledonian Railway
cyclic	working arrangements for locomotives spread over several days
damper	method of controlling flow of air
diagrams/turns	working arrangements for locomotives
down	direction of travel and/or men away from London
ecs	empty coaching stock
EE	English Electric company
fitted goods	goods train having some or all vehicles fitted with vacuum brakes
FL	Full Load basis for timing in a timetable
GER	Great Eastern Railway
GJR	Grand Junction Railway
GNR	Great Northern Railway
GSWR	Glasgow and South Western Railway
GWR	Great Western Railway
HMR	Huddersfield and Manchester Railway
L&MR	Liverpool and Manchester Railway
LBR	London and Birmingham Railway
LCR	Lancaster and Carlisle Railway
links	arrangement of enginemen based upon route knowledge
LL	Limited Lead basis for timing in a timetable
LMA	Locomotive Manufacturers' Association
LMR	London Midland Region
LMS	London Midland & Scottish Railway
LNER	London and North Eastern Railway
LNWR	London and North Western Railway
L&PJR	Lancaster & Preston Junction Railway
LYR	Lancashire and Yorkshire Railway
MBR	Manchester and Birmingham Railway

MR	Midland Railway
MS&LR	Manchester, Sheffield & Lincolnshire Railway (later Great Central Railway)
MT	mixed traffic (passenger and goods)
NB	North British
NBL	North British Locomotive Co Ltd
NER	North Eastern Railway
NSR	North Staffordshire Railway
NUR	National Union of Railwaymen
outshopped	locomotive/vehicle completed in a works and released for traffic
pilotman	engineman with knowledge of a route to assist driver who does not
PWR	Preston and Wyre Railway
Q	train that was run only if required
RE	Railway Executive
reverser	driver control to adjust rate of steam entering valves/cylinders
Sectional Council	forum for meeting between management and representatives of particular groups within the workforce
Shopping Bureau	office of CME that determined the input of locomotives into works
Shopping Proposal	form submitted by shedmaster describing condition of locomotive and mileage run with a request for a works repair
SL	Special Limit basis of timing in a timetable
sparks effect	the relative attraction to commuters of an electrified railway
STN	Special Traffic Notice issued weekly to advise changes to arrangements for following period
superheating	method of passing saturated steam under pressure through flue tubes allowing efficiency of steam to increase
TSSA	Transport Salaried Staffs Association
TUCC	Transport Users Consultative Committee
TVR	Trent Valley Railway
up	direction of travel towards London or as defined locally for east-west
washing out	periodic cleaning out of scale and impurities in boilers
working timetable	internal use timetable showing detailed workings at junctions and restrictions applicable
XL	XLimit basis of timing in a timetable
12/15	railway operating method at indicating times between midday and midnight

Listing of Maps

To assist the understanding of the manuscript, a selection of maps has been included. The maps cover the main route of interest in general, centre areas and traffic centres in detail and include station layouts.

Preface

In 2016 Pen & Sword Books Ltd published a book titled *Midland Main Lines to St Pancras 1957-1963*. This book is a companion to it and pursues a similar style for the same period of change and capital investment. Where the two volumes differ is that the route mileage covered here is greater, the traffic flows more varied and the operational challenges were different, though certainly no less interesting.

During the time period covered by the book, lives were being transformed; rationing was at an end, the general population lived in an era of peace and relative prosperity, family holidays at the coasts were extremely popular and the development of the electricity industry brought to many better lighting, heating and the availability of household appliances such as refrigerators and televisions. Ownership of private cars was growing rapidly and, with the growth of the road haulage industry encouraged by the Transport Act 1953, the railways were facing an era of competition. That the railways were not so well prepared to meet that competition resulted from internal, organisational matters which arose after nationalisation under the Transport Act 1947 and a need for capital investment that was several years overdue. Cleaner industries were attracting from the railways artisan staff who no longer needed the unsocial hours of working in a generally dirty environment. Challenges for railway management included modernisation with diesel and electric traction, improvements to the infrastructure, a need for fewer footplate staff, retraining and new methods of working, redundancy for some, opportunities for others, traffic flows to protect, new flows to pursue, competition from road and air to be challenged.

Improvements would include safety by means of an automatic warning system on all types of traction, an extension of fast goods trains fitted with a continuous braking system, the use of welded sections of track, an extension of colour light signalling and a major electrification scheme linking the three most populated cities in England. The Modernisation Plan of 1955 – some £1.2 billion worth of capital investment – had been accepted by the Conservative government in the expectation that it would enable the British Transport Commission (BTC) to restore its business fortunes.

The Transport Act 1953 had made it clear that the role of the BTC included that it must provide railway services for Great Britain. The word 'for' was of particular relevance as it replaced the expression 'within Great Britain' in the 1947 Act. The 1953 Act went on to state that 'In performing … duties the Commission must have regard to efficiency, economy and safety of operation and to the needs of the public, agriculture, commerce and industry'. In practice that meant meeting the peaks and troughs of demand for passengers, goods and of being a common carrier (i.e. obliged to convey what it was offered and being available on every day and night of the year).

The book starts with a review of the origins of the routes of interest and the main characteristics of each. However, it does not attempt a history of the very fine railway company that was the London and North Western Railway (LNWR) and seeks only to identify the strength of that Company in the period to 1922 when it formed part of the London Midland and Scottish Railway (LMS).

The following chapter sets the scene for the review, year by year, of what was a fascinating period of change.

I feel that I was fortunate to have been born into an extended railway family, to have been brought up living close to the ever-changing railway and to have enjoyed a career of almost 40 years within the railway industry. Not only did I benefit from a rewarding career, my work was very closely linked to a deep interest in all things railway at home and overseas which has sustained me now through years of contented retirement.

I do have to declare at this early stage that I was born in Derby and hope that will not be held against me by any still promoting the Crewe and Euston ways.

My exposure to the LNW main lines started with loco spotting trips to Tamworth – a very popular place for Derby lads – Lichfield and Crewe. The father of a school friend was involved with the planning of power stations and frequent trips to Rugeley were enjoyed. My father was something of an understated enthusiast and, despite his employment with the railways keeping him away from home for too long, he found time and patience to take me to the London termini. A typical long day was Derby to London, mid-morning departures and arrivals at Paddington, quick visit to Waterloo, mid-afternoon to Euston for the departure of *The Caledonian* to Glasgow, King's Cross for the 5-6pm rush and finally back to Derby.

For a boy brought up watching short passenger trains over the steeply graded Derby-Manchester (Central) route, the fascination of the LNW lines included the vast length of passenger trains – sometimes 16 or 17 carriages – the powerful and impressive locomotives, the speed of the trains and what seemed like efficient operation.

I guess that many readers will still remember very clearly the excitement of railways in the late 1950s/early 1960s and I hope that this book will recall happy days at the lineside and maybe answer a few questions along the way.

John Palmer
Allestree, Derby
2022

Map 1: The Routes of Interest

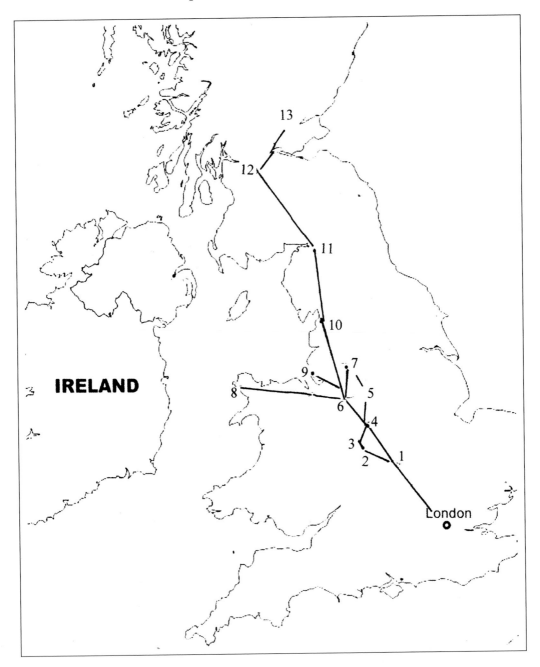

Key

1 Rugby	6 Crewe	11 Carlisle
2 Birmingham New Street	7 Manchester London Road	12 Glasgow Central
3 Wolverhampton High Level	8 Holyhead	13 Perth
4 Stafford	9 Liverpool Lime Street	
5 Stoke-on-Trent	10 Preston	

Chapter 1

Origins and Characteristics

The LNWR was formed in 1846 out of three railway companies: the Manchester and Birmingham (MBR), the Grand Junction (GJR) and the London and Birmingham (LBR). At the time of the amalgamation, each of the three companies contributed sections of track that, in total, provided most of the routes of prime interest to this book. Those sections were:

- London (Euston) to Birmingham via Rugby (LBR)
- Birmingham to near Warrington via Wolverhampton, Stafford and Crewe (GJR)
- Warrington to Wigan (GJR)*
- Wigan to Preston (GJR)
- Crewe to Chester (GJR)
- Crewe to Manchester (MBR)

At the time of the amalgamation agreement, statutory powers were in place for the construction of new lines or extensions to new lines already under construction:

- Chester to Holyhead
- Stafford to Rugby via Trent Valley
- North Union Railway Wigan/Preston
- Lancaster to Preston
- Lancaster to Carlisle
- Huddersfield to Manchester
- Leeds to Huddersfield

Developments of railways in Great Britain occurred in phases which were influenced by recessions in trade, a lack of privately held finance for investment and poor harvests. The three companies that eventually formed the LNWR each benefitted from the real growth in the wealth of the country in the early 1830s. The earlier general level of investments in manufacturing, docks and harbours, the machinery of production in centres of industry, a fall in the price of copper and iron together with a mood of financial optimism and low level of returns available elsewhere, combined to encourage some speculation in new ventures.

The railway 'boom' of the mid-1830s was followed by a lengthy depression in trade and a succession of poor harvests, but the time lag between the new companies being incorporated and physical completion meant that the network continued to grow. The network of lines was developing without any serious planning and with a parliamentary position that competition was always good and railway companies could never be totally trusted.

When the investment cycle turned more favourable in the early 1840s, the possibilities for promoters were more easily identifiable, the competition for profitable routes more intense,

---

* connection for Liverpool/Manchester via existing Liverpool and Manchester Railway, opened 1830.

the short lines capable of being formed into a more co-ordinated system, railway companies at times content to work as partners with reciprocal running rights over each other's tracks while, at other times, being consumed with protectionism and reprisal actions. All of those characteristics were present as the MBR, GJR and LBR made their way towards eventual amalgamation. Each company will be considered in turn.

The MBR was incorporated in 1837 and opened its 31-mile railway through Stockport and Sandbach as far as Crewe in 1842. Along the way, it disturbed the grounds and commercial arrangements of the Belle Vue zoological gardens and pleasure grounds then being enjoyed by the middle-classes of Mancunians. Although the successful enterprise objected and had been on the site from 1836, it was a wrong that was not corrected before 1848 when Longsight station was re-sited closer to the attraction. At Crewe the MBR had its own modest station and a connection was made by a single line to the tracks of the GJR which was already established. That Crewe was as close to Birmingham as the MBR reached suggests that the promoters and proprietors were well satisfied with their efforts. That was not the case. In 1835, the Engineer for the line – George Stephenson – suggested that, although the GJR had a line from Crewe to Birmingham via Stafford and the LBR was making progress with a line from London (Euston) to Birmingham via Rugby, there was an opportunity for a shorter, direct route to London by linking Stafford (originally Stone) and Rugby and avoiding the Wolverhampton/Birmingham area and necessary change of trains at the latter. The idea was referred to at an MBR meeting in 1838 and quickly received support from not only within the company, but also from other merchants, manufacturers and traders of Manchester. The private Bill submitted to Parliament in 1839 met with considerable opposition, mainly from the LBR and, as a further submission in 1841 fared no better, the project lapsed until 1844.

The GJR was an amalgamation of the Liverpool and Manchester Railway (L&MR) opened in 1830, the Bolton and Leigh and the Warrington and Newton-le-Willows Junction Railway which was merged into the GJR in 1830. In 1833, the GJR was authorised by parliament to build a line from Birmingham via Wolverhampton and Stafford to near Warrington where it would form a connection with the L&MR, a distance of 82 miles. Services commenced from the terminus station at Curzon Street, Vauxhall, Birmingham in July 1837. As part of the building of the line, the GJR had built a very modest station where the turnpike road between Nantwich and Sandbach was crossed by the new railway. The name Crewe was assigned in acknowledgement of the local dignitary Lord Crewe. During the following year, the LBR reached Birmingham and sited its facilities adjacent to the GJR and thus enabled passengers for the north of Birmingham to join a GJR train and vice versa for travellers heading south to Rugby and London. The GJR was also active in pursuing opportunities to the west of Crewe, the 21-mile Chester and Crewe railway being merged with the GJR in 1840, and north of Newton Junction where several lines and ownerships were involved.

The LBR had a difficult beginning. Due to widespread opposition from influential landowners, the first attempt by the promoters failed during the parliamentary session of 1832. Following modifications to the proposed route, a second Bill was successful in the 1833 session. With the Act in place, construction started in November of 1833 under the overall direction of Robert Stephenson and with individual contracts put in place for works along the way. The first section to be opened was 24½ miles as far as Hemel Hempstead, in July 1837, and had involved tunnelling at Watford to appease landowners. Although the contractor engaged for the tunnel at Kilsby (77 miles from Euston) had correctly driven bore holes that suggested no causes for concern, he was unfortunate when a serious flooding occurred causing a delay to completion of the line

Map 2: Euston – Weaver Junction Section

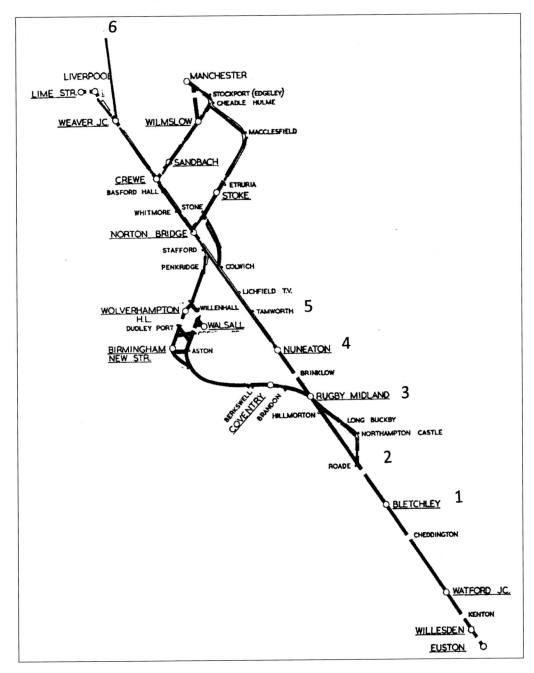

Key

1 Links to Cambridge and Oxford
2 Incoming coal traffic from South Yorkshire and Nottinghamshire
3 Links to Stamford/Peterborough and to Leicester
4 Links to Leicester and Birmingham
5 Links to Derby and Birmingham
6 Main line to Warrington

and arrival of the first services into Curzon Street to coincide with the start of GJR services. The 112 miles of the route opened throughout in 1838. A journey time of some 5½ hours was longer than it could have been due to refreshments being taken at Wolverton (52½ miles).

The timetable offered connecting omnibuses from Charing Cross (45 minutes journey) and other trains in conjunction with the GJR, MBR, Birmingham & Derby, North Midland, North Union/LPR, Midland Counties and the Birmingham & Gloucester. At Hampton (Derby Junction) a connection could be made for Derby and north thereof.

By 1842, therefore, all three railway companies were functioning and, as such, had formed part of a largely uncoordinated wider activity with little regulation as to accounting. By using the services of the three companies, the government's most populous centres of production could be reached (London, Birmingham, Liverpool and Manchester) with journey times unthinkable only a few years before. Journey times were, in fact, variable due to different centres being several minutes at variance to Greenwich time, a matter addressed later by the LBR/LNWR. Parliament had recognised the potential of railways to convey mail (the Railways [Conveyance of Mails] Act 1838) which gave wide powers to the Postmaster General, had established the Railway Department within the Board of Trade, had made a start with regulations to apply to the conduct of railway companies and had, in 1842, levied a tax on passenger receipts.

For the capital of the L&MR, opened in 1830, the Marquess of Stafford subscribed nearly a quarter of the total, 20 per cent from London, 47 per cent from Liverpool and the balance from a still unsure at that time Manchester. Some 85 per cent of the finance for the LBR and GJR was drawn from Lancashire. There is little to suggest that any of the three companies that formed the LNWR struggled to raise the necessary capital with which to build their railways. There is far more to support a theory that the capital, when 'called up' following the Act of Parliament, came in the main from small groups of well-informed, successful businessmen and landowners who, far from being speculators, were committed to a long-term investment to support their wider interests.

The parliamentary sessions 1845-6 and 1846-7 produced 219 and 112 Acts respectively, new capital authorised at £133 million and £39 million, with 4,538 and 1,354 miles of new track. Calling up capital became more difficult, the bank rate was increased as large imports of grain were necessary because of crop failures and abnormally high imports of cotton.

Into this maelstrom of activity were drawn the LBR, GJR and MBR. The lines of particular interest were between Chester and Holyhead, plus the Trent Valley line as proposed to link Stafford with Rugby. To provide some perspective, at the end of 1844, only 11 of the 104 railway companies which had attained legal status were operating more than 50 miles of track and those 11 accounted for over half of the track in use. The LBR and GJR were within the 11, with its Trent Valley line the MBR would have a total of 82 miles.

A new railway to link Chester with the port of Holyhead (CHR) represented an attractive proposition. The LBR board was particularly keen, to the extent of asking for and receiving the backing of the proprietors of an additional £300,000 to make a total contribution of £1m. The attraction lay in mail contracts with the Postmaster General, government support for movement of personnel, the possibility of shipping services and for livestock from Ireland (Dublin). For reasons of a wider nature involving other lines, the GJR was not quite as keen as the LBR and held the 'key' to the route with the Chester and Crewe Railway which had been amalgamated with the GJR in 1840.

The 85 mile route held several engineering challenges; a need for a bridge across the Menai Straits to Anglesey, a possible need for a new bridge arrangement at Conwy, sections

Map 3: Weaver Junction – Liverpool and North to Carnforth

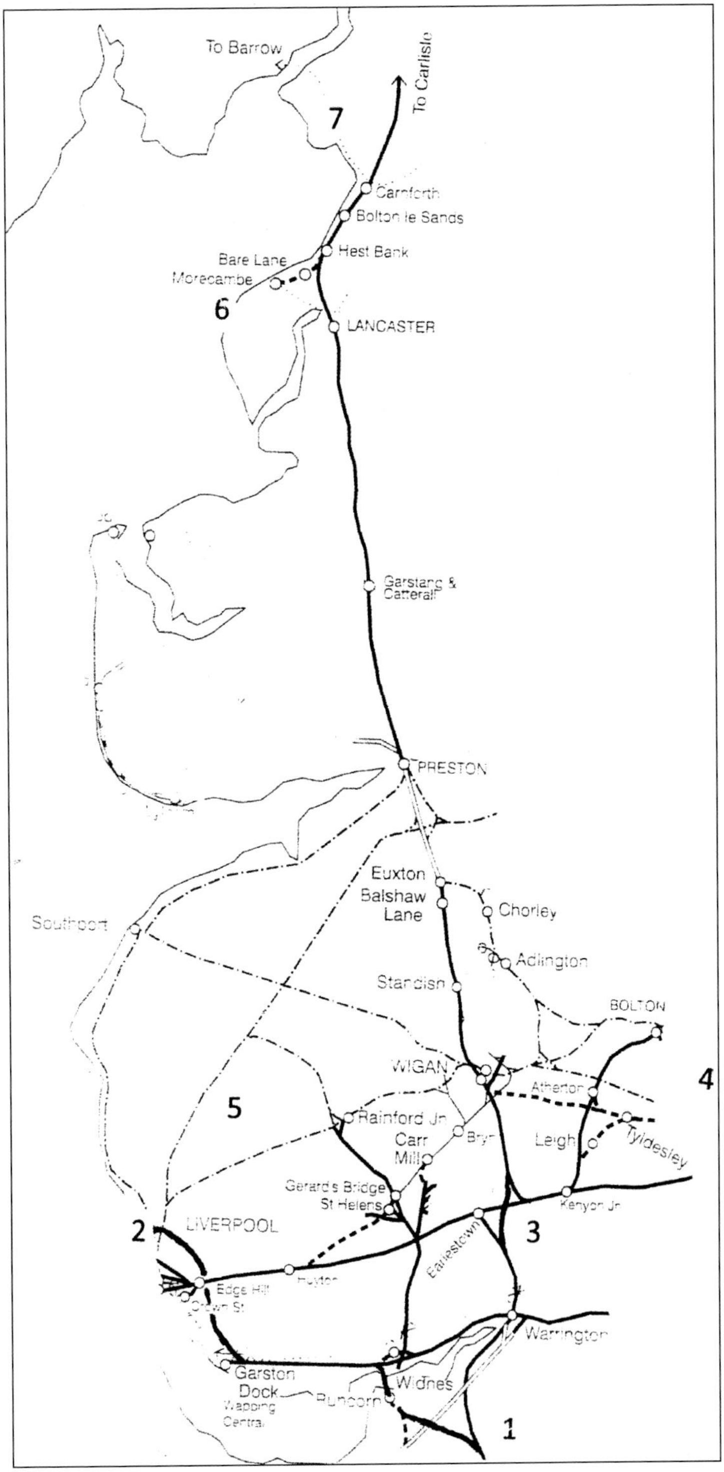

To Barrow

To Carlisle

7

Carnforth
Bolton le Sands
Hest Bank

Bare Lane
Morecambe

6

LANCASTER

Garstang &
Catterall

PRESTON

Euxton
Balshaw
Lane

Chorley

Southport

Adlington

Standish

BOLTON

WIGAN

4

5

Atherton

Rainford Jn
Carr
Mill

Bryn

Leigh

Tyldesley

Gerard's Bridge
St Helens

Kenyon Jn

2

LIVERPOOL

3

Earlestown

Edge Hill
w St

Huyton

Warrington

Garston
Dock
Wapping
Central

Runcorn

Widnes

1

Key

1   Weaver Junction
2   Liverpool Lime Street
3   1864 connection
     Winwick/Golborne
     Junctions
4   Alternative routes from
     main line to Manchester
     Victoria
5   Alternative routes from
     main line to Liverpool
     Exchange
6   Heysham
7   Furness route to Barrow
     and Workington

Map 4: Crewe – Manchester and Crewe – Holyhead

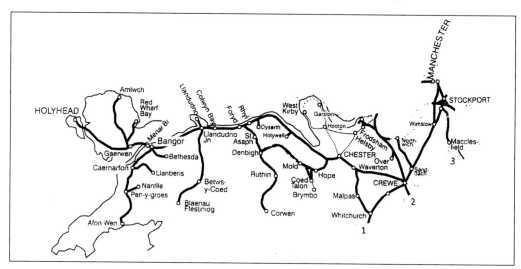

Key

1 To Shrewsbury
2 Main line to Stafford
3 North Staffordshire route from Macclesfield to Stoke-on-Trent, Norton Bridge/Colwich
4 Liverpool

of cliff-side running beyond Bangor and the bishop of that diocese requiring that the route be changed to take the railway away from the grounds of his palace. At Holyhead the Irish Steam Navigation Company was already offering a sea passage service. The government contract proved difficult in terms of the amount they were willing to pay, the bridges demanded new civil engineering challenges, the GJR wanted the railway to take a route more inland and for their Engineer, Joseph Locke, to work alongside the nominee of the LBR, Robert Stephenson. As matters between the GJR and LBR worsened, the provisional board of the CHR, including the Chairman of the LBR, George Carr Glyn, informed the GJR that it intended to purchase the Chester to Birkenhead Railway just across the River Mersey from Liverpool and would use it to take traffic that was currently taken by the GJR via a longer route and then shipped across the Mersey. That move was interpreted by the GJR as a hostile act and their support for the CHR would be withdrawn.

At a time when both the LBR and GJR were engaged in various ventures and other aspirant companies had an eye on linking centres of production, it was clearly in their mutual interest to come to some form of agreement. At a meeting held on 3 July 1844 – and with the Act for the CHR hanging in the balance – agreements were reached that included:

- the two companies would remain independent but would unite for mutual defence.
- the LBR could promote the Holyhead and Birkenhead lines, and any branch line to the south of Birmingham.
- the GJR would not reduce its rates for Chester to Birkenhead traffic routed via Liverpool and would …
- not work with the Irish Steam Navigation Company.

- neither company would develop interests in any new venture without the consent of the other and would assist each other in the conveyance of joint traffic.

Word travelled quickly and on the following day the CHR was incorporated. The line was opened in 1850 and allowed the then LNWR to develop plans for a steamer service over the 66-mile passage to Kingstown for passengers and 70 miles to Dublin for livestock and merchandise. Thus started 70 years of intense competition between the LNWR and the Irish Steam Navigation Company for the contract to convey mail.

Map 5: Rugby – Stafford

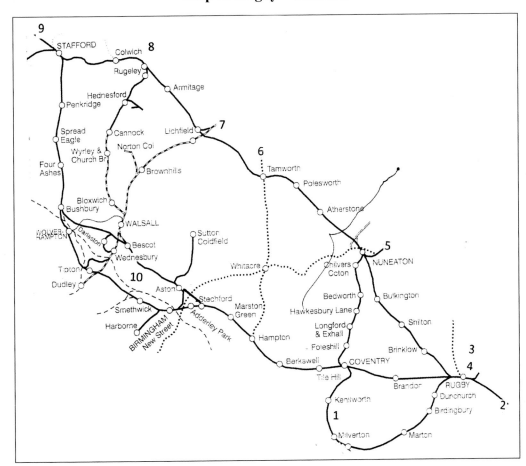

Key
1 Diversionary route during electrification works
2 Main line to Bletchley, Euston
3 Links to Stamford/Peterborough
4 Link to Leicester
5 Links to Leicester and Birmingham
6 Change for High Level services to Derby and Birmingham (mail interchange station)
7 Links to Burton-upon-Trent and Birmingham
8 Junction for Stoke, Macclesfield, Cheadle Hulme
9 Junction for Stoke, then as for 8 Main line to Crewe
10 Broken line indicates close proximity of Great Western/Western Region line

The GJR had shown great initiative by producing, in 1838, a converted horse box for the conveyance of mail and the sorting of it while on its journey between Birmingham and Liverpool. The Railways (Conveyance of Mails) Act of that year gave the Postmaster General powers to direct railways to convey mail on trains and at times to suit the requirements of his organisation. For mail to and from Ireland, the part of the journey over Welsh and English soil was a contract for the CHR and the company was also interested in the sea passage. However, when the contract was put out to competitive tender, the City of Dublin Steam Packet Company submitted the bid that was considered the better of the two. The CHR vessels plied their way back and forth with passenger, cargo and livestock using Holyhead and two Irish ports: Kingstown (later renamed Dun Laoghaire) and North Wall, Dublin. In 1853, the parliament agreed to the Steam Packet Company investing in four new ships with a sailing time of 3¾ hours for mail and passengers.

In 1859, two years after the LNWR acquired the CHR, the company ceased sailings to and from Kingstown and concentrated its efforts more on increased livestock tonnage from North Wall. On the Irish side of the sea passage, the (Irish) North Western Railway extended its line from Dundalk to a newly established port facility of Greenore, operated by the LNWR. The LNWR was very keen to develop its Irish traffic, invested in a hotel and new inner harbour, goods shed facilities and a splendid clock tower at Holyhead and in its own facilities at North Wall (1877).

The mail contract was again put out to tender in 1883 but, despite seemingly having submitted the better bid, LNWR representations to parliament still resulted in the Steam Packet Company prevailing again. The LNWR had to wait until after the First World War – during which the Steam Packet Company's fleet suffered losses, but with no financial recompense from the government – before it finally had the main contract.

The last LNWR route paddle steamer was sold in 1906 and the last ship purchased by the LNWR in 1921 – the *Slieve Donard* – sailed on until 1954.

The backers of the MBR had twice seen their proposals for a line between Stone/Stafford and Rugby rejected, but undaunted returned in 1844. By that year and having the six years of experience of London-Birmingham (change trains)-Crewe-Newton Junction-Liverpool-Crewe-Manchester, the LBR and GJR could each see the benefits from a direct line avoiding Birmingham/Wolverhampton. Far from objecting to the Bill, the LBR and GJR threw behind it their financial support. However, the Earl of Lichfield, through whose estate the line as projected would run, was an influential objector who was eventually appeased by the building of Shugborough tunnel with suitably impressive adornments on the portals. Another man of influence was the prime minister, Sir Robert Peel, Member of Parliament for Tamworth, who clearly faced a conflict of interest. The Bill passed through parliament and the Act (July 1845) allowed for the company to be leased to any or all of the LBR, GJR and MBR. While still under construction and after tactically turning down several offers, the Trent Valley Railway Company (TVR) was sold in spring 1846 to the LBR acting on behalf of itself, the GJR and the MBR. The 51 miles of new railway were opened in 1847 and, from December of that year, was used for all 'through' trains for north of Stafford. Interestingly, that also brought a unification of times applying at various stations and previously at variance to Greenwich time which was adopted as standard.

The jigsaw of the LNWR was beginning to take shape and with eyes more to the north and, perhaps a little surprisingly, also to the east. To the north was a core of several short sections followed by one large section. The GJR had a junction with the L&MR at Newton. The Wigan

Branch Railway (WBR) also made a connection with the L&MR at nearby Parkside and had been incorporated in 1830; its nearly seven miles of railway to Wigan was authorised by the Act to include an additional three miles of colliery lines known as Springs Branch. The WBR found difficulty in calling in the share capital as initially subscribed and construction was delayed. However, the Springs Branch, as built by engineers of the L&MR, was able to open in September 1832. Some two years later the WBR was still struggling and an amalgamation with the slightly more prosperous Preston and Wigan Railway (PWR) under the title North Union Railway, the first railway company amalgamation. The line to Wigan was opened in October 1838 and for its passenger services and some, not privately owned, colliery traffic used locomotives, rolling stock and staff of the L&MR.

The Preston and Wigan Railway Act of 1831 had authorised the building of a new railway between the two towns some 15½ miles apart. Amalgamation with the WBR was agreed by the board of directors in 1833 and gained Royal Assent in May 1834. Amongst the challenges was the fact that Preston stood on a ridge, with the River Ribble to be bridged, and for gradients to be manageable as the ridge was climbed. The line opened in 1838 with a station in Butler Street, Preston. With the later formation of the LNWR in 1846, the North Union was absorbed with a logical split of the Newton (Parkside station) to Euxton Junction (some six miles south of Preston) on the main line to be under the ownership of the LNWR and the Bolton and Preston Railway (BPR) as far as Euxton Junction to be under the ownership of the LYR. The through working between Warrington and Wigan, without the difficulty of the earlier L&MR/ North Union curves, junctions and stations, was achieved in 1864 when the LNWR built a 'cut off' between Winwick and Golborne.

Following the electrification works south from Manchester and Liverpool little of the original architectural style of the stations remained to be seen. The style adopted for the Trent Valley can be glimpsed here at Atherstone as a Jubilee calls with a Liverpool-Rugby stopping service. Note also the LNWR style of signal box. Curzon Street terminus at Birmingham is (at the time of writing) being restored to form part of the new complex for the railway (photo1).

The Lancaster and Preston Junction Railway (L&PJR) developed from a public meeting in the former town in April 1836. The distance between the two places was 20 miles and, without undue civil engineering challenges, would not hinder Joseph Locke for too long. Authorised in 1837, the line was ready for opening in June 1840 to Duke Street. However, the tracks were poor from the start and the locomotives of the North Union Railway suffered damage. The L&PJR was not a commercial success and John Hargreaves (who worked for the WJR) took over the working of goods and mineral traffic, including along a branch line, to the Preston docks. In due course, they acquired the LPR locomotives and took over the workings in their entirety. In July 1842 the Lancaster Canal Company took a 21-year lease on the railway which, although effective locally from September 1842, was not ratified by parliament until April 1843.

If Joseph Locke had found the largely flat section between Lancaster and Preston to lack challenges, his later challenge starting from the northern end was more towards the opposite end of the spectrum; the 90 miles to Carlisle. While the WBR, LPR and Northern Union had been struggling with the sections between Newton and Lancaster, well informed eyes were on a bigger prize. The prize would be the Lancaster to Carlisle Railway (LCR) through terrain very different to that encountered south of the former place; largely undeveloped and untouched by the heavy industries of industrial, Victorian Britain. On 6 November 1843, a meeting was held at Kendal (later known, on the railway at least, as Oxenholme) which

Map 6: Carnforth – Carlisle

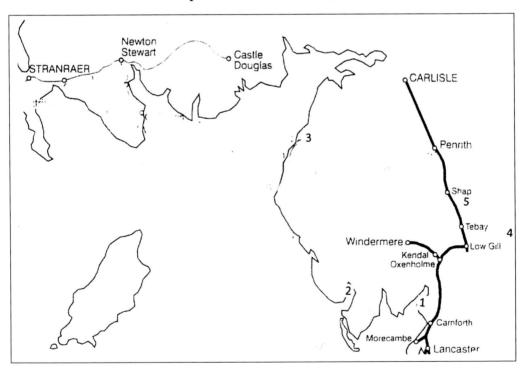

Key

1 Furness route to Barrow (2) and Workington (3)
4 Diversionary route away from main line
5 Shap summit

confirmed considerable local support for a railway. As the proposal was developed, the GJR and LBR offered to subscribe £250,000 and £100,000 respectively, the North Union and the LPR £65,000 each. Clearly the GJR and LBR wanted to push north to Carlisle and with a probable intention of contributing to a first all land travel route between London and Glasgow; at that time a sea voyage was a necessary part of any such venture.

Locke's preferred route, partly driven by an avoidance of the cost of tunnelling, was Lancaster-Oxenholme-Grayrigg-Tebay and then ascending to Shap summit at 914 feet above sea level, via a four-mile climb at a rate of one foot for every 75 travelled. Beyond Shap summit the northbound descent would be via Thrimby Grange and Penrith. Two railways were already at Carlisle (from Maryport in the west and Newcastle in the east) and agreement would need to be reached with regard to a shared station with an eye to another railway or railways from the north. Matters proceeded quickly and in the parliamentary session of 1843-4, Royal Assent was received on 6 June 1844 and with an authorised capital of £900,000 to allow a single line construction (later doubled throughout). The good burghers of Kendal – who after all had started the process – were dismayed to find the route did not pass through Kendal, but Kendal Junction (Oxenholme) to Kendal itself and Windermere was served by a two-mile branch line.

The line was opened in two stages; to Kendal Junction on 22 September 1846 and to Carlisle on 17 December 1846, double tracked from January 1847. During 1846, the LNWR had been formed and that company inherited an earlier agreement between the GJR and LPR that allowed through trains running between north of Lancaster and south of Preston, though without legal authority, for some time. To round off the convoluted Preston-Lancaster-Carlisle section, the L&PJR, the LCR and the lease of the Kendal Junction-Windermere branch were all leased to the LNWR in 1859 for a period of 900 years. The shareholders in the two former companies were guaranteed handsome dividends.

The Gladstone Act of 1844 had sought to protect the travelling public by requiring railway companies to erect mileposts at one side of the track and for fares to be mileage based. Because of the history of the building of the London-Carlisle main line (299 miles) there were four individual sections that started from milepost zero: Euston to Golborne Junction (189), Golborne Junction to Preston (209), Preston to Lancaster (230) and Lancaster to Carlisle. The mileposts still in situ can be spotted to this day; they are on the Down side; that is left-hand when in the direction of travel.

The formation of an Anglo-Scottish route had moved a step closer in July 1845 with the Act for the Caledonian Railway (CR) to build a 102-mile line between Glasgow and Carlisle via Beattock. That line was opened in two stages; Glasgow to Beattock being opened in September 1847 and to Carlisle in February 1848. By agreement between the railway companies using it, the station at Carlisle was named Citadel.

The LNWR and CR thus created the first Anglo-Scottish railway route. In so doing they were ahead of a route up the north-east coast of England from York/Newcastle to Berwick and Edinburgh. Until the Royal Border bridge at Berwick was available from 1850 this had necessitated a road journey; in that year things were markedly improved by the GNR service from London to Askern (near Doncaster) from where the North Eastern Railway took over to Berwick. The North British Railway had completed their Edinburgh to Berwick section in 1846 and, from the following year, had received the passengers having been inconvenienced by the course of the River Tweed. The same North British company made a foray south from Edinburgh to Hawick in 1849 and, as part of a challenge to the supremacy of the CR, proceeded through difficult terrain to reach Carlisle in 1862. A third railway company for Anglo-Scottish

Map 7: Carlisle–Glasgow and Carlisle–Dumfries

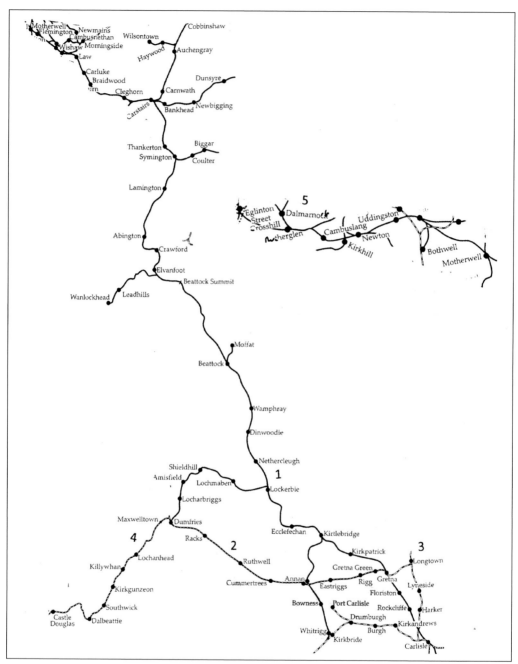

Key

1 Main line Carlisle-Lockerbie-Beattock-Carstairs
2 Glasgow and South Western route to Glasgow
   via Dumfries and Kilmarnock
3 North British route to Edinburgh (Waverley route)
4 Joint line to Castle Douglas (see map A4 for
   Castle Douglas-Stranraer)
5 Main line Motherwell – outskirts of Glasgow

Map 8: Glasgow Area Showing Goods Yards

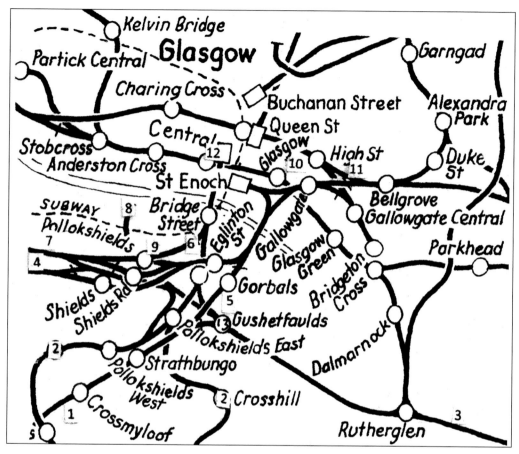

Key

1 Glasgow and South Western route to Kilmarnock
2 Cathcart circle route
3 Main line to Motherwell, Carstairs
4 To Paisley
5 South Side Goods and Gushetfaulds Goods
6 West Side Goods
7 Kinning Park Goods
8 General Terminus Goods
9 Eglinton Street Goods
10 College Goods
11 High Street Goods
12 Glasgow Central Low Level
13 Gushetfaulds

traffic was the Glasgow and South Western that ran from Glasgow via Kilmarnock and Dumfries to join the CR at Gretna Junction 8½ miles north of Carlisle.

Turning to the east of Manchester may seem illogical but is perhaps better understood against a background that the Great Northern Railway did not open its main line to the north until 1850 (15 years after the LBR) and Leeds represented the fifth most populated centre of production in the England of the late 1840s. Any route between Manchester and Leeds would be faced with a barrier formed by the Pennines. The one gap between contours – the Calder Valley – had already been surveyed and used for the Manchester and Leeds Railway (MLR) which was opened in 1841 and in 1847 became part of the LYR. The route chosen was

Map 9: Glasgow–Perth

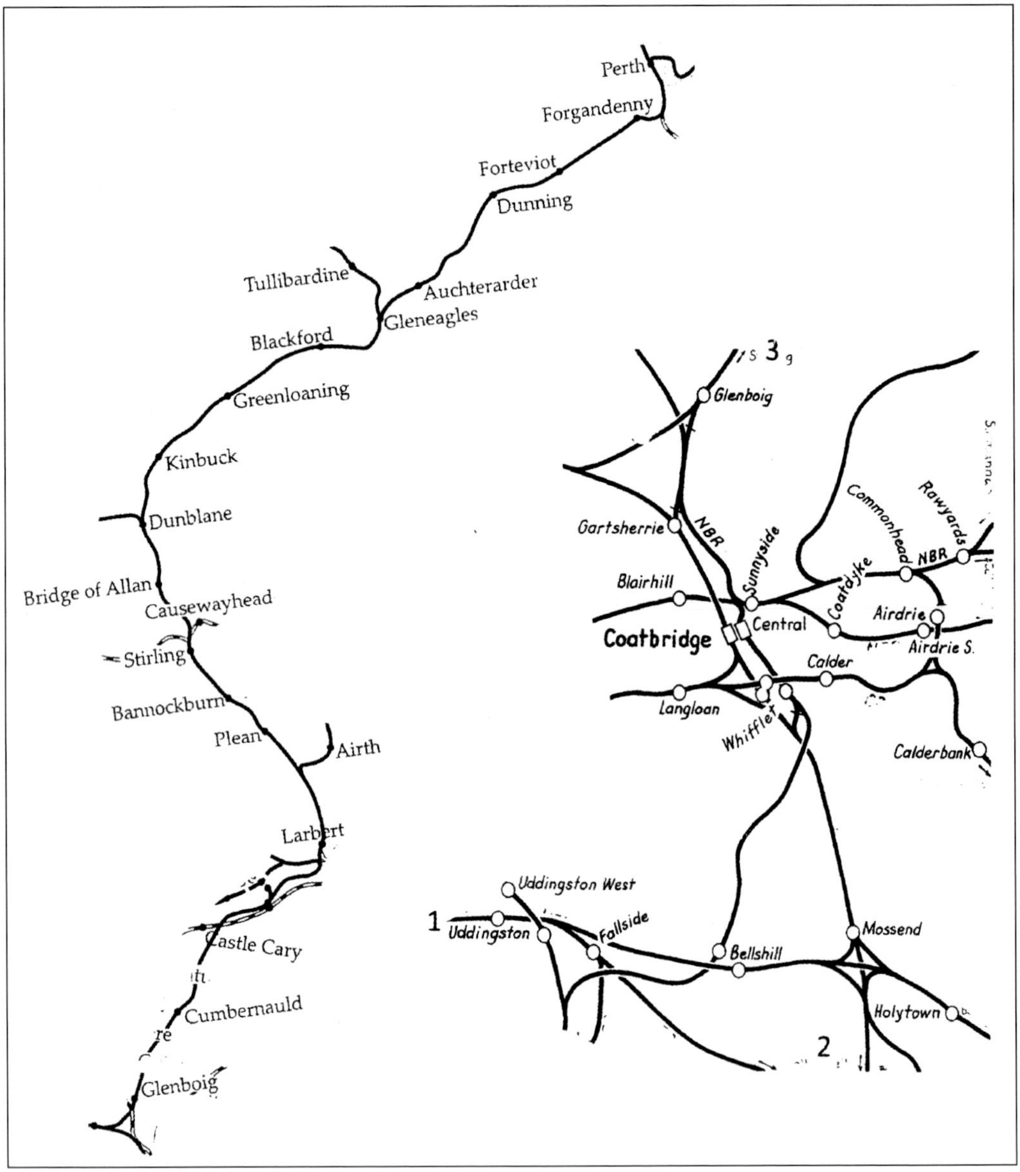

Key

1 Main line from Glasgow Central
2 Main line continuation to Carstairs, Carlisle
3 To Stirling, Perth

commercially weakened by access to the prosperous town of Huddersfield being considered worthy only of a branch line; a fact that upset the good folk thereabouts. Local dignitaries formed a group to promote a railway and canal to Manchester (26 difficult miles) and their Bill (HMR) was eventually approved in the parliamentary session of 1844-5. The line was completed in 1849 and, during its construction – including the three-and-a-half-mile tunnel at Standedge – was acquired by the LNWR. The station at Huddersfield was quite something to behold; a fine, Grecian façade with a central portico supported by Corinthian columns and a smaller replica to each side. Huddersfield announced itself and while opinion locally was still not favourable to the LYR, the two railway companies worked together in that the station became Huddersfield Joint. For the LNWR having Huddersfield was good and Leeds would be a strong addition. While the acquisition of the HMR was a work in progress, proposals for a Leeds, Dewsbury and Manchester railway developed and came partly into use in July 1848. Coming west from Leeds via Morley and Dewsbury, the line reached Thornhill Junction, 11 miles from Leeds, and from which point the LNWR enjoyed running rights over the LYR to Heaton Lodge (Huddersfield). Thus, the LNWR had a main line through the Pennines which could be developed before the GNR arrived into Leeds via Doncaster and the Midland developed a route to Lancaster.

Having use of another existing railway by trading running rights was a popular tactic and the LNWR was keen to use the route of the North Staffordshire Railway (NSR) between Cheadle Hulme, Macclesfield and Stoke-on-Trent to Colwich, north of Stafford. By use of the NSR, the LNWR gained a second route south from Manchester via Crewe and via Stoke-on-Trent, with the latter being eight miles the shorter. While NSR/LNWR locomotives were changed at Stoke-on-Trent, all tickets were checked and 'punched' with an identifying 'P' in order that at a later audit the NSR could be credited with its fee for conveying through passengers on LNWR trains.

A watershed in development of railways was reached in the 1850s. The second of the three routes from London to the north was established by the GNR from its terminus at King's Cross, opened in 1852. In that year there were 6,628 miles of railway in Great Britain, up from 2,236 miles as recently as 1844.

The number of railway Acts passed in the 1850s was very similar in total to the 1840s (831), but in the 1850s the emphasis was more on short lines to connect others, to consider amalgamations and to seek authority to raise additional capital. Amalgamations were often tactical proposals rather than strategic; a method of testing the strength of feeling without giving too much away as to the future intentions. The MR had aspirations towards Scotland and, while it eventually had to wait until the mid-1870s, it did establish a northern outlet at Lancaster in 1850, arriving there by means of Leeds, Shipley and Skipton, and gave a connection with the Lancaster to Carlisle. In 1852, the MR proposed amalgamation with the LNWR and for a while it looked promising, but resulted in failure and the MR acquiring the Skipton to Lancaster line, known as the Little North Western, including the Lancaster to Morecambe line. Also, in 1852 both the LNWR and GNR approached the MR with offers of a friendly union and a Bill was introduced to parliament in 1853 for the proposed amalgamation of all three into one company controlling all traffic between south and north. Parliament was having none of it and the Bill was rejected on 'national grounds'.

There were also joint lines (owned by two or more companies), one of which was of particular use to the LNWR, was with the MS&LR over the short line between Manchester South Junction and Altrincham. Between 1850 and 1863 the number of passengers conveyed annually increased by over one million and goods traffic from 114k tons to 679k. Another joint line – and one which damaged the trading position of the LNWR – the Cheshire Lines Committee involving the MS&LR, GNR and MR, will be introduced later in this chapter.

The LNWR developed through the 1850s and 1860s and its interests were far wider than are within the parameters of this book. Those interests of relevance to this book may be summarised as:

- Northampton to Market Harborough, 18 miles (1853) of relevance for coal traffic to London.
- Hampstead Junction connection to North London Railway (1853). Cross London traffic and route to docks.
- West London Extension, jointly with Great Western Railway (GWR) (1859). Route to Battersea and connection with London and South Western Railway.
- Warrington and Stockport (1859), leased.
- GNR, Manchester, Sheffield & Lincolnshire Railway (MS&LR). Agreement on interchange of traffic at through rates and on utilisation of London Road station, Manchester (1858).
- GWR. Use of LNWR lines for its Manchester traffic.
- NSR (1860). Traffic agreement for passage of LNWR trains between Manchester and London via Stoke-on-Trent.
- New Works (1859). New line Edge Hill to Garston (dock), Liverpool, 4½ miles.
- New Works (1861). New lines Stockport to Cheadle and from Chelford to Knutsford. 13 miles.
- New Works (1861). New line Edge Hill to Bootle, new line Winwick to Golborne (through route Warrington – Wigan), a branch line to Runcorn and a bridge over the River Mersey (the latter to be built within seven years). 13 miles. Enlargement of Lime Street station, Liverpool.
- New Works (1861). Citadel station improvements, Carlisle.
- New Works (1861). Lease or purchase of St George's harbour, Holyhead.
- New Works (1863). Abandonment of section of Chelford to Knutsford line.
- Station rebuilding (1867) Crewe station, with widened platforms and bays to keep main line through services clear of terminating/originating shorter trains.

That listing contains two items of particular relevance to the changing competitive nature of the LNWR around the commercial honeypot of Lancashire, Merseyside and Cheshire. From the time of the formation of the LNWR in 1846 until the late 1850s, the company had enjoyed a dominant trading position with only the MS&LR (which had use of three platform faces at London Road station and its own goods depot) actively in competition for eastbound and some northbound traffic. That started to change when the MS&LR worked closely with the GNR to allow access to through traffic from London via Retford and Sheffield and then entered a 50-year agreement with that company on traffic. Also, into the Manchester area came the Midland Railway (MR) after years of struggle through the Peak District (1862) and, while the MR did not at that time have a London terminal station, it would do so from 1866-7. The MS&LR, GNR and MR together represented the greatest challenge yet faced by the LNWR. The commercial arrangements were disturbed when the practices of Captain Mark Huish of the LNWR forced him to resign his position with the company, having been involved since GJR days of very little meaningful regulation. The two items of interest were the new line from Edge Hill to Garston dock and the agreement with the MS&LR and GNR on through traffic rates and use of London Road station.

Map 10: Manchester Area

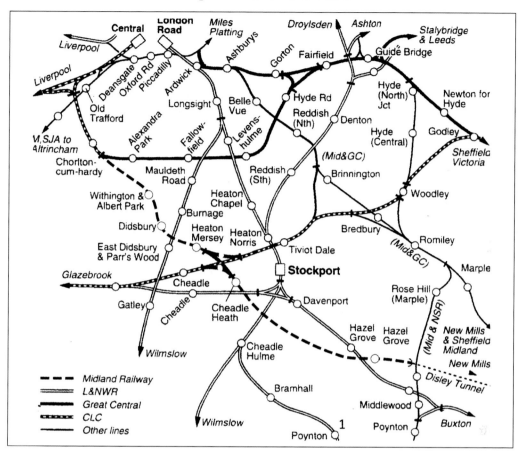

Key

l To Macclesfield, Stoke-on-Trent

The map shows the attraction of Manchester as a major trading centre in the nineteenth century.
The manuscript outlines how the dominant position of the LNWR was weakened over time.

Access to docks was an important consideration and very useful in 'trading' reciprocal rights with some and not with others. For access to Garston, which was to become an important centre for export of coal to Ireland and import of cotton and, later, fruit, the LNWR agreed an arrangement with the MS&LR and GNR, but not the MR and, at the Manchester end of the traffic flows, utilised the MSJ&A in joint ownership with the MS&LR. The Manchester Ship Canal linking the River Mersey at Liverpool with Manchester was opened in 1894 and with a Director, later Chairman, of the MS&LR/Great Central Railway as a major shareholder, the largest railway beneficiary was the MS&LR and not the LNWR.

Within its own organisation, the LNWR concentrated its engineering activities into separate workshops; from 1853, the wagon department was relocated from Crewe to Earlstown, in 1859 the carriage department was relocated to Saltley, Birmingham, where it remained until transfer to Wolverton. In 1877, the construction of locomotives at Wolverton ceased and thereafter was centred at Crewe. While both Earlstown and Wolverton benefitted as places

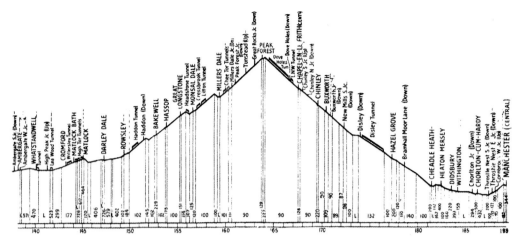

The lure of the commerce and industry of Manchester, Lancashire and Cheshire caused the Midland Railway to carve a route over and through the Peak District. With every hindrance from the LNWR which sought to protect its dominant position it took 31 years for the Midland to achieve its aim. The rivalry extended to the establishing of the Cheshire Lines Committee; an alliance of the Great Central, Great Northern and Midland companies.

from the presence of the LNWR, Crewe was the very epitome of a railway town that owed its development and relative prosperity to the LNWR; its housing, its schools, its hospital, its gas and water supplies, its Crewe Arms Hotel, its employment and its skilled workforce that attracted Rolls-Royce to set up a factory in 1938.

Later in this book there are references to services and traffic from places not yet detailed in this first chapter. Their origins lay with various companies later absorbed or taken over by the LNWR solely as part of a joint venture or under reciprocal running rights arrangements. The lines were:

Area	Notes
Preston & Wyre Railway (main line services to and from Blackpool)	Opened 1840, Preston to Fleetwood from where (1841-48) coastal steamers took passengers to Ardrossan. Taken over by LYR and LNWR (1849) and used to develop Fylde (Blackpool, Lytham). LYR developed Fleetwood as a port for Ireland and the Isle of Man.
Workington/Whitehaven/Barrow (main line services to and from London via Carnforth)	Northern end opened 1840-45 to tap coalfield and later serve iron and steel works. Around Whitehaven/Barrow opened from 1846. Absorbed into the Furness Railway 1866. Prosperous in 1870s in particular as steel-making flourished.
Liverpool – Runcorn – Weaver Junction (main line services to and from London joining 16 miles north of Crewe)	LNWR development in 1860s including bridge over River Mersey (and later Manchester Ship Canal) at Runcorn, opened 1869.

Area	Notes
Liverpool – Wigan and Liverpool – Preston (main line services to and from Scotland; portions attached/ detached from/for Manchester)	Used LYR routes by agreement prior to amalgamation with LNWR.
Liverpool to Southport (through carriages on main line services to and from London)	Vehicles detached/attached at Edge Hill/Allerton/ Wavertree, thence LYR.
Liverpool Riverside (through trains or carriages on services for shipping)	Riverside station opened by LNWR in 1895. Connection to main line at Edge Hill mainly in tunnel.
Lancaster – Heysham Harbour (main line services to and from London/Manchester)	Used MR branch.
Stockport – Colne (through carriages to and from London attached/detached)	Used LYR route via Manchester Victoria and Bolton.
Rugby – Northampton -Roade (loop off main line from Rugby to re-join main line at junction 13 miles south of Rugby)	Opened by LNWR in 1883 to serve fast-growing centre of production.
Gretna Junction – Stranraer (main line services to and from London/ Carlisle mainly for shipping)	Originally an extension of the Castle Douglas – Dumfries line, opened 1861/62. Acquired in 1885 by CR, GSWR, LNWR and MR.

The 1870s brought forth proposals for a further amalgamation, the start of a lengthy trade depression and the arrival of a third competitor for Anglo-Scottish travel.

In 1872, the two railway companies that dominated much of industrial Lancashire – the LNWR and LYR – asked parliament to consider allowing them to amalgamate. While amalgamations were useful for retaining lines which linked or supported others and may otherwise have ceased to operate, the creation of a near complete monopoly of traffic for prosperous Lancashire was hardly in that category. Parliament was more strongly minded towards competition with a choice of carrier and rejected the request not once, but twice as the request was repeated in 1873.

A financial crisis in 1866 claimed several railway contractors, the failure of a bank which had over extended the extent of its risk, a panic in the money markets, an increase in the Bank of England lending rate and a collapse in confidence. Capital expenditure in the 1870s by the leading companies, such as the LNWR, was directed more towards improvements to the infrastructure to cater for increasing traffic, extending facilities and building short lines to usefully connect others. Major improvements to the handling of goods traffic in the Liverpool area were made with a new yard at Edge Hill employing a method of sorting wagons using gravity rather than shunting engines.

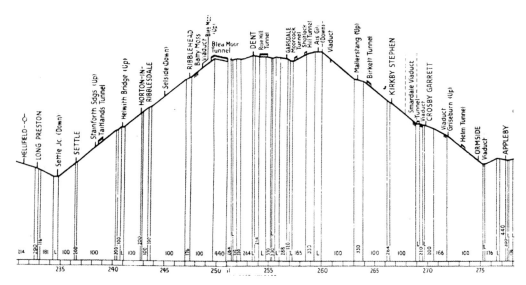

Glasgow, as being the second great industrial city of the Empire, attracted the Midland Railway. That Company made extraordinary efforts to reach, first, Carlisle via a route over and through the Pennines and there joined forces with the Glasgow and South Western Railway.

One area in which capital expenditure by the LNWR was less than expected was for new carriages; operations and lengths being hampered by a traverser arrangement at Euston station. From the middle 1880s, it was possible to introduce some eight-wheel, non-bogie carriages but, overall, the company was losing ground to its rivals. As an example of the competitive spirit of the late 1880s, there were three expresses leaving London termini at Euston, St Pancras and King's Cross (less than one mile apart) for Manchester at 2/0 and due to arrive at Manchester within five minutes of each other. The 78-mile MR route from Settle to Carlisle, built between 1866 and 1876, encountered and overcame significant geographical barriers to progress, but finally achieved its intended purpose of providing a third route between London and Scotland. From Carlisle, it utilised the GSW between Gretna Junction and Glasgow via Dumfries and Kilmarnock. Also, in Scotland, the LNWR/CR Anglo-Scottish traffic flow for Aberdeen was dealt a blow when, in 1890, the Forth Bridge was opened and allowed the NB an advantage of 34 fewer miles between Edinburgh and the granite city.

Out of chronological context, but similarly relevant to a weakening of the LNWR's position, was the opening of the last main line to be built in Great Britain; that between Annesley Junction and Aylesbury (95 miles) that formed part of the Great Central Railway (GCR) line linking Manchester and London (Marylebone) from 1900. The GCR was a new name for the MS&LR. To round off the increasing competition along LNWR routes, the GWR's direct route from Paddington to Birmingham and Wolverhampton via Princes Risborough, Aynho, Banbury and Leamington Spa was a very similar mileage to that offered from Euston.

A final outbreak of rivalry developed in summer 1895 and involved the LNWR and CR route from London with the GNR/NER/NB route up the east coast, both aiming to reach Aberdeen (540 miles from Euston, 516 from King's Cross) before the other. A nonsense, of course, involving lightweight trains not covering their costs, but demonstrated the capabilities of locomotives and their enginemen. On the final night, 23 August, the west coast men achieved the run at an average speed of 63.3 miles per hour.

The following tables will enable an understanding of the position of financial strength that was earned by the Directors, Officers and staff of the LNWR.

Dividends (per cent) declared to holders of ordinary shares						
Company	**1891**	**1892**	**1893**	**1894**	**1895**	**1896**
LNWR	7	6½	5⅜	6¼	6⅜	7⅛
MR	6⅜	6	3⅞	5¼	5⅛	6
LYR	3⅞	3⅝	3⅛	4	4½	5⅜
CR	4¼	4⅛	4⅜	3⅝	6	5

So much for origins, developments and finance. What were the characteristics of the physical railway that influenced journeys and the travelling public?

For a company that was formed out of three others and which later acquired/had running rights over many more, it would not be a surprise to discover a variety of architectural styles along its routes from Euston, as portrayed in stations, bridges, viaducts and tunnels.

Map 11: Manchester London Road Station

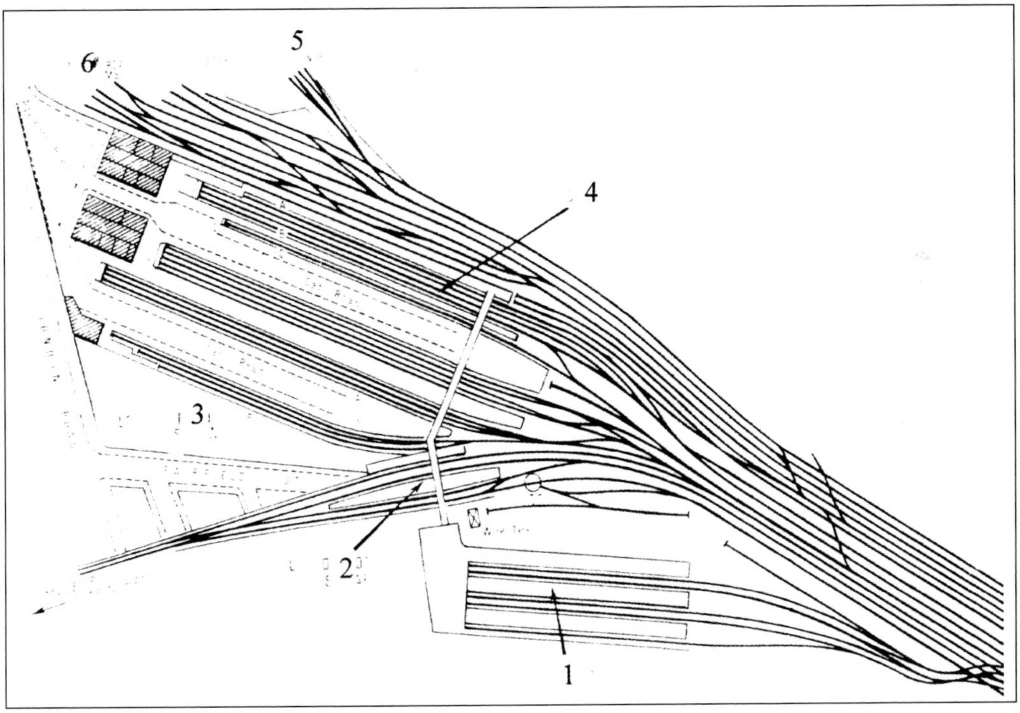

Key

1 Mayfield station
2 Platforms for Manchester South Junction and Altrincham services
3 London Road station used by LNWR/LMS
4 London Road station used by GCR/LNER and later electrified services to Sheffield Victoria via Woodhead
5 LNER Goods
6 LMS Goods

Map 12: Liverpool Lime Street Station

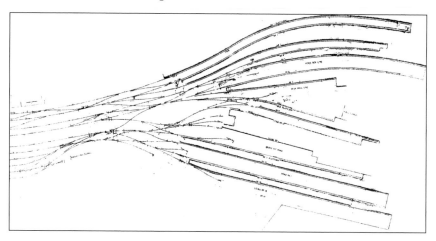

Map 13: Euston Station

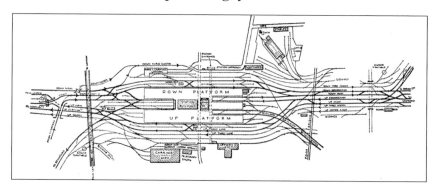

Map 14: Rugby Station

Map 15: Carlisle Area

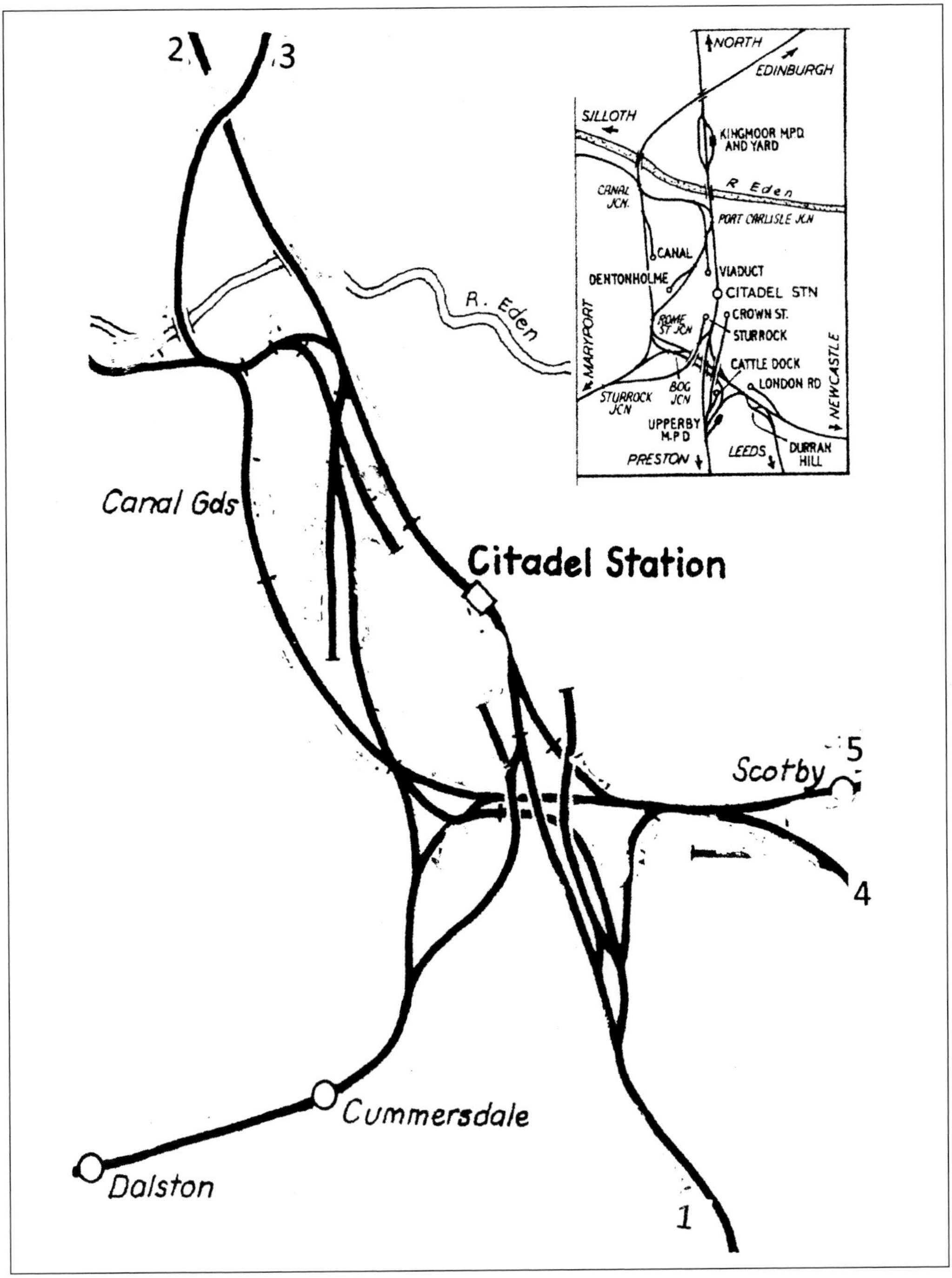

Key

1 Main line to Shap and Lancaster
2 Main line to Gretna Junction, Beattock, Carstairs
   and Glasgow/Perth
3 North British route to Edinburgh
4 Midland route to Appleby and Leeds
5 North Eastern route to Newcastle

Stations ranged from the grand statements of presence and solidity such as Huddersfield as already described, Euston, Liverpool Lime Street, Curzon Street at Birmingham and Chester; smaller but similar at Bangor and others between Chester and Holyhead; to purely functional, but with some style like those of Lancaster, Carlisle, Preston; those with a fine overall train shed – Rugby, Manchester London Road – and those about which the less said probably the better including Crewe, Birmingham New Street, Wolverhampton and Coventry.

The approach to Euston – in the form of Hardwick's Doric Arch of granite (1837) for the LBR, with two lodges flanking on each side – was far more impressive than the station itself. The LNWR employed Gerald Horsley in 1901 to design stations at Harrow and at Pinner in a style half way between a bank and a country house. Harrow was even given a tower. Francis Thompson was engaged for Chester and stations along the line towards Holyhead; at Chester the influence of Hardwick could be seen and, at the smaller stations, a cantilevered platform veranda contained between two terminal blocks projecting out from the station building. Thompson also designed the approach structures to the Britannia tubular bridge near Bangor and a station in the gothic style at Conway. In Liverpool, the City Corporation insisted that Lime Street station must harmonise with the St George's Hall which stood nearby. The architect John Franklin's work featuring Corinthian columns was so popularly received that the GJR engaged him to design a more modest terminus for the Birmingham end of their line. Sadly, the station at Lime Street did not survive beyond the 1870s, by which time functionality was of a greater priority. Carlisle Citadel station was designed by Sir William Tite who was the architect for the Royal Exchange building and – like Thompson – later favoured the gothic style so stunningly applied at St Pancras station in London. Lancaster's appeal owed much to the castle adjacent to it and the use of attractive locally hewn stone.

The Great Hall at Euston – in LNWR days – was another work by Phillip Hardwick and sheltered many a waiting passenger and those just in need of a resting place. Hardwick also designed what became known as the Victoria Hotel and Dormitories which consisted of two separate buildings with a total of 40 bedrooms, a coffee room and a lounge. In 1881 the

The Doric Arch

two buildings were connected by a central block to give 141 bedrooms and the place was renamed the Euston Hotel – it closed 13 May 1963.

Beyond the 'gateways', the intending passenger would probably have found a bookstall selling newspapers and journals. The LNWR was quick to identify the commercial attraction of large numbers of people with a journey in prospect and put out to tender the contract to operate bookstalls. All the morning and evening newspapers were on offer though at a premium of one penny above the published price. The LNWR was also quick to see the opportunity from

The LNWR was quick to spot the opportunity from having a captive audience at stations and on trains. The richly coloured, stove enamel advertising signs proclaimed all manner of products and remedies and of those signs placed under cover many outlived the lives of the products themselves.

selling space upon which advertising boards could be placed, including on the vertical faces of steps over bridges. Amongst the early signs were Virol (a health food) in its characteristic bold style of an orange background and some of these lasted for 70-80 years. Other commonly seen signs were for Stephen's pens and inks, Spratt's dog and cat foods, Brooke Bond Tea (which copied the Virol style), the marvellously titled Mazawattee Tea and Swan Soap. Advertising seemed to work; the British Army of 1914-18 purchased millions of dog biscuits from Spratt's.

For the comfort of passengers, vendors along the departure platforms would offer cushions, blankets and footwarmers for hire and tea, coffee, cakes and chocolate for purchase. During 1896, the LNWR carried nigh on 76 million passengers; some 2 million of whom travelled in the greater comfort of first-class. At that time there were three classes of travel but, as the distinction between second and third-class was barely noticeable, there was a move – initially by the MR, the GWR and the London & South Western – to withdraw second-class facilities and fares. Third-class lasted until 1956.

Once on the move, the seated passengers would not be aware of the gradient profile of the line, at least after the initial slow climb of the first mile to Camden. The LBR/GJR/MBR were engineered wherever possible to an evenness of grading which extended also to Stafford via the outskirts of Birmingham, via the Trent Valley line and onwards to Crewe, Manchester and Warrington. Apart from a few miles between Madeley (150 miles from Euston) and Betley Road (153) and again between the latter point and the approach to Crewe, there was no gradient more than one foot in every 330, all the way for 175 miles towards Warrington, or between London and Manchester via Crewe (188 miles). There were some lengthy spells at 1 in 330; 7½ miles between mileposts 7 and 14½ (Carpenders Park), between 22½ and 31 (near Tring), between 32 and 38, 54 and 60 (near Roade where the line to Northampton deviated) with less of a gradient between 71 and 75½ (Welton) and finally for six miles from the northern end of Kilsby tunnel through Rugby to Newbold water troughs. A ruling gradient of 1 in 330 equates

The Edwardian era brought together a society that was more relaxed than that of the Victorians. Coinciding then with the pre-First World War 'golden age' of railway travel the LNWR entered into the spirit of things by offering charabanc tours. (2)

to a rise or fall of 16 feet in a mile and, while that was helpful to the locomotive engineers and train weight planners, it paled in comparison to Brunel's 'carpet' of four feet in a mile for stretches of the Great Western (1 in 1320). The Midland tried for 1 in 200 (26.4 feet in a mile) and the Great Central 1 in 176 or 30 feet in a mile. To achieve such a stretch of track so favourable to consistent running speeds and sighting of signals, the cost was in the physical form of deep cuttings. Of the gradients listed, some were favourable, others adverse depending upon the direction of travel. Beyond Newbold water trough (84) there was nothing of great concern to enginemen for the next 64 miles.

As far as the Northern Fells the civil engineers for the routes of interest to this book were faced with few physical barriers except the crossing of rivers and canals and boring of several tunnels. Here a **Royal Scot** *is crossing the Weaver Navigation by means of a 16-arch viaduct at Dutton. (3)*

At the southern end of the route the decision to adopt a ruling gradient of 1 in 330 (or 16 feet per mile) necessitated some lengthy cuttings with finely graded embankments. Here, one of the five BR prototype diesels assigned to the route from 1956 (10202) sweeps past. (4)

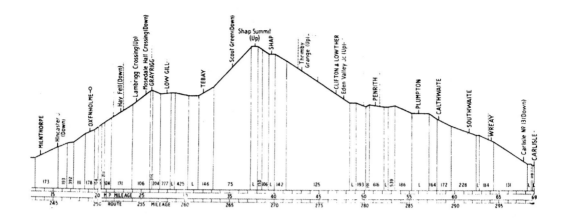

The nature of the line northwards then changes and becomes more undulating with some short, sharp climbs. The harder work for the locomotive (as described in chapter 2) began after Carnforth, as shown on the accompanying profile and the visual delight of the valley of the River Lune would be lost on the fireman as he prepared his fire and steam pressure for the task ahead. For some 30 miles, the locomotive and fireman had little respite but, beyond Shap summit (268), had a similar distance for recovery. In the southbound direction the challenging sections were, of course, reversed and with a 'cold' locomotive from Carlisle could be particularly difficult.

To reach Carlisle from Lancaster Joseph Locke opted for a route over Shap and, in so doing, provided for locomotives and their crews a test of ability that extended throughout the steam era. Here a Black 5 has been obliged to take the assistance of a banking engine as it leaves Tebay. The railway on the far side of the river formed part of the North Eastern Region cross country line to County Durham via Kirkby Stephen. (5)

The physical challenge and scenic grandeur of the fells around Shap still provide a spectacle today. A long way from its previously natural habitat a Merchant Navy Class locomotive (35018) makes excellent headway on an unusually calm winter day and made worthwhile the 360 mile trip of the photographer. The M6 motorway is to the left of the picture; Tebay beyond the bottom right hand corner. (6)

Close to the location where 35018 is shown in picture 5 the photographer would have been watching the clouds as the Royal Scot became due. He was fortunate to capture this classic scene as City of Bristol worked towards him; the Carlisle Upperby crew nearing the end of a lodging turn to London that would probably be repeated the next day. (7)

The fireman of 46237 in picture 7 would have been able to relax after his train breasted Shap summit; 31 miles of favourable gradients and a change of locomotives at Carlisle would allow him some respite. However, his contemporary on a Patriot still had some five miles to go between Thrimby Grange and the summit. Each shovelful of coal is registering in the exhaust and with the sanders on the driver is taking no chances of a slip with a heavy, unbraked train. (8)

The line through Northampton included gradients both favourable and adverse though, if routed south via Blisworth (rather than directly to Roade), involved a short climb at 1 in 100. Trains passing through Birmingham New Street and between there and Wolverhampton faced short gradients as severe as 1 in 58/77/100.

For trains taking the NSR route from Colwich (127½) via Stoke and Macclesfield to Manchester, there was a continuous, though gentle, climb for 23 miles, but with the final 3 miles or so to and near Macclesfield at 1 in 176, where the gradient becomes favourable. The hard work was then over, at least in the northbound direction, with descents at 1 in 137/154/192/240 to the junction at Cheadle Hulme.

Coming south out of Liverpool Lime Street, trains faced a climb at 1 in 93 for the tunnelled section of 1¼ miles to Edge Hill and again to a summit at Wavertree. Beyond Wavertree, the gradients to the junction at Weaver were fairly equally shared between adverse and favourable with a difficult climb southbound from Ditton Junction through Runcorn to Halton Junction.

Crewe to Holyhead did not excite the civil engineers in terms of gradients but did include a climb either side of Llysfaen (217) and a dip between 247 and 251.

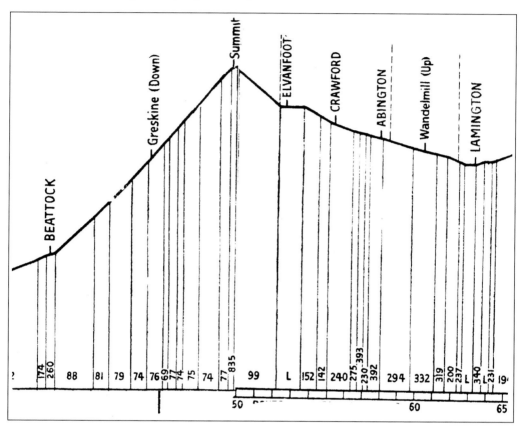

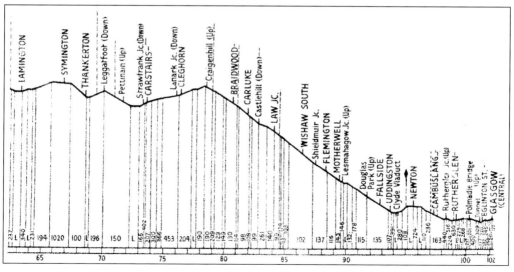

Beattock bank. There were at least three happy people here; the fireman of Princess Royal Class **Lady Patricia** *(who has matters well under control and can afford to take in some cool fresh air), the driver (who has an abundance of steam and the assistance of a banking engine) and the photographer (who has been patiently awaiting his opportunity as dawn broke). (9)*

Of the two routes between Carlisle and Glasgow – the CR via Beattock and the lengthier, by 14 miles, via Dumfries and Kilmarnock – that of the former included the most challenging gradients in each direction. Having faced northbound, nothing more severe than a sharp 1 in 193 near Gretna Junction (306/8), trains were faced with 11 miles at 1 in 69/88 between Beattock (where banking locomotives were available) and the summit, before a generally favourable descent into and along Clydesdale. Southbound was, of course, the opposite. The GSW route northbound featured a climb of 14 miles between near Holywood (36½) and Carronbridge and from the stop at Kilmarnock (91) to between Stewarton and Dunlop (98). Southbound also featured Hurlford (89½) to Garrochburn (84) at 1 in 100. Against the background of what has been described, the switchback to Stranraer from Carlisle was murderous. Spare a thought too for the Crewe North firemen who, from the 1930s, worked through to Perth including a final effort with the shovel for the six miles up through Dunblane to Kinbuck at between 1 in 78 and 100.

For a passenger between London and Carlisle, it was an opportunity to pass through ten counties of England, to see the varying geological structures ranging from London clay, to chalk, green sand, red sand, clay again, limestone, marl, sandstone, an intrusion of granite, red sandstone, coal, red oxides of iron, salt workings, coal again, millstone grit and limestone again, each of which drove the industry of the localities passed through; the bricks, the cement, the potteries, the collieries of Warwickshire and Lancashire, the chemicals of Warrington and the cotton of Lancashire.

The spectacular three spires of Lichfield cathedral and the single towering spire of St Walburge's church at Preston, the castle at Lancaster could be enjoyed, as could a glimpse near King's Langley of the birthplace of the sole English pope and at Warton where the ancestors of George Washington lived. Perhaps above was – and still is, though passed through now at too high a speed – the topography of the route north of Lancaster all the way into Scotland with its two great valleys, Annandale and Clydesdale.

The route between Chester and Holyhead also held visual attractions, as it does still; Conway beside the railway and the river of its name, south of Llandudno, and Chester itself.

As at the start of the twentieth century, the routes of interest to this book were well established and would remain largely undisturbed, except for large-scale remodelling and electric signalling at Crewe and war-time improvements for traffic movements, up to the late

Map 16: Crewe Station

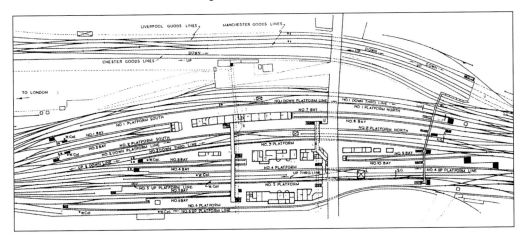

Map 17: Glasgow Central Station

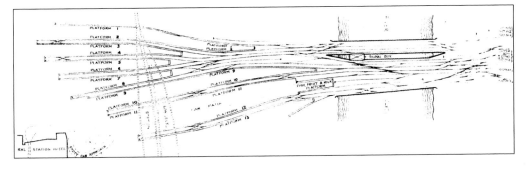

Key

1 Crewe North motive power depot

*Crewe: north end, Chester line to the left, Liverpool/Preston straight ahead, Manchester to the right, goods line in a tunnel beneath, Crewe Works area starting above the rear carriages of the train, Crewe North depot to the left of those carriages. Royal Scot, **The Royal Horse Guardsman** brings in a train of portions from off the Chester line; perhaps Holyhead/Llandudno and Birkenhead. A smaller than was often the case group of spotters has made use of some empty pigeon baskets and will be occupied by plenty of interest. (10)*

1950s. There is, therefore, little to add here for the period 1900-22 when, following the First World War, the multiple private railway companies were grouped into just four. The LNWR, LYR (which merged in 1922) and MR formed the majority of what became the London Midland and Scottish Railway (LMS) which, together with the Great Western, Southern and London and North Eastern, provided railway services up to nationalisation in 1948.

Chapter 2

Setting the Scene

This chapter seeks to identify the position of the railways and particularly the London Midland Region just prior to the era of interest to this book. The chapter is presented in three sections. First comes demand and competition, second comes supply and efficiency and finally the way in which the Region was organised and managed.

The statutory obligations of the British Transport Commission (BTC) were clearly stated in The Transport Act 1953. The railways, as being the dominant part of inland transport, had been nationalised from 1 January 1948 and became the third industry after coal and electricity to be taken into public ownership. The role of the Railway Executive was to provide railway services within Great Britain. The Act of 1953 followed a General Election held on 25 October 1951 in which the Conservative Party won a majority of seats, though not the highest number of votes cast, and replaced the Labour Party which had been in power since 26 July 1945. The arrival of the Conservative-led parliament put an end to a proposed further programme of nationalisation, reversed that for the steel industry and ushered in a policy of competition. Provisions within the 1953 Act paved the way for a rapid growth in the number of holders of 'C' licences. The 'C' licence holder was a manufacturer or trader who used his own fleet of vehicles for the transport of goods and could do so with low overhead costs and a choice of loads/destinations. Holders of 'A' and 'B' licences included those who plied either wholly or partly for hire or reward. The BTC had its own substantial fleet of vehicles as a Public Carrier and as such were similar to holders of 'A' and 'B' licences. Although the Act allowed the railways much more flexibility in charging than previously, it left the railways burdened by an obligation to be a common carrier; in other words, it had to accept whatever it was presented with. The holders of 'C' licences logically invested in larger vehicles, identified the economies of distances/times/return loads and conveyed the loads of their preferences.

Beyond the question of competing with a fast-developing private road transport industry, the Act made clear that the general duty of the BTC was that it must provide railway services for Great Britain. The key word was 'for' and replaced 'within Great Britain' which had been used in the 1947 Act. In simple terms, the BTC was to meet the needs of the nation and to do so while acknowledging the needs of efficiency, economy and safety. In 1954 the post-war recovery of the national economy allowed the government scope for capital investment in the three nationalised industries. The Treasury was willing to consider proposals from the BTC. When that programme was submitted it resulted in the Modernisation Plan 1955 which was accepted by the government at a cost of £1.24 billion and was perceived by the government to be the best available way for the railways to shape their own future in a competitive environment.

In 1953, British Railways and London Transport carried around 20 per cent of the total passenger miles travelled in total by private cars, public buses and coach services and railways in the UK. For 1956/57 that proportion of the total remained around the same figure – the total passenger miles travelled had increased by 12 per cent. After 1953, the proportion of the total tonnage of freight carried by the railways followed a downward trend; from 44.3 per cent to 26.4 per cent in 1962 (and 18.1 per cent in 1973).

By any measure the volume of business on offer was huge and, under the provisions of the Act of 1953, the public expectation was that a train would be available to destinations throughout the kingdom. For the LNW main lines to and from London there was a pattern of services for passengers, conveyance of mail, parcels/newspapers and for goods traffic.

Starting with express passenger services the summary was:

Route	Direction	Daytime departure 6 am to 9.00 pm	Night 9.01 pm to 5.59 am
Scotland	north	5	5
	south	6	5
NW England	north	7	2
	south	7	-
Manchester	north	6	2
	south	8	1
Liverpool	north	6	1
	south	5	1
N Wales	north-west	2	-
	east-south	3	1
W Midlands	north	8	1
	south	9	-

The following notes apply to the summary:

a) Winter Timetable 1956/57
b) the imbalance in the Scotland traffic was due to the carriages for Stranraer being conveyed on a Perth service, but southbound as a separate train
c) north-west England includes Crewe as a destination
d) trains for Manchester were routed by either Stoke-on-Trent/Macclesfield or Crewe/Wilmslow
e) some trains for Manchester/Liverpool conveyed carriages for Colne and Southport detached/attached en route
f) certain business trains for Manchester/Liverpool ran as one to Crewe and were separated there
g) the Scotland summary excludes the mail only service in each direction, no passengers conveyed
h) services to Birkenhead Woodside were offered using carriages attached to N Wales services and detached at Chester General.

The spread of trains throughout the day was uneven; examples being two departures for Scotland at 1/30 and 1/35 then nothing until 7/20 and 7/30, for Manchester nothing between 6/0 and 10/45, for Liverpool nothing after 6/10 until after midnight and for the West Midlands nothing between 7/0 and 9/35 (except via Paddington and the former Great Western route).

For the departures from Euston, a total of 564 vehicles were rostered and marshalled into train formations that, for examples, allowed detaching, placement of catering vehicles to allow ease of service to first-class passengers in dedicated class restaurant cars and, where portions of a train were detached, for it to have a hand-braked vehicle. The coaching stock sets generally stayed within a route, for example the 7/30 Euston-Perth set returned from Perth at 8/15 on the evening of day two and then formed the 7/30 departure on day three and, therefore, two identical formations were required to work the service, being serviced during the day at either Perth or Willesden carriage sidings/laundry. To cater for the business traveller, some of the sets included a high proportion of first-class seating; for example the 9.45 Euston-Manchester London Road service was marshalled as two first-class corridor compartments, guard's brake plus second-class compartments, two first-class open (tables) seating laid up as necessary for breakfast, kitchen car, first-class open, second-class open laid up as necessary, a second-class restaurant car, another second-class open, a second-class corridor compartment carriage and, finally, a guard's brake plus second-class compartments. A total of twelve carriages in a fixed formation, with reservations available for first or second-class seating, smoking or non-smoking areas, dining as an option. Following arrival at Manchester at 1/19, the set went empty to Longsight for servicing, seat reservation tickets, catering car re-stocking/gas bottle changing and then returned to Euston at 5/45, due 9/25 then empty to Willesden. Out via Stoke-on-Trent, back via Crewe, seating for close on 500 passengers, some 375 miles in the day. Despite its history and title, the *Royal Scot* 10.0 from Euston to Glasgow Central had only 108 first-class seats (within the total of 406) compared to 210 on the Manchester service (*The Comet*).

For completeness of record, Scotland enjoyed through services to and from Birmingham, Manchester and Liverpool, the latter two cities having their individual portions, attached or detached at either Preston or Wigan (North Western). Day and night services were available and further details are given later in chapter 3.

Sharing the tracks between Roade (59¾) and Euston were passenger trains routed either via Northampton (65¾) or originating/terminating there (five southbound, four northbound) and Bletchley (46¾), eight/fourteen.

Having four tracks as far as Roade helped with the regulation of traffic. Here 42573 passes South Kenton with an evening Euston-Bletchley stopping service formed of a standard set of predominantly non-corridor stock. The external appearance of such carriages was enhanced from 1960 by the addition of lining at waist and below the gutter strip levels. (11)

Between Watford Junction and Euston, the suburban service was provided by electric multiple units using the direct current system powered from the (LMS) Stonebridge Park power station. The two tracks ran on the Down (west) side on the main lines as far as Willesden (7¾), then passed under the main lines to emerge and then run on the east side to eventually gain access to platforms nine and ten at Euston.

In the 1950s BR was a willing partner with publicity departments of coastal resorts.

A summer Saturday morning; Camden bank and Jubilee **Implacable** with its banking engine have the 8.05 to Holyhead (W48) on its way. Also in the picture are three locomotives engaged with coaching stock duties and a class 7 awaiting access to Euston station with the stock of a later departure. The pollution of a still morning is evident, imagine that scene on a foggy/smoggy winter night. (12)

At the top of Camden bank, close to the motive power depot, Princess Coronation **City of Glasgow** has clearly tested to maximum extent the limits of the loading gauge. (13)

At certain times of the day and night Carlisle was an excellent location at which to enjoy the sight of several ex-LMS pacifics. W106 was a seasonal extra service from Glasgow and it would seem that **City of Lichfield (46250)** 'with at least one strengthening carriage' is waiting to relieve **Princess Alexandra (46224)** which will have brought the service from the north. Meanwhile, **City of Lancaster (46243)** has the 9.00 from Perth, its return through working as far as Crewe. (14)

In steam days any visit to Euston station was likely to deliver immediate interest at the buffer stops of the arrivals platforms. It was usually 20 minutes or so before the empty stock was cleared and the train engine either accompanied the empty train as far as near the entrance to the motive power depot (where it was uncoupled) or followed it as a light engine. Either way there was an opportunity to ask permission to have a look in the cab of the locomotive. Here a Royal Scot and a Britannia have arrived and await release. (15)

Passenger expectations for travel changed in accordance with the holiday season, religious festivals and bank holiday long weekends. As far as the railway authorities were concerned, summer was fixed between mid-June and mid-September (and the season for the heating of carriages 1 October to 30 April). During the Summer Timetable period, additional trains were operated either as shown in the public timetable or as Q (run as required) in the Working Timetable only. The running of the Q trains was often weather dependent and/or based upon the level of reservations made for the advertised services. The peak of the season was in line with the main school holidays when 'dated' services were operated. To cater for the demand many year-round services were strengthened by the addition of vehicle(s) within the maximum weight of train allowing particular point to point timings in the Working Timetable (see later reference in this chapter) to be adhered to by a single locomotive.

The build up of expectations started on Fridays and additional services ran as follows:

Time	Destination	Reporting number
12/20Q	Liverpool Riverside	W175
2/25	Liverpool Lime Street	W113
4/23	Birmingham New Street	W187
4/45	Liverpool Lime Street	W181
5/12	Preston	W191
5/55	Manchester Hayfield	W133
6/15	Heysham	W247
7/22	Inverness	W149
7/30	Oban	W307
8/15	Holyhead	W245
11/15	Blackpool North	W183
11/25	Holyhead	W481

A popular business train to the West Midlands is shown here with Jubilee **Thunderer.** *Timed at 79 minutes to pass Rugby it should by then be close on the tail lamp of the proceeding heavier 5.35 from Euston with a class 7 locomotive. Bushbury crews liked those challenges. (16)*

Friday evenings and weekends provided a higher probability of seeing Patriot Class locomotives on express passenger trains. W697 (with 45510) was a busy Euston-Holyhead relief service to the 8/50 Irish Mail which, despite its weight and length, conveyed seating accommodation insufficient to meet demand from London, let alone Crewe. (17)

The heavy 2/45 Euston-Manchester was usually hauled by a Longsight Royal Scot but, on this occasion, a Britannia (Byron) has the working and is seen passing Hatch End in fine style; first stop Rugby. (18)

As an example of the demand in summers, the following were main line departures from Euston between 8.0 and 1/30 for 1956:

Time	Destination	Reporting number
8.05 Q	Holyhead	W49
8.05 SO	Holyhead 21 July – 1 Sept	W49
8.15	Holyhead	W37
8.37 QSX	Crewe	
8.50 SX	Wolverhampton	W51
9.0 SO	Wolverhampton	W55
9.05 QMSX	Liverpool Riverside	W489
9.20 SO	Llandudno	W51
9.28 MO	Manchester London Road	W59
10.10	Glasgow Central	W57
10.20 QSX	Perth	W65
10.20 SO	Perth	W65
10.30	Liverpool Lime Street	W71
10.40	Carlisle	W251
10.48 SO	Blackpool Central	W127
10.50 SX	Blackpool Central	W77
10.55 SO	Blackpool Central	W77
11.15 SO	Portmadoc	W89
11.15 SX	Portmadoc	W89
11.22 SO	Liverpool Lime Street	W181
11.30 SO	Wolverhampton	W81
11.52	Workington	W121
12.00 SO	Workington	W179
12/01 SX	Crewe	W95
12/07 SO	Crewe	W95
12/37 SO	Manchester London Road	W45
12/50 SX	Wolverhampton	W91
1/15 SO	Glasgow Central	W97
1/20 SO	Perth	W99
1/30 SX	Glasgow Central	W97

The reporting number would be paper decals pasted onto a wooden board which would be attached to either the top lamp bracket on the front of the locomotive or to the handrail above the number plate. The same reporting number would be pasted onto at least one vehicle of the train, usually a guard's brake. Any reporting number in the block 1-499 was a timetabled train, odd for the Down direction, even for the Up and the use of W indicated Western Division (M for Midland Division and C for Central Division). The reporting numbers were of particular value to station staff and signalmen in contact with Controllers and the letters assisted at such places as Crewe (where W and M could be seen) and Preston (W and C). The LNWR had followed other railway companies in meeting the attraction of south coast resorts by running 'through' services. In the case of the LNWR Hastings was the destination of choice. In the late 1950s seasonal services (routed from Willesden via Kensington Olympia and Clapham Junction) ran from/to Leicester and Manchester, one from each.

Festivals and bank holiday weekends brought yet greater demands as, for example, half of Dublin seemed to wish to head for Holyhead at Christmas, the Scots home for Hogmanay, the Welsh for the Eisteddfod. The days in the approach to Christmas were particularly demanding with the additional expectation that all the parcels would arrive on time. The only Special Traffic Notice I have available was for 1958, but gives an idea of the position at Crewe in the middle of 20 December. The detail applies only to the line from the direction of Euston/Stafford/Shrewsbury and is for additional services only.

Time at Crewe	Train and remarks	Reporting number
10.59 – 11.1	Birmingham – Holyhead relief	W999
11.7 – 11.13	6.30 Euston – Windermere retimed	W33
11.14 – 11.20	Euston – Holyhead relief	W697
11.25 – 11.30	8.5 Euston – Holyhead relief	W49
11.20 –	Q relief from Birmingham	W995
11.43 –	Parcels ex Euston	W15
12/7 – 12/13	Q 9.10 Euston – Holyhead relief	W965
12/20 – 12/27	8.55 Cardiff – Manchester, first portion only	W283
1/44 – 1/50	12/5 Rugby – Barrow relief	W693
1/52 – 1/58	10.30 Euston – Crewe retimed	W251
2/27 –	10.47 Euston – Crewe extended to Holyhead (second portion of 10.40 Euston – Holyhead)	W89
2/31 –	Football Special ex Whitchurch	D2 (dmu)
2/45 –	11.42 Euston – Crewe (second portion of 11.35 Euston – Crewe)	W179
2/55 – 3/7	Military leave special to Manchester	W653
3/23 – 3/30	Paignton – Manchester relief	W309
3/55 – 4/2	9.45 Bournemouth West – Manchester retimed	M236
3/43 – 4/8	8.0 Plymouth – Liverpool retimed	W263
– 4/13	4/2 Crewe – Manchester retimed	W261
4/9 – 4/14	1/0 Euston – Glasgow relief	W685
4/15 – 4/22	1/20 Euston – Glasgow retimed	W97
4/35 –	1/32 ex Euston (second portion of 1/25 ex Euston)	W243
5/11 – 5/20	2/15 Euston – Liverpool relief	W941
5/15 –	Parcels ex Birmingham	W271

To compound the operational challenge arrangements for certain timetabled trains were amended, examples having been to divide the following to Crewe:

11.35 Euston – Manchester (W91, load 15). Second portion 11.42 to run to Workington (W179, load 12 to Crewe then ten).

1/25 Euston – Perth (W99, load 12). Second portion 1/32 to run to Blackpool (W243, load 11).

4/55 Euston – Blackpool (W159, load 13). Second portion 5/2 to run to Holyhead (W145, load 14, five to Llandudno only).

While the Down side platform Inspectors were dealing with the progress of these trains, passengers and parcels, their colleagues on the 'up' had at least an equal challenge. While the activity continued additional empty stock passenger trains were being positioned or repositioned. Examples were:

6/10   Euston – Carlisle to run to Morecambe E Rd (W3)
10/43   Leicester – Stafford to be extended to Rhyl (W241)
2/0   Penzance – Crewe to be extended to Rhyl (W61)

Additionally, there were certain goods services that were afforded a high priority for seasonal, perishable traffic:

3/20   Palethorpes Sidings – Dudley Port
6/15   Palethorpes Sidings – Dudley Port
8/20   Southampton Docks – Crewe, perishable fruit

Behind these lists were detailed planning lessons learned from previous Christmas periods and included some rare routings around Crewe. For example, the 8/45 (Friday) Euston-Holyhead (W161) was always solid with passengers and was diverted around Crewe by means of the independent lines between Basford Hall and just north of Crewe station onto the Chester line.

With railway planning, timetabling and rostering of men, locomotive and stock it was a continuum. While passengers alighted, parcels and goods were collected at the end of their journeys, the railway simply continued with disposing or arranging the next move for the men, locomotives and stock.

Overnight travel was catered for by sleeping cars and those built with six-wheel bogies and to the maximum permitted dimensions (note inlaid door handles and end grab handle) were about as good as it got anywhere. Reserve a berth in the centre of the vehicle and a better night's sleep was assured, away from the bogies. (19)

The expectations of business travellers in particular included sleeping car and catering services. Some splendid services were available:

Train		Notes
7/20	Euston – Inverness	Three sleeping cars (two first-class). Restaurant cars as far as Crewe and from Perth
7/30	Euston – Perth	One sleeping car, plus three to Carlisle for Stranraer. Restaurant car as far as Crewe
8/50	Euston – Holyhead	Two sleeping cars plus a restaurant car
9/10	Euston – Glasgow C	11 sleeping cars (seven first-class). No other passenger accommodation
9/25	Euston – Glasgow C	One sleeping car
10/52	Euston – Perth	Two sleeping cars
11/10	Birmingham – Glasgow	Three sleeping cars (two first-class)
11/05	Euston – Windermere	Three sleeping cars (two first-class)
11/50	Euston – Glasgow St E	Seven sleeping cars (six first-class). Restaurant car from Carlisle
0.20	Euston – Glasgow C	Five sleeping cars (four first-class). Restaurant car from Carlisle
0.30	Euston – Liverpool	Three sleeping cars (two first-class)
0.40	Euston – Manchester	Four sleeping cars (three first-class)
0.45 1.03	Liverpool Lime St - Glasgow C Manchester – Glasgow C	Trains combined at Wigan North Western. Four sleeping cars (two from each originating station and two of which were first-class)
Each working was balanced with an equivalent working south.		

Eating while on the move was another expectation of many. Of the 29 main line departures from Euston between 7.55 and 6/55, all but one included catering vehicles and 17 included a full-length kitchen only car for the preparation of meals.

Along the route were several ports from which passenger ship sailing times were supported by connecting railway services. The sailings were for both near coastal and international destinations. Short duration sailings were to Ireland (Dublin, from Holyhead and Liverpool), Northern Ireland (Belfast, from Liverpool, Heysham and Stranraer) and to the Isle of Man (Douglas, from Liverpool and Heysham). Liverpool was served by seven shipping lines:

Anchor Line	sailings to Port Said, Aden, Karachi and Bombay
Bibby Line	to Rangoon
Booth Line	to Lisbon, Barbados, Trinidad and North Brazil
Canadian Pacific	to Montreal, Quebec (summer) and St Johns (winter)
Cunard Line	to Montreal (summer) and New York (winter)
Elder Dempster Line	to Lagos
Pacific Steam Navigation Line	to South American ports via the Panama Canal

The ships deployed on the short crossings were:

to Dublin	*Cambria, Hibernia* Both had been built in 1948, entered service 1949 and replaced ships of the same names dating from 1921
to Belfast and Larne	*Duke of Argyll, Duke of Lancaster* built in 1956 *Hampton Ferry* (as a short-term replacement for *Princess Victoria* which sank during a severe storm in January 1953 when sailing Stranraer-Larne) *Caledonian Princess*, entered service new in 1961
to Douglas	*Lady of Man* used at Dunkirk and for the D-Day landings *Ben-my-Chree (IV)* which means in English My Fair Lady (also used at Dunkirk and for D-Day landings) *King Orry (IV)* *Tynwald (V)* *Mona's Isle (V)* *Snaefell* *Manxman (II)* new in 1955 *Manx Maid II* (a car ferry, new in 1962)

For the longer voyages, the expectation of passengers was for a connecting train service to and from Liverpool (Riverside) station, reached from the main line near Wavertree. Where demand did not justify a complete train, several carriages attached to a Liverpool Lime Street service from Euston would be detached at Wavertree and worked to Riverside. The BTC entered into the spirit of a profitable business by naming some of the then new diesel locomotives after the names of some of the ships used:

Aureol	of the Cunard line
Empress of Britain	of the Canadian Pacific fleet
Empress of England	of the Canadian Pacific fleet

Other locomotives used carried names of ships associated with Liverpool and a full listing is in Chapter 8. The Public Relations department was let down by *Carmania* (named such only after it was transferred by Cunard to Southampton in 1957), previously *Saxonia* when sailing from Liverpool.

The period covered by this book would witness a decline in international shipping of passenger traffic. For the profitable Irish routes – where a virtual monopoly existed – the BTC/BTB responded to expectations by the introduction of a roll on/roll off ship for Stranraer-Larne for road vehicle traffic (see later reference for containerised traffic and ships conveying livestock): *Caledonian Princess.*

If your local football or rugby league team was fortunate to progress to the annual cup final played at Wembley stadium, north London in early May, your expectation would have been for a special train to take you and your fellow supporters/family for a grand day out. For the savvy spotter in the London area, Willesden and Neasden depots would be ideal for seeing locomotives not normally seen in the capital. Those spotters probably did far better for the Rugby League finals than the Association Football:

Year	Rugby League	Association Football
1957	Leeds v Barrow	Aston Villa v Manchester Utd
1958	Wigan v Workington Town	Bolton Wanderers v Manchester Utd
1959	Wigan v Hull FC	Nottingham Forest v Luton Town
1960	Wakefield Trinity v Hull FC	Wolverhampton Wanderers v Blackburn Rovers
1961	St Helens v Wigan	Tottenham Hotspur v Leicester City
1962	Wakefield Trinity v Huddersfield	Tottenham Hotspur v Burnley
1963	Wakefield Trinity v Wigan	Manchester United v Leicester City

While the Association Football final was always a full house of 100,000, the attendances for the Challenge Final of Rugby League attracted between 66,109 and 94,672 and generally produced plenty of Black 5 4-6-0s. Some years were good for the spotters along the route, others not so as either the motive power came from depots that normally supplied the route or the trains were routed along the Midland, Great Central or Great Northern lines.

The then bi-annual football meeting of England and Scotland at Wembley/Hampden Park produced many overnight trains which were spread across the West Coast, East Coast and Great Central routes. A similar bi-annual exodus, from South Wales to Scotland for the rugby union international, involved more than thirty special trains sent mainly down the route to Crewe and thence to Carlisle and Edinburgh while a minority took the Midland route via Gloucester and Leeds to Carlisle. Care was taken to get the returning trains away in an order that allowed those from West Wales home at about the same time as those for Cardiff and Newport who left Edinburgh later.

Hockey matches at Wembley were also well supported and brought Southern Region and Western region power to either the stadium station or nearby and, when the former was closed, the turning of the locomotives with their trainsets produced some unusual sights.

Expectations for the provision of special trains for passengers extended to:

• day/half day/evening excursions for ramblers/illuminations
• Glasgow Fairs specials

The FA Cup Final at Wembley was a special occasion to which BR contributed by provision of train headboards and attention to the external condition of the locomotives. For what was 'Stanley Mortensen's Final' but which became 'the Matthews Final' Blackpool triumphed 4-3. (20)

- city or town holiday week(s) excursions with a different destination each day
- flower shows (Southport)
- miners' welfare specials
- Sunday school excursions
- invalid specials to Lourdes
- Billy Graham Crusader tour trains
- enthusiasts' tours

While the route generally met passenger expectations, it left to others the relative attractions of cheap fare Starlight Specials between Scotland and London and also the developing market for those families who wished to take their car by train overnight to a place where they could start/finish their holiday motoring tour. The families were accommodated overnight in sleeping cars. The 7/20 Euston-Inverness conveyed cars which were loaded off a ramp at platform 17 (that train becoming *The Royal Highlander*). Another similar service was the Sutton Coldfield-Stirling/Inverness service (three times a week in each direction) routed via Derby, Leeds and Carlisle.

> This is the Night Mail crossing the Border
> Bringing the cheque and the postal order,
> Letters for the rich, letters for the poor,
> The shop at the corner, the girl next door …

The expectation of the British public was that if a letter was posted before a certain time it would be delivered the following day in either the first or second round by a friendly postman or woman. In turn, the expectation of the Royal Mail was that the railway would operate a fleet of vehicles dedicated to the collection, sorting and exchanging of mail along key routes. Our route of interest included the Night Mail trains that produced W.H. Auden's poem *The Night Mail*, quoted from above, and due to the vagaries of the railways' accounting arrangements one of the 'cheques' (as in the poem) went invariably to the London Midland Region and never to the Scottish Region. Crewe was the place where most interchanges of vehicles/mail took place in various directions as follows:

Train (down)	Reporting number	Arrive	Depart	Note
7/20 Cardiff – Manchester	–	11/03		A
6/30 Swansea – York	W201	11/27	0.05	see I
10/10 Birmingham – Crewe	W297	11/31		B
8/30 Euston – Glasgow	W157	11/44	0.10	C
10.30 Crewe – Liverpool			0.30	D
10/52 Euston – Perth	W195	1.55	2.15	E
2.05 Crewe – Holyhead	W1		2.05	F
10/10 Liverpool – Crewe – Cardiff	W142	11/25	1.25	G
7/35 Holyhead – Birmingham	W170	11/35	0.45	
6/30 Glasgow – Euston	W148	0.25	0.37	H
9/50 York – Swansea	487	1.7	2.15	I
10/0 Stranraer Hbr – Euston	W68	4.38	4.48	J

Notes

A. Post Office van ex Pontypool Road off noon Penzance – Manchester (W297) service
B. Post Office vans forward to Holyhead at 2.05
C. Picked up mail bags at speed from Harrow, Watford Junction, Hemel Hempstead, Berkhamsted, Cheddington, Bletchley and called at Rugby (mail ex Peterborough route) and Tamworth (Lincoln, Nottingham, Derby). Change of locomotive 8P/8P. Portion of train for Aberdeen
D. Included Post Office van off 11/03 arrival
E. Picked up mail bags at speed from Leighton Buzzard, Bletchley, Rugby and near Nuneaton. Called at Nuneaton to pick up bagged mail (Leicester/Birmingham). Post Office vans detached (see J)
F. Included Post Office vans off 11/31 arrival
G. Post Office van forward to Pontypool Road/Penzance
H. Changed locomotive 8P/8P. Portion of train from Aberdeen
I. Post Office vans to Shrewsbury (returned following night on 6/30 Swansea-York)
J. Post Office vans off 10/52 Euston-Perth attached for return to Euston

Additional notes

- The 10/52 Euston – Perth service also conveyed Post Office vans to Carlisle (5.16) returned that evening (9/0) attached to the 6/30 Glasgow-Euston
- The 6/27 Workington – Preston conveyed a Post Office van, returned on the 11/5 Euston – Windermere to Lancaster
- Birmingham New Street was also busy as an interchange point with cross country services Bristol-Newcastle and vice versa
- Post Office employees travelled with these trains to either sort individual items of mail, receive bags collected en route, stow sorted bagged mail for specific destinations and unload bagged mail en route
- Sorting vans had a post box into which letters could be posted for an additional (small) amount though it helped to know in which direction the train was travelling.

Parcels and newspaper traffic were also in the category of mail as having a sense of urgency. There were, up to 1959, multiple parcels handling/forwarding points on the London Midland Region with each London terminal station involved. From Euston the main parcels trains were to Bletchley, Northampton, Rugby, Crewe and Manchester and with those for north and west of Crewe taken forward by a similar service to Carlisle/Holyhead. There were two principal centres for the English press – London and Manchester – from where printed newspapers were taken by road between 10pm and midnight for loading into vans. Trains were then taken as far as the 'boundary' cities and towns between the southern and northern print run distribution areas. From Euston, the 1.30 went to Wolverhampton via Northampton and with stops to unload at all significant intermediate stations for local distribution.

Goods traffic was classified into three groups; coal, coke and patent fuels, other minerals and merchandise. The geology of the UK meant that there was a need to bring coal south for consumption in the home counties, London and the south-east. The markets were industrial, domestic and for the railway itself (some 12 million tons annually for the latter alone).

The demand for London and the south-east was such that no single route from the coalfields of South Yorkshire, Nottinghamshire, Derbyshire and Leicestershire, could meet the total demand. Each weekday, some 81 loaded coal trains were dealt with at yards at Temple Mills, Ferme Park and Neasden (Eastern Region), Brent/Cricklewood (Midland Division of London Midland Region) and Sudbury Junction/Brent yard at Willesden. The latter yard received 15 loaded trains which had originated in Yorkshire (and routed via Newark, Welham/Market Harborough and Northampton/Roade), Nottinghamshire (via Leicester, Market Harborough) and Leicestershire (via Rugby). To provide power from the BTC's Stonebridge Park (near Willesden) power station for the Watford Junction – Euston d.c. electric service 'block' trains of purpose-built, bogie wagons with vacuum brakes ran south from Toton (between Nottingham and Derby) on three nights a week.

The Clean Air Act of 1956, together with the rapid development of clean, cheap electricity via the National Grid, combined to make 1957 the peak year for demand for coal for the industrial and domestic markets. With capital investment having been directed to Temple Mills, routes such as the Newark-Market Harborough, Great Northern/LNW Joint were quickly at risk and cross London transfer flows via the North London line came more into short-term usage.

Demand for other mineral traffic was less at the southern end of the route than in centres of production consuming primary materials (the marls, clays, salt and iron ore) which tended to be local or flow east-west and emerge from the production process as merchandise traffic. For examples, the sanitary ware from the Potteries, cotton, agricultural chemicals, refined salt and detergent from Warrington, almost anything from the Black Country of the West Midlands, footwear from Northampton and Nuneaton. That left perishable traffic in the form of meat (from Scotland and Ireland), fish (Scotland and Fleetwood), fruit, vegetables and milk. The use of containers for particular products had been developed by the LMS and LNER in the 1920s and such a method of transport, with loading/off-loading onto a railway flat wagon for journeys exceeding 250 miles, made it ideal for the BTC.

Goods trains having all, or a proportion of, wagons marshalled next to the locomotive fitted with continuous vacuum brakes, gave a greater braking force and allowed faster timings in

Any lull in passenger traffic would attract the planners of goods train services. The most interesting working was the thrice weekly Toton-Sudbury Junction/Stonebridge Park coal train which was usually powered by a Toton 8F. Stonebridge Park power station was a BR plant which supplied the 'juice' for the d.c. Harrow-Euston multiple units. (21)

As the shadows lengthened so did the stream of brake fitted goods trains. (22)

The mid-afternoon lull in departures from Euston allowed two fully brake fitted long distance goods services to use the fast line for some of the journey to Roade and beyond. Here Jubilee *Vindictive* has been denied an opportunity to cross to the fast line, but nevertheless makes good progress; note the containers used for meat/fish from Scotland. (23)

A considerable volume of cattle and sheep traffic from Ireland was conveyed forward from Holyhead. Here a Black 5 has a valuable load under way skirting the sea near Penmaenmawr. (24)

Londoners were well provided for by provision of fresh milk from Ayrshire/Westmoreland (as well as Derbyshire, Cornwall and Devon) in glass-lined, six-wheel tank wagons. The external condition of the tank wagons was in stark contrast to the purity of their contents, but intensive usage and the shape of the wagons made cleaning of all but the interiors difficult. Afforded a high priority, the trains enjoyed express status and the use of class 7/8 locomotives. **City of Birmingham.** *(25)*

the Working Timetable. A 'C' was completely fitted with vacuum braked wagons, 'D' and 'E' proportionately less. The route handled on weekdays up to 30 'fitted' goods trains from/to London:

'C' trains Time	Service
2/40 SX	Camden (in London) – Glasgow Buchanan Street
2/55 SX	Camden – Crewe
7/0 SX	Camden – Manchester London Road
7/35 SX	Camden – Liverpool Edge Hill
8/37 SO	Broad Street – Stockport
8/50 SX	Camden – Carnforth
8/55 SX	Camden – Manchester Brewery Sidings
10/02 SX	Broad Street – Stockport
10/15 SX	Broad Street – Carlisle Viaduct Yard

'D' trains	Service
12.45 MX	Camden – Carlisle
1.50 MX	Brent Sidings – Crewe
10.50	Camden – Crewe
12/25	Brent Sidings – Northampton
3/45 FOQ	Brent Sidings – Crewe
7/0 SO	Camden – Manchester London Road
7/35 SO	Camden – Liverpool Edge Hill
7/45 TThO	Brent Sidings – Toton (coal empties)
9/10 SX	Broad Street – Hooton
9/20 SX	Camden – Manchester
9/25 SO	Camden – Carlisle Kingmoor
9/28 SX	Camden – Crewe
9/45 SXQ	Camden – Hillhouse
9/55 SX	Camden – Warrington
10/50 SX	Camden – Birmingham Curzon Street
'E' trains	**Service**
12.15 MO	Camden – Carlisle
1.05	Brent Sidings – Birmingham Curzon Street
3.20 MX	Willesden – Crewe
8.45 SX	Brent Sidings – Crewe
3/25 SO	Brent Sidings – Crewe
5/30 SO	Brent Sidings – Crewe
8/15 SO	Camden – Walsall
10/15 SO	Brent Sidings – Crewe

Note: Northampton also produced two 'D' trains, being the 1.52 to Manchester Adswood and the following 2.0 to Warrington.

Beyond the 'E' trains were unbraked goods trains and engineers' trains (civil engineering materials, signal and telecommunications materials, coals for stations and signal boxes), 'pick up' goods trains and minerals which were fitted into the Working Timetable for the slow lines whenever available.

An interesting, if niche, expectation was that of Federations of Homing Pigeon Fanciers. Breeding pigeons for competitive racing had been a popular pastime since the 1920s and the GWR, LNER (and possibly the LMS) built vehicles especially for conveyance to far off destinations where the birds would be released at a specific time. In the 1950s, Federations joined together to request that seasonal specials be run between for example South Wales and Scotland, the north-east and south coast of England and Wolverhampton to Frome/Weymouth. These trainsets grew at times to around 20 bogie vehicles and were an inter-Regional challenge to the railway operators. Working the empty trainsets home was hardly a priority and any available route was taken.

From time to time, a national emergency would place demands upon the railways. One such occasion was between the end of October 1956 and mid-May 1957. After it was opened in 1869, the Suez Canal in Egypt offered to shipping a direct route between the North Atlantic and Indian oceans via the Mediterranean and Red seas. The alternative was the longer route via the tip of Southern Africa and the need for re-fuelling/stocking. A short conflict resulted in the closure of the Canal and necessitated longer voyages via Cape Town.

Above all else, the expectation was that the railways would run. The only times the railways did not run were when railway workers became so disgruntled with the treatment they received from the BTC that they took the ultimate action by voting to withdraw their labour. The level of disgruntlement had been growing as transport workers progressively slipped down the pay league in comparison with others. A Court of Inquiry effectively avoided a strike over Christmas/New Year 1954/55 and in its judgment the Court made a 'hint' that in that instance the BTC should receive finance from the Government to meet the legitimate demands of the men. There were three trade unions representing railway workers; the National Union of Railwaymen (NUR), the Transport Salaried Staffs Association (TSSA) and the Associated Society of Locomotive Engineers and Firemen (ASLEF). Thus far the case and proposed settlement had been progressed by the NUR, but when the details of the settlement became clearer, ASLEF recognised that it weakened the traditional relativity of locomotive enginemen in the pay hierarchy. ASLEF called a strike to commence on 1 May 1955. The strike actually started on 28 May and lasted for 17 days; both the NUR and TSSA stood aside from the dispute though the latter made a donation to ASLEF funds. It was the first railway strike for 30 years and the 68,000 strong membership of ASLEF were in solid support. The strike was called off on 14 June following agreement between the union and the BTC that the matter should be decided by an independent referee and that his decision would be binding on both parties. The referee's decision increased the weekly rate of pay for drivers by either one, two or three shillings dependent upon the length of time during which the driver had become qualified (one, two or three years+). Firemen and locomotive cleaners received nothing at all.

No railwayman or woman could take much comfort from the strike. It soured internal relationships at all levels and damaged the commercial trading relationships and trust with those who depended upon speed of movement in accordance with market demands. The fishing industry in particular was badly affected and prompted thoughts as to their future transport arrangements.

The London Midland Region (LMR) had some 18,000 miles of track (5,000 route miles) and, just prior to the declaration of a state of war in September 1939, the LMS had in its West Coast main line one of the two best maintained lengthy stretches of track in the country. Together with the LNER, it had tracks and signalling capable of supporting the streamlined, high speed services that formed part of the emergence from the years of depression, during which the four railway companies had benefitted from finance made available by the government for approved new works to reduce unemployment and improve transport facilities. The Railway Finance Corporation made loans available to the railways at 2½ per cent interest and, in taking advantage of that, the LMS invested in a major re-signalling scheme (colour light signals, electrical point changing machines, track circuits, route indicators, ground signals controlled from two signal boxes) at Crewe. Other works included improving telecommunications linkages and improving locomotive servicing facilities by new (cenotaph type) coaling and ash plants. Wartime had resulted in improvements to refuge sidings becoming loops (i.e. no need to propel back into a refuge) and the authorisation by the Ministry of War Transport for the quadrupling of a section of the main line north of Carlisle.

The task of restoring the main line infrastructure to pre-war standards was initially hampered by material shortages and between 1948 and 1953 the total mileage of track renewed for the entire railways system averaged only 1,575 miles. However, with lengthy sections of four track railway and the ability to divert traffic via Northampton, via the West Midlands between Rugby and Stafford while work along the Trent Valley was progressed and via Stoke-on-Trent to Manchester and north and west thereof if necessary while work was progressed between Colwich and Crewe/Cheadle Hulme were all useful to the engineers.

While main line departures from Euston usually benefitted from a helpful push up most of Camden bank by whatever locomotive had brought in the empty stock, the arrangements for the northbound ascent of Shap (from Tebay) and Beattock involved small allocations of locomotives stationed purely for the purpose of banking trains. During the period of interest to this book both Tebay and Beattock had handful numbers of 2-6-4 tank locomotives to Fowler and (development by) Fairburn designs. Through the earlier years Beattock shed also had use of Caledonian 0-4-4 tank locomotives.

Not all express passenger trains required the assistance of a banking locomotive but in every case and often dictated by how the locomotive was steaming, the prevailing weather and railhead conditions the decision was entirely at the discretion of the driver. The relevant Sectional Appendices detailed the whistle codes to be sounded in advance in order that the signalman could telephone through the request for, or decision to not require a banker, the latter being used more for goods trains fitted with vacuum brakes.

The two Anglo-Scottish expresses that took a banker from Beattock were both bound for Glasgow Central; being the 11/10 from Birmingham and the 0.20 from Euston, both being allowed 29 minutes for the climb and one of perhaps seven or eight ascents made daily by a banking locomotive.

Signalling was for the major part of the route of the semaphore type controlled from manual signal boxes. Spacing between signals had, over some sections, been adjusted for the high-speed services of 1937-39. No automatic warning system was installed to alert drivers to the fact that a signal at caution had been passed and safety of trains relied heavily on the eyesight and professionalism of the enginemen and maintainers of the track.

*The headboard on the **Black 5** announces the passage over Moore troughs of a returning day excursion from probably Blackpool or maybe Morecambe. The train went to a different destination each weekday and was popular with families. (26)*

Once on the move, trains at speed could save time by their locomotives picking up water from troughs placed between the rails. From Euston to Carlisle, the troughs were at Bushey (15¼ miles), Castlethorpe (54), Newbold (84), Hademore (114), Whitmore (148), Moore (179), Dillicar/Brock (217), Hest Bank (233½) and Tebay (261) and were generally one quarter of a mile in length. A passenger steam locomotive at speed would consume over 30 gallons of water per mile. When trains were headed by two locomotives, the drivers would agree beforehand at which trough a 'dip' would be made by each as may be necessary, but as most tenders of the 1950s/60s had a capacity of 4,000 gallons (a few such as the Holyhead allocated *Britannias* had more) the need for constant 'topping up' was rare.

In terms of safety, there was one horrendous accident at Harrow & Wealdstone on 8 October 1952 with loss of 112 lives; derailments due to the state of the track at Polesworth on 21 July 1947, a locomotive defect at Weedon on 21 September 1951, an unknown condition within Watford Tunnel (Up) on 3 February 1954 and a rear end collision at Winsford on 17 April 1948, when, due to a signalling error, the 6/25 Glasgow Central-Euston ran into the rear of the 5/40 service between those stations.

In terms of the basics of track, capacity, overcoming geological factors and telecommunications, the expectations as in the Transport Act 1953 were being met. Safety remained a concern across all Regions and the progressive introduction from 1957 of an automatic warning system was welcome and overdue.

To move the trains, there was a heavy reliance upon steam motive power. Far more detail is given in Chapter 3, but it is relevant here to summarise the position. Steam locomotives were grouped into classes of power and signified F for freight haulage, P for passenger and MT for passenger or freight. The main lines of interest to this book were fortunate to have a fleet of locomotives suitable for passenger train work with a relatively low average age. A summary is:

Power	Quantity allocated to route	Note
8P	51	2 from 1933 10 from 1935 36 from 1938 2 from 1947 1 from 1954
7P	81	Rebuilt between 1943 and 1955 2 new in 1942
6P	109	33 from 1930 76 from 1934
7MT	13	13 from 1952
6MT	10	10 from 1952
5MT	354	1934-48

For freight work, the 5MTs were ideal for the brake fitted trains, a fleet of 8Fs (from 1934-46) ideal for mineral and unfitted merchandise trains and 7Fs (from 1912) still dependable particularly in the West Midlands and within the former Lancashire and Yorkshire Railway system.

A measure of efficiency is the percentage of days on which locomotives were available for traffic. For the passenger types a figure around 72 was an average and this will be developed in detail at Chapter 3. A further measure was reliability when in traffic and the higher average figure achieved reflected the maintenance and overhaul periodicities assigned to these machines.

The maximum daily mileage for these steam locomotives very rarely exceeded around 400 miles. The average mileages and the figures for availability and reliability ranked well when compared to what other Divisions of the London Midland Region and other Regions were achieving.

In setting the scene at end 1956, the allocation of the front-line fleet of steam locomotives was:

Depot	Code	Power class	Quantity
Camden, London	1B	6	7
		7	15
		8	15
Willesden, London	1A	6	6
		7	–
		8	–
Bushbury, Wolverhampton	3B	6	10
		7	–
		8	–
Crewe North	5A	6	20
		7	21
		8	17
Longsight, Manchester	9A	6	17
		7	22
		8	–
Edge Hill, Liverpool*	8A	6	15
		7	14
		8	6
Holyhead	6J	6	–
		7	7
		8	–
Carlisle Upperby (LNW) Note: 12A to 1958	12B	6	16
		7	8
		8	4
Carlisle Kingmoor (CR) Note: 68A to 1958	12A	6	23
		7	–
		8	–
Polmadie, Glasgow (CR)	66A	6	5
		7	10
		8	9

* also supplied power classes 6 and 7 for other route

The allocation of the go anywhere, do anything 5MT (the Black 5s) to London Midland Region depots along the route was as follows:

Aston, Birmingham 18, Bangor 3, Blackpool 19, Bletchley 7, Bushbury 6, Carlisle Kingmoor 52, Carlisle Upperby 40, Carnforth 23, Crewe North 41, Crewe South 25, Edge Hill 25, Holyhead 2, Llandudno Junction 7, Longsight 15, Monument Lane, Birmingham 7, Preston 3, Rugby 17, Springs Branch, Wigan 9, Warrington 10 and Willesden 25.

In summary, the class 7Ps and the class 5MTs were the 'go to' locomotives as and when high levels of expectations were headed towards the route of interest.

From 1955 until 1959 the route also had use of six diesel locomotives:

Number	Power	Year built	Configuration	Builder
10000	1,600hp	1947	Co – Co	EE/LMS
10001	1,600hp	1947/48	Co – Co	EE/LMS
10201	1,750hp	1951	1 Co – Co – 1	EE/SR
10202	1,750hp	1951	1 Co – Co – 1	EE/SR
10203	2,000hp	1954	1 Co – Co – 1	EE/SR

Notes

Co-Co	three powered axles, plus three powered axles
1 Co – Co – 1	one unpowered axle, three powered axles plus three powered axles, plus one unpowdered axle
EE	English Electric

*As a shop window enticement, the English Electric **Deltic** and its performance in traffic proved irresistible to even an initially unwilling management. The locomotive is preserved in the National Collection and is normally at Shildon. (27)*

The sixth was a prototype built by English Electric to demonstrate the capabilities of a high performance, high powered (3,300hp) Co-Co diesel and also to promote the company itself. The locomotive was attractive to the civil engineer as having no unsprung weight. Unlike the other five, *Deltic* was not sold to the BTC; it was made available with the commercial future and investment monies within the Modernisation Plan of 1955 in mind. Throughout its time on the Region (deployed only within the Western Division) the locomotive was accompanied by representatives of the Company and the London Midland Region Chief Mechanical and Electrical Engineer. Statistics for availability and reliability are not available.

All five of the other English Electric diesels received a major overhaul in 1955/56 and emerged in the dark green lined with horizontal bands of orange, black, orange livery then standard for passenger locomotives. The working environment of a steam railway was not supportive of maintaining diesels at depot level and frequent visits to main works in Derby reduced the availability to less than 70 but, on the days they were available, they accumulated net annual averages of 91,000 miles each, at the very top end of what a London Midland Region main line passenger steam locomotive could achieve. The operators were confident to let 10203 work alone on principal expresses, though 10000 was paired with 10001 (5P5F) and 10201 paired with 10202. All five experienced problems with steam heating boilers and were more regularly seen on express passenger duties between May and the end of September. Any of the five could be seen on shorter haul passenger services to Northampton and Birmingham. The conclusion is that with its steam and diesel locomotive fleet, the expectation of travellers could be consistently met.

In terms of coaching stock, the route had a mix of vehicle types and age profile. For a few years after nationalisation, the six Areas/Regions continued to build carriages to the designs of the former companies. However, due to the backlog of maintenance from the years of wartime, very little new build during that time and material shortages combined to give a fleet with 22 per cent having an average age of 35 years. In 1948-53 an average of 1,653 new carriages were built, with the new British Railways' Mark 1 design appearing from 1950 and in production quantities from 1951. There were two basic types, both with a gauge profile able to pass over all principal routes without restrictions; a step forward. Underframes for vehicles having corridor connections were 63 feet 5 inches and, for non-gangwayed stock, 56 feet 11 inches. The longer vehicles were produced as compartment or open (i.e. with tables), first and third-class seating and later production builds were authorised for sleeping cars, catering vehicles with either a kitchen only or cooking facilities to serve a restaurant car or buffet, and also a luggage van. From introduction to 1956 the livery was carmine and cream, the latter covering the upper part of the steel bodyside.

As a route with high traffic and passenger densities, the West Coast route quickly received an allocation of the newer builds and, wherever possible, formed them into complete trainsets. From 2 June 1956, third-class was abolished, though with the existing carriages no changes were made to the seats. Also, in 1956 a change of livery occurred with carmine and cream giving way to maroon and the emblem on locomotives becoming a red lion holding a silver locomotive wheel. The lion had a crown upon which was a rose (England), thistle (Scotland), a leek (Wales) and an oak leaf (for all Great Britain). With the words *British* and *Railways* to either side, the lion, crown and wheel were circled within a gold perimeter.

From the commencement of the 1956 Summer Timetable, some trainsets were formed of maroon stock (either new or re-painted), mostly Mk1 though with LMS design kitchen cars. Examples included:

Name	Feature
The Royal Scot	Carriage roof boards had a green tartan background
The Midlander	Light blue background edged in cream and with red lettering and the coat of arms of Birmingham at each end
The Mancunian	Light blue with red edges and red lettering plus coat of arms at each end
The Merseyside Express	Grey with white lettering plus the motif of Merseyside flanked by Liver Birds.

Each trainset was dedicated to that particular service, two sets being needed for *The Royal Scot* as each worked a two-day circuit.

The use of named trains promoted the incoming, newer stock and the appearance and upkeep of them was supported by a team of rolling stock inspectors. Other named services included *The Comet, The Irish Mail, The Lakes Express, The Manxman, The Mid-Day Scot, The Midlander, The Red Rose, The Shamrock* and *The Ulster Express.*

For other services in the winter timetable, and additional services run only in the summer, for relief excursion special, run as required, shipping and control authorised used services, the Western Division had an adequate stock of vehicles held at carriage sidings and depots. A listing of main line departures from Euston for winter 1956 is at Appendix 3.

For local services to and from Bletchley, some non-gangwayed stock was deployed. Diesel multiple units were introduced with great success into the Birmingham area and would follow into other areas as the Modernisation Plan was progressed.

A national railway system that did not make it a requirement to pre-reserve a seat had a consequence of loadings in excess of seating capacity. Friday nights, Bank Holiday weekends, Summer Saturdays all provided examples of clamour for seats but, in more normal circumstances, expectations of passengers were met. It was a similar story of a range of ages and types for catering vehicles. The route had call upon a total of 51 older kitchen-only carriages, being 50 feet long, 16 cafeteria cars, 120 first-class 'open' restaurant cars, 110 second-class 'open' restaurant cars (of which 8 were specifically for Liverpool Riverside traffic) and 31 composite 'open' restaurant cars. Starting to arrive new were some 63 feet 5 inch kitchen cars. The restaurant cars included 59 that had 6-wheel bogies and, at 68 feet long, were route specific. Additionally, there were hybrid vehicles; three buffet cars, three pantry cars (for use with sleeping car services) and eight kitchen buffet cars (seven being the twelve-wheel, route restricted type).

The Winter Timetable 1956-57 included a need for only 19 kitchen cars and, as such, left more than adequate scope to meet expectations.

I have to admit being in the dark as regards the extent and age profile of the fleet of sleeping cars, but new Mk 1 BR types were built to initially augment and then replace the older, twelve-wheeled LMS designed types.

The times of arrival were more important than departure and, for all, it was possible for passengers to not vacate their berth immediately.

Arrivals at Euston	Empty stock to Willesden
ex Manchester 5.24	6.10
ex Liverpool 5.57	6.45
ex Holyhead 6.30	7.10
ex Glasgow 7.03	7.40
ex Perth 7.13	7.45
ex Glasgow 7.20	8.01
ex Stranraer 8.05	9.0
ex Inverness 8.20	9.20

A similar arrangement applied for early morning arrivals at Glasgow Central but arrivals at Perth and Inverness were later in the morning. Passengers for Dublin had to vacate at Holyhead at 2.35 off the 8/50 from Euston and Manchester/Liverpool arrivals were at very unsocial hours (4.45/4.34). My research has not identified any indication of expectations not being met, though it is my experience they were rather like saunas. The trains run solely for the Royal Mail were contract based, and afforded high priority and given class 8 power throughout in each direction, with a change at Crewe.

Having now considered demand and supply for passenger and mail services, it is appropriate to identify how different services to destinations at different times of the day/night/year were

Empty stock of main line passenger services was taken to Willesden for servicing and by the look of things here at Kensal Rise the driver of 47483 will also be looking for coal at the adjacent depot. (28)

planned in terms of number of vehicles. For examples, a lot of business travellers wanted to reach Liverpool/Manchester in the morning, passengers of all types seemed to wish to get to Liverpool in the evening, traffic to Holyhead needed to convey more than just passengers, while the volume of traffic to and from the West Midlands was less and more evenly spread. The result was trains of various numbers and types of vehicles and, therefore, of various weights travelling along the route. The express trains made few stops en route and, except for those routed via Northampton, very few called anywhere before some did at Rugby (82½ miles) and few then stopped again before either Stafford (133½) or Crewe (158); the Trent Valley stations being particularly badly served. Not necessarily badly served, but not quite so well served were southbound passengers originating in the North-West of England from whence there was an imbalance of through trains compared with northbound. The carriages kept returning but not in complete trainsets.

Heavy express trains between Euston and Rugby and lighter weight express trains between the same points could be expected to take different durations unless the more powerful locomotives were assigned to the former. For the planners and timetablers of the day, their challenge was not a new one and how the response had evolved will be described in Chapter 3. Clearly, part of the challenge was to avoid fast trains being hindered in their progress and that all trains could progress as best they could without having to await platform capacity at stations.

For each section of the route, sets of timings were laid down and, within each set, the weights of trains that were expected to keep to these timings when hauled by locomotives of different power. As an example:

Section	Weight tons	Timing (mins)		
		With class 6	With class 7	With class 8
Euston – Rugby	350	79		
	405		79	
	510			79
	415	86		
	475		86	
	600			86
	430	92		
	495		92	
	655			92
	495	97		
	550		97	
	700			97

Notes
350 tons = 11 vehicles
405 tons = 13 vehicles
510 tons = 15 vehicles

In the Working Timetable, the timings were expressed as XL (the fastest), SL, LL and FL, meaning Special Load, Limited Load and Full Load.

Taking as examples our morning and evening trains to Liverpool, Holyhead and the West Midlands, it was clearly desirable to keep the passengers on the move in accordance with their expectations.

Train	Weight (tons)	Locomotive power class	Timing to Rugby (mins)
7.55 to Liverpool	440	8	79
6/10 to Liverpool	522	8	86
8/50 to Holyhead	486	7	92
2/20 to Wolverhampton	357	6	79

In compiling the Working Timetable, other factors had to be taken into account and the actual times for one of the trains used as an example was 86 minutes rather than the 79 allowed but, in most other cases, the 'booked' time was expected to be kept. Seventy-nine minutes start to pass for 82 miles was well within the capability of a class 8 and, as the infrastructure was upgraded (track signalling and automatic warning system), further improvements could be expected if the management so desired and directed.

During the course of each winter weekday, 14 departures from Euston were assigned to class 8 power.

As can be seen from the two tables giving weights of trains (timetable basis and actual loads) there was sometimes a margin allowing for additional tonnage; for example, the 7.55 to Liverpool could have taken on additional 70 tons (two vehicles) and still have been expected to keep to 79 minutes. However, the 8/50 to Holyhead with a class 7 was within a few tons of maximum (and, on Fridays, that was invariably accounted for by Irishmen standing in the corridors).

The margins varied from train to train and, during the Suez Crisis and other busy times, were taken up by attaching additional vehicles, often to the limit of platform lengths at Manchester and Liverpool.

In the event of a shortage of motive power, the driver of a train timed beyond the capability of his locomotive could request the provision of an assisting locomotive; for example, with a Wolverhampton train loaded to 13 vehicles for commercial reasons and timed XL with a class 6 he could request assistance and would normally be provided with a class 5 (or 4, as still then available) assisting (pilot) locomotive.

Steam locomotives were not fitted with speedometers, but drivers were in possession of the timings, knew the weight of train (as advised before departure by the guard, for example 11 for 355 tons), knew every inch of the route and knew where all the clocks were along the way … XL 21 mins to Watford, 35 to Tring, 58 to Roade and 67 to Weedon. They knew it by feel, heart and head.

As outlined earlier in this chapter, the Working Timetable for passenger trains looked very different in the summer and at times of holidays/sporting events. The response was generally to insert additional trains at seven-minute headways and to time the train in line with class 5 power singly or in pairs. In order to save 'paths', some unnecessary piloting occurred rather than have light engines vying for track access. An example of a Working Timetable is in Appendix 1. The same approach to timing of trains based upon their weight and the power classification of the locomotives also applied in other sections of the Western Division.

Between Preston and Carlisle ,timings ranged between 97 and 114 minutes dependent upon those two influencing factors, but excluded the demanding section between Carnforth and Shap Summit. What that meant was that, while a class 8P was timed 97 minutes with up to 450 tons, it would be allowed 4 minutes extra with 500 tons and another 10 minutes if with 570 tons (Special Limit, Limited Load and Full Load respectively). A refinement was that on the less demanding sections, the more powerful locomotives could be timed at Special Limit between Preston and Carnforth plus between Shap Summit and Carlisle while being timed at either Limited Load or Full Load between Carnforth and Shap Summit. With a train of 570 tons a class 8P would be expected to take 26 minutes to Carnforth, 49 minutes between Carnforth and Shap Summit and 30 minutes between Shap Summit and Carlisle, 105 minutes in total. When *The Caledonian* was introduced the class 8P, with just eight carriages (280 tons maximum), the timing was in total 89 minutes (25/35/29 by sections). In the Up direction the timing sections were Carlisle to Shap Summit and Shap Summit to Preston and gave timings of 101, 107, 122 and (for *The Caledonian* only) 93. As with the northbound runs, the effect of climbing to Shap was allowed for; 45, 48 and 55 (39 for *The Caledonian*) being applied.

While most of the planning could be done well in advance and committed to paper books, shorter term planning had to be undertaken, for example for football matches that were dependent upon which teams progressed to a semi-final or final. Those arrangements appeared in Special Traffic Notices printed weekly and distributed from Thursday and others in sheet form. In the continuum that was the railway, the starting points at change of shift (10pm, 6am, 2pm) were the Working Timetable, the STN and any paper Notices and the handover of whatever the position with traffic and arrangements happened to be. Detailed knowledge of the 'book', the sectional timings, the availability of loops, the crucial junctions, needs for connections to be made, forward provision of power and stock and, above all else, experience and calm were the basic requirements for what was a totally absorbing profession.

The planning for and timetabling of goods traffic included challenges associated with sectional times for braked and unbraked trains, the need to match power to weight and necessary brake power and, particularly for perishable traffic, to find suitable 'paths' for loaded and empty wagons/containers. Arrivals at ports of ships containing perishable traffic needed special attention; bananas arriving in quantity were generally received at the Commission-owned Garston dock at Liverpool.

The details for C, D and E class trains show most to be timetabled to take advantage of the quieter times. Two class C trains that ran on weekdays (SX) and left Camden for Glasgow and Crewe respectively at 2/40 and 2/55 were exceptions that caught my eye. Both were afforded good paths with the 2/40 due to pass Lichfield (114¾) at 5/19 (159 minutes) and with the following, lighter 2/55 reducing the headway between the two trains by six minutes to pass Lichfield at 5/28 (153 minutes). The 2/40 had use of the fast line throughout from Willesden while the 2/55 gained the fast line at Tring, milepost 32.

Within the mineral train category, the only fitted train (the Stonebridge Park-Toton) attracted adverse publicity in the national press due to what was perceived as inefficient use of manpower. Three sets of enginemen were involved with the working; Willesden to Northampton (3 hours 6 minutes) then home as passengers, Northampton to Welham Junction/Market Harborough (1 hour 58 minutes) then home as passengers and Welham Junction to Toton (69 minutes). Although linked to traditional railway operating boundaries and being a service which ran only three times each week, it made for a representation of the facts in such a way that did the railway management no favours at all. The average trip time for a coal wagon (colliery loaded to colliery return empty) was some 12 days, but as the National Coal Board also used the railway's wagons for stockpiling, that organisation did not complain though consignees did, particularly in the winter.

The management of the London Midland Region was made difficult by nature of its size in relation to that of the other five Regions.

Indicators of relative size were:

Region	Route miles	per cent	Train miles per cent
London Midland	4,993	26	29
Eastern	2,836	15	17
North Eastern	1,823	9	8
Scottish	3,730	19	12
Southern	2,250	12	17
Western	3,782	19	17

Of the total of 689,514 employees at nationalisation, the LMR was responsible for 228,569 of them, the Commercial Department alone numbering over 20,000.

Financially the key figures were gross receipts and how much was left after all operating expenses had been deducted. For 1953-56 the net receipts of the LMR were £10.9m, £8.2m, £7.1m and £3.0m. For the other Regions the figures were:

Region	1953	1954	1955*	1956⁰
Eastern	7.7	5.0	5.4	1.3
North Eastern	11.5	11.3	9.5	7.7
Scottish	-2.4	-4.2	-5.5	-7.2
Southern	6.2	5.1	-2.9	-3.5
Western	0.6	-9.1	-11.8	-17.8

Notes
* strike in May
⁰ Suez Crisis effect November/December

While these figures show a worrying trend, they also reflected the difficulties faced by the BTC in seeking agreement of the government to raise passenger fares in line with cost increases and adjusting to road competition for goods. At Divisional/District level, the greater commercial freedom under the Act of 1953 resulted in lower rates to retain business being agreed without knowledge of the true costs involved. The scale of business though was huge; the gross receipts of the LMR in 1956 were £148.9m. (£100 in 1956 was equivalent to £2,090 in 2019).

Following nationalisation, the size and shape of the Areas/Regions had been a concern; the eventual result seemingly having one (North Eastern) too small and one (LM) being too big. South of Carlisle (at which place the Scottish Region boundary applied) the LM retained the majority of the area of the former London Midland and Scottish Railway's major constituents (LNWR, MR, L&YR), though the London, Tilbury and Southend route had found a more logical home within the Eastern Region and that Region also extended its influence over the Pennines from Sheffield to Manchester and into the lines of the Cheshire Lines Committee extending to Liverpool and Chester. Operating and motive power complexities were such that they precluded a decision to define Areas/Regions in purely geographical terms.

As it evolved, the LMR had three Divisions; Western, Midland and Central based respectively on the former LNWR, MR and L&YR systems. Originally each Area/Region had a Chief Regional Officer, which sounded authoritative, but in reality limited, while the Railway Executive wrestled and wrangled with the BTC over matters of policy direction, delegation and decentralisation. That resulted in a lack of clear responsibility between departments and a lack of co-ordination of initiatives being proposed to headquarters. In summary, it was a very grim time for railwaymen and women at operational level.

In summer 1956 the General Manager of the LMR, J.W. Watkins, was appointed a member of the BTC and his role was taken by David Blee, appointed to the newly-formed Railway Executive in 1948. He became the Member for commercial matters and remained in that role until the 1953 Act abolished the Executive. At that time, he transferred to a role within the BTC and, as a member of the General Staff, was Traffic Adviser (a mix of commercial and operating matters), one of nine such Advisers who provided a service to Members of the Commission by reviewing and commenting upon proposals from the six Area/Regional Boards within his areas of expertise.

In performing that and his previous role, he would have become fully aware of the complexities of the processes to adjust fares and goods charges, the difficulties of the extent of delegated authority to allow local management to manage, despite a lack of meaningful costings and statistics. He would also have seen the development of Regionally proposed schemes for the Modernisation Plan and been able to assess and advise upon the relative merits of each. The input of the LMR was actually very lacklustre and, with regard to dieselisation, offered a trial replacement of steam at one depot (Devons Road). With the elevation of Watkins to the BTC, Blee was invited to become General Manager of the LMR, a post he held until being asked to retire in 1961.

Rather than his previous role to consider and advise, Blee now had to 'do'. Amongst his many challenges were to resolve, with other GMs, the conundrum since 1948 of 'penetrating lines', geographical boundaries and operating/motive power arrangements, within the LMR to organise a method of decentralisation of management responsibilities and, thirdly, to prepare for one of the biggest 'cherries' in the Modernisation Plan, the electrification of the LNW route between Manchester/Liverpool and London.

Taking these in turn, the Railway Executive had contained advocates for a retention of the status quo of arrangements as for the four grouped companies and others (including Blee) for a geographical division of the system. What emerged was a compromise, perhaps best shown by reference to the Midland St Pancras to Carlisle route via Leicester, Chesterfield, Sheffield, Cudworth, Leeds, Skipton and Appleby.

Section	Geographical region	Regional responsibility for:	
		Motive power and operating	Civils, signals and telecommunications
St Pancras to Chesterfield	LM	LM	LM
Chesterfield to Cudworth	E	LM	E
Cudworth to Skipton	NE	LM	NE
Skipton to Carlisle	LM	LM	LM
Any significant changes for the route would necessarily involve the General Manager of each of three Regions			

The BTC directed that this and other similar examples be resolved by the Regions and, in due course, a 'basket' of agreements emerged. The LMR gained from the Eastern the former Cheshire Lines Committee and the former Great Central route south from near Chesterfield to Woodford Halse, while the Midland and Great Northern system was transferred in entirety to the Eastern. The Eastern and Western Regions took responsibility for motive power at the extremes of the Midland cross-country route between Sheffield and Bristol but the Western and LMR were unable to agree a way forward for the Birmingham/Wolverhampton industrial heartland in the West Midlands leaving the two competing for the same markets.

The delegation of authority and decentralisation of management and the extent of each had been a problem since nationalisation. Most Regions had distinct lines of operation of trains; on the LMR from Euston to Carlisle/Manchester/Liverpool/Birmingham/Holyhead, St Pancras to Manchester/Sheffield and across the Pennines between Liverpool/Manchester and Leeds. Together with their networks that fed into and from these main routes, there was a basis upon which to organise the generation and retention of traffic both passenger and goods. The challenge was to find a way of coordinating the three main departmental responsibilities – commercial, operating and motive power – to empower a single manager to be fully responsible for 'his' line. Those three departmental responsibilities were separate, not only at Regional headquarters level, but also at Divisional and District level and disturbing such arrangements would be a major change. Having successfully trialled the approach on the Fenchurch Street-Southend line, the Eastern Region made that change by creating Line Managers for the former Great Northern route from King's Cross to Doncaster and for the former Great Eastern route from Liverpool Street to Norwich; two distinctly separate systems which, initially at least, benefitted from the planned improved utilisation of motive power, rolling stock, presentation, promotion and publicity and staff morale.

As an advocate of geographical boundaries, David Blee had other ideas on decentralisation and established six Divisions; London, East Midlands, West Midlands, East Lancashire, West Lancashire and Northern. The Divisional Managers did not enjoy the status of Line Managers as a post of Director of Traffic Services was created for headquarters. The attempt to improve coordination of traffic matters involved six Divisional Traffic Managers and, within each Division, there were in the varying number of Districts, officers for each of operating, commercial and motive power. It was a three-tier organisation – Headquarters, Division, District – still centralised and cumbersome at local level. The new arrangements did, though, eliminate the post of Chief Commercial Manager and the three Operating Superintendents at Crewe, Derby and Manchester. Euston had the concentration of power and authority and, while his organisation was criticised, it could be better understood when viewed against what the next few years held in prospect for large parts of the Region.

The Modernisation Plan of 1955, as endorsed by the government, had included a sum for electrification of some main lines and suburban routes. As at end of 1956, preparatory work on adopting a standard (except for the Southern Region with its long installed d.c. system) 25 kV a.c. overhead catenary system. Although there were concerns as to costs and the ability of contractors to support more than one major scheme, at that time both the East Coast and West Coast (LNW) routes, for distances up to 190 miles from London, were included. The final decision to back the LNW route project was based upon availability of capital and traffic flow density. Blee would have recognised the impact and demands to be made upon his engineers (civil, signal & telecommunications and mechanical), planners, personnel and, in time, motive power arrangements, while his commercial team sought to at least maintain revenue. Having a second main line to Manchester (St Pancras-Derby-Matlock-Cheadle Heath) and the potential of a third (the ex GC main line) as a diversionary route made having a single Director of Traffic Services with authority spanning the Region look far more pragmatic.

With the reasonable expectation in mind of the largest railway project since the constituent companies of the LNWR built their railways in the 1830s, it is understandable that Blee did not seek to make major changes for the LNW main lines in the next few years. For varying periods of time, until electrification encroached, the LNW main lines south of Crewe would provide a feast for train watchers; those watching north and west of Crewe would be able to enjoy the show for longer.

The 1957-1963 era was characterised by a huge interest in railways and particularly steam locomotives. Here, at Lichfield, a typical gallery is excited by the high-speed passage of **Princess Louise** *on* **The Merseyside Express.** *In a very busy half hour from 9.30 five expresses were due with motive power, usually three class 8, one class 7 and one class 6. It was a similar story at Tamworth though in school holidays a much larger gallery. (29)*

Chapter 3

Motive Power for the Route and Motive Power Depots

Chapter 2 included references to the challenges of matching expectations to a timetable and suitable motive power. This chapter shows that many of the locomotives that could be seen at work along the line, in 1957-61 at least, had their origins up to some 45 years earlier and outlines how the front-line steam fleet was maintained and utilised.

The development of motive power is well documented elsewhere and the images here serve to show early examples.

The formation of the LNWR brought together motive power that had originated with the various original companies, including the Liverpool and Manchester and Grand Junction. A replica of **Planet** *(built for the LMR) was built for the Manchester Science Museum and was given a run or two with* **Rocket** *(also a replica) at the Great Central Railway. (30)*

Lion was built in 1838 eight years after the original **Planet** and illustrates the pace of early development. It became LMR 57 and later LNWR 116 and, following withdrawal in 1859, was sold to Mersey Docks and Harbour Board. In 1928 the locomotive was presented to the Liverpool Engineering Society, and, after a spell of 39 years during which the locomotive starred in three films, it was first loaned and then gifted to Liverpool Museums. Last steamed in 1980, the locomotive is now for museum display only. (31)

Cornwall was built in 1847 as a 4-2-2 but was later (1859) rebuilt as a 2-2-2 in which form it was preserved in the National Collection. The widespread use at that time of locomotives with a single, very large diameter driving wheelset reflected the pre-piston valve era. The picture was taken during a rare venture outside at the Shildon Museum. (32)

The progressive need for new or modified locomotives to cater for increased weights of trains at higher average speeds over sections of the route was constant. Added to that was the element of competition between rival railway companies in meeting the changing aspirations of the travelling public. A review of express passenger main departures from Euston in 1898 and 1908 reveals how the LNWR offering changed to accommodate the Edwardian love of leisure activities; at Appendix 2.

The majority of the front line passenger fleet of the era of prime interest in this book was built new from the 1930s, though some were rebuilt from their original form of the 1920s (the Royal Scots) and others (the Patriots) developed from the time of arrival of William Stanier in 1932.

Stanier, a Swindon, GWR man (and boy) and, at the time of being invited to consider joining the LMS as Chief Mechanical Engineer, was Principal Assistant to the CME, GWR, Charles Collett. The total stock of LMS locomotives was around 9,000 and only a very small proportion displayed evidence of something close to Stanier's engineering heart; standardisation of proven components. He was also used to a better organised main workshop than the topsy-turvy Crewe that had grown enormously over the previous 60 years. His appointment – an outsider to the LNW/LMS – broke the chain of 'successor in waiting' that had been the Crewe way since the days of Webb.

On the first day of the tenure of Stanier as CME (1 January 1932) it was agreed that fifteen (later increased to forty) Claughtons would be modified as they became due for replacement boilers and then be classified as 5X. However, the 15/40 would differ from two earlier rebuilds in that the spacing between the driving wheelsets would be as for the Royal Scot Class. A further fifteen locomotives were then agreed and, while ten of those were included in the 1934 programme of work, the other five emerged in a very different form (see later). Thus, the rebuilt/modified Claughtons became 42. In 1937, 5500 gained the name *Patriot*. Although unofficially referred to as Baby Scots, the class of fifty-two (forty-two rebuilds and ten new using some old components) officially became the Patriot Class and *Patriot*

The 130-strong Claughton Class entered service between 1913 and 1921. With a varied selection of carriages, 5936 is shown at Tring passing a G2 0-8-0.(33).

became the company's publicly seen recognition of the sacrifice made by many servants of its constituent companies between 1914-18.

Five 'spare' slots in the 1934 programme of work were taken up by the building of the first few of a Stanier design for a 4-6-0 (later known as the Jubilee Class). The LMS was keen to find the most suitable power for its West Midlands express services (the rival GWR then boasting the fastest train in the world, the *Cheltenham Flyer*) and tests were held involving a modified Claughton and a new Stanier 4-6-0. The Stanier 4-6-0s had tapered boilers (at the top only) and one had two rows of superheater tubes and the other with three rows (of eight flue tubes) while the Claughton had three rows. The trials demonstrated firstly the relatively greater efficiency achieved with a higher amount of superheating within a taper boiler and, secondly, that further gains could be made with the 4-6-0s by making further modifications to the boiler.

The progression of the Claughton Class from 1925 was as follows:

Year	As built	4-cylinder with Caprotti	4-cylinder with large boiler & Caprotti	4-cylinder with large boiler & piston valves	3-cylinder rebuild 5X
1925	130				
1926	129	1			
1927	129	1			
1928	110		10	10	
1929	109		10	10	
1930	107		10	10	2
1931	107		10	10	2
1932	83		10	10	17
1933	65		10	10	42
1934	30		10	10	42
1935	0		8	8	42
1936			4	6	42
1937			2	2	42
1938			2	2	42
1939			2	2	42
1940			2	1	42
1941			0	1	42

As more of the Stanier 4-6-0s were delivered (eventually totalling 191) they became the 5XP and were popularly known as the Jubilees – in honour of the 25 year reign of George V. Their arrival and use on all Divisions of the LMS prompted re-allocations of the 5X Claughton rebuilds; fifteen in the West Midlands, eight at Manchester depots, fifteen at Camden/Willesden, three at Polmadie and just three on the Midland Division. There were several short-term allocations of interest; two to Shrewsbury for just four weeks in 1935, one just prior to that to Bristol Barrow Road for nine weeks, both possibly with working the Liverpool-Plymouth via Hereford service.

The story of the original Claughtons was not yet complete. The successful application of taper boilers to the Jubilee 4-6-0s resulted in a proposal to at least re-boiler the Royal Scots, using as a basis the one designed in 1935 for fitment to the side-lined *Fury*. The Second World War delayed progress, but benefitted from a more comprehensive programme of work

The developmental link to the front line motive power in use during 1957-61 was the Claughton Class rebuilds to Patriot Class. In turn, eighteen of the Patriot Class were rebuilt, leaving 34 in the form of 45547 as seen at Willesden and for which an adequate supply of spare boilers negated any capital investment for new taper boilers and other modifications. (34)

The introduction of what became known as the Jubilee Class coincided with the Silver Jubilee year of the reign of George V. 5552 was suitably adorned and was replicated (with 5593) by the Great Central Railway for its own 25th year of operations celebrations. (35)

The LMS favoured maroon for its passenger locomotives although here (in the era of preservation) 5593 found itself on a breakdown train. (36)

to involve the taper boiler plus a double blastpipe, new frames, new driving wheelset axle centres, improved cylinders and replacement of the small Fowler tenders with the Stanier higher sided 4,000 gallons/nine tons capacity type profiled at the top to match the contour of the cab roof. Taper boilers were first fitted to two Jubilees (5735/36) in 1942 and their eventual appearance came very close to the Royal Scot locomotives to be modified; with the engineering enhancements they were classified BR 7P. It was not until 1943 that the first Royal Scot was modified and it was 1955 when the final one was completed. The success with the work resulted in a further proposal to extend the programme to include some of the 5X (three-cylinder Claughton) locomotives. A total of eighteen 5Xs were modified between 1946 and into the BTC era of 1949. Quite how many of the eighteen incorporated Claughton components is unknown, but the first eight through works retained the main section of frames above the horns of the driving wheelsets. In 1949, consideration was given to modifying the other thirty-four Patriots, but that did not proceed because sufficient spare parallel boilers existed as a 'float' to allow re-boilering as and when required. When final withdrawal came for the thirty-four unmodified Patriots, four carried boilers dating from 1928.

In 1937, the express passenger services of the LMS were worked predominantly by the three cylinders, Royal Scots, Patriots and Jubilees, totalling 313 (70 Royal Scots, 52 Patriots & 191 Jubilees) and the vast majority less than a decade old. The arrival on to the scene also of two classes of pacific 4-6-2 locomotives placed the management of the route in as good a position for motive power suitable for its needs and expectations as they (or their predecessors) had ever known. A listing of main line departures from Euston in 1935 is at Appendix 3.

While the developments with the Claughtons were proceeding, the management of the LMS advised Stanier of a need for yet more powerful express locomotives capable of taking a 500 ton train single-handedly along the entire Scottish route. The response was a small class of twelve four cylinder 4-6-2s with a tractive effort equivalent to a GWR King, a much larger diameter boiler driving wheels 6ft 6in diameter and a length overall of 74ft 4¼in. In his first three years in office, Stanier consistently faced a single locomotive engineering challenge; finding the amount of superheating in relation to the firegrate area and size of boiler. When the first two locomotives appeared in 1933, the intention had been to put them on the *Royal Scot* train in each direction. However, the amount of superheating did not allow sufficient 'dried' steam to the cylinders and 'wet' steam would not do the job. The locomotives very quickly became known for being poor in steaming and the need for the fireman to counter that by continually having 45 square feet of raging fire producing steam at maximum pressure before the safety valves lifted. The same problem occurred with the first 5XP Jubilees. An engineering reassessment for the 4-6-2 resulted in a new design of boiler with four rows of eight superheater elements passing through 32 flue tubes, the length of the boiler barrel (that is between the front of the firebox and the rear of the smokebox) was reduced by 18 inches, the diameter of the smoke tubes was increased and boiler pressure lifted to 250lbs/sq.in. In summary, the 45 square feet of fire grate would produce heat that would pass more easily along the smoke tubes to the smokebox, steam generated would collect and would build to a higher level, when the driver opened the regulator, the wet steam would pass through a header and then be dried while passing along the elements themselves, being within the 32 flue tubes. Having completed its rapid journey, the dried steam would pass into the cylinders where its main purpose would be fulfilled. The new boilers were a success as evidenced by recorded runs in summer 1935 between Liverpool and Euston and a round trip Crewe to Glasgow. All twelve of the Class (known as Princess Royal) were fitted with the new boilers and, with the benefit of enhanced superheating, the performance had been significantly improved.

The increase in superheating had been applied first in another Stanier design; a mixed traffic 4-6-0 known as Black 5s introduced in 1935 and the first of a class that eventually became 842 in total.

The general economic conditions of the early to mid-1930s were hardly conducive to the spirit of optimism displayed by the LMS in pursuance of a locomotive policy of scrap and invest in new. That policy had been supported, to some extent, by the government making available capital at low interest rates in order that projects to reduce unemployment could be continued. Those projects had included improving locomotive maintenance and servicing facilities at principal depots. A Princess Royal took ten tons of coal compared to the much lower amounts into a Fowler tender and turning a Princess needed either new turntables or time taken in use of busy triangular junctions. By late 1936, there were signs that economic conditions at home and abroad were improving and, following the abdication in December 1936 of Edward VIII, it was expected that 1937 would include the coronation of George VI. It was a time to lift the spirits of the nation and the railways – particularly the LMS and LNER – would be at the forefront.

When the CME of the LNER – Nigel Gresley – returned in 1934 from a visit to Germany where he had seen the high speed running of a diesel unit, he considered the possibility of introducing a similar service between King's Cross and Newcastle. The maker of the railcar could, though, offer only an average speed for the journey of 63 miles per hour. Gresley thought that could be improved by use of steam power and with finance underwritten, it was

Also at the Great Central Railway, privately owned Black 5 5231 was turned out in early LMS black lined out in red. (37)

decided to proceed with the aim of a high speed, streamlined train ready for service in the autumn of 1935. The train would be named *Silver Jubilee* in honour of the 25 years of the reign of George V. For the train, a new class of locomotive – also streamlined – was designed (the A4) and the first (*Silver Link*) appeared in September 1935, followed by thirty-four more before the end of 1938. The *Silver Jubilee* train was deemed a commercial success and was followed by two further streamlined services, the *Coronation* and *The West Riding Limited*. The LMS needed to be seen to be responding.

The Directors of the LMS realised that their competitors in the road and air transport industries were also intent upon further encroachment into the market. There was also the public and therefore publicity interest in streamlining. The result was the authority given to Stanier to design and have built a class of locomotives capable of producing steam for sustained, high-speed running over distances up to 400 miles. He produced a design that incorporated eight additional superheater element sets and, before leaving for a trip to India, provided guidance on improving the steam passageways as had impressed him on French locomotives designed by André Chapélon. While Stanier was away, responsibility for the detailed design and construction was delegated to Robert A. Riddles (whom Stanier had appointed as his Locomotive Assistant plus 'eyes and ears' around the LMS) as being his Principal Assistant and T.F. Coleman, the Chief Draughtsman. The diameter of the driving wheels was increased (compared to a Princess Royal) by 3in (6ft 9in) and the diameter of the cylinders by one quarter inch. To assist firemen in their arduous duties, particularly towards the end of each run, Stanier introduced a steam-operated coal pusher which had the desired effect of pushing forward coal towards a point when the slope of the steel plating above the water space would allow it to fall towards the shovelling plate. With 50 square feet of grate to feed, any help was appreciated. The profile adopted for the streamlining was accentuated by a silver chevron that extended horizontally along the entire length of the engine and tender in four stripes, the top and bottom ones being broader than the top in the centre. Midway along the side of the casing over the boiler, a nameplate was aligned with the top stripe. The main livery was a Caledonian blue. Technically and mechanically (except for the maintenance staff) the new locomotives were an immediate success, with locomotive *Coronation* achieving 114mph on a test run. Five locomotives were built in this form and livery in 1937. In parallel the civil engineer was undertaking work on the track to allow the timing of six hours to Glasgow.

The trains to be hauled by these new locomotives would be promoted as the *Coronation Scot*, the nine vehicles having the same livery and stripes as for the locomotives. With seating capacity for 232 passengers (82 first-class) and two kitchen cars in each of three sets, the total of twenty-seven vehicles were built by the LMS at Wolverton (nine), Derby (three) and for the LMS by Gloucester Railway Carriage & Wagon (six), Birmingham Railway Carriage & Wagon (six) and Metropolitan Cammell (three), all but six having been built between 1934 and 1936 as part of the annual carriage building programme and refurbished for use in the *Coronation Scot*. The *Coronation Scot* train commenced public service on 5 July 1937 and then ran until the outbreak of the Second World War in September 1939. Stopping only at

The preservation era has allowed a look back to what an LMS trainset would have looked like. Here at the Severn Valley Railway the visiting **Princess Elizabeth** *completes a fine scene. (38)*

Above: The improvement of economic conditions from around 1936 allowed the government of the day to lift the general mood of the population. The railways responded with higher speed passenger train services and the streamlining of some locomotives. William Stanier designed his Princess Coronation Class for services including the Coronation Scot; a blue and silver livery being applied to that trainset. (39)

Left: Other members of the Princess Coronation Class received a maroon and gold livery, in which 6229 as 6220 toured parts of the United States of America. In preservation 46229 Duchess of Hamilton was restored to the appearance of the original streamlining and is seen here at the National Railway Museum. (40)

Wartime put an end to the short-lived age of the high speed streamlined services. **City of Leeds** *and other members of the Class received an all over coat of black. (41)*

Carlisle for a crew change – Camden or Upperby men exchanged with Polmadie men – in each direction, the trains were allowed six and a half hours for the 401 miles to and from Glasgow.

As with *Royal Scot* in 1933, it was decided that a *Coronation Scot* trainset plus locomotive would be shipped to America for a tour in 1939 to culminate in exhibition at the World Trade Fair in New York. The set of vehicles shipped consisted of eight carriages; three articulated twin sets, a club saloon and a sleeping car, all built at Derby. Two of the articulated twins and the club saloon survived until 1963-65. To haul the train, locomotive 6229 masqueraded as *Coronation*.

Wartime conditions meant that the three standard sets were placed into store and never ran again in that form or livery. The vehicles and locomotive sent for the tour of parts of America were stored until shipping capacity enabled their return (6229 in 1942, vehicles in 1946).

The five locomotives new in 1938 became the Princess Coronation Class and others followed from Crewe:

Year	Quantity	Number series	Streamlined?
1938	5	6225-29	Yes
1938	5	6230-34	No
1939	5	6235-39	Yes
1940	5	6240-44	Yes
1943	4	6245-48	Yes
1944	4	6249-52	No
1946	3	6253-55	No
1947	1	6256	No
1948	1	6257	No

The late 1930s were, therefore, characterised by two very skilled locomotive designers, both of whom learned developments from the wider world of traction development. While Sir Nigel Gresley had little time for the development of diesel technology, Sir William Stanier embraced such for shunting locomotives. Both diesel mechanical and diesel electric types were tried, the first from Hunslet Engine Co (1932), thirty diesel electrics in 1936 (twenty from Armstrong Whitworth and ten from English Electric) with the latter working at Crewe for 82 per cent of a week of 168 hours. A further order for thirty sets of power equipment was placed with English Electric for use in a further batch of 350hp shunters built at Derby in 1939.

Articulation of carriages to save money and weight was an idea that Sir William adopted following LNER practise and was applied to eleven three-carriage sets and fifty-five two-carriage sets. The technique was extended in 1938 to a streamlined 750hp diesel engine train of four vehicles weighing just 78 tons with seating for 162 passengers and intended for use on the Cambridge-Oxford via Bletchley service. The lightweight nature of that train owed much to the use of high tensile steel and welding technology, both being developments of Sir Harold Hartley, Vice-President and Director of Scientific Services for the LMS and the officer who had invited Stanier to join the LMS.

Mention needs to be made of two classes of goods locomotives. The Stanier designed 8F from 1935, which eventually totalled 852, was another early success and the timing of its availability (and the role of Riddles, then in the War Department) made it a favourite for selection for mass production as part of the war effort. The other class was the further

The final design of Stanier was developed by Charles Fairburn and was for a 2-6-4 tank locomotive; the Fairburn designed examples having a reduced driving wheel spacing that allowed ease of use around track having a radius of five chains (rather than six). 42085 at Haverthwaite adequately demonstrates the capability. (42)

development of the ex LNW 0-8-0 (G2a) mentioned earlier in this chapter as being rebuilt. The 8Fs and surviving 0-8-0s remained in service well into the 1960s.

Knighted in 1943, Sir William was elected a Fellow of the Royal Society in 1944 upon his retirement as CME. A summary of designs of LMS locomotives attributable to Sir William is in Appendix 4.

Sir William was succeeded by Charles Fairburn, who had been Deputy CME (1938), was Acting CME after Sir William was called away on war effort work in 1942 and appointed CME in 1944. Sadly, Fairburn died in 1945, aged 58. At that time there were two possible successors; Riddles, who had by then been released from wartime duties, and Henry G. Ivatt, who had been Principal Assistant to Stanier in 1937 and, therefore, followed Riddles in that role. As it turned out, Ivatt got the job and Riddles was promoted to the Board of the LMS as a Vice-President.

At the outbreak of war, the LMS's scrap and build new policy for locomotives had been placed into a position where it had a fleet of front-line locomotives that could be expected to see it through much of the next quarter century. During the course of the war, the class which saw the most commitment was the 8F 2-8-0, with multiple production builds in various workshops. Authorisation was given in 1942 for twenty conversions of the Royal Scot Class and a further authorisation was given in 1944 for the remaining fifty to be similarly treated; the final one not emerging in modified form until 1955 (46137). Classified 7P, they were one of the 'go to' locomotives of choice. The other 'go to' saviour of many a day, the Black 5 4-6-0, had 111 locomotives added to its considerable ranks during wartime. There was time in Fairburn's short stewardship to see the first of 277 2-6-4T locomotives (a Stanier design modified).

Ivatt was CME until retirement in 1951. During that time, the railways were nationalised and he probably expected to have little authority or budget after that occurred (1 January 1948). However, post-nationalisation wrangling and organisational strife allowed him time to be involved with the following:

Class	Work
Stanier/Fairburn 2-6-4T	Production 1946-51 (277)
Patriot	Rebuild of 18 as for *Royal Scot* Class 1946-49
Princess Coronation	Modification of two, plus fitment of roller bearings
Class 5 4-6-0	Production of later new build batches and experimental fitments of roller bearings, double blastpipe and chimneys, valve gear, motion in various combinations
Royal Scot	Rebuild in progress
Class 4 2-6-0	Design and build of 162 2-cylinder for ease of maintenance
Class 2 2-6-0	128, 2-cylinder
Co-Co	Production of 10000/1
Bo-Bo	Development of, with British Thomson-Houston

The General Election of summer 1945 resulted in a win for the Labour Party and heralded a programme of nationalisation; of the coal, electricity and inland transport industry. The four grouped railway companies had campaigned against such a move from 1943 and were less than enamoured when the Transport Bill of 1946 progressed through parliament and received Royal Assent in August 1947 with a vesting date of 1 January 1948. The five nationalised inland transport organisations each had an Executive body. Riddles was appointed the Member of the RE for Mechanical and Electrical Engineering. He also had a shared responsibility for motive power. The other 'share' was held by Sir Victor Barrington-Ward, a strong advocate of Regional structures following operating and motive power arrangements rather than geographical territories proposed by others. Assisting Riddles were two prominent ex LMS men; Roland C. Bond, Chief Officer for locomotive construction and maintenance, and Ernest S. Cox, locomotive design. Collectively, the three were CME and worked together in producing the Standard class designs and, in so doing, to apply a lot of hard lessons learned along the LMS way.

In theory, at least, the RE was accountable to the BTC, but was reluctant in the extreme to accept that it, comprising individuals who had helped the railway through the years of war and knew a great deal about operation, planning and getting the job done, was a subservient body. In the ensuing period of five troublesome years until the Transport Act 1953, Riddles was allowed almost a free hand to develop the use of steam traction by the design and build of 999 locomotives in 12 classes of varying power and using standard components wherever possible. He saw main line electrification as being the natural successor to steam and, in that regard, he had similarly minded civil servant supporters at the Treasury.

The final BR steam passenger design was **Duke of Gloucester,** *built 1954 at Crewe. The photographer must have been thrilled by its approach in low, clear autumn sunshine just after 6pm at Oxenholme. Despite its appearance of commanding strength, the technical performance of the locomotive was a disappointment and it was generally confined to the Crewe-Euston section. (43)*

Also a disappointment was the performance in traffic of the ten Clan Class locomotives based in equal quantity at Polmadie and Carlisle. Over a short period of use the locomotives were used more on parcels and fitted brake goods trains than express passenger. **Clan Macleod** *is seen leaving Perth. (44)*

Between 1948 and 1953, a total of 2,061 new locomotives were built plus – on the decision of the BTC not the RE as represented by Riddles – 602 second-hand ex War Department for wartime use. In the view of the RE, the Austerity 2-8-0s were surplus to requirements and the London Midland would not take any of them. The Scottish Region took twenty-three Austerity 2-10-0s and these found useful employment on short, heavy haul from docks to steelworks in the Glasgow area and also clumped their way south on occasions as far as Carlisle.

With the investment of the LMS in its passenger fleet between 1932 and 1939, then continuing with class 7 rebuilds (Royal Scot and Patriot plus two Jubilees) the Western Division's ex LNW main lines were not at the head of the queue for the BR Standard types that appeared from 1951. The BTC, though, was keen that it be seen to be benefitting. The LM received Class 7 Britannia 4-6-2s for work from Longsight and later five more for Holyhead, the Scottish Region received five Britannias and all ten class 6 Clans and later a batch of class 5 4-6-0s. All were mixed traffic rather than being specific to a particular type of traffic, all had two cylinders and all followed similar design characteristics to allow ease of maintenance, including rocker arm firegrates and drum reversers. The enginemen were provided with the best seats that had ever been provided on the ex LNW main lines. The design was found wanting in regard to the connection between engine and tender; three coming adrift at speed on passenger trains (70012 on the Great Eastern, 70014 at Hazel Grove and 70033 at Macclesfield). Crewe North was allocated to the sole Class 8 pacific to be built (71000 in 1954), though many would say its best work did not start until the 1990s, by which time it had been withdrawn and languished for two decades in a scrapyard prior to an heroic restoration and technical re-appraisal.

A picture full of interest at Birmingham New Street. 10001 has W82, the 1/55 Wolverhampton-Euston, running in to the LNWR side of the station. In parallel, the **Pines Express** *(9.45 Bournemouth-Manchester) is running in on the MR side whilst, between the two trains, an early Derby lightweight dmu awaits its next move. (45)*

Elsewhere along the route, Birmingham and Carlisle were recipients of early examples of lightweight diesel multiple units which quickly gained favour with the public.

The introduction and allocation of main line diesel and electric locomotives, other than those listed at chapter 2, are noted in the chapters for the respective years 1959 onwards.

Attention now turns to how the front-line fleet of passenger locomotives was maintained, overhauled and deployed along the route of interest. The classes of prime interest and their principal duties are:

Class	Main Duties
8P *Princess Coronation*	1B Camden: Euston – Carlisle 5A Crewe N: Euston – Crewe – Carlisle – Glasgow/Perth 12B Carlisle Upperby: south to Crewe/ Euston 66A Polmadie: south to Carlisle
Duke	Crewe: Crewe to Euston
Princess Royal	8A Edge Hill: Liverpool – Euston Crewe N: Euston – Crewe – Carlisle – Glasgow/Perth Polmadie: south to Carlisle
7P/MT *Britannia*	9A Longsight: Manchester – Euston 6J Holyhead: Holyhead – Crewe – Euston Polmadie: south to Carlisle/Manchester/ Liverpool
Royal Scot/Patriot/ *Jubilee*	Camden) Anywhere along Crewe N) Euston - Carlisle Carlisle Upperby) Longsight: Manchester – Euston Edge Hill: Liverpool – Euston and cross Pennine Holyhead: N Wales – Crewe Polmadie: south to Carlisle

Class	Main Duties
6P *Jubilee/Patriot*	3B Bushbury: Wolverhampton – Euston Camden:) Anywhere along Crewe N) main lines Carlisle Upperby) Longsight: Manchester – Euston Edge Hill: Liverpool – Euston and cross Pennine Carlisle Kingmoor: north from Carlisle Polmadie: south to Carlisle
6MT *Clan*	Polmadie: south to Carlisle/Manchester Carlisle Kingmoor: north to Perth/Glasgow

As at 1 January 1957, these 261 locomotives of those classes were allocated to the depots as listed. In addition, Willesden had six Patriot Class 6 4-6-0s for vacuum fitted goods work. The main concentrations of power were Crewe North (58), Longsight (39), Camden (37), Edge Hill (35) and Carlisle Upperby (28). The allocations reflected long-standing arrangements for the provision of power, traffic flows and enginemen working arrangements. Each 'home' depot was responsible for maintaining its allocated fleet of locomotives in accordance with the Standard Examination Schedule Circular MP11 of the BTC/RE and for recording mileages run and accumulated.

Disposal work at depots was a filthy occupation. Here, at Camden, a Bushbury Jubilee has its smokebox cleared of soot and particulates that have worked along the boiler tubes en route from Wolverhampton. Blocked tubes, usually at the lower part of the boiler barrel, became a bigger problem as the quality of the coal used was also lowered. (46)

The physical characteristics of Edge Hill depot were such that disposal was undertaken close to the coaling plant. Here the paraphernalia of firegrate and ashpan cleaning is evident together with the constant need for clearing the area of ash and tools of the trade. The rocker arm firegrates and self-cleaning smokeboxes of the BR Standard locomotives were a step forward though 'self-cleaning' was something of a misnomer. (47)

MP11 stipulated that there were two types of examination to be carried out in between the times each locomotive was in works for more extensive overhaul work; one type was time-based in terms of days/weeks in traffic, the other type being based on mileage run.

The time-based examinations were undertaken every six to eight days and every twelve to sixteen days; the difference being that, after the longer period, the boiler was required to be washed out and the locomotive not being in steam. The list of work to be undertaken varied for the examination of the locomotive with the boiler empty or full; X day exams.

For the mileage-based examinations of prime interest were components that would, over a period of time, suffer from mechanical wear. Those examinations were undertaken at intervals of 5-6,000 miles and up to the third such examination (15-18,000) would not involve dismantling the motion (e.g. connecting rods). For the four-cylinder ex-LMS pacifics, the big ends (i.e. the connecting rod at the centre driving wheel) were dismantled at the third examination, piston rings were changed at the fourth exam and at the sixth exam the cylinder end covers were removed, all rings were replaced and other work undertaken in parallel. The sixth exam would take eight working days and all London Midland Region allocated ex-LMS pacifics were attended to at Crewe North where teams of fitters were deployed in shifts and, for expediency, two locomotives were on occasions dealt with simultaneously. The choice of Crewe North was influenced by its proximity to the inventory of components held at Crewe Works.

At the average weekly mileage run in traffic of 1,500 and, making allowance for the time on lesser examinations, the ex-LMS pacifics would receive two 36,000-mile examinations before the time to consider a visit to the main works (Crewe) for an overhaul of the locomotive. The procedure was for a Shopping Proposal to be submitted by the Mechanical Foreman/ Shedmaster to the Regional CME for consideration; the usual time was around eight months since the locomotive last emerged from works following a classified repair. The decision on timing of shopping could be based upon the work for a third number six exam being undertaken while the locomotive was in works, rather than lose eight days under examination at Crewe North. The Shopping Proposal may have been returned endorsed 'Resubmit at such and such a mileage' to enable maximum time in traffic/maximum beneficial level of overhaul in works.

For the time-based examinations, MP11 stipulated the work to be undertaken. The following is the list for a Britannia pacific, BR7MT:

six-eight day, boiler full (see later list for X day) examination.

- water gauges: examine, test
- vacuum brake/steam brake: test
- vacuum brake ejector operations
- large ejector operation
- non return valve
- vacuum relief valve
- drain top sieves, check, clean
- train brake cylinder
- carriage warming apparatus
- buffer beams shut off valve
- injectors
- feed water valves for live and exhaust steam injectors
- top feed water trays
- safety valves
- wheels and tyres/tyre profiles
- connecting and coupling rods
- bogies and pony truck
- intermediate drawgear and buffers
- valve gear
- main frames stays, nuts and brackets

Over the years there were three serious failures of locomotives due to maladjusted water gauge frame assemblies (46224 on 10 September 1940 and 7 March 1948, 46238 on 24 January 1962) and in each case the inner firebox ripped away from the roof stays. To provide extra assurance, an additional fusible plug was inserted into the lower part of the water space of the fireboxes of Princess Coronation Class locomotives.

In a 12-16 day, boiler washout examination, upon arrival in the depot and the fire being dropped, the boiler was filled to capacity and remaining boiler pressure was used to enable the steam test examination to take place. The steam remaining in the boiler was then blown down through the live steam injector overflow pipe. After being allowed to cool for six hours, the boiler was then flushed using cold water at an increasing rate of pressure. The washing down of the water spaces started at the highest point (the firebox crown sheet), then the boiler barrel and tubes (from the mud hole doors in the smokebox tubeplate). The front of the tubeplate in the firebox was washed down and then the waterspaces at the sides and back of the firebox. Scale and sediment disturbed by the process of flushing and rodding naturally fell to the lowest point; for the firebox this could be raked out through the mud holes at the front corners of the foundation ring forming the base of the firebox. The stage had then been reached where the boilersmith could examine all the visible waterspaces and then go inside the firebox to check all accessible stay heads by 'sound' using a hammer and a lot of experience. Firebox work could then extend to removal/replacement of cracked or leaking stays, removal or replacement of firegrate bars and the brick arch around which the heat of the fire was directed. In parallel with this activity, the X day examination was undertaken. Again, for a Britannia, the following applied:

tender:
tender tank: draining and washing out
external water feed valve and sieve cleaning out
water scoop: no lower than one inch below rail level
engine:
graduable steam brake valve: strip down
steam manifold shut off valve
oil pipes and clips: check all unions
axlebox underkeeps: drain/refill
piston rod swab box: change swabs
grease nipples: examine/replace/re-charge
springs and spring gear: check clearance top and bottom
brakegear: brake blocks change as necessary
brake pull rods: adjust
sanding apparatus: check valve/pipes
roller bearings (oil fed): re-charge/record volume
water tank level indicators: examine/replace joints as necessary
blast pipe, blower pipe and ejector exhaust pipe
smokebox internal deflector plates
rocking grate mechanism functions
hopper ashpan and fittings functions
damper gear functions
cylinder cocks: clean, check for any signs of broken piston rings

After the boilersmith had made known to the Mechanical Foreman the results of his examination and, assuming he was content with the condition, all the washout plugs and mud hole doors would be replaced, boiler fitted with treated Alfloc water, a fire lit and steam raised in line with traffic requirements. If a locomotive was brought into the shed in an afternoon, at the end of a booked duty it could be ready for traffic before 10/0 the following day, thus not 'losing' a day's availability.

The valve and piston exams (at 30-36,000 miles) was much more demanding on labour and time. For the Princess Coronation Class, two teams of fitters were deployed solely on this work with an elapsed time of approaching 200 hours (between seven and eight days per locomotive), somewhat less for three-cylinder (Royal Scot, Patriot, Jubilee, Duke) and two-cylinder (Britannia and Clan) classes. The work involved much stripping, checking, changing piston rings, measuring and reassembly work, mechanical lubricators and lubrication systems to cylinders, valves and motion checking and adjusting and associated fittings such as anti-vacuum valves and piston packings.

The final examination to be noted was that undertaken by the Examining Fitter before a locomotive was authorised to commence a duty.

The end result of this activity was a front-line fleet of locomotives that delivered a high level of reliability in its day to day performance. However, it came at the cost of a loss of days when locomotives were not available for traffic.

From the earliest days of railways, the department of the government of the day responsible for overseeing and regulating the activities was the Board of Trade. Over a period of time, all manner of definitions were formed to improve safety, record-keeping and books of accounts. For overhauls of steam locomotives, works repairs were either classified or non-classified; the latter being for modifications such as fitment of a speedometer or the automatic warning system apparatus or re-painting. Classified repairs were either:

Heavy

- General (HG)
- Service (HS)
- Overhaul (HO)
- Intermediate (HI)
- Casual (HC)

Light

- sub-divided as above

A 'Heavy' repair was either

- when a boiler was replaced or had it temporarily lifted and then replaced in situ
- when any two of these applied; new tyres to four or more wheels, fitment of new cylinders, new axles, profiling the wheels, machining/refitting axleboxes, removing and renewing motion/brake gear, re-tubing/repairing a boiler in situ with 50 plus stays replaced with new.

On many occasions, the decision on the type of repair to be undertaken would be taken locally at Crewe with the representative of the Shopping Bureau when the locomotive had been stripped of its major components. Heavy General repairs were carried out within a balance of time/mileage estimated to have run and, upon completion, the traffic department could expect a machine in 'as new' condition. The average mileage run by the Princess Coronations between Heavy General repairs (1951-59) was 192,539. Intermediate repairs were more concerned with particular components known to be likely in need of attention.

With a small total of ex-LMS pacifics concentrated at only a few depots and the vast majority of overhauls being undertaken along the same 'belt' within Crewe Works, anything that was out of the expected normal condition would be spotted and reported. The men knew their locomotives. A summary listing of works visits made by the Princess Coronation and Princess Royal Classes is at Appendix 5. There appears to have been no attempt to achieve an even spread of the load and there are some strange sequences of overhauls involving the same

Crewe Works with **City of Leeds** on one of the two 'belts' reserved for the classes of larger passenger locomotives. It would seem to be a Heavy General in progress with the engine having received a replacement boiler and also having been re-wheeled.

Compared to photograph 48, the environment in Derby Works with diesel traction is a sign of things to come with easier exchange of major components. The three prototype 10201-3 each received a major overhaul at Derby in 1956 and then worked on the Western Division of the LMR alongside 10000 and 10001; a change of livery to green lined out orange, black, orange also being applied. (49)

locomotive. For the ex-LMS pacifics between 1950-1957, the average number of weekdays each year that locomotives were under and awaiting classified repairs at works was 64 for Princess Royals and between 38 and 56 for modified or unmodified Princess Coronations.

By adding the average number of days not available due to both shed examinations/repairs and works overhauls, that gave overall availability of 60.4 per cent and 68.9 per cent respectively. In simple terms, the traffic planners and timetablers would need to work on the basis of having 7 or 8 Princess Royals and 26 or 27 Princess Coronations available; 35 out of a total of 50 8Ps.

Of the other classes of front-line passenger locomotives, a majority of the seventy Royal Scots, all the eighteen rebuilt Patriots and ten Clans as well as 71000 *Duke of Gloucester* were allocated to the principal depots along our route of interest. The Jubilee Class was allocated across the Divisions of the London Midland Region and formed the prime power for the Midland Division services from St Pancras to Nottingham, Sheffield and Manchester.

Data for these locomotives is less comprehensive than that for the ex-LMS pacifics, but as MP11 was applicable to all of them, the time-based exams would be very similar, albeit only two or three cylinders (rather than the four of the ex-LMS pacifics) and sets of motion were present. The mileage-based examination periodicities would have varied with the characteristics of the services worked by the locomotive, for example a return Wolverhampton-Euston service compared to a Euston-Blackpool turn overlapping two days.

Mileage figures for Princess Royal and Princess Coronation Classes allocated to the LM Region averaged (in thousands of miles run):

	1956	**1957**	**1958**	**1959**
Princess Royal	56.4	56.5	52.2	n/a
Princess Coronation	74.6	73.2	72.1	71.2

For the Princess Coronations allocated to the Scottish Region, the averages for 1956-59 were 53.8, 49.9, 54.7 and 50.1 respectively.

The average mileage accumulated by the SR/LMS built line diesels working on the LM Region between 1 January and 30 September 1957 was 91,000, although none was available for more than 70 per cent of that time. The annual mileages for *Deltic* are not available.

The calculation of availability of any or all of the non-route specific classes of locomotive is not possible but, based upon what data is available, an average figure of around 70 per cent is suggested.

Each Region and route within each Region had unique characteristics and, to draw comparisons between how comparatively well the management of the Western Division of the LM Region maintained and deployed its fleet of locomotives, is of limited value.

Each route was different, but the mileages run and availability statistics for the Scottish Region in comparison with the same classes allocated to the LM Region were inferior; a round trip Glasgow to Carlisle via Beattock being just 204 miles while Carlisle-Perth return was just over three hundred. Not only was each route unique; so too were the traffic flows, state of the infrastructure, the gradient profile, route capacity over critical sections and gross weight of trains.

Focus now turns to the deployment of locomotives along each main passenger traffic flow. The following order is followed as it 'builds' the picture from the most straight forward to the most complex and is depot based for the various power classifications. The listing is separate for workings in England/N Wales and for complex Anglo-Scottish through services.

Time/train	Reporting number W	Route worked	Miles	Note
Longsight Britannia Class 7MT 10.0 Man – Euston 10/45 Euston – Man	50 283	Throughout, 1/55 Throughout, 2.42	181 189 370	1 2, 3
2/0 Man – Euston 9.45 Euston – Man	94 69	Throughout, 5/54 Throughout 1/19	181 181 362	1 1, 4, 5
4/0 Man – Euston 8.30 Euston – Man/Lpl	118 39	Throughout, 7/52 Man portion 12/43	181 189 370	1 3,4
5/45 Man – Euston 11.45 Euston – Man	130 91	Throughout, 9/25 Throughout, 3/40	189 189/158 378/347	3, 6 3, 4, 7
Longsight ex-LMS Class 7P 11/58 Man – Euston 3/45 Euston – Man	322 199	Throughout, 5.24 Throughout, 8/0	183 181 364	8 1,4
7.45 Man – Euston 2/45 Euston – Man	20 117	Throughout,11.25 Throughout, 6/50	189 181 370	3 1, 2
9.35 Man – Euston 10/0 Euston - Man	58 -	Throughout, 1/05 Throughout	189 181 370	3 1, 2, 9
10/28 Man – Euston 9.45 Euston – Man	- 69	Throughout, 3.09 Throughout, 1/19	189 181 370	3 1, 4, 5
Longsight Jubilee Class 6P Noon Man – Euston 0.40 Euston – Man	64 9	Throughout, 3/45 Throughout, 4.45	181 189 370	1 3,4

Notes

1. via Stoke
2. same day return
3. via Crewe
4. following day (turn extends to day two)
5. control arrangement to double head due to weight of trains/timing of train
6. on Fridays only worked by Crewe North 8P
7. on Saturdays only worked to Crewe by loco off W130 on Friday
8. via Stoke and Northampton
9. parcels trains

Time/train	Reporting number W	Route worked	Miles	Note
Edge Hill Princess Royal Class 8P				
0.10 Lpl – Euston	152	Throughout, 5.37	194	
2/30 Euston - Lpl	115	Throughout, 6/0	<u>194</u>	1
			388	
8.10 Lpl – Euston	36	Throughout, noon	194	
6/10 Euston – Lpl	137	Throughout, 9/50	<u>194</u>	1
			388	
10.10 Lpl – Euston	54	Throughout, 1/45	194	
0.30 Euston – Lpl	213	Throughout, 4.34	<u>194</u>	2
			388	
9/50 Lpl – Euston	-	Throughout, 2.40	194	3
12/30 Euston – Lpl	83	Throughout, 4/0	<u>194</u>	2
			388	
Edge Hill ex-LMS Class 7P				
2/10 Lpl – Euston	92	Throughout, 5/45	194	
8.30 Euston – Lpl	39	Throughout, 12/25	<u>194</u>	2
			388	
4/10 Lpl – Euston	114	Throughout, 8/20	194	
4/55 Euston – Lpl	87	Throughout, 8/22	<u>194</u>	2
			388	

Notes
1 same day   2 following day (turn extends to day two)   3 parcels train

Time/train	Reporting number W	Route worked	Miles	Note
Camden Princess Coronation Class 8P				
7.55 Euston – Lpl	29	Throughout,11.36	194	
5/25 Lpl – Euston	122	Throughout, 8/50	<u>194</u>	1
			388	
6/20 Euston – Heysham	141	Throughout,11/06	236	2
7.0 Heysham – Euston	32	Throughout,11.35	<u>236</u>	3
			472	
6/30 Euston – Preston	131	Eus–Crewe 9/22	158	
7.48 Crewe – Euston	24	Throughout,11.09	<u>158</u>	3
			316	

Time/train	Reporting number W	Route worked	Miles	Note
Camden Royal Scot Class 7P 0.02 Euston – Crewe 8.30 Carlisle – Euston	189 74	Throughout, 5.04 Crewe 1/0 – Eus 4/12	167 <u>158</u> 325	4
– Eus/M'bone – Preston 8/30 Windermere – Euston	- 370	London – Preston Preston 10/39 – Eus 3.39	209 <u>209</u> 418	5 3
10/50 Eus – Blackpool C 8.0 Blackpool C - Eus	77 296	Throughout, 4/41 Throughout,12/55	229 <u>229</u> 458	3

Notes

1. same day
2. locomotive overnight at Carnforth mpd
3. following day (turn extends to day two)
4. via Northampton, Birmingham to Stafford
5. parcels train
6. via Northampton
7. return working n/a

Time/train	Reporting number W	Route worked	Miles	Note
5/5 Eus – Blackpool C 10.0 Blackpool C – Eus	159 330	Throughout, 10/0 Throughout, 3/05	229 <u>229</u> 458	3
Camden Jubilee Class 6P 6.24 Euston – Wolv 1/55 Wolv – Euston	- 82	Throughout Throughout, 4/34	127 <u>127</u> 254	5
8.50 Euston – Wolv 3/55 Wolv – Euston	51 104	Throughout,11.25 Throughout, 6/30	125 <u>125</u> 250	
9/35 Euston – B'ham	173	Throughout	<u>114</u>	6
12/50 Euston - Wolv 17/40 Glasgow C – Euston	81 146	Throughout, 3/22 LE to Stafford Stafford – Crewe Crewe – Euston 5.05	125 15 25 <u>158</u> 323	 5 3

Time/train	Reporting number W	Route worked	Miles	Note
Bushbury Jubilee Class 6P 10/50 Wolv – Euston 9.0 Euston – Wolv	- 55	Throughout, 137 Throughout, 12/11	127 <u>128</u> 255	1, 2 3, 4
6.45 Wolv – Euston 2/20 Euston – Wolv	160 115	Throughout, 9.56 Throughout, 4/55	125 <u>125</u> 250	5
9.45 Wolv – Euston 4/37 Euston – Wolv	44 125	Throughout,12/41 Throughout, 7/56	125 <u>130</u> 255	1, 4, 5
11.0 Wolv – Euston 5/50 Euston – Wolv	116 135	Throughout, 1/30 Throughout, 8/30	125 <u>128</u> 253	4, 5
11.55 Wolv – Euston 6/55 Euston – Wolv	452 123	Throughout, 2/30 Throughout, 9/29	125 <u>125</u> 250	5

Notes

1. via Northampton
2. parcels train
3. following day (turn extends to day two)

4. via Bescot after Birmingham New Street
5. same day
6. ? unbalanced

Time/train	Reporting number W	Route worked	Miles	Note
Carlisle Upperby ex-LMS Class 7P 8.30 Carlisle – Euston 10/52 Euston – Perth	 74 195	 Carlisle – Crewe, 12/51 Crewe 2.5 Clsle 5.16	 141 <u>141</u> 282	 1

Note

1. following day (turn extends to day two)

Time/train	Reporting number W	Route worked	Miles	Note
Holyhead Britannia Class 7MT 1.10 Holyhead – Euston 8/50 Euston – Holyhead	4 157	Throughout, 6.50 Throughout, 2.35	264 <u>264</u> 528	1
7.30 Holyhead - Euston 10/52 Euston – Perth 9.20 Crewe – Holyhead	48 195 55	Throughout, 1/20 Euston – Crewe 155 Throughout	264 158 <u>106</u> 528	2
Holyhead Royal Scot Class 7P 11.00 Holyhead – Bangor/ Euston 5/35 Euston – Holyhead	100 145	Holyhead – Crewe 3/17 Crewe 8/45 – Holy 10/55	106 <u>106</u> 212	1

Notes
1. same day
2. following day (turns extend to day two)

Time/train	Reporting number W	Route worked	Miles	Note
Blackpool Jubilee Class 6P 5/5 Blackpool C – Euston Noon Euston – Crewe/ Blackpool C	136 243	Throughout, 11/02 Throughout, 7/0	229 <u>231</u> 460	1, 2

Notes
1. following day (turn extends to day two)
2. via Northampton (portion added at Crewe)

Time/train	Reporting number W	Route worked	Miles	Note
Preston Patriot Class 6P - ? – Camden 6.40 Eus – Windermere	- 33	? Euston – Preston 12/23	209 <u>211</u> 420	1 2,3

Notes
1. worked a fitted goods
2. following day (turn extends to day two)
3. via Northampton

Time/train	Reporting number W	Route worked	Miles	Note
Crewe North Princess Coronation Class 8P 9.10 Lpl – Plymouth 8.0 Plymouth – Lpl	210 263	Crewe 10.36 – Shrewsbury 11.11 Shrewsbury 2/54 – Crewe 3/42	33 <u>33</u> 66	1 2
Crewe North ex-LMS Class 7P 9.10 Llandudno – Eus. 11/05 Eus – Windermere	56 193	Crewe 11.31 – Euston 3/37 Euston – Crewe 2.08	160 <u>158</u> 318	3 4
12/50 Bangor – Euston ? Eus/M'bone – Crewe	100 -	Crewe 3/24 – Euston 6/21 Throughout	158 <u>158</u> 316	5
6/35 Kendal – Euston 7/0 Euston – B'ham	- 147	? Crewe – Euston 4.25 Throughout, 10/15	158 <u>127</u> 285	2, 3, 6
8/50 Crewe – Euston 5/35 Euston - Holyhead	- 145	Throughout, 1.10 Euston – Crewe 8/27	158 <u>158</u> 316	4

Notes

1. used as a running in turn for locomotives, outshopped from Crewe Works
2. same day
3. via Northampton
4. following day arrival (turn extends to day two)
5. return details n/a
6. arrangements for working forward to Crewe, relief to 11/10 Birmingham – Glasgow/as pilot/parcels

On weekdays between mid-September and mid-June, there were sixteen passenger (and one postal sorting) services between England and Scotland, seventeen on Fridays only. A majority of those services involved at least one change of locomotive en route and some involved locomotives working to complex cyclic diagrams over periods up to four days. A summary of the arrangements is:

Time/train	Reporting number W	Locomotive arrangement	Note
0.20 Euston – Glasgow C	5	1B 8P Euston – Carlisle 66A 8P Carlisle – Glasgow	15
0.45 Liverpool Ex-Glasgow C } 1.03 Manchester Ex-Wigan NW}	7	66A BR7 throughout	1,2

Time/train	Reporting number W	Locomotive arrangement	Note
9.25 Crewe – Perth	27	66A 8P Crewe – Carlisle 63A 5 Carlisle – Perth	3
9.30 Manchester V – Glasgow C } 9.43 Liverpool Ex – Preston	314	26A 6P throughout	4 1,2
10.0 Euston – Glasgow C	63	1B 8P Euston – Carlisle 66A 8P Carlisle – Glasgow	7
11.25 Birmingham – Glasgow C	67	5A 7P B'ham – Crewe 5A 8P Crewe – Glasgow	2, 5, 15
1/30 Euston – Glasgow C	97	5A 8P Euston – Crewe 1B 8P Crewe – Glasgow	6 7
1/30 Manchester V – Carlisle	400	26A 5 throughout	8
1/35 Euston – Perth	99	12B 7P Euston – Carlisle	9
4/15 Manchester Ex-Glasgow C} 4/25 Liverpool Ex-Preston }	39	66A BR7 throughout	1
7/20 Euston – Inverness	151	1B 7P Euston – Crewe 5A 8P Crewe – Perth	10
8/30 Euston – Glasgow C	157	5A 8P Euston – Crewe 5A 8P Crewe – Glasgow	12 13
9/10 Euston – Glasgow C	169	1B 8P Euston – Carlisle 66A 8P Carlisle – Glasgow	16
9/25 Euston – Glasgow C	171	12B 7P Euston – Carlisle 66A 8P Carlisle – Glasgow	
10/52 Euston – Perth	195	6J BR7 Euston – Crewe 12B 7P Crewe – Carlisle	9
11/10 Birmingham – Glasgow C	299	5A 7P B'ham – Crewe 66A 8P Crewe – Glasgow	7
11/50 Euston – Glasgow St E	21	1B 7P Euston – Carlisle 66A 8P Carlisle – Glasgow	14

Notes

1. two portions
2. through carriages for Edinburgh detached at Carstairs
3. six carriages forward
4. via Bolton
5. conveyed carriages from Crewe for Perth, detached at Carlisle
6. 5A BR8 used if available
7. formed part of cyclic diagram (see later reference in text)
8. on Fridays only was extended to Glasgow Central
9. Scottish Region motive power forward
10. 2 x ex-LMS Class 5 forward from Perth
11. conveyed carriages for Stranraer detached at Carlisle; forward with 12A BR6
12. Royal Mail (no passengers)
13. conveyed vans for Aberdeen, detached at Carstairs
14. via Dumfries/Kilmarnock
15. assistance of banking locomotive Beattock to summit
16. locomotives changed at Carlisle Kingmoor
26A Manchester (Newton Heath) depot
63A Perth depot

For southbound services, the pattern was very similar, though with a through train from
Stranraer to Euston. A summary of the trains and the 'balancing' or cyclic working that
proceeded the particular working where applicable is:

Time/train	Reporting number W	Locomotive arrangement	Note
9.0 Perth – Euston	110	ScR power to Carlisle 1B 8P off 169 to Euston	
10.0 Glasgow C – Euston	96	66A 8P to Carlisle 1B 8P off 5 to Euston	
10.05 Glasgow C – B'ham	98	1B 8P off 97 Crewe 5A 7P off 67 Crewe – B'ham	7 1
10.55 Glasgow C – Man V/Lpl Ex	282	26A 6P off 93	2
12/15 Perth – Euston	484	ScR power to Carlisle 12B 7P to Euston	
1/30 Glasgow C – Euston	126	5A 8P off 67 to Crewe 1B 8P off 98 Crewe – Euston	3
4/05 Glasgow C – Lpl Ex/Man	140	66A 7MT through	
5/15 Inverness – Euston	138	5A 8P off 153 ex Perth to Crewe 5A 8P – Euston	
5/40 Glasgow C – Euston	148	5A 8P off 299 to Crewe 1B 7P off 81 Crewe – Euston	
6/30 Glasgow C – Euston	148	5A 8P off 157 to Crewe 5A 8P Crewe to Euston	4 5
8/15 Perth – Euston	12	5A 8P off 151 to Crewe 1B 7P off 151 Crewe to Euston	
9/25 Glasgow C – Euston	10	66A 8P to Carlisle 12B 8P Carlisle to Euston	
10/0 Stranraer Hbr – Euston	68	12A 6MT to Carlisle 1B 7P off 21 Carlisle – Euston	
10/20 Glasgow C – Euston	6	66A 8P to Carlisle Upp 1B 8P off 63 Carlisle – Euston	6, 7

Time/train	Reporting number W	Locomotive arrangement	Note
10/25 Glasgow C – Euston	224	66A 8P to Carlisle 1B 8P off 251 Carlisle – Euston	7
11/15 Glasgow C – B'ham	18	66A 8P to Crewe 5A 7P Crewe to B'ham	
11/30 Glasgow C – Lpl Ex/Man V	22	66A 7MT throughout	

Notes

1. locomotive worked earlier B'ham. Crewe leg
2. on Saturdays only (return Sunday) was a 66A BR6 MT
3. locomotive paused at Crewe 3/22 – 6/28
4. Royal Mail (no passengers) Aberdeen vans attached at Carstairs
5. BR8 used if available, return with 1/30 (97)
6. train did not call at Carlisle Citadel station. Locomotives changed near Upperby depot
7. Formed part of cyclic diagram

The use of cyclic diagrams was an attempt to improve the utilisation of locomotives and took them away from their home depots for varying periods of days. As an example, Camden had a diagram involving four class 8P pacifics extending over a period of 84 hours. As it resulted in a different locomotive on the northbound *Royal Scot* for four consecutive days, it found as an incidental consequence much happiness at the lineside.

The diagram required the four locomotives to start day one at different locations:

A   Camden, to work the 10.0 Euston to Carlisle
B   Carlisle, to work the 0.45 (ex Glasgow at 10/20) to Euston
C   Crewe, to work the 4/22 (ex Euston at 1/30) to Glasgow
D   Glasgow, to work the 10.05 Glasgow-Birmingham as far as Crewe.

At the start of day 2, locomotive A would be at the position as for locomotive B on day one, locomotive B at the position as for locomotive C on day one and locomotive C and D as for D and A. The cyclic diagram followed this pattern until locomotive A reached Camden 84 hours after it started and, if due for a time mileage or X day exam/boiler washout, would be withdrawn and replaced by another 8P resuming work. The time within the 83 hours and 50 minutes actually engaged upon working trains was 28 hours 42 minutes.

Locomotive A	Locomotive B	Locomotive C	Locomotive D
Day 1 10.0 Eus – Glsgw to Carlisle arr Carlisle 3/28	Day 1 0.45 from Clsle with 10/20 Glsgw – Eust (7.03), then 7/20 Eus – Inv to Crewe 10/16	Day 1 4/22 from Crewe with 1/30 Eus – Glasgow arr 9/10	Day 1 10.05 Glsgw – B'ham to Crewe (3/21), then 7/0 from Crewe to Euston with 12/15 from Perth (arr 9/50)

Locomotive A	Locomotive B	Locomotive C	Locomotive D
Day 2 As for locomotive B			
	Day 2 As for locomotive C		
		Day 2 As for locomotive D	
			Day 2 As for locomotive A
Day 3 As for locomotive C			
	Day 3 As for locomotive D		
		Day 3 As for locomotive A	
			Day 3 As for locomotive B End at Euston at 9/50 then to Camden. END
Day 4 As for locomotive D			
	Day 4 As for locomotive A		
		Day 4 As for locomotive B	
			Day 4 As for locomotive C

The mileage accumulated by each locomotive over the four-day cycle was 299 + 457 + 243 + 401 = 1,400. Dependent upon the recent history of time/mileage-based examinations and boiler washout, locomotives A, B, C and D could repeat the four-day cycle; being then withdrawn for necessary eight-day examination as part of Camden depot resource planning.

In similar vein, the 11/15 Glasgow-Birmingham was a very useful way of working Polmadie locomotives to Crewe when due for works attention and the usual following duty for the locomotive (the 11/10 Birmingham-Glasgow forward from Crewe) taken by another Polmadie locomotive recently outshopped from the works; one in, one out and without affecting the daily availability figures.

Based upon the utilisation of the fifty-one strong class 8P locomotives as tabulated, it is possible to identify work on a daily basis for thirty-five of them. That equates to a required availability of just under 70 per cent and aligns with the time taken on average for depot examinations and workshop repairs. At depots where specific classes of locomotive were assigned to work along the route (Longsight Class 7MT, Bushbury 6P and Holyhead 7MT) the position – at least for the basic timetable – was 'comfortable'. However, as detailed in chapter 2, the pattern of passenger services changed to meet the expectations of travellers and the Transport Act 1953 placed upon the BTC/the Regions an obligation to meet the requirements of the nation.

Although the utilisation of the class 8P locomotives is identifiable, it is not so for the large allocations of classes 6P and 7P at Longsight, Edge Hill, Crewe North, Carlisle Upperby and Camden. Longsight provided power for passenger services via Crewe and Shrewsbury to the west of England, Edge Hill for cross-Pennine traffic to Leeds, Crewe North was always something of a giant depository, Carlisle provided power for parcels and heavy goods trains and Camden was always expected to be able to find a class 7. The size of the total fleet reflected the balloon-like nature of the West Coast route; inflated to capacity when demand arose, but much of the time living well within its resources.

Before moving on to consider the human side of these locomotive arrangements, the opportunity will be taken to review the extent of the use of the Clan Class BR6 MT. The key letters there are MT – mixed traffic. Once the locomotives had demonstrated an early and consistent inability to maintain steam pressure for hard, fast running, it was towards other duties that the attention of the planners turned. The allocation within the Scottish Region was for the entire class of ten; five at each end of the Caledonian main line between Glasgow and Carlisle, 102 miles via Beattock. Polmadie, at the northern end, initially turned out two of its five for the long run to Manchester, returning the following day, but soon substituted *Britannia* Class 7MT, except at weekends when a Clan could be used in the Newton Heath 6P turn. The Perth workings could have involved any of Polmadie, Carstairs, Perth or Carlisle Kingmoor and (two) Clans from the first listed worked a two-day cycle involving the 7.0 Glasgow C-Carlisle, then taking over the 9.25 from Crewe through to Perth, returning the following day with the 12/15 from Perth to Carlisle, thence the 7/42 via Dumfries and Kilmarnock home.

Kingmoor sent a Clan to Stranraer, with a pilot locomotive if the load was marginal for the adverse gradients, and that prompts a painful personal memory. In those now distant days, I had a pal in my home town of Derby. In his happy, young life he had an annual treat in the form of a long journey by train to visit his aunt who lived at Newton Stewart on the Stranraer line. That in itself should have been sufficient to irritate me, but to compound my angst, I was then gleefully sent a postcard advising me that his train from Carlisle had been hauled by Clan something or other plus an extremely rare (in Derby at least) Jubilee as pilot. It still hurts!

The next categories of train were the parcels/newspapers (on a par for the operators), the class 'C' fully fitted goods for Glasgow and the class 'D' partially fitted goods. Kingmoor also had a cyclic diagram involving four *Clans* over four days (89 hours and 50 minutes, of which 40 hours and 9 minutes working trains and a total of 894 miles), but upon which a Patriot or Jubilee could equally be found. The diagram followed the same principle as for the Camden 8Ps, with the starting points and workings being:

Locomotive	Working
A start at Carlisle	10.50 parcels to Perth
B start at Perth	12.51 to Aberdeen
	9.35 Aberdeen – Perth 11.47
	4/50 (fish) to Carlisle 9/33
C start at Carlisle (K)	2.52 class 'C' to Glasgow College yard 7.10
	6/5 'D' Glasgow – Carlisle Durranhill
D start at Carlisle (V)	4.57 'D' to Glasgow Buchanan St
	11/30 'E' Glasgow – Kingmoor arr 3.57

Notes
K-Kingmoor
V-Viaduct yard
The Glasgow College yard workings were through services from/to Birmingham via the Midland route and worked by Saltley men to and from Durranhill.

The Scottish Region was frequently noted as achieving low mileages with its front-line passenger fleet between Glasgow and Carlisle. The Region could work only with the traffic that was on offer. Along the route via Beattock on weekdays there were just sixteen express passenger trains in each direction. The pattern was skewed by eight trains leaving Carlisle northbound between midnight and 6am, plus the Royal Mail train, while in the southbound direction there were three departures from Glasgow in mid-morning and then a concentration of sleeping car services in the late evening. A glance to Edinburgh provides a clue as to what could be done if your main line went to the north as well as south. Two diagrams for Haymarket depot A4 Class pacifics:

(A) Haymarket LE 6.35
     Edinburgh (Waverley) 7.40 to Perth 9.13
     Perth 12/8 to Edinburgh 1/50 (to depot)
     Edinburgh 8/10 to Newcastle 11/5
     Newcastle 0.39 to Edinburgh 5.9 (to depot)   (346 miles)

(B) Haymarket LE 11.20
     Edinburgh noon to Newcastle 2/12
     Newcastle 3/42 to Edinburgh 6/2 (to depot)
     Edinburgh 11/10 to Newcastle 2.4 (to depot)
     Newcastle 3.40 to Edinburgh 6.10 (to depot)   (500 miles)

During the period of the Winter Timetable the Euston arrivals on typical Mondays – Thursdays would produce the following. Power provided by:

Locomotives allocated to	Power classes		
Camden	7 8P	8 7P	3 6P
Longsight		7 7P	1 6P
Edge Hill	3 8P	3 7P	
Holyhead		3 7P	
Crewe North	3 8P	4 7P+6P	
Bushbury			4 6P
Carlisle Upperby	1 8P		
Blackpool			1 6P

Note
Preston 6Ps at weekends

For the main line services into and from Euston, the majority of the enginemen worked lodging turns and, between the outward and homeward legs, would be accommodated in hostels and dormitories offering basic facilities for sleeping, eating and washing. During the course of each week, men from Crewe North, Longsight, Edge Hill, Carlisle Upperby, Holyhead, Bushbury, Blackpool, Carnforth and Preston worked into Euston and Camden/Willesden men lodged away in similar circumstances. At each depot, drivers, passed firemen, firemen and passed cleaners were grouped into 'links' based upon route knowledge and seniority within the grade. At Camden there were five main line links and with very few exceptions were based upon lodging:

a)   one night turn to and from Carlisle and two day turns to Blackpool. That was the 'top link'
b)   Manchester via Stoke
c) & d) Manchester, Liverpool and Crewe main line
e)   Wolverhampton, Crewe, miscellaneous.

Between Crewe and Euston, a large proportion of the trains were worked by men of Crewe North. Edge Hill had six passenger links for routes south to Birmingham and London and east to Leeds and six links for goods. Similar arrangements at the other depots listed and the number of sets of men in each link was generally quite small at around twelve to fifteen (Holyhead fewer, Crewe more). Men in the top passenger links would normally be contract mileage men. What that meant was a working day mileage of 140 with each 15 miles being equivalent to one hour's pay. A lodging turn spread over two working days for Euston-Liverpool would produce a mileage of 388; two days at 140 miles plus two lots of 54 miles equivalent to nearly eight hours pay. The top link contract men were the senior men of their days, usually drivers at the end of long careers. Men not working to contract rates worked an 11-day fortnight. Whatever the arrangement, some unsocial hours work was unavoidable; the top link Camden crew who booked on duty late at night on a Monday for the 0.20 departure to Carlisle did not see their own bed again until mid-morning on the Wednesday, having worked the 0.08 departure (9/25 from Glasgow) from Carlisle. Two lodging turns a week would produce a contract mileage of 560 plus a handsome bonus of 35/36 hours pay. By comparison, the lodging turns to Blackpool were easier with northbound departures of 10.50 and 5/5, returning from Blackpool at 8.0 and 10.0 respectively.

The eight-hour shift arrangement had been agreed in 1919 (prior to that it was twelve) and, to provide some flexibility for local workings within the wider network, men were required to assist with preparation and disposal duties with locomotives, but that unpopular obligation was avoided if individuals were prepared to work lodging turns. Arrangements on the LMS had been strengthened in the 1930s when non-stop workings between Euston and Carlisle had been started. As a result of Crewe North missing out on some main line work, its men were offered lodging turns to Perth. While lodging turns predominated on the Western Division, their application elsewhere was far less prevalent. Neither the Scottish nor Western Regions had lodging turns and, on the Eastern and North Eastern Regions, they were a constant base for discontent, particularly at Grantham, York, Gateshead and Heaton where the NUR had a strong membership. Irrespective of trade union representation, each depot was protective of its turns and continually fought for at least an ongoing status quo. With the operating arrangements being accepted as the stronger basis for organisation following nationalisation, the circumstances supporting an ongoing status quo were allowed to remain unchallenged while the nation it served changed beyond recognition. Apart from it representing a problem too large for any one Region to disturb, I can find no logical explanation as to why it was necessary in the 1950s/60s for Holyhead and Carlisle men to work south of Crewe, for Camden men to work north and west of Crewe, for Bushbury men not to be exchanged on some turns at Coventry or Rugby, why Preston (approximately half way between London and Glasgow) was not afforded a higher operational status and why men worked on Jubilees from Manchester to Glasgow.

The working arrangements for enginemen, guards and catering staff added more layers of planning effort. Enginemen worked a basic eight hour shift, were allowed a break of at least nine hours if 'lodging' prior to working home.

This is the arrangement for Polmadie enginemen working the afternoon service to Manchester from their home station of Glasgow:

Book on duty 2/35 (prepare locomotive)
Polmadie engine sidings 3/35
Glasgow C depart 4/5
Manchester Vic arrive 10/10. Relieved at 10/26
Travel passenger to Dean Lane (dormitory) at 10/50
Rest

Next day book on duty 12/8 (prepare locomotive)
Newton Heath engine sidings 1/8
Chatham Hill (carriage siding) 1/38
Manchester Vic depart 2/0
Glasgow C arrive 7/50 (relieved by Polmadie men)
Book off at Glasgow Central station 7/50

Hours on duty:
Day one 8 hours 39 minutes
Day two 7 hours 52 minutes
Time away from home: 29 hours 15 minutes
Bonus miles end day: 143

Locomotives:
Day one, BR 7MT or BR 6MT
Day two, ex-LMS 6P Jubilee.

All of the arrangements were guarded by the management, the unions and at each depot. Other depots and 'links' of enginemen watched too as they expected to benefit from increases in services for the Summer Timetable, additional services and relief trains. The matters were dealt with as necessary at the Sectional Council, a meeting between the management and elected representatives of the men. While there was no logic to why Holyhead men or Carlisle Upperby men should work beyond Crewe, or Polmadie and Crewe men work beyond Carlisle, the complexity of any major changes was enormous. As soon as the senior management of the LM Region were told that electrification of the Manchester/Liverpool to Euston route had been underwritten as part of the Modernisation Plan (1955) they knew that would bring massive change. Revising long standing arrangements for locomotives and enginemen for the ex-LNW main lines was a low priority, though not for the Midland Division of their Region (see chapter 4).

For the next few years, linesiding along the ex-LNW main lines to Euston would be a wonderful experience.

Chapter 4

1957: Opportunity Knocks

For the management team of the Western Division of the London Midland Region, the challenges for 1957 could be placed into two very different categories; firstly, to meet the immediate expectations of the travelling public and industry as latterly enhanced by the Suez Crisis and rationing of petrol, and secondly, to plan for the early benefits accruing from the Modernisation Plan. The second of those challenges had implications for the Midland Division of the Region which would require a degree of mutual support to assist initially in the short-term. While these challenges were within the control of the Regional Board and General Manager, neither had direct influence over decisions taken by the BTC with or without influence from the government.

Within days of the imposition of the rationing of fuel on 7 November 1956, the effect of Suez had been apparent in the increased number of passenger journeys made on railway services and on revenue. That increased volume of demand – in a month that was normally relatively quiet for passenger travel – required decisions and actions for the higher level of traffic on weekdays, at weekends and at religious holiday times.

For some of the weekday, timetabled, trains, the solution would be as was usually applied in the summer months; trainsets would not be disturbed except to the extent of attaching

The need for an assisting locomotive on tightly timed West Midlands services with a tonnage exceeding the limit for a Jubilee was met up to 1959 by the use of Monument Lane Compounds. Compounds were no strangers to the route having been entrusted with fast services in LMS days. Here, Connaught has an easy time of things. (50)

additional carriages at the front or rear to provide, say, an extra 112 second/third class and 36 first-class seats. While that solution could be applied to the Wolverhampton and some Manchester and Liverpool services, the marshalling of trainsets for some other services precluded that application. For example, the Holyhead and Windermere services included the conveyance of non-passenger carrying vehicles at front and/or rear for detachment along the route. Similarly, some trains conveyed portions or through carriages for detachment at Crewe, Stockport, Preston and Carlisle, in particular, with restaurant cars being included at some stages of overnight services.

Additional carriages also increased the weight of the train and the revised tonnage may well have resulted in the power class of the normally rostered locomotive to be expected to meet the timings as laid down in the Working Timetable. For example, a Jubilee Class 6 would be expected to work the 8.50 Euston-Wolverhampton (357 tons, 11 carriages) train and pass Rugby in 79 minutes. That tonnage was already marginally over the maximum of 350 and the provision of one or two additional carriages would have allowed the driver to request the provision of an assisting locomotive; usually a class 5, but in 1957 possibly a class 4, 4-4-0. As the year progressed, the 4-4-0s which had been placed into store, serviceable, at Rugby were re-introduced to traffic while those at Monument Lane, Birmingham resumed seasonal duties to North Wales.

The use of pilot assisting locomotives made the task of finding power for secondary passenger and vacuum brake fitted goods traffic that much more difficult, reduced net revenue but made many a footplate crew happier by being in receipt of a mileage worked bonus payment. Having

Ex-LMS pacifics were not allowed over the Stoke-on-Trent route, but they did appear at Manchester from Crewe. On Fridays the strengthened tea time express to Euston was usually a pacific with a return to Crewe on the Saturday 11.45 down. Here **Lady Patricia** *arrives as a Jubilee prepares to depart. On the east side of the station an electric locomotive awaits a duty. (51)*

available up to five BTC owned main line diesels was extremely useful as if their train heating boilers were defective the locomotives could be deployed on goods workings.

The weight of the fixed formation trainsets, which could not be disturbed by the addition of more carriages, varied and may or may not have been even close to the maximum allowed for the rostered locomotive to maintain timings. The use of a Princess Coronation Class 8 on the 6/20 Euston – Heysham (ten carriages for 326 tons) timed at 86 minutes to Rugby was eight carriages (274 tons), less than that for which the locomotive was deemed capable of; while seemingly inefficient, the return working of the locomotive was the much heavier 7.0 Heysham-Euston the following morning (fourteen carriages, timed to XL non-stop from Crewe and in between the important business trains from Manchester and Liverpool due to pass Stafford within the space of seventeen minutes).

A summary of the dilemma for the train planners for departures from Euston is:

Trains having spare tonnage capacity for locomotive/timings		
Time	**Destination**	**Spare capacity (carriages)**
0.02	Crewe	6
0.20	Glasgow	7
0.30	Liverpool	11
0.40	Manchester	3
6.40	Windermere	1
7.55	Liverpool	2
9.0	Wolverhampton	2
10.40	Carlisle	6
10.50	Blackpool	1
noon	Crewe	6
12/30	Liverpool	5
2/30	Liverpool	1
3/45	Manchester	4
4/30	Manchester	1
4/37	Wolverhampton	4
6/0	Manchester	2
6/10	Liverpool	2
6/20	Heysham	8
6/30	Preston	5
7/30	Wolverhampton	1
6/55	Birmingham	2
7/0	Inverness	2
7/20	Perth	6
9/10	Glasgow	3
9/25	Glasgow	9
9/35	Birmingham	2
10/45	Manchester	4
10/52	Perth	5
11/50	Glasgow	1

Trains not having spare tonnage capacity for locomotive/timings	
Time	**Destination**
8.30	Liverpool
8.50	Wolverhampton
9.45	Manchester
10.0	Glasgow
11.45	Manchester
2/20	Wolverhampton
2/45	Manchester
4/30	Manchester
4/55	Liverpool
5/05	Blackpool
5/35	Holyhead
5/50	Wolverhampton
8/50	Holyhead
11/05	Windermere

At first glance, the trains with spare capacity would seem to offer a favourable solution, but a closer inspection reduces that due to the complexities of the usual arrangements with through carriages and non-passenger carrying vehicles. As an example, the 7/30 to Perth conveyed a restaurant car as far as Crewe, two non-passenger carrying vans to Carlisle and had attached at Bletchley a van to be detached at Crewe. Further complications were carriages on other trains for Colne, Southport, Birkenhead, the Furness line and for the Scottish Region to attach catering vehicles at Carlisle. As usual, Holyhead services were in constant jeopardy of serious overcrowding and the lack of spare capacity for most departures between 4/30 and 6/0 was particularly troublesome.

The solution was to introduce 'relief' trains with or without catering on all or some weekdays as in the summer (and listed in chapter 2). The timing, and therefore motive power arrangements of these trains, needed to avoid a mix of XL and SL trains and most trains ran to SL with a timing headway of seven minutes (having grown from three to five to seven over a span of twenty years). For its additional traffic, British Railways was able to quickly adjust by use of coaching stock that would not normally see usage during the majority of the nine months of the Winter Timetable and applying proven 'paths' within the Working Timetable. The effect against the measure of passenger receipts was:

Comparison with previous year (per cent)		
	1956	**1957**
December	+11.2*	-
January	-	+22
February	-	+23
March	-	+16
June	-	+8

* 8.2 million extra journeys made

With goods traffic, the Suez Crisis presented to the Regions an opportunity to, at the very least, regain some larger share of the total demand for movement. Of the three categories as defined by the Board of Trade (coal/coke/patent fuel, other minerals and merchandise) the one that had ebbed to road during the period of growth 1952-55 was merchandise. Merchandise included manufactured goods, cement, timber, and perishable produce such as fruit and vegetables. Of the three categories, the Midland lines carried the higher Regional proportion of the coal markets' traffic. The Western/ LNW lines received some of that coal and moved additional tonnage from the coalfields of Warwickshire, Staffordshire and Lancashire, and moved the higher proportion of the merchandise that originated in the main centres of production that characterised the routes. When set against the wider measure of the growth of UK production, the trading performance of the railways in total was poor; the national increase in tonnage produced had risen between 1948, an index figure of 100, and 1956 to an index figure of 137. During that time, the corresponding increase in tonnage carried by the railways had increased by some 2 per cent for minerals, while the tonnage of merchandise had shown a decline of some 14 per cent. That latter depressing statistic came about for a number of reasons including post-war shortages of materials and staff, years of wrangling between the RE and the BTC, a desire by the BTC to acknowledge the needs of the nation under the Act of 1947, a slow adjustment to the new world of the Act of 1953, confusion at Goods Agent level regarding the commercial effect of reducing tariffs in order to retain traffic, the rapid growth of 'C' Licence road haulage operations and an unwillingness of the government to concede in full submissions by the Commission to the annual Railway Rates Tribunals. In the years of growth of the economy, an increasing consumer confidence and development of the electricity industry left the railways behind and having lost the advantage that containerisation in particular should have given them. The third category – coal/coke/patent fuel – became progressively larger in proportion and, while profitable, against a measure of direct operating costs was never allowed to be used to subsidise losses elsewhere in the portfolio. 1957 was the year in which demand for coal in the domestic and industrial markets of the National Coal Board peaked, leaving that Board (and the railways as carrier) with only power station demand as a growth market.

In parallel with the loss of total market share, the railways were also facing increased costs for materials and labour and, dependent upon a government that reacted only slowly; the strike in 1955 was a sign of distress for the industry. To compound the financial woes, the central charges for the Commission were an increasing burden, as was the obligation to repay with interest the capital loaned for the programme of modernisation.

Overall, British Railways traffic volumes and market share were:

Years (average)	Passenger traffic mileage '000m	Market share per cent	Freight traffic tons, mileage '000m	Market share per cent
1951-53	24.2	23.4	22.7	45.3
1954-56	24.2	18.9	21.7	40.5

Traffic trends for British Railways 1948-56 (millions)				
Year	Passenger miles	Coal/coke/ patent fuel tons	Minerals tons	Merchandise tons
1948	21,022	9,662	4,959	7,041
1951	20,561	10,660	5,164	7,078
1953	20,578	10,715	5,261	6,790
1954	20,712	10,489	5,059	6,542
1955	20,383	10,191	5,075	6,087
1956	21,133	10,248	5,217	6,008
1957	22,591	9,869	5,068	5,944

The benefit for British Railways freight business from the Suez Crisis was short-lived between January and March 1957; thereafter the additional tonnage for merchandise ebbed away again as the nearly one million holders of 'C' road licences regained commercial control (up from 327,000 in 1948). A Wigan-Glasgow vacuum fitted merchandise service formed a part of a very short list of newly introduced railway services that arose out of Suez.

The rationing of petrol ceased from 14 May 1957, by which time the UK had a newly appointed Prime Minister, Harold Macmillan, who had replaced Anthony Eden when the latter's health deteriorated. Macmillan was fortunate to inherent a buoyant and confident consumer-led economy, leading him to declare that many people had never had it so good. For the railway it would prove to be a busy summer.

If anything, the arrangements for passenger traffic for summer 1957 were easier than for the previous two years; much of the stock was already in place and many of the relief and Q train services were more established than usual. From 3 June, the third-class seating and fares were officially abolished and replaced by a new second-class. The seven months had not resulted in any significant re-allocations of front-line passenger locomotives but, for the summer, the usual changes affecting Edge Hill, Crewe North, Carlisle Upperby and Camden depots were affected and, in the case of Carlisle Upperby, were more extensive.

To meet the requirement for the relief to the southbound *Royal Scot* to be hauled from Carlisle by a Princess Coronation Class 8, it was usual for an additional such locomotive to be re-allocated from Crewe North which, in turn, received from Edge Hill a Princess Royal Class 8, leaving the latter depot to use a class 7 for one turn. Camden usually received a handful of Royal Scots for use on the seasonal extra services, particularly those on Fridays and Saturdays. For 1957, the re-allocation of class 8 locomotives was more extensive and resulted in the main from changes made by the Scottish Region involving a change of locomotive at Carlisle and the introduction of a new Anglo-Scottish service, *The Caledonian*.

The Caledonian was a lightweight, eight-carriage trainset which ran on Mondays to Fridays between Glasgow and Euston and vice versa, to fast timings of 6 hours 38 minutes, including a two-minute stop at Carlisle in each direction. Blessed with a class 8 Princess Coronation from Polmadie and Camden depots, it was timed to leave Glasgow at 8.30 and 4/15 from Euston. The introduction of the train southbound had the result of negating a need for a relief to the *Royal Scot* and that train calling at Carlisle station rather than changing locomotives alongside Kingmoor depot. The southbound *Mid-Day Scot* was re-timed to leave at 3/0 (instead of 1/30) and to run non-stop from Carlisle to Euston, due at 10/20. However, an additional service was run in the path of the 1/30 to join at Carstairs with the 12/15 Perth-Euston. On Mondays to Thursdays, the through carriages from Glasgow to Plymouth were conveyed to Crewe as part of the 10.05 Birmingham service. On Fridays and Saturdays those carriages formed part of a separate through 10.15 train to Plymouth which also offered a restaurant car and was a balanced service with a Fridays only Plymouth-Glasgow service. There was also a daily through train between Aberdeen and Manchester with carriages from Dundee (West) which balanced the 9.50 SX/9.25 SO Manchester/Crewe-Aberdeen service. For travel on these services, full fare tickets would be issued, i.e. not discounted in any way as applicable to excursion trains or to the Starlight Specials. The Starlight Specials catered for a different market and, for a return fare of £4, a guaranteed seat would be provided on Friday night special services between Glasgow/ Edinburgh and London termini, more usually to St Pancras and Marylebone than Euston. The trains commenced on 18 April from London, the 19th from Scotland and then ran weekly in each direction until 20 September. These trains proved to be popular and none more so than at the start and end of the Glasgow Fairs holidays which started in June and caused an exodus south of magnificent proportions. Any number up to eight and still counting trains would run, requiring in excess of 100 carriages with reserved seating and colour coded tickets for specific outward and return dated and timed services. The Scottish Region sent the trains via all three routes to Carlisle, requiring up to fourteen locomotives with some continuing south at least as far as Leeds/Sheffield. Three or four of the trains on those exceptional evenings were directed to Euston, with a subsequent return flow of the same proportions a fortnight later. For the final week of the season, a general sort out of coaching stock of a 'foreign' Region was arranged as was also for motive power, explaining why mid-September was a good time to spot Polmadie allocated Britannias way down south. Sporting fixtures too generated special traffic in bulk and, when Scotland hosted England/Wales and vice versa for Association Football or Rugby Union internationals, locomotives would frequently stray beyond the usual boundaries.

Arising from this, Edge Hill lost half its winter allocation of six Princess Royals to Crewe North (46200/4/5) which then had an allocation of nine of that Class, but lost one Princess Coronation (46242) which joined 46226/8/51/5 at Carlisle Upperby. With four non-stop London services (two day time, two night time) in each direction, Upperby needed additional high power.

The shopping into Crewe Works did not cease during the summer but, in 1957, no single depot suffered disproportionately. The detail is at Appendix 5 but, in summary, Camden lost the services of two Coronations while classified repairs were undertaken, Crewe North three, Carlisle Upperby two and Polmadie two. In addition, they all lost locomotives of that Class for periods of a few days while speedometers were fitted.

The concept of *The Caledonian* owed much to what had been happening 'next door but one' along the Euston Road, i.e. at King's Cross, where they already had on offer the summer non-stop London-Edinburgh service *The Elizabethan*. Rumour had it that, from September 1957, the planning provided for a fast, through service to and from Perth to be named *The Fair Maid*. Furthermore, the Eastern Region was fitting a set of carriages with roller bearing axleboxes and intended using that set on a round trip King's Cross-Edinburgh to achieve 786 miles in the working day. The attendant promotion and publicity did nothing to improve the mood at Euston where 1956 had passed without an appearance by a new service.

That there was a need for an additional day-time service between Euston and Glasgow was not in doubt; the timing, market, capacity and stopping points along the route were. Main line departures for Scotland left Euston at 10.0 (*Royal Scot*), 1/30 (*Mid-Day Scot*), 1/35 for Perth,

7/20 for Inverness and 7/30 for Perth. The 10.0 called at Rugby, Crewe and Carlisle and reached Glasgow in seven and a quarter-hours with three vehicles for Perth detached at Crewe and taken forward on the following Birmingham-Glasgow service as far as Carlisle, finally reaching Perth at 8/14. The 1/30 also called at Rugby, Crewe and Carlisle and reached Glasgow at 9/10. The 1/35 conveyed thirteen carriages as far as Crewe where five were detached (for Blackpool) leaving eight to go forward to Carlisle where one was detached and two attached; Perth was reached at a quarter after midnight. The 7/20 spent nearly fourteen hours over its 568-mile journey with catering at either end of the long journey, three sleeping cars and five seating carriages plus two non-passenger carrying vehicles. South of Carlisle the train called only at Crewe. The 7/30 to Perth conveyed more carriages for Stranraer (eight) than for its ultimate destination (five) which was reached at 7.13 and with stops south of Carlisle at Bletchley, Rugby, Crewe and Wigan North Western.

In terms of seats available:

Service	First	Second	Note
10.0	102	304	1
10.0	18	48	2, 3
1/30	132	295	4
1/35	84	144	2, 4
7/20	36	144	5
7/30	18	90	2, 3, 6

Notes
1. Glasgow portion
2. Perth portion
3. also conveyed restaurant car to Crewe 12/18
4. also conveyed restaurant car to Crewe
5. also conveyed sleeping car(s)

All of these services were 'full fare' basis, with the *Royal Scot* attracting, by its departure times in each direction, sufficient second-class fare paying traffic to generate a need for a Summer Timetable relief train. One of the commercial risks of *The Caledonian* – with a departure from Glasgow at 8.30 – was to draw passengers who would, in any event, have taken the 10.0 *Royal Scot* or its relief. That risk was balanced by the relief service being cancelled and, therefore, no extra train crew or coaching stock costs were incurred. The trainsets offered 84 first-class and 120 second-class seats. The marketing efforts centred on speed and comfort, a time of 6 hours 40 minutes in each direction was better than the *Royal Scot* and the northbound 4/15 caught up and overtook the 1/35 at Carstairs to arrive in Glasgow just as the pubs closed. Two sets of carriages were used, with maintenance and heavy cleaning at weekends.

The questions of the marketing and filling a new service – any new service – is a challenge. Apart from the Scottish services originating/terminating at Birmingham/Manchester/Liverpool, the thriving business centres of Warrington and Preston were particularly ill served by the Anglo-Scottish services of the London Midland Region. The insertion of a pause at Preston northbound at around 8/0 would surely have appealed to a Lancastrian businessman returning from five hours in London, having left on the Up service that morning.

A problem with high speed, long distance trains with just one stop is that, if you leave with a lot of empty seats, the tendency is to arrive at the destination in a similarly disappointing, commercial situation. *The Caledonian* did not make an immediate impact, but received good publicity including the use of *City of Glasgow* on the first departure from Euston, accompanied by a pipes and drums send off. Operationally, the timings for the southbound service allowed it a good path from Warrington. Once clear of Crewe, the only impediment to consistent fast-running ahead of schedule was the preceding Blackpool-Euston service due into London at 3/05. The service from Blackpool was heavy – fifteen vehicles – and booked for a *Royal Scot* to an SL timing of 138 minutes from its last stop at Stafford. If anything, the train was slightly overweight for a *Royal Scot* on those timings and, once *The Caledonian* settled down within its path, it was not uncommon for the Blackpool to be double-headed from Crewe. In the event of late running of the Blackpool, it could be 'put inside', usually at King's Langley/Watford.

Something must have stirred at Euston as, in the late summer, *The Caledonian* was allowed some official leeway to achieve headline catching runs southbound arriving at a time when the newspaper sub-editors were putting their copy into a final format. Railways were still news of interest and the Public Relations and Publicity Office of the London Midland Region was always close to a reporter. Before tipping off reporters, it is as well to be confident that a good story will unfold as hoped. As part of the planning, arrangements were quietly made for 7 August, upon which date the timing from Crewe to Euston was reduced by 15 minutes and the Blackpool service kept well clear to allow *The Caledonian* a clear run. With a Camden footplate crew of driver Starvis and fireman Wills, *The Caledonian* arrived at Euston 6 hours 27 minutes after leaving Glasgow hauled by 46229 *Duchess of Hamilton* which had been a regular performer on the train that summer. That clearly went down well at Euston and arrangements were again made for 5 September, but with the aim of truly exceptional timing harking back to the days of the streamlined trains of the 1930s. Delayed at Penrith, 46244 *King George VI*, driven by Starvis (fireman Tumilty), recovered to the extent of being allowed a clear run through at Crewe, passed at 12.34, 13 minutes early. Progress unhindered by anything other than permanent speed restrictions, the train covered the 116 miles between Stafford and Watford in 84 minutes at a (pass to pass) average speed of 83 miles per hour. The 119-minute run from Crewe exactly equalled that of the record-breaking run with *Coronation* in 1937. A further exceptionally fast run was recorded on 20 September with 46239 *City of Chester* (Court/Vigo) worked hard to recover time lost north of Oxenholme. If nothing else, Euston had spiked the balloons and banners next door but one along the Euston Road.

High speeds and derring-do also bring managerial concerns. Just how fast was the train travelling at any given time (probably around 100mph near Castlethorpe), what was the safe stopping distance from that speed in the event of a signal at caution being sighted in the prevailing hours of daylight and clear visibility? The high speed streamlined trains were 'double blocked', i.e. signalled two sections ahead rather than one and the same arrangements probably were applied on 7 August and 5 September. On 20 September the train was probably a block behind the noon service from Manchester from Watford. Neither of the locomotives used on 7 August and 5 September were then fitted with a speedometer, although 46239 was fitted with one by 20 September. The notional upper speed limit on the London Midland Region was 90mph. Men and their machines were on top of the job.

For the Winter Timetable, *The Caledonian* service was retained and the only other alteration of note was to reinstate the southbound *Mid-Day Scot* departure time to 1/30 (Euston 9/0). With the availability of more of the BR Mark 1 carriages, a further service received a title;

the 7/20 to Inverness became *The Royal Highlander*, as did the 5/15 return service to London. Two Princess Royals went back from Crewe North to Edge Hill and three Princess Coronations back to Crewe North. The usual re-distribution of Royal Scots back from Camden took place but, by the time the reallocations settled, the Western Division was six of the class short and the Midland Division had gained all six at Kentish Town (London) depot.

The Midland Division services to Leicester/Nottingham/Derby/Sheffield/Manchester were greatly improved in 1957. Forming part of a plan to offer and establish a good foundation for the times ahead when the Euston lines were expected to be affected by electrification works, the speed up of services had been maintained during the months of petrol rationing and the summer at the expense of double heading. Timings on the Midland Division were on the same principle as for the Western Division (XL, SL, FL), but around the use of class 6 Jubilees. The necessary strengthening of most services, the demands of the gradient profile and the fact that the pilot locomotives were frequently aged 4-4-0s had made it a very hard year for the Midland. As the Winter Passenger Timetable was equally demanding on the Midland, as for the summer and matters eased somewhat on the Western Division, Euston deemed that the Midland would be relieved by the provision of six class 7 locomotives. The usual arrangement at depot level was for the locomotive(s) with the highest mileage to be put forward for re-allocation. However, in this case all six locomotives (46110/6/27/31/52/7) had received a general repair at Crewe in the recent past. It helped the Midland out, but could be only short-term. While the winter set in, efforts were directed to find alternative sources of class 7 power and allow the six Royal Scots to be returned (see chapter 5). As evidence of the enhanced status of the Midland, the 7.55 from St Pancras and 2/25 return from Manchester, received a title, *The Palatine*. At the same time, the 7.55 from Euston became *The Lancastrian*, 4/0 return.

Chester, with Royal Scot Civil Service Rifleman *leaving with a train conveying three horse boxes. Race horse traffic with accompanying grooms from/back to Ireland via Holyhead was regular, seasonal traffic on passenger services allowed to take four wheeled vehicles. (52)*

Mixed emotions for the photographer here alongside Kingmoor depot, Carlisle where the summer Royal Scot changed locomotives and did not call at Citadel station. Princess Coronation **Queen Mary** *has brought the train from Glasgow and would normally have been replaced by a classmate. However, on this occasion a Royal Scot has been provided* (**The King's Royal Rifle Corps**) *and is making a confident start for its 300-mile journey. (53)*

The second challenge facing the management of the Region was to plan for the early benefits accruing from the Modernisation Plan. To prepare the content of its submission to the government, the BTC had established nine sub-committees to seek and consider specific areas to improve. Amongst the sub-committees were those for forms of motive power, modernisation of stations, rolling stock, marshalling yards and the recruitment of staff having technical skills for rolling stock, infrastructure and management. The London Midland Region contributed proposals to the sub-committees and those for motive power electrification and infrastructure are of greater relevance here.

A fuller description of the torment surrounding the schemes for the main line diesel locomotives is offered in chapter 6 but, as 1957 saw the arrival at the London end of the LNW lines of the first batch of diesel locomotives, it is appropriate to make reference here. There had long been an acceptance within the RE/BTC and London Midland Region that diesel locomotives should be used for shunting work. A logical development of that was for a more powerful, bogied type with low axle weight and generous route availability to undertake local trip and train marshalling work. With the difficulties of maintaining the prototype main line diesels within steam infrastructure at Willesden and elsewhere in mind, the proposed new locomotives would be allocated to a single depot built or converted solely for the use of diesels. With the potential of twenty-six diesels to replace forty-one steam locomotives and a conversion of the modest depot at Devons Road, the case proved to be persuasive. Devons Road depot was near Bow, East London and was used to supply power for the former North London Railway route which was used by goods trains transferring across London, particularly between Temple Mills, Ferme Park, Willesden, Cricklewood, Acton, Battersea and Hither Green. The depot was designated 1D, a sub-shed of Willesden. The Region also submitted plans for diesel hauled main line services between London, Birmingham, Manchester and Liverpool.

After the sub-committee had completed its work and parliament had underwritten the Modernisation Plan, the BTC drew up outline specifications for diesel locomotives of varying power. Widespread interest was shown by industry in tendering to build initial batches and resulting from a consideration of offers received, the BTC placed contracts for fourteen separate pilot scheme builds of a total of 174 locomotives. The fourteen builds featured seven different main contractors, eight different suppliers of engines of varying types and eight suppliers of transmission equipment. Over a period of two/three years in operational service conditions, the locomotive that emerged as being most suitable would form the basis for a smaller number of production quantity build programmes.

Of the main contractors, two – English Electric (EE) and Brush Associated Oil Engine Group/Brush Electrical Engineering (Brush) – had the advantage of greater experience of diesel traction development, build and operation; each had (within the group of companies in the case of Brush) an ability to build the body, bogies, engines and transmission systems and source mainly 'in house' the mechanical parts.

Three pilot scheme orders were potentially suited to the London Midland's Devons Road depot proposal; ten 800hp from British Thomson-Houston (BTH) with their own design of transmission powered by Paxman engines, ten 800hp from North British Locomotive Company (NBL) with General Electric Company (GEC) transmission and Paxman engines, and twenty 1,000hp from EE with their own transmissions, engines and mechanical parts.

NBL was, traditionally, a builder of steam locomotives for overseas and the home markets, but it had accepted from the LMS an order for a single 827hp diesel locomotive which was delivered in 1950 and given by BR the number 10800. The locomotive was equipped with a Paxman engine and BTH transmission and, after initial trials in Scotland, it spent time on the London Midland, Southern and Eastern Regions before returning to the LM in 1955 when it was allocated to Rugby and frequently worked the Leicester line. The locomotive was fitted with a steam generating boiler. For its invitation to tender for locomotives in the 800-1,000hp power band, the BTC used the NBL design as a basis.

It was decided that the EE and NBL (numbered D82XX) products would work from Devons Road and, like the BTH products of Bo-Bo configuration, not equipped with train heating equipment. The weights in working order were 68 tons (NBL/BTH) and 72 tons 14cwt (EE).

The first to arrive was the EE product numbered D8000 which arrived in the London area in mid-June 1957 and was put on display at Battersea together with a few more examples of progress and use of capital investment. Turned out in a dark green livery with grey roof, the EE product D8000 paved the way for an eventual class of 228 in total. Progressively they worked more in multiple to provide 2,000hp braking power for heavier trains and with cabs at the outer ends which gave improved visibility. Prior to acceptance by BR, the locomotives were given proving runs from the Vulcan Foundry works between Warrington and Wigan; the tests typically involving a run to Penrith and back with eight empty carriages taken over Shap. The design feature that was similar to steam locomotives was that with the cab being at one end, the bulk of the body limited forward visibility and made the sighting of signals/hand instructions difficult on occasions.

Until September 1958, Devons Road depot was shared with a dwindling number of steam shunting 0-6-0s and then became the country's first all-diesel depot.

Amongst the reasons for being satisfied with the EE early products was a need for the BTC to be seen to be trying to meet the provisions of the Clean Air Act 1956.

For motive power of the future for main line traffic, there were three bodies of opinion which centred around considerations beyond the method of propulsion:

Electrification

- high capital cost
- extensive disruption over a long period of time
- overhead 25kv a.c. systems successfully installed in post-war France
- dc system used extensively on Southern Region
- economists considered application to suburban lines would provide a better return on investment than main lines
- clean technology

Diesel

- lower capital cost than for electrification
- offered greater flexibility of use over electrification
- fuel costs high
- experience from use of five prototype units on Southern Region considered by that region to be favourable
- higher daily utilisation than for steam would offset in the medium/long-term the high, initial, capital cost

Steam

- low first cost
- further technical developments offered potential to increase availability and speed over improved infrastructure (track/signalling)
- existing policy was to develop (Standard classes then being built) and progressively switch to electrification

The adoption of an overhead system using 25 kv a.c. supply had been recommended by Riddles in 1951. That recommendation followed a visit to France to see such a system in use on a 55-mile section between Aix-le-Bains and Laroche-sur-Foron. Accompanying him was S.B. Warder who, following Riddles' retirement, became Chief Electrical Engineer on the Central Staff of the BTC, and representatives of UK firms including EE and British Insulated Callender's Cables Ltd (BICC). Riddles was so impressed with what he had seen that he asked for support from the firms to supply equipment for a trial of the a.c. system on the nine-mile Morecambe and Heysham line. The firms agreed and the work was carried out under the direction of Warder and in conjunction with the British Electricity Authority (later CEGB). Using an ex-LNWR three coach electric set, trials were started in November 1952 and full passenger services from August 1953.

The BTC was faced with a dilemma. In 1951, a Technical Committee had endorsed the use of 1,500V d.c. and the Manchester-Woodhead-Sheffield line had been so equipped and opened in grand official style in 1954. It was a case of continue as before or accept that the French system was better and its adoption as recommended by Warder – lighter overhead equipment, few electrical supply sub-stations, more economical locomotive control, offset by a need for larger clearances under overbridges through tunnels and under station structures. For schemes to electrify the main line from Euston, there was an estimated saving of £6m from the use of 25 kv a.c. over d.c. with a projected total cost of £118m.

The BTC Technical Committee accepted Warder's recommendation to adopt the 25 kv a.c. system and, together with the cost estimates for the Euston main line project, was reviewed by the Commission in October 1955 (Euston/Manchester/Liverpool).

At its meeting on 15 March 1956, the BTC authorised work for the first phase of the Manchester to Crewe section; the Styal line between Slade Lane Junction and Wilmslow, a further £3.4m by the end of that year and £14.3m more in April 1957 for Manchester-Crewe Works and preparatory work for the Crewe-Liverpool line. In spring 1956, tenders were invited from contractors for forty mixed traffic and twenty express passenger locomotives and for the equipment for a further twenty of each type to be built in BR workshops, a total of 100 locomotives and half of the expected total requirement. The specification called for locomotives capable of hauling 475-ton passenger trains at speeds up to 100mph and 950-ton freight trains at up to 55mph. The total weight would be limited by the maximum axle weight of 20 tons, as stipulated by the Chief Civil Engineer. In the short-term it was envisaged that train heating would be by steam generated in vans forming a part of each train; electric train heating would follow as suitable coaching stock became available.

The potential needs for south of Crewe caused a change of mix of types and a revision of the specification for the mixed traffic type (designated B) to have a maximum speed of 75mph and be capable of hauling 1,250 tons at 55mph.

Arising from the evaluation of bids, orders were placed for five pilot scheme classes.

Main contractor	Mechanical parts	Drive	Type/Quantity	
			A	B
BTH	BRCW	BB	20	5
MV	BP	BB	5	5
EE	EE	Als	10	5
GEC	NBL	Als	5	5
BTH	BR Doncaster	BB	40	-

Notes

Als	Alsthom (France)	BB	Brown Boveri (Switzerland)
BP	Beyer, Peacock	BRCW	Birmingham Railway Carriage and Wagon
BTH	British Thomson – Houston	GEC	General Electric Company
EE	English Electric	NBL	North British Locomotive Co.
MV	Metropolitan Vickers		

Type B locomotive specification abandoned in 1962 and converted to type A.

E3035 (English Electric with Alsthom drive) was selected for preservation and is seen here in the yard of the National Railway Museum, York. (54)

The Modernisation Plan had included an amount of £120m for electrification of main lines (and £65m for suburban) and had identified King's Cross to Leeds/possibly York as a proposed route. The decision to favour the Euston line was based upon studies of traffic density, limitations on capital investment available and the ability of private sector contractors (particularly BICC) to service multiple projects.

A number of observations can now be made:

- EE had deployed *Deltic* on the route it expected to be dieselised and not electrified. The locomotive was transferred to the Eastern Region in 1959 and quickly convinced the management of its potential
- the loading gauge dictated by the overhead line equipment would be 13ft 1in at its lowest points and that would preclude certain classes of steam locomotive from being operated over those sections south of Crewe
- the London Midland Region had ahead of it a monumental task. Of a total of 1,434 track miles included in the scheme, 1,329 needed some form of improvement, 705 overbridges would need raising and, in tunnels, the track level would need to be lowered (including the West Midlands Rugby to Stafford route and the Trent Valley route)
- dieselisation (as a short-term expediency of the BTC) in the short-term would need to be managed in parallel
- the Midland Division and former Great Central routes from Manchester to London would be called upon; in the case of the former to offer an alternative, equivalent level of passenger service and the latter for goods and as a diversionary route.

While this book is primarily concerned with main lines, it is relevant to record that thirty-five new four-car a.c. electric multiple units for Manchester/Liverpool to Crewe services were ordered (BR works with BTH power equipment). In addition, 57 new three-car d.c. (ground level supply) electric multiple units for London area (Euston/Broad Street/Watford/Richmond) built at BR Eastleigh with GEC equipment started to replace LMS stock. The latter units carried two-character headcode panels; when running in service 'A' indicated limited stops and 'B' all stations, while the numbers 1-7 inclusive indicated the route. When running empty, the single codes were 0, 4, 8, 9, X, Y, Z to signify destination, station or depot.

During the course of the year, confidence in modern traction seems to have increased and, by December, the former Southern Region allocated 1,600hp diesels were being entrusted with the *Royal Scot*.

The year ended with the BTC recording a working deficit of £27.1m, £10.6m more than in 1956. The early results from the introduction of diesel multiple units on cross-country and suburban services had been extremely positive and encouraged thoughts that the Modernisation Plan would place the railways in a good position to continue to meet the needs of the nation.

Chapter 5

1958: The Last Great Year of Steam

During 1958 there were three main demands placed upon the management; to at least maintain the improvements made in recent years for main line and suburban passenger services and for merchandise goods traffic, to adapt to new technological developments in the physical forms of diesel locomotives in quantity and for the first stage of overhead electrification works, and to develop detailed plans for other works that were authorised under the provisions of the Modernisation Plan.

At the beginning of January 1958, the allocations of front-line steam power across the motive power depots showed only minor changes from a year previously.

Depot	Power class		
	6	7	8
Camden	+1	–	–1
Crewe North	+2	–1	+3
Longsight	–3	–4	n/ap
Edge Hill	+2	–3	–1
Carlisle Upperby	+2	+1	–1
Carlisle Kingmoor	–3	n/ap	n/ap
Polmadie	–1	–	–

Notes
1. n/ap none allocated at either 1957 or 1958
2. four *Clan* Class in process of re-allocation to Edinburgh Haymarket
3. Willesden, Bushbury and Holyhead unchanged

The biggest change affected the Western Division in total and was due to the transfer of the six Royal Scot Class 7 locomotives to help out on the Midland Division. The events of 1957 had caused a huge increase in the amount of double heading on the London Midland Region. During the Winter Timetable, the demands placed upon the depots between Camden and Polmadie were somewhat less than during the summer and, in the short term, six Royal Scots (two from Edge Hill and one each from Camden, Crewe North, Longsight and Carlisle Upperby) were re-allocated to work from Kentish Town, London on the principal expresses out of St Pancras to Manchester (Central). An out and home turn for the locomotives accumulated a very similar mileage to the Euston-Manchester route though with much harder work through the Peak District. The re-allocation was within the control of the London Midland Region, but with no main line diesels beyond the five prototypes plus *Deltic* in prospect for the Western Division in 1958, could be seen as providing only a short-term solution.

The move of the six Royal Scots was not the first attempt to improve matters on the Midland. The Region's difficulties – or perhaps more likely its costs – had prompted an earlier move south of a Clan Class 6 (72009) in June 1957 for trials on the Great Eastern section of the

Eastern Region. The large stud of Britannia Class 7 locomotives allocated to that section from 1951 had been an outstanding success for the Norwich main line services. In order to maximise the potential for the route, it had been pencilled in to receive an early allocation of main line diesels and thus release some of the Britannias. The Eastern Region management and its locomotive footplate crews liked the Britannias and, given any choice, would redeploy some of them onto Clacton expresses rather than let them go. The thought at the BTC was that if a Clan proved suitable on a Clacton duty, it would be useful in finding a better use for the class in total than that available in its native Scotland and also release a batch of Britannias for the Midland. The limitations of a Clan were very quickly made apparent to a willing management at Liverpool Street, 72009 was sent home, the Great Eastern retained its Britannias, planned its 1958 timetable around them and ten 2,000hp diesels. Lucky them.

February 1958 ushered in several long overdue changes to Regional boundaries and responsibilities. One of these changes involved Carlisle becoming a part of the London Midland Region, Kingmoor depot becoming code 12A (previously 68A) and Upperby becoming 12B (previously 12A). The other changes included the London Midland Region becoming responsible for the southern end of the former Great Central main line extension from near Chesterfield to London (Marylebone) via Nottingham (Victoria), Leicester (Central), Rugby (Central) and Aylesbury. With the transfer came the motive power then resident and that included a quantity of V2 2-6-2 class 7 locomotives, three of which were then allocated at each of Neasden (depot for Marylebone) and Woodford Halse and with seven more at Leicester. The prompt withdrawal of through expresses between Marylebone and Sheffield/Manchester via the Great Central route meant that the BR class 5 4-6-0s could handle the remaining passenger traffic, thus making the V2s available for passenger work elsewhere or on vacuum fitted goods traffic on the Great Central route.

The London Midland Region authorities decided to hold trials with a V2, influenced more by civil engineering concerns rather than mechanical and performance. The concern of the civil engineer was based upon its axle weight and wheelbase between driving wheelsets. Trials were held in March and involved 60855 venturing as far as the outskirts of Leicester with moves being made over various points, crossings and alongside various station platform faces. As no further V2s were seen, it can be concluded that the civil engineer and/or capital cost implications had prevailed over operational need. Back to the drawing board, or BTC headquarters, to seek a solution that would necessarily involve another or other Regions. The Southern Region seemed overly blessed with class 7 power, but with no provision for water pick up apparatus and low coal capacity in its tenders plus a ravenous hunger for coal and thirst for water not ideal, the Western Region locomotives would not fit and were not considered. That left the Britannia Class as a strong favourite option and that is what emerged. The Southern Region was relieved of its two prestige examples (70004/14), the Western Region donated three (70015/7/21) and sent a fourth to Derby (70016, returned) and the Eastern Region grudgingly gave up a high mileage one (70042). In addition, Polmadie saw two of its Britannias re-allocated to Leeds (Holbeck) (70053/4), thus releasing two Royal Scots (46103/33) to work south from that city. The Britannias were allocated to Kentish Town, but very shortly after were reallocated to Trafford Park, Manchester where fitting staff from Longsight could attend as required to provide their knowledge gained with the upkeep of 70031-3/43/4.

For the start of the Summer Timetable it would have been possible for the Western Division to receive back its six Royal Scots. However, the moves involving Leeds (Holbeck) took rather too long and delayed the return of 46110 (to Crewe North from Kentish Town) and 46116/31/52 (to Camden from Trafford Park). 46127 went to Holyhead and 46157 to Camden, both from Kentish Town, and were available from the start of the Summer Timetable. Given the eventual level of availability of the Britannias on the Midland, the Western Division enjoyed the better part of the arrangement.

Of the two football final matches played at Wembley in the spring, that involving an oval ball and Workington Town produced the most interesting motive power. The Town was well supported against Wigan and, late on the night of the final, a succession of four specials left Euston for Lancaster, Carnforth, Barrow and stations to Maryport, for Egremont Woodend and Workington, for Maryport and for Penrith, each headed by a Carlisle Kingmoor Black 5. The supporters of Wigan were catered for by specials from Euston and St Pancras, serving Bolton, Bury, Rochdale and Daisy Hill, also for Todmorden and Hindley, Wigan, Pemberton and Orrell. The Football Association final involved Bolton Wanderers and Manchester United, but did not produce anything out of the ordinary on the special trains.

Another annual sporting occasion that attracted an increasingly large attendance at Wembley was the women's international hockey match. The increased attendance was due in part to the efforts of commercial teams of the Southern and London Midland Regions to promote special trains for school groups. For the match on 8 March, the interesting feature was a succession of trains headed by Bulleid pacifics which were worked to Watford for turning.

For the Summer Timetable, a new weekdays (Saturdays excepted) service between Euston and Glasgow Central was introduced. This was the 7.45 from Euston, titled *The Caledonian* and timed to reach Crewe under XL timings in 147 minutes with a class 8 pacific hauling a maximum of 270 tons. Running ten minutes ahead of the heavier Euston-Liverpool/ Manchester, the train (W47) paused at Crewe (10.12-10.15) and made possible a connection for passengers off the 8.25 Birmingham-Liverpool. Due through Preston at 11.12, the train was due into Glasgow 6¾ hours after leaving Euston, including a brief pause at Carlisle to change footplate crews. To accommodate *The Caledonian*, the timings of the portions of morning trains from Manchester and Liverpool to Glasgow and Edinburgh were adjusted to leave earlier and gain their destinations in early rather than mid-afternoon. To balance the northbound working, there was a new 4/0 from Glasgow due Euston at 10/45 including stops at Carlisle and Stafford. Camden and Polmadie Princess Coronation Class locomotives were deployed and worked through. As such, the workings placed additional demands on availability of the locomotives and, in support of that, the level of shoppings into Crewe Works during the summer was less than in 1957 (as at Appendix 5).

For the summer, Princess Royal 46204 went from Edge Hill to Crewe North and 46201/10 went (July) from Edge Hill and Crewe to Polmadie. The latter moves were to cover for the transfer away of the two Britannias as already mentioned (70053/4) and lasted until March 1961. As long as availability remained high, the additional working for *The Caledonian* could be accommodated by Polmadie class 8 power. The transfers of Princess Coronation Class for part of the summer also involved two of that class moving from Polmadie to Crewe North (46220/1) in the July and left seven of that Class at Polmadie. Transfers to Carlisle Upperby for the Summer Timetable involved 46236/7/50 being moved from Camden and 46233/4/43/4 from Crewe North. Edge Hill fared better in summer 1958 and, until the move of 46210 in July, had four Princess Royal Class, plus one Princess Coronation on loan (46241) to cover the London workings with shed pet 45527 *Southport* (rebuilt Patriot Class 7) in reserve, plus three Royal Scots received from Crewe North. Camden and Longsight also benefited from a re-distribution of Royal Scots from the general depository that Crewe North had a tendency to become. The additional Royal Scots at Camden were used on seasonal trains; the 8/52 relief to Holyhead (a through working) returning with the corresponding train the following night, on the 9.20 (SO) to Llandudno returning on the 9.10 the following day, also the 10/50 to Crewe thence local arrangement to Chester, returning with *The Welshman*. The Anglo-Scottish services – apart from the Jubilee Class 6 Newton Heath working which continually missed out – were very well placed for class 8 use and perhaps better placed than at any time since the heydays of the late 1930s.

During the peak of the summer, no single depot was disproportionately disturbed by shoppings into Crewe Works and provided a basis for a good all-round performance.

As part of a move to allow the Regions more freedom of decentralised control, the BTC was agreeable to a relaxation of the corporate livery of maroon for coaching stock as applied to all Regions except the Southern which had been allowed to retain green for its stock. The Western Region promptly reverted to chocolate and cream for its titled trains and also proceeded to paint any locomotive that could conceivably work a passenger train into a lined out livery similar to that of the Great Western Railway. The London Midland Region was content with maroon as being close to that applied by the LMS, but took the opportunity to repaint twenty class 8 pacifics from green into a maroon and lined out on the perimeter of the tender, around the cab side, along the edge of the running plate vertically on the outside cylinders and at the

Writing captions before seeing the printed picture is fraught with risk, but I selected this picture as portraying, to best effect, the maroon livery as applied to ex-LMS pacifics in 1958/59. Seen here at Carlisle, the fireman has created maximum steam pressure and is trying to prevent loss at the safety valves by use on the live steam injector and coal pusher. A spotter checking his book completes the scene. (55)

As also visible in photograph 15 it was standing practise at Camden to fill to the maximum extent possible the space in tenders. It looks as though the loading gauge has self trimmed the top of the layered heap on **City of Lichfield** waiting to go back down to Euston to work an evening service. (56)

At nearly 74½ feet long the Princess Royals only just fitted the turntables and, where the required length of table was not available (as at Longsight), a triangular junction was used. The length of the driving wheel base also made use in certain yards very difficult and hastened some withdrawals. **Princess Margaret Rose** never carried maroon in BR days. (57)

front and rear of the boiler barrel. There were some variations including tenders and cab sides being lined out as for the green liveried examples, but between December 1957 (46245) and November 1958 (46251) the following re-appeared from visits to Crewe Works in their freshly applied new livery:

46200/4/7/8
46225/6/8/9/36/8/40/3-8/51/4/6

When clean and matched with maroon coaching stock, the locomotives looked magnificent and, for those many who looked back to the days before nationalisation as representing something preferable, had the added advantage of lifting morale. The call of the past was evidently strong as, at their next shopping for a classified repair, the livery/lining out was based upon that applied by the LMS.

In July, Holyhead's Britannia 70048 received the name *The Territorial Army 1908-1958*, adding to *Lord Rowallan* (the Chief Scout) and *Anzac* as late namings and leaving 70047 as the sole un-named Britannia.

All this activity at the edge of operations helped with what the ex-military Chairman of the BTC knew as esprit de corps. He would doubtless have been pleased when invited to name a new diesel locomotive at Paddington and find his own name thereon: *Sir Brian Robertson*.

The London Midland Region had a strong public relations and publicity department which, as with other Regions, produced a monthly magazine for staff. The magazine featured, under the nom de plume *Tempus Fugit*, an item 'Clipping off the Minutes'. Perhaps seeking to make several points, one article referred to a run of the afternoon Glasgow-Euston (*The Caledonian*) worked forward from Carlisle by a class 7 rebuilt Jubilee (45736) which was deputising for a class 8. The train was 18 minutes late when the Carlisle Upperby (named) footplate crew took over and, written in a derring-do style, the article described how time was recovered despite temporary permanent way speed restrictions … four minutes recovered by Preston, but eleven late at Wigan, ten at Crewe, eleven passing Whitmore and ten late into Stafford. At Stafford the station staff were credited with saving a minute and then two minutes were gained in the section to Tamworth, another two to Rugby, two more to Tring and another by Watford. A clear run into Euston brought the train to a stand 'on the dot or as near to it as makes no difference'. You may wonder, as I do, why a 270-ton train usually needed a class 8 locomotive throughout, but I also wonder how much coal was left in the tender of 45736 and who helped fireman Johnson off the footplate!

With the motive power arrangements for the main line routes being very similar to 1957, interest in new developments was concentrated into specific areas at different times of the year. There were four classes of steam locomotive to attract the eye, two of which were quite novel in their use and one of which was a pleasant reminder of the past. Made surplus to requirements by the introduction of diesel multiple units in the Midlands, eleven examples of the Fowler 2-6-4 tank locomotives introduced from 1927 (BR 423XX) found themselves re-allocated to Willesden for working empty stock trains between the carriage sidings and Euston, plus some suburban train work. With a coal capacity of three and a half tons and water capacity of 2,000 gallons, they offered advantages over the Camden 3F 0-6-0 tanks for empty stock workings in between visits to the water cranes. The number of 3Fs in the area was being reduced also as a result of another home depot (Devons Road) being converted for short-term shared use with new diesels and then total use (from summer 1958) by the new traction. Although the Fowler

2-6-4 tank locomotives were more than adequate for the job, the tenure of most of them was truncated by a need for them to cover passenger duties in the Midlands and Manchester areas. The short-term problem was caused by a postponement of a diesel multiple unit service linking Birmingham, Stafford, Stoke and Manchester due to a need for a programme of modification work – during the year, two new diesel multiple unit maintenance depots were opened, at Crewe and at Stoke-on-Trent. The Fowler 4P tanks that remained were joined by two other tank locomotives of a class introduced less than a decade earlier for use on the Eastern Region. The transfer of Neasden depot referred to earlier made available to the London Midland Region a number of L1 Class 2-6-4 tank locomotives, known as 'cement mixers' due to their unfortunate riding qualities. Nevertheless, with their age, capacities of four and a half tons of coal and 2,630 gallons and for use solely over very short distances, they needed to be used and 67740/7 were loaned to Willesden.

Occasionally heading into Euston that summer were three Compound 4-4-0s taken out of store at Rugby plus one of the same Class from Monument Lane, Birmingham supplemented by another on loan from Crewe North. In terms of their capabilities, the Compounds had nothing left to prove and were well liked anywhere along the main lines from Euston to Birmingham, Wolverhampton, Crewe and Carlisle. 41168 was the one transferred from Crewe North and when, on the first Saturday of the Summer Timetable, it appeared from Birmingham and headed for North Wales, it may well have been 'taken hostage' for use from Crewe on better things. During the following few days it was used as a pilot locomotive assisting heavy passenger trains over Shap and was returned on the Wednesday as pilot to the locomotive on *The Mid-Day Scot*. Less arduous duties on Saturdays involved the holiday trains from the West Midlands to the resorts of North Wales, Morecambe and Blackpool.

On summer Saturdays between 1957-60 Class 9F goods locomotives were used on passenger trains to coastal resorts, particularly Llandudno and Blackpool, from the Midlands and Sheffield. 92058 has passed through Chester and is on its way to Llandudno. (58)

Holidaymaker trains were plentiful at Crewe and also at Preston. The latter dealt with a large volume of passenger train traffic to and from Blackpool. In 1957, the operating authorities of the Eastern and London Midland Regions (later also the Western Region) had arranged to use 9F 2-10-0 heavy freight locomotives on seasonal passenger services. On the London Midland Region, 9Fs from depots such as Wellingborough would be despatched on Friday nights to work passenger trains that night or during the weekend towards the West Country and to Blackpool/North Wales. The services that typically produced 9Fs through Preston were the three from Sheffield (6.50, 8.10 and 8.50) with a balanced working for the first two at 2/55 and 2/20 respectively and one from Desford, Leicestershire.

Interest in diesel traction was mainly at the southern end of the routes. By the end of March, all twenty of the EE 1,000hp type had been delivered (D8000-19) and the early examples of the NBL 800hp type (D82XX) were arriving to join them at Devons Road. To oust the few remaining steam locomotives at that depot, a few NBL 300hp diesel hydraulic (MAN of Germany engines) 0-4-0 type (D29XX with a Class total of 14) also arrived. The arrival of the EE type 1s had a consequential effect upon the demand for continued use of the 3F 0-6-0 tank locomotives allocated to Camden for shunting and coaching stock duties. Popularly known in parts of the London Midland Region as Jinties, they attracted the term Dobbins in the London area. When the locomotives were re-allocated away from Camden some went surprising distances; to Carnforth, Crewe South, Carlisle Kingmoor, Wigan, Speke and Bidston, while others (moved from Devons Road) stayed local at Willesden and at Bletchley.

Sometimes photographers and caption writers get lucky. The transition from steam is shown to good effect at Northchurch tunnel (near Berkhamsted) as Royal Scot **Old Contemptibles** *briefly runs parallel with an EE type 1.* **Old Contemptibles** *was a military riposte to the Kaiser who referred to the British Expeditionary Forces (the forerunner to the British Army) as 'that contemptible little army'. (59)*

In the preservation era, an EE type I is in a livery that closely resembles that of its original introduction. The photograph also shows to good effect the LMS trainset of the Severn Valley Railway. (60)

As the quantity of the EE type increased towards the expected total allocation of fifteen and then exceeded it, a need for footplate crew and maintenance staff training was met by a combination of theory and practice courses over several weeks. The locomotives found work on empty coaching stock moves and local trip goods trains plus, in the summer, on the passenger workings to Watford, Tring and Bletchley. The introductory phase was not without its difficulties and tended to confine the passenger work to off-peak services. The locomotives were not fitted with any method of heating the coaching stock and that limited their use on empty coaches being worked to Euston from Willesden for later departures. The D82XX class were engaged on cross-London exchange traffic (goods) between Temple Mills (Eastern Region) and Acton (Western Region) yards; by mid-year seven of the Class were available.

The operating authorities quickly realised that, by pairing two of the D80XX nose to nose, they would have the equivalent of 10203 and with a combined braking force adequate for working the fast, fully vacuum brake fitted goods trains, such as the 2/0 Camden-Glasgow (Buchanan Street) as far as Crewe, usually a Longsight Jubilee balancing turn. The training in use of the Class was extended to Rugby, at which depot three pairs were based from the spring plus a spare usually used for crew training on the line to Market Harborough. Confidence in the Class grew and, with the allocation of fifteen settled at Devons Road, D8002 was re-allocated to Rugby, D8000 went to Toton (near Nottingham, Midland Division) for tests and D8001/3 went to Crewe South for training and balancing of fast freight workings to and from Camden and D8006 to Scotland for trials.

The English Electric Company pursued a policy of evolutionary designs which, once proven, would be adapted for use with later builds for various track gauges. The early design for the railways of Queensland can be seen to have influenced the later type 1 D8000 series for BR, as can the front end designs of export orders at the time Deltic was being progressed.

Testing was very much in vogue and also involved *Deltic*. In some ways the choice of the London Midland Region for the demonstration of its capabilities became unfortunate in that the decision to electrify that Region's main lines south of Manchester and Liverpool meant that EE had to demonstrate those same capabilities also to the management of the Eastern Region. The initial proposal of the London Midland Region, within the Modernisation Plan, was to use Deltic type locomotives. With nothing left to prove to the London Midland Region, EE were content to let *Deltic* be used for wider applications, partly as a 'shop window' product. One such usage was with a trainset made available by the BTC for the use of a trade delegation of businessmen from Canada. Overnight the train was used as a travelling hotel with several first-class sleeping cars added to the day-time use and catering carriages. As such, EE were agreeable to *Deltic* going to Glasgow and it found no trouble in accelerating its 400-ton train from a standing start in Beattock station to breast the summit at 52mph. That was in late 1957 and in the new year the locomotive was put through its paces over another route featuring long, demanding, adverse gradients; in that case Carlisle to Leeds with a load of 642 tons. At that time the reasons for such a test – during which *Deltic* performed very adequately – were unclear to uninformed linesiders, but it emerged later that it formed part of the planning for a diesel hauled goods service over the same route.

In the period 1955-58, the number of at least partly vacuum brake-fitted goods trains run each weekday increased from 529 to eight hundred and fifty. While that helped to increase the average speed of trains and therefore route capacity, it caused difficulties where such trains needed to be split/re-marshalled en route. In most yards the staff were skilled at lifting coupling hooks while wagons were on the move but, with vacuum brake hose connections between wagons, it was more time-consuming. Wherever individual wagon load traffic for the same destination could be marshalled together, it helped when trains were re-marshalled en route, for example Crewe was an important 'staging post' for trains, train crews and locomotive purposes, but rarely was it the final destination. The Scottish Region was making progress with blocks of wagon load traffic being marshalled together from the earliest time in their journey and placed into the train in a pre-planned way for later detaching/attaching. The London Midland Region was very keen to develop and introduce a concept that was long overdue, but very welcome; with the co-operation of the Scottish Region and the use of a fully vacuum brake fitted train, a train in excess of 500 tons could be run overnight between the major production centres of London and Glasgow. Any distance over 300 miles for such a load would provide a good economic case for the movement of time-sensitive traffic. The concept was strengthened by the train being formed of flatbed wagons with screw couplings and roller bearing axleboxes, onto which containers packed by consignees and collected/ delivered by BR, could be securely loaded. The flatbed wagons used allowed two containers of different sizes to be carried. The West Coast route would have been ideal, could have avoided any stops for other than train crew purposes and could have been timed to fit into the established pattern of sleeping car and postal service trains. However, as the needs of the civil and signalling engineers were likely to disturb route and timing arrangements, the route from London was agreed to be from Hendon via Leicester, Sheffield and Leeds to Carlisle. From Carlisle to Glasgow (Gushetfaulds) the trains were able to use the former Caledonian Railway route over Beattock. To power the trains, the plan was to use pairs of new 1,200hp diesel locomotives to be built by Metropolitan Vickers as a pilot order of twenty. The economic case was one thing, the commercial case another and reliability day in/day out a third. In the event of non-availability of diesels, the alternative was to be a pair of Black 5s (later a 9F). The traincrew arrangements involved men of Polmadie working to and from Carlisle and Carlisle Kingmoor through to Hendon as a lodging turn. Kingmoor men, within a particular link, worked to Sheffield with Starlight Specials and car-sleeper trains and to Leicester with a goods, but Hendon was a new destination. During a working week, the Kingmoor men worked two round trips for 1,200 nocturnal miles. From Glasgow (depart 7/50) the train was due to change traincrew at Carlisle (10/0-10/03), pass Leeds at 12.38, Chesterfield at 2.0 and reach

Hendon at 5.40. In the return direction it was 7/23 from Hendon and into Glasgow at between 5 and 6 am, in time for perishable traffic being in the markets by 9 am. The trains were titled *Condor*. The timing of the trains over the particularly difficult section between Carlisle and Hellifield in each direction owed something to the testing of *Deltic*.

Birmingham also generated sufficient merchandise traffic to allow a conventional vacuum fitted train of 50-55 van wagons and that also used the Midland route rather than that of the LNW. The originating yards were Water Orton (9F locomotive from Saltley depot) and College (Glasgow), with examination of the train at Skipton. Saltley men worked through to Carlisle, exchanging there with Kingmoor men and working to a similar lodging arrangement as applied to *Condor*. In due course the *Condor* concept was extended to a Birmingham-Glasgow service via Stafford, Crewe and Preston to Carlisle.

Elsewhere along the routes from Euston was some merchandise classification traffic that was full or part trainload. Meat and fish from Scotland/Heysham/Fleetwood, sheep and cattle from Ireland and seasonal produce from Garston Docks (bananas/other fruit), seasonal fruit, flowers and seed potatoes. The prime need in an increasingly competitive market was to keep pace with change, an example being refrigeration of meat and fish, invest in better facilities/methods of handling and, once was on the move to avoid lengthy operational lag.

The Modernisation Plan had included a large amount of capital for investment in facilities and improved methods of operation. A legacy of multiple small-scale yards at places such as Carlisle dated from before the 1923 grouping; Carlisle having been served by, for examples, the North Eastern, Maryport and Carlisle, Lancaster and Carlisle, Furness, Caledonian, Glasgow and South Western, North British and Midland Railway companies, each with its own yard receiving, sorting, exchanging, despatching to another yard locally or at distance using its own service or that of another. Sadly, Carlisle was not alone in that regard and Manchester, with its history involving the London and North Western, Manchester, Sheffield and Lincolnshire/Great Central, Lancashire and Yorkshire, Great Northern, Midland and the Cheshire Lines Committee was greatly in need of a single yard with modern facilities. Birmingham and Wolverhampton had a legacy of competition between the London and North Western, Midland and Great Western companies where, in the late 1950s, the London Midland and Western Regions were in competition with each other as well as the road hauliers.

Taking our routes of prime interest, the planning centred upon new yards at Carlisle and on the Cambridge-Oxford line at Swanbourne to the west of Bletchley. Bescot (for the West Midlands conurbation) emerged later while Willesden, Crewe, Warrington, Wigan, Preston, Liverpool Edge Hill and Glasgow received less attention than they needed. Manchester was left wondering, while Northampton, Nuneaton and Stoke-on-Trent were expected to be able to support their staple traffic flows. The heavy mineral traffic at the southern end of the routes was principally coal in slow moving, unbraked, loose coupled wagons and, despite efforts to improve matters by improved braking and couplings, the only thing that flowed faster was outgoing investment capital with no return.

The proposed new yards fell into two distinct categories; new, on greenfield sites and new, near centres of production and population. Examples of interest of the former category were Swanbourne and Carlisle, of the latter Bescot.

In the eyes of the London Midland Region, Swanbourne offered great opportunities. Situated along the Cambridge-Oxford line (east to west) it had connections with the main line to and from the Willesden and Camden yards at Bletchley and with the former Great Central main line (both running north-south). The strategic value of Swanbourne was proven during the Second World War in avoiding the heavily bombed areas of London and its development for use from the late 1950s was envisaged as saving mileage and time for the considerable tonnage of cross-London inter-Regional traffic. Further factors were that the former Great Central line connection at Calvert could form part of a diversionary route for traffic while electrification work on the Euston line was progressed and was in mind for a parcels depot concentration scheme involving Marylebone (Goods) depot and depots at Nottingham, Leicester and Birmingham. Three night parcels trains departed from Marylebone for Preston (one) and Crewe (two) and gained the ex-LNW main line at Bletchley. As with other greenfield and new sites proposed for marshalling yards, the proposed development of Swanbourne would require planning permission and could be expected to raise objections.

From the perspective of the Eastern Region, Swanbourne represented a threat to their own aspirations to finally improve matters at Temple Mills. That yards, operators, staff and customers would benefit from rationalisation/investment was not in doubt; what was in doubt was the strength of each Regional case and with no co-ordination from the centre. The Eastern Region let it be known to the London Midland Region that westbound traffic from Cambridge would not be forthcoming and, as such, torpedoed the case for Swanbourne, later confirmed by the BTC. A reorganisation of some Regional boundaries in 1958 helped ease some of the inter-regional problems, though not for Swanbourne. The Scottish region agreed to a change that extended the territory of the LM Region some nine miles Down the former Caledonian Railway main line from Carlisle to Gretna Junction. That enabled the LM to start the planning process for acquisition of land intended for a vast new marshalling yard to the west of Kingmoor and involving 72 miles of tracks. The change also included responsibility for Kingmoor motive power depot (Scottish 68A) which became LM 12A and relegated Upperby, south of the city, to 12B. It provided for the LM an opportunity, albeit at a capital cost of over £4m.

Carlisle was another greenfield site and, while a new yard would solve the localised problem and inefficiency of multiple small yards, trip workings between yards and consequential delays, the city of Carlisle was hardly a big centre of either population or production. Sorting traffic at Carlisle would make sense for railway operating, motive power and staffing purposes, but would also put in place an impediment to Anglo-Scottish traffic. As such, Carlisle was rather like Crewe and the effect was to harm the railways' pursuit of traffic retention and growth from Glasgow and Manchester respectively.

The Scottish Region opted for new yards at Perth and at Edinburgh, Millerhill and another to serve industrial Fife at Thornton. Glasgow, with eight small yards dating from pre-grouping days, was a loser.

While it was obvious that the BTC was ill equipped to form a national strategy for freight, private industry was not so constrained. Unlike the BTC, private industry knew their costs, their markets, the economics of alternative forms of transport and the yield they required to seek funding for a long-term commitment. All that was required was a locomotive and crew to collect their trainload of wagons from point A (production) to point B (consumption) and return at agreed times and within an agreed journey time. Early examples included frozen food in containers (Birds Eye), cement (Blue Circle) and petroleum products (Shell Mex and BP, Esso) with car components (Ford) an interested onlooker for the future. Disappointingly, the railways themselves had let slip during the last years of internal wrangling (1948-53) the concepts they had developed with industry; trainload coal and limestone, containerised traffic on flat bed wagons for perishable and merchandise goods. Revenue and tonnage statistics for merchandise traffic made for depressing reading. In the twenty weeks to mid-May 1958, the railways carried overall over nine million tons – 8.1 per cent – less freight than in the same Suez-influenced period of 1957 and 14.9 per cent of the merchandise carried in the corresponding period. A recession in the steel industry compounded the worrying decline.

Progress in relation to the electrification work as authorised in spring 1957 became evident in terms of signalling and overhead work, two types of traction, civil engineering work and alterations to the direction of travel over certain lines on the final approach to Manchester (London Road) station.

Heading south out of London Road station, the first divergence on the Down side was after two miles, at Slade Lane Junction, where trains could be routed towards Crewe by travelling via Heald Green and Styal to Wilmslow or via Stockport to Wilmslow (12 miles from Manchester); the distance by each route being very similar. Traffic to and from Stoke-on-Trent diverged from the route via Stockport at Cheadle Hulme (eight miles from Manchester). The route via Styal was chosen as the one for early progress to be made as it did not feature tunnels in need of opening out and because it carried less traffic. The Styal line was re-signalled with colour light signals, track circuiting throughout and with electronically controlled ground frame apparatus for various sidings, controlled throughout by two signal boxes, Wilmslow and Manchester (London Road), with the latter having the benefit of improved train regulation and track capacity. To avoid as many conflicting movements as possible, the direction of travel between London Road and Slade Lane Junction was changed for the two centre tracks. As a consequence of that decision, there was no longer a use for the station at Longsight and, as a distant echo to the complaints of the 1842 proprietors of Belle Vue Pleasure Gardens, their 1950s successors again complained, though without success. Work on the re-signalling of the 22-mile section between Cheadle Hulme and Crewe was planned for winter 1958/59. For future use on the Manchester-Crewe passenger stopping services, fifteen four-car electric multiple units were authorised to be built at the BR workshops at Wolverton.

With the pilot orders for the a.c. electric locomotives (as described in chapter 4) some way off being available and with hundreds of train crew to be trained/familiarised, a survey was launched to find an existing locomotive that could be modified for short-term use. The best available option was a gas turbine diesel locomotive numbered 18100, a Co-Co, 3,000hp ordered in 1946 by the Great Western Railway to be built by Metropolitan–Vickers and delivered in 1951. The locomotive had been used mainly on the easily graded main line between Paddington and Bristol and was compared with a similar locomotive (18000) produced by Brown Boveri. The experimental use of 18100 showed that it consumed as much fuel when idling and stationary as when under power. Withdrawn in 1958, the locomotive was converted by Metropolitan-Vickers Electric Company to have only four of its six axles powered (therefore A1A-A1A) and being able to connect via a pantograph to either 25kv or 6.25kv supply. The locomotive was re-numbered E1000.

The structures and overhead catenary were put in place between Manchester and Wilmslow via the Styal line with the 14-mile section from Sandbach coming east towards Wilmslow and then extending through to Cheadle Hulme. That left the final two miles at the Crewe end and the challenging section between Cheadle Hulme and Stockport to Slade Lane Junction to be completed.

With work at night, Sundays and wherever possible working via the alternative Styal or Stockport routes, disturbance to the travelling public had been minimised. The complete remodelling of Manchester (London Road) station and works associated with electrification was on a wholly different scale and would require a closure of sections for several months. The people of Manchester were not impressed by the prospect of a lengthy disturbance, nor were they impressed by having to read about it first in the local press. Naturally, the Chamber of Commerce wanted re-assurances as to the plans. The latter body was placated by an intention to introduce a high-speed diesel Pullman service to be routed by the Midland route through the Peak District and East Midlands to supplement the improved steam worked service via that route with the Britannias. For good measure the operating authorities somehow managed to find a class 7 locomotive for the business folk who used the early evening train from Central to Buxton and its morning return service.

Because of the history of the lines that formed the Manchester-Crewe and Crewe-Liverpool sections, there was no single architectural style of station building. Within the electrification project was a proposal to introduce, at intermediate stations, prefabricated buildings erected on site, a total of 18. As such, they represented the new age and, unfortunately, provided examples of a fairly dreadful decade of architectural design.

The planning work had produced a likely scale of unavoidable disruption that would disrupt the travelling arrangements of the public between Manchester, Liverpool, Stafford, the West Midlands and London with the Stafford – Rugby Trent Valley route expected to be last to be dealt with. With that in mind it was not surprising that the route was not included in some of the important technical developments of the year.

In December 1957 there had been an horrendous accident on the Southern Region with considerable loss of life. The accident occurred in fog on a winter night when the driver of a steam locomotive hauled train passed a succession of three signals; two of which progressively were at caution and the final one at danger. Having belatedly spotted the signal at danger, the driver applied the brake, but not before his train ran into the rear of the preceding train and, as ill luck would have it, the ensuing derailment caused a pillar supporting an overbridge to be dislodged, bringing the overbridge down onto the scene of carnage. The Inspecting Officer drew attention – not for the first time in the 1950s – to the need for an automatic system of warning for drivers when passing signals. The BTC had been developing a standard system (the Western Region and London, Tilbury and Southend lines were, at that time, equipped with other systems, atc and the Hudd system respectively) and, when it became available in 1958, it was first installed along the 105 mile high speed main line route between King's Cross and Grantham. There was by then an acceptance that the proposed electrification of the ex-Great Northern line from King's Cross to Leeds/York would not proceed. In due course, *Deltic* would be transferred from the London Midland Region to the Eastern Region (where one of the first things they requested was a speedometer for up to 105mph) for train crew training. In spring 1958, an order was placed with EE for twenty-two production deltic type locomotives.

Another development was the introduction of a method of welding together the traditional 60ft track units to form lengths of up to 300 feet but, while such lengths were trialled on the London Midland Region, their widespread use on the main line from Euston would await a campaign programme of track rationalisation, remodelling and relaying.

The arrival of production batches of main line diesels will be covered in chapter 6, but it is of interest here to record a second attempt to introduce Clan Class pacifics to the Great Eastern lines. The four Clans transferred to Haymarket had not found favour on the east coast of Scotland and the two pairs had been returned to Polmadie and Carlisle Kingmoor. The introduction in the spring of EE type 4 diesels (D200 Class pilot order examples) onto Liverpool Street-Norwich express passenger services had been successful and had released several Britannias for the Clacton services. A change of Operating Superintendent at Liverpool

Street may have encouraged the BTC to try again as 72009 was sent south again. It was no good; Stratford would have none of it but, at least, *Clan Stewart* made it further south than did Bonnie Prince Charlie. The Clans had few friends; even Haymarket would have no good words or work for them and sent them home again after the potato traffic ended for the year.

The Winter Timetables of the London Midland Region reflected the growing demands of the engineers for access to the infrastructure south of Crewe. To facilitate the overhead catenary and structures, the options were limited; lift bridges or lower the track under bridges/through tunnels with improved drainage. Synchronising the production of the Working Timetable with the programmes of work planned by the engineers was difficult in the extreme. The result was the insertion into the Working Timetable of recovery allowances for time lost over particular sections south of Crewe and beyond to Manchester and Liverpool plus adjustments to the Passenger Timetable, as publicly available. As the civil and signalling engineering teams conducted their work in specific locations, the detailed arrangements of temporary speed restrictions were detailed in Weekly Notices displayed at signing on duty locations for footplate crews and which they were required to read. To limit the effect at the important junctions and passenger changing station at Crewe, timings of trains reaching there from the north, west and south were disturbed as little as possible; achieved by departures from Euston being moved back by ten minutes (the *Royal Scot* for example moving from 10.0 to 9.50) and all trains between Manchester and Crewe had an additional allowance of ten minutes.

For the Euston main line, the recovery allowances in the Working Timetable were:

Section	Direction	Allowance (minutes)
Main line to Stafford via Trent Valley:		
Tring – Bletchley	Down (north)	4
Rugeley – Milford	Down	4
Whitmore – Crewe	Down	4
Norton Bridge – Stafford	Up	4
Roade – Bletchley	Up (south)	4
Watford J – Willesden	Up	4
Main line Rugby – Wolverhampton – Stafford		
Rugby – Coventry	Down	3–4
Wolverhampton – Stafford	Down	4
Wolverhampton – Birmingham	Up	7
Birmingham – Coventry	Up	4
Main line Crewe – Liverpool		
Winsford J – Weaver J	Down	3
Runcorn – Liverpool	Down	3
Liverpool – Weaver J	Up	5
Winsford – Coppenhall J	Up	4

The effect was to extend all journey times, trains frequently standing waiting time when work on the track was not, or had not, been taking place within particular sections, drivers opting to work their trains within the revised timings rather than run early and then be held at signals. It was a recipe for operational malaise and very difficult for staff along a route that had enjoyed considerable improvements in recent years. The business communities of

London, Birmingham, Manchester and Liverpool voiced their concerns through Chambers of Commerce. To reach Manchester from London in mid-morning, the better alternative to the 11.35 (formerly 11.45) from Euston was the 11.20 Pullman lunch service from King's Cross to Sheffield, a change of train there to reach Manchester via the electrified Pennine route and arrive as the Euston train was leaving Stockport. Similarly, and for the first time, the journey from Manchester to London via the Peak District and East Midlands with Britannias was marginally quicker than via the LNW/NS routes. For Mancunians it was the start of a lengthy period of disturbance.

To effect the long-term improvements, the engineers needed possession of the track and the availability of the Styal line as an alternative to Stockport was useful, as was an ability to divert trains that would normally have been routed via Crewe to Stafford, onto the alternative North Staffordshire route via Stoke. Saturday nights and Sundays gave reasonable possession times. With only one Sunday evening passenger train via Stockport and Crewe to consider, several extra hours of work could be planned if that train – the 5/15 from Manchester complete with restaurant service and stopping only at Stockport – could be diverted via Stoke. It could be diverted, but work between Stoke and Stafford meant it could not regain the main line. The answer was to send a pilotman driver from Derby to join the Longsight engine and crew at Stoke and for the train to be routed via Blythe Bridge, Uttoxeter, North Staffs Junction, Stenson Junction to Sheet Stores Junction, where it joined the Midland main line to Leicester and London (St Pancras). A journey time of five hours and five minutes with an arrival after 10 pm was bad enough; the withdrawal of the catering facility was for some even worse. The empty stock and Longsight engine/crew were then worked around to Willesden/Camden via Dudding Hill for resumption of their usual return working.

Also, for the Winter Timetable the Down morning and Up afternoon workings of *The Caledonian* were withdrawn and reduced demands for the availability of two class 8 pacifics each weekday. To enable *The Caledonian* to have a clearer run between Preston and Scotland in the late morning and early afternoon, the Manchester and Liverpool to Glasgow/Edinburgh services had been retimed to depart earlier. Those re-arrangements were left in place and gave earlier arrivals than had previously been the case.

Any consideration of the financial performance of the London Midland Region needs to reflect more on its day to day operation of the timetable of passenger and goods services (i.e. revenue) than with investment (i.e. capital) that was outside its control and would take time to produce returns. The revenue position was:

Year	Gross revenue £m	Working expenses £m	Net revenue £m
1954	139	130.8	8.2
1955	140 (a)	132.9	7.1
1956	148.9 (b)	145.9	3.0
1957	153.1 (b)	153.6	(0.6) (c)
1958	141.5	155.6	(14.1) (c)

Notes
(a) 1955 ASLEF strike
(b) 1956/57 Suez effect
(c) ( ) loss

For comparison, over the same period the Scottish and Western Regions were in deficit throughout, the Southern Region slipped into deficit from 1955 and similarly the Eastern Region from 1956. Only the small North Eastern Region was profitable throughout the period and during which the national Gross Domestic Product (based upon an index of 100 at 1948) rose from 119 to 126.6. Whitehall noted such things.

Right: *It was unusual for a locomotive withdrawn from traffic to be photographed by BR. However, 58926 was destined for preservation. (61)*

Below: *A quarter of a century later, 58926 re-appeared as LNWR 1054 and made a fine spectacle leaving Ingrow at the Keighley and Worth Valley Railway. (62)*

Chapter 6

1959: Start of Change

While 1958 had provided early evidence of physical progress from the capital investment, 1959 brought an acceleration of the pace of change. This chapter outlines the arrival of the first production batch of one class of main line diesel locomotives (the EE type 4) and the initial build of another as a pilot scheme (the BR/Sulzer type 4). The main line diesel theme is then extended into the case made by the London Midland Region for capital investment in the Manchester/Liverpool – Euston routes. The effects of investment upon the predominantly steam worked services is explained. Finally, the chapter covers the increasing political concerns of a newly re-elected and strengthened Conservative Government intent on change.

The policy of having pilot orders committed with multiple constructors and with various combinations of equipment could, and was, justified by being aligned to a period of several years, during which the alternative designs would be evaluated in traffic prior to standardisation with a small number of 'standard' classes. The policy was jettisoned by the Commission as it came to terms with its worsening financial position. The earlier promise to give diesels a thorough and selective trial was abandoned in February 1957 when the Commission decided on the elimination of steam power with diesels, though still with the ultimate long-term objective of electrification of all main lines. The need for diesel locomotives was considered by the Commission to be immediate in order that the financial target to break even in 1961/62 might be fulfilled. The Regional Boards were asked to produce revised plans and these were made available in April 1957 and a programme of 750-800 locomotives for 1959 was then approved. Three years later the electrification strategy was negated by intervention from a concerned Government, leaving the railways with a diesel fleet of 41 designs. Of that excessive number of designs, some had been authorised for production build programmes even before the trial with the pilot order batch had started and others that were expensive failures. Against this background the London Midland Region was fortunate to be favoured by a decision to allocate the first production batch of type 4 2,000hp diesel electric locomotives produced by EE and for them to be deployed on the Western Division. A second type 4 class intended for use on the LM Region was the BR workshops/Sulzer 2,300hp diesel electric of which a pilot order of ten was initially authorised. At a lesser power was a batch of twenty type 2 1,160hp produced by BR workshops with Sulzer engines as a pilot and also a batch of twenty 1,200hp locomotives produced by Metropolitan-Vickers with Crossley engines and destined for the Midland Division.

With EE, the Region had grounds for optimism that with the first production batch of twenty-seven type 4 locomotives, they – as for the type 1 class received in 1958 – would prove to be successful. The grounds for optimism would have been based upon the facts that EE had several years' experience of producing diesel electric locomotives for main line use on railways at home and overseas, had within well laid out production facilities, had used the bogies and engine in earlier builds and the production batch of twenty-seven followed on from a pilot order for ten introduced on the Eastern Region from spring 1958. Further factors included that the operating department of the London Midland Region had gained confidence with *DELTIC*,

10000/1 and 10201-3, all of which used EE major components in total or part, and with the D8000s working from Devons Road.

When compared to most of the other builders involved with the pilot orders, EE was in a far better technical and commercial position in not having to manage different suppliers of mechanical parts, engines and transmissions. EE was formed in 1918 from Dick, Kerr & Co of Preston, an early supplier of electrical equipment for trams, light railway systems and main line carriages, Willans & Robinson of Rugby, the Phoenix Dynamo Manufacturing Co of Bradford, the Coventry ordnance factory and also took over a post-war distributed part of the Siemens dynamo works at Stafford. The rapid development of the private electricity and electrical equipment of the 1920s was followed by the years of depression of the 1930s. An interesting development between the LMS and EE during the 1920s involved railcars equipped with Beardmore airship engines trialled in the Preston-Blackpool area. During the 1930s, EE became involved by the LMS in the development of early diesel shunting locomotives. For those locomotives, EE was in competition with Armstrong Whitworth, but emerged as being the preferred contractor with an engine of 300-350hp not only for the LMS, but also from the mid-1930s, the SR and GWR. Just prior to nationalisation, the LNER was considering the purchase of 176 diesel shunting locomotives and, following nationalisation, the EE product formed the basis for the standard BR diesel electric shunting locomotive (later BR TOPS class 08). During 1939-45, production at the various centres of production was given over to work in support of the war effort but, upon cessation of hostilities, the company was again able to support the LMS, plus the SR with diesel electric engines and bogies for the five early prototypes: 10000/1, 10201-3. During the course of the war, EE acquired D. Napier & Sons, a manufacturer of diesel engines for naval vessels, and, shortly after the war, the firm of Marconi.

Influenced by EE being the foremost UK supplier and having received an order from Egypt for 12 1,600hp diesel electric locomotives (to a very unusual 1A-Do-A1 configuration), H.G. Ivatt of the LMS chose the same power equipment to be used in 10000 and 10001. The engine was the 16 SVT, 16-cylinder, four-stroke vee configuration with turbo-superchargers, the generator being EE type 823A supplying six traction motors on a Co-Co wheel configuration. The weight in working order of the locomotives was 127 tons and with a capability expected to enable a top speed of 93mph. The SR locomotives numbered 10201 and 10202 emerged from Brighton works in 1950 and 1951 respectively and both used the EE equipment as for 10000 and 10001. Their weight in working order was 135 tons and, with such a high (six) axle weight, were given an additional unpowered wheelset at each outer end to give a configuration of 1 Co-Co 1. The third SR locomotive – 10203 – was more powerful (2,000hp) and used the 16 SVT engine at 850 revolutions per minute, i.e. medium speed.

In the early 1950s, while Riddles was pursuing his policy of building 999 standard steam locomotives of various power classes, many other parts of the world were shunning steam and turning to diesel traction. EE was very much at the forefront of that transition and was dealing at its Preston works with small production batch contracts for the railways of New Zealand, Rhodesia (now Zimbabwe), Nigeria and (electric locomotives) for South Africa. Following Riddles' retirement in 1953, his successor R.C. Bond initially propounded the same strategic policy for main line traction of steam to electric but when, in summer 1954, it was reported to him that a 2,000hp diesel electric locomotive was likely to prove more economical than a steam class 7 for annual mileages over 70k without taking into account a higher level of maintenance, the case for steam was effectively obsolete.

The manner in which the transition was then effected can be seen in the following table of acquisitions to 1960:

Year	Steam	Diesels		Electric	Total
		main line	All (a)		
1954	208	1(b)	60	6	275
1955	174	-	136	-	310
1956	138	-	156	-	294
1957	144	20	195	-	359
1958	65	83	400	1	549
1959	15	318	601	14	948
1960	3	416	751	50	1220

Notes
(a) including shunting locomotives
(b) *DELTIC* on trial, owned by EE

In 1954/55 EE took the considered risk of designing and producing *Deltic*. Its purpose was to demonstrate to a wavering BTC what could be achieved with a powerful (3,300hp) diesel electric locomotive which could run as a Co-Co with an axle weight more acceptable to the civil engineers; by using two Napier engines each developing 1,650hp the locomotive weighed in at 106 tons.

When the BTC decided to pursue the pilot orders for 174 diesel locomotives, EE increased its level of co-operation with the nearby Vulcan Foundry at Newton-le-Willows, a traditional builder of steam locomotives for the export market but which built railcars for New Zealand in 1956, shunting locomotives for Malaya in 1948 and had built the EE locomotives for Egypt as previously mentioned, prior to acquisition in 1957. In 1955, EE acquired Robert Stephenson & Hawthorn, another traditional builder of steam willing to turn to diesel traction. The company had two sites for production: Darlington and Newcastle.

By comparison with EE (and Brush), the other UK based producers for the pilot orders were not so advanced either commercially, technically or organisationally. The BTC wished to maximise the use of its own workshops wherever equipment could be sourced on a competitive basis; for components other than engines and transmissions, which would have to be sourced externally, that was well founded and for diesel electric locomotives, the Commission's costs were lower than for some private contractors. Of the 100 locomotives ordered in the medium power range, twenty were to be built in BR workshops and, of the twenty of the higher power range, half were to be built in BR workshops (D1-D10) and the other half by EE (D200-09). The Locomotive Manufacturers' Association (LMA) represented the UK based private traditional builders who were trying to adapt to a reduced demand for steam locomotives. The LMA made a strong case to government that success for the traditional producers for the home market would strengthen their marketing efforts to secure export orders. While the government influenced the BTC decision to reject any option of buying diesel locomotives from America, where General Motors (GM) was the leading manufacturer, there were other factors including a need for GM to adapt its designs to meet the UK loading gauge, the economics of small pilot orders and a reluctance to consider a licencing agreement for production in the UK. By 1958, GM were prepared to consider joining with Leyland under a licence arrangement; by then the production batches using Swiss and German equipment were already at least pencilled in, if not committed. Although the LMA achieved a short-term success at home, GM proceeded to develop standard designs for export orders around the world that were at delivered prices lower than those offered from the UK. With the exception of EE and Brush, locomotives built by the private British manufacturers for the BR Modernisation Plan did not provide the marketing platform for future export orders. By the end of the 1960s, North British had gone into liquidation and the private company locomotive building industry in the UK was insignificant in world production terms.

The introduction of the pilot order of D200-09 to the Eastern Region (Great Eastern and Great Northern lines) from spring 1958 had not been without technical problems that affected reliability (for example traction motor flashovers), maintenance problems due to sparks from brake blocks igniting oil on bogie sides and mechanical parts such as sticking fan shafts. Introduction during the spring/summer meant that the train heating boilers were not used until October. The traction motor problem was solved later by use of a six-pole version and the use of the discarded four-pole version on the production batches of D8000 1,000hp class.

Both the Great Eastern and Great Northern lines sought to utilise their five examples to maximum effect. The diagrams were spread over seven days and, if completed, produced mileages of 3,842 and 4,516 respectively. On the GE the locomotives were used on eleven carriage Norwich-London express passenger trains and provided a comparison with the 2,600 miles and nine carriage trains entrusted to the steam class 7 Britannias. The GN line management were more interested in 3,300hp power than 2,000hp, but were nevertheless keen to use the 2,000hp types on turns such as two return trips to Sheffield on weekdays with a lighter weight Pullman train.

The decision taken by the BTC in 1957 to press ahead with the faster elimination of steam by diesel locomotives denied the mechanical and electrical engineers an opportunity to evaluate the 174 locomotives as ordered for the pilot schemes and to identify the types best suited to the individual needs of the six Regions. It also resulted in orders for production quantities of some types being considered and even committed before the pilot orders had been completed. The BTC perpetuated the practice of the former companies in having costed annual building programmes authorised well in advance. The proposed acceleration of the production of main line diesels placed unexpected demands upon the builders. An indication of the disparity between the aspiration of the BTC for 410 main line locomotives for the build programme of 1959 and the locomotive building community may be gauged by actual production in 1959 totalling 315, of 12 different main line classes. The BTC programme called for EE to provide 30 power sets for type 1 locomotives and 90 for type 3 (D6700 services) and for Sulzer to provide 90 power sets for each of types 2 and 4. It was improbable that Sulzer could produce 90 power equipment for type 4 and the capacity of EE was dependent upon the priority that the BTC assigned to any order for a production quantity of deltic type locomotives for the Eastern, North Eastern and Scottish Regions (contract award agreed in February 1958). The actual production in 1959 using EE and Sulzer equipment was 80 and 64 respectively.

Throughout this difficult, if largely self-induced, period for the BTC, EE, in both the Preston works and the Vulcan Foundry, found its way through orders for the home and overseas markets for diesel and electric locomotives, for various gauges and generally small production batches. The Vulcan Foundry contracts for Vulcan Foundry 1957-59 were:

VF No.	Customer	Number service/class	Qty	Gauge
6553/57	BTC/ER	D5900	5	4'8½"
6554/57	BTC/ER	D5900	5	4'8½"
6568/57	Argentine Rly	D-	21	metre
6794/57	BTC/LMR	E3XXX	5	4'8½"
6795/57	BTC/LMR	E3XXX	5	4'8½"
6796/57	BTC/LMR	E3XXX	5	4'8½"
6804/57	Spanish Rly	E-	5	5'6"
6865/57	Spanish Rly	E-	5	5'6"
6570/57	Peruvian Rly	D-	6	4'8½"
6571/57	Peruvian Rly	D-	10	4'8½"
6816-2057	South African Rlys	E-	55	3'6"
6598-6600/58	BTC	D9000	22	4'8½"
6589-91/58(a)	BTC	D2XX-3XX	95	4'8½"
6620/58(b)	East African Rlys	D-	10	metre
6589-91/58	BTC	D2XX-3XX	10	4'8½"
6653-4/59	Sudan Rly	D-	15	3'6"
6665-68/59	BTC	D67XX	42	4'8½"
6646/59(c)	BTC	D8XXX	15	4'8½"
6837-8/59	Polish Rlys	E-	20	4'8½"

Notes
(a) later batch D305-24 produced by Robert Stephenson & Hawthorn
(b) Robert Stephenson & Hawthorn production
(c) transferred from Robert Stephenson & Hawthorn

Actual deliveries of the first production batch of EE type 4 main line diesels were:

Painted number	Period to	Initial allocation to
D210	16 May 59	Willesden 1A
D211-14	13 June 59	Willesden 1A
D215	8 August 59	Willesden 1A
D216-23	8 August 59	Crewe North 5A
D224-6	5 Sept 59	Crewe North 5A
D227/8	5 Sept 59	Longsight 9A
D229	5 Sept 59	Carlisle Upperby 12B
D230	3 Oct 59	Carlisle Upperby 12B
D231-5	3 Oct 59	Crewe North 5A
D236	31 Oct 59	Crewe North

Note
D215 to Edge Hill 8A via Crewe North

At the London end of the routes, the early arrivals were allocated to Willesden depot; the reasons being that Camden was being readied for examination, fuelling and changing of consumable inventory purposes and Willesden was on the main line (unlike Devons Road where the EE type 1s were) and had gained experience with 10000/1, 10201-3. For crew training purposes in June and July, D210/1 were based at the London end, D212/4 at Crewe, D213 at Carlisle Upperby, D215 at Edge Hill and D216 at Holyhead. That left Longsight as the only depot not involved at that time and its exclusion was due to civil engineering concerns particularly between Stockport, Slade Lane Junction and Manchester (London Road) station.

All the indications were that rather than concentrate the diesels on the Crewe-Euston section and plan a timetable around the acceleration and braking characteristics of the diesels, the London Midland Region intended a straight substitution of diesel for steam. Even allowing for the extent of planned civil engineering and re-signalling work, that was a far more cautious approach than adopted by the Eastern Region, influenced by concerns about reliability, availability, a perpetuation of depot lodging turns/mileage bonus payments and the number of trained footplate crews as may be available. In other words, the management intended to do with D210-36 much the same as had been the case with 10203 and *Deltic* in single mode (both being away in works for part of the summer) and the other two pairs working in tandem. No comparison trials appear to have been held.

The first production batch of main line diesels arrived in 1959 in the form of 26 EE type 4s. Surprisingly few colour pictures of the early years seem to be available. D212 (Aureol) was photographed at the Midland Railway Centre. (63)

For reasons of intended comparison between two pilot orders for type 4 diesels, ten BR/Sulzer types were used on the Western Division. The placement of orders for production builds before the pilot quantities had settled down rendered such comparisons largely irrelevant. D4 Great Gable was one of the first ten BR/Sulzers and has survived into preservation. (64)

The BR/Sulzer type 2 diesels also saw service on the Western Division, with duties ranging from empty coaching stock, to suburban passenger and – in pairs – longer distance brake fitted goods services. D5061 is in preservation at the North Yorkshire Moors Railway. (65)

In June the first of the other class of type 4 diesel/electric locomotives intended for use on the London Midland Region appeared. D1 had been built at BR Derby works and, like D210-36, was a 1 Co-Co 1 configuration with certain design features that owed much to the early prototypes; the bogies of 10201-3 and the cabs/noses of 10000/1. D1-3 had been listed in the aspirational build programme of the BTC for 1958, but had been delayed by a combination of factors and somewhat overtaken by the D5000 type 2 pilot order. D1-10 were to form the pilot order for the type 4 equipped with a Sulzer (built in Switzerland) 12LDA28 engine, a Crompton Parkinson main generator and traction motors to produce 2,300hp. D1 tipped the scales at 138 tons 3cwt and, as such, was 5 tons and 3cwt heavier than D200, both being fitted with a train heating boiler and water tank (5 tons in the case of D1) though D1 did not have water scoop pick up apparatus. D1 was despatched to Carlisle for a naming ceremony there (*Scafell Pike*) and en route was used on trials over obtuse (i.e. blunt ended rather than pointed and, therefore, more exposed to damage from heavy, unsprung wheelsets) crossings in the vicinity of Preston station.

Following acceptance trials, D1 was taken into London Midland Region stock in period ended 5 September 1959. The other nine of the pilot order were received as follows:

Painted number	Period to	Initial allocation to (a)
D2-4	3 Oct 59	Camden 1B
D5	31 Oct 59	Camden 1B
D6/7	5 Dec 59	Camden 1B
D8/9	2 Jan 60	Camden 1B
D10	27 Feb 60	Camden 1B

Note
(a) all subsequently transferred to Derby 17A during the same or next period and not released for
    traffic until spring 1960

The BR Derby works/Sulzer type 2 1,160hp diesel electrics pilot order of twenty emerged in 1959 and, following acceptance trials, the first fifteen (D5000-14) were allocated to the Southern Region. D5015-19 were delivered in June and July and allocated to Crewe South, but later in the year they went south to work empty stock and local services into and out of Euston. A sensible decision was taken to concentrate EE type 1s at Devons Road and, with this in mind, the D8200s were re-allocated to the Eastern Region and Devons Road received a further batch of new D8000s (D8036-44) from the follow-on production batch.

One of the many challenges of the time was axle load weight. Route availability (main lines, branch lines, goods only lines) depended upon individual axle load, total weight and axle spacing, the latter for the distance between outer axles when locomotives were running in pairs/multiples. Stress on rails and rail joints caused by weight carried on small diameter wheels was a further factor of civil engineering concern. To address those concerns, a balance had to be found while accommodating the needs of the designers of the diesel electric locomotives requiring either a wheel diameter of under four feet or, alternatively, to have additional wheelsets to spread the load or – at increased costs – to adopt the North American practise of running locomotives in multiple over heavier rails. The Civil Engineer proposed that the axle weight in tons divided by the wheel diameter should not exceed 4.5. The Chief

Mechanical Engineer was concerned to have locomotives that allowed maximum access to the tracks. The dilemma was:

Maximum axle load (tons)	Route availability	Civil Engineers minimum wheel diameter
13	Nearly all	2'5"
16	All except small branch lines	3'3"
18	90 per cent passenger or goods	4'0"
20	83 per cent passenger, 48 per cent goods	4'7"
22½	Certain main lines only	5'1"

With the BR/Sulzer and EE type 4 locomotives having axle loads of 18 tons 16cwt and 18 tons respectively and each having a wheel diameter of 3ft 9in, that was a problem. The problem was overcome by the Civil Engineer holding trials initially with D207 on a test track laid at Willesden, trials with D210/1 over the section to and then beyond Bletchley and then into Manchester London Road following the planned remodelling. Where restrictions applied, they were detailed in the Sectional Appendix, a copy of which was made available to all staff involved. The clear need was for locomotives developing high power with a lower total weight and axle load; Co Co *Deltic* at 106 tons had achieved that for EE with the use of two Napier engines developing a total of 3,300hp and with a wheel diameter of 3ft 7in. The later (1962) introduction of the Brush type 4 Co-Co (of which 512 were eventually built) developing 2,750hp from a Sulzer 12LDA28C engine, a wheel diameter of 3ft 9in and an axle load of 19 tons was also a compromise. In the shorter term, axle load was a problem that had to be lived with and, for the production builds of the BR/Sulzer and EE type 4, would not go away.

There was also a healthy debate about where best on the Western Division of the London Midland Region to deploy the EE type 4s and, by extension, where best to deploy the class 8 steam power. A good Princess Coronation (that is, all of them) could shift very adequately the heavy expresses between Euston and Carlisle/Glasgow and with an ability to generate a much higher horsepower than the 2,000 maximum of an EE type 4. On that basis, a case could have been made for a concentration of steam over the more heavily graded line north of Crewe, leaving the type 4s to maximise their powers of acceleration between Euston and Crewe/Manchester/Liverpool.

The front-line passenger fleet as allocated at the start of 1959 compared to the start of 1958 was:

Depot	Power class					
	6		7		8	
	1958	1959	1958	1959	1958	1959
Camden	8	7	15	14	14	8
Crewe North	22	22	20	22	20	19
Longsight	14	10	18	21	-	-
Edge Hill	17	18	11	17	5	7
Carlisle Upperby	18	15	9	8	3	8
Carlisle Kingmoor	20	22	-	-	-	-
Polmadie	4	2	10	8	9	9

The big changes in numbers were for power classes 7 and 8. The return of the Royal Scots loaned to the Midland Division lifted the total available at the start of 1959 and were to the benefit of Longsight and Edge Hill. Planned work at Camden to be ready for the arrival of the EE type 4 diesels necessitated a reduction in the total number of steam locomotives requiring 'home depot' examinations and washouts. Unfortunately, the artisan workforce establishment was also reduced and made recruitment of locomotive cleaners (the first step on the traditional ladder for promotion to the footplate links) that much more difficult at a time of high employment. The reduction of six class 8 power locomotives was to the benefit of Carlisle Upperby which had not previously had such a quantity during the months of a Winter Timetable.

The spring season of sporting fixtures at Wembley brought forth variety in motive power. The women's hockey international brought six Bulleid pacifics and a Schools, the FA Cup Final was between Nottingham Forest and Luton Town, the Rugby League Challenge final paired Wigan with Hull and the football international England versus Scotland. It was a shame that, for the Cup Final on 2 May, the wonderful run of Third Division Norwich City was halted by Luton Town as a stream of B17s would surely have come from Norfolk; as it was Immingham B1s helped out with the trains from Nottingham (GC and Midland). Immingham B1s were rare but, anyone who missed seeing them on 2 May had a second chance the following Saturday when Hull visited Wembley. The Scots always turned out in large numbers for the bi-annual match at Wembley and all routes south were used. As an aside, there were four specials from east Scotland that were routed up the east coast main line to Doncaster, then to Mexborough where locomotives were changed for the run to London up the former Great Central line. Haymarket turned out two A4s and two A3s and all four stood on Mexborough shed; anyone who knew Mexborough shed with its mineral locomotives will pity any local spotter who turned up at school on the following Monday with the unbelievable story of seeing four Haymarket pacifics.

For the Summer Timetable, the arrangements for passenger services were very similar to those for 1958 but, as they incorporated the recovery times inserted between Euston and Crewe from September 1958, there were some adjustments to the times of the seasonal extras, reliefs and Q trains. Irrespective of the state of Camden, that depot was allocated five class 7 (Royal Scots) and two class 8, two Princess Royals went from Edge Hill to Crewe North and one each of classes 7 and 8 to Carlisle Upperby. Also of note was the transfer of seven class 6 to Crewe North.

With the EE type 4 diesels which arrived in the first half of the year being involved in acceptance and crew training, the first half of the Summer Timetable was almost totally dominated by steam. A storm was brewing in terms of high mileage Princess Coronation pacifics which resulted in nine of the class of thirty-eight being in Crewe Works during the first half of August, and all but one granted either Heavy General or Heavy Casual classified repairs. Of the nine, seven were allocated to the London Midland Region and with Heavy General repairs taking an average 47 days, the route inevitably suffered. The problem extended beyond power class 8 into power class 7. The Midland Division was in a high degree of strife due to its Britannias managing to average weekly mileages varying between 500 and 1,200 (a single St Pancras-Manchester return run being nearly 400), the introduction of the Metrovick type 2 diesels being protracted and their utilisation being prioritised for Condor, Moorgate services into central London leaving two pairs available for other work. To help out and reduce costly double heading Longsight provided its Britannias (70031-3), the first two of which averaged 5,000 miles/week and, during the summer, 70033, fresh from a Heavy Intermediate classified repair. Further support was provided by short-term loans of four Royal Scots; one arriving in each of February and March and leaving in May, replaced by two more that stayed until July. To round off references to the Midland Division, the settling in of the EE type 4s allowed the transfer later in 1959 of seven class 7 (six Royal Scots, including four to Nottingham, and one Patriot) to leave the Division at the end of the year with twenty-three class 7 locomotives (14 in 1957 and 16 in 1958).

The effect on the Western Division during the peak of the summer was to increase the amount of double heading and to work the available fleet harder than was normally the case. Despite its high profile the 9.50 *Royal Scot* became an unexpected candidate for haulage by a pair of class 6 or a 6 plus a Black 5 pilot, but this was solved for most of the summer by one of the Upperby class 8 locomotives working through each previous day. An alternative for SL and LL was the use of a class 7. By contrast with the Princess Coronations, the Princess Royal Class did not suffer any shoppings and it was, therefore, a good summer in which to see them, including the two still at Polmadie (46201/10). The planning for the year had envisaged the BR/Sulzer type 4 diesels helping out on the Euston-Liverpool workings but that was on hold.

As the EE type 4s were progressively accepted and crew training established sufficient footplate crews in the various links the locomotives were placed into a succession of workings, the most regular of which were as follows:

A schoolboy's early passion for railways and venture into photography at Hatch End in 1959 resulted in a lifelong interest (see photo 86, 2015). **Royal Inniskilling Fusilier** *has an up express. (66)*

Train	Working	Return
10/20 Glasgow – Eus	Carlisle – Eus	10/0 Euston – Glasgow to Carlisle
5/15 Lpl – Eus	Throughout	7.45 Eus – Lpl
7.45 Crewe – Eus	Throughout	5/25 Eus – Holyhead to Crewe, or
		8/30 Eus – Glasgow TPO to Crewe
9.0 Perth – Eus	Carlisle – Eus	0.10 Eus – Glasgow to Carlisle
5/15 Inverness – Eus	Carlisle – Eus	5/25 or 8/30 as above

The summer of 1959 was, therefore, dominated by steam haulage on the main routes of the Western Division and, with the large number of class 8 in works, a need for high availability of those in traffic. My visits during that time noted Princess Coronations on the heavier trains of over fourteen carriages and class 7s on several Liverpool workings interspersed with Princess Royals and EE type 4s. Even 71000 was turned out for the heavy 10.15 Glasgow-Euston from Crewe. Sadly, however, diesel multiple units were used for Saturday West Midlands to Llandudno and Morecambe services for which the two 4-4-0s at Monument Lane had been held in reserve.

By September, all of the Liverpool-Euston and return workings, except the 4/0 Up and 2/20 return, were diesel diagrams and, during that month, a northbound journey on the *Royal Scot* could produce anything from a pair of Jubilees to an EE type 4. The allocation of the type 4s was Camden six, Crewe North five, Carlisle Upperby three, Edge Hill seven, Longsight four and Holyhead one. For footplate crews who had completed their training on the type 4s it was a case of coming dressed for steam and exposed to the weather conditions, but ready for a diesel in one or both directions of travel; a national level agreement on manning arrangements for diesel locomotives having been agreed.

The end of the summer dated passenger services, reliefs and Q trains did not prompt the usual re-allocation of locomotives between Crewe, Edge Hill and Carlisle Upperby, plus a reduction in class 7 at Camden. What happened was far more extensive and was spread over a period of weeks from mid-September to early December. The operating department was far more organised than the Winter Timetables, delayed by a strike in the printing industry and not publicly effective until 2 November. Of particular interest were the allocation of six Royal Scots to Preston (including taking over the former Camden working of Blackpool services), four Jubilee Class 6 to Willesden (fitted goods trains), the transfer of all five Holyhead Britannias to Crewe North and their replacement by two Royal Scots (plus type 4 diesels), a concentration of Patriot class 6 at Carnforth and Preston (for vacuum fitted goods trains) and the transfer of most of the Bushbury Jubilees to Carlisle Upperby with replacement Royal Scots to work a reduced London service. For the Patriots this was to be their redoubt. For the record, the allocation of the Princess Royals and Princess Coronations was:

Depot	*Princess Royal*	*Princess Coronation*
Camden	46207	46221/9/34/9/40/2/5/7/54
Crewe North	46200/5/6/9/12	46220/8/33/5/41/3/6/8/9/51-3/6
Edge Hill	46203/4/8/11	-
Carlisle Upperby	-	46225/6/36-8/44/50/5/7
Polmadie	46201/10	46222-4/7/30-2

Note

46234/56 to Carlisle Upperby for winter 59/60

For the Winter Timetable, type 4s were allocated to work all but three of the principal named express services including the Travelling Post Office. The exceptions were *The Comet, The Emerald Isle Express* and *The Ulster Express*. By that time, the concerns of the civil engineers had been met at Chester, Manchester, Crewe and Preston allowing access to all routes, subject to adherence of particular restrictions. All trains were given recovery times for engineering work and for most, the public arrival time as in the printed timetable allowed ten minutes more than that in the Working Timetable. On Sundays the Trent Valley route between Rugby and Stafford was closed for engineering works, all passenger trains being routed via Coventry, Stechford, Bescot to the Wolverhampton area, thence to Stafford and adding 35 more minutes to times for 83 through trains.

The weekday arrangements for the principal trains were:

Euston dep	Destination	Due		Recovery (mins)	Load	Note
		wtt	**public**			
7.45	Lpl	11.37		21	12-14	1
	Man	11.40	11.50	23		
9.05	Glsgw	2/31		38	14	2, 3
9.35	Man	1/20	1/30	15	12	4, 5
12/20	Lpl	4/08	4/20	21	13	6
1/05	Glsgw	6/31		38	8	3, 7
3/45	Glsgw	9/11		38	8	3, 8
4/45	Lpl	8/33	8/45	21	14	9
5/25	Holy	10/55	11/05	12	12	5, 10
5/50	Man	9/40	9/50	19	12	11
6/0	Lpl	10/01	10/15	22	15	12
6/10	Hey	11/13		20	10	5, 13
7/10	Inv	1.39		20	12	14
8/30	Glsgw/Aber	3.22		17	14	15
8/45	Holy	2.35		18	15	16
10/0	Glsgw	4.09		20	14	17

Notes: Recovery time for LM Region only

1. *The Lancastrian*
2. *Royal Scot*
3. due time is for Carlisle
4. *The Comet*
5. steam
6. *The Red Rose*
7. *The Mid-Day Scot*
8. *The Caledonian*
9. *The Shamrock*
10. *The Emerald Isle Express*
11. *The Mancunian*
12. *The Merseyside Express*
13. *The Ulster Express*
14. *The Royal Highlander*
15. TPO
16. *The Irish Mail*
17. *Night Scot.* Trains 2, 7 and 8 non-stop to Carlisle

The business community was far from happy with these developments and let it be known. The burghers of Manchester were assured that their needs would be met by a diesel Pullman service by the Midland route and, in the meantime, their evening train to Buxton would be given added status by the allocation of a class 7P locomotive. For travellers to Manchester from London the Midland route offered *The Palatine* (7.55 from St Pancras due Manchester

Central 11.48), returning at 2/25, due 6/15, with the prospect of the faster diesel Pullman service from early 1960.

The planning for the electrification of the route between Stockport and Manchester included a provision to remodel the junctions to allow a reduction in the number of conflicting movements across tracks. For example a train seeking to access the west side platforms at Manchester London Road station needed as clear an approach as was possible without other trains having to cross over its tracks. The final few miles involved four main tracks and a junction at Slade Lane. The revised arrangements involved changing the direction of travel over certain tracks and the installation of three aspect colour light signalling with direction indicators for crossovers (known as feathers). On the evening of 23 November 1959, two trains were running on the adjacent Down lines towards Manchester; *The Pines Express* on the fast and a diesel unit on the slow. The express was signalled to cross over and precede the unit, but the driver of the latter misinterpreted the signal and assumed it was for him to take precedence. A side on collision occurred as *The Pines Express* crossed over, but thankfully at slow speed and with less of an impact upon passengers and rolling stock. It was a reminder of the need for route re-learning.

The need for catering to a high standard was recognised by the BTC in an order for thirty new kitchen cars (series 80000) to be built for the Eastern and London Midland Regions by Charles Roberts Ltd.

With the way that the London Midland deployed the diesels, that left a majority of express passenger trains with steam; the untitled Manchesters, the Blackpools, the Workington/Windermere, the Crewe/Carlisle, the Birmingham-Glasgow, the Manchester/Liverpool-Glasgow, one Holyhead, the Crewe-Perth and the few Wolverhamptons that remained.

From 2 November there was a reduction of passenger services between Euston and the West Midlands, though not between London and the West Midlands. To allow the civil and signal engineers more possessions, it was decided to reduce the service on the LM route and augment that along the Western Region between Paddington and Wolverhampton via High Wycombe, Banbury, Leamington and Birmingham (Snow Hill). Coventry became the biggest loser from this re-arrangement.

The timing of the enhanced Western Region service reflected the two (rather than four for much of the LM route) track infrastructure and the need to accommodate other traffic flows; an average time to Birmingham being around 2¼ hours. Worked by King Class 8 steam power from Stafford Road (Wolverhampton) and Old Oak Common (London) depots (some re-allocated from Plymouth following the arrival of pilot diesel orders) there were fifteen Down and fourteen Up services (plus two Fridays only Up) and required 70 per cent weekday availability of the ten Stafford Road Kings. Just behind the Kings in ability to handle the services were Castle class 7; loads varying between nine and twelve carriages. To support a high level of catering, some LM catering vehicles and staff were transferred and caused some disturbance to the Western's attempt at unified chocolate and cream livery. The services were generally timed to leave Paddington at ten minutes after the hour and on the hour from Wolverhampton; all train reporting numbers from Wolverhampton being in the range 008 to 103 and from Paddington in the 807-920 range, the latter for trains destined for Birkenhead.

The services that remained on the LM route were 6.40 and 9.30 Wolverhampton-Euston trains and the 5/0 and 7/40 Birmingham-Euston trains, all but the 7/40 being for a Bushbury class 7 locomotive. The workings were not very well balanced and involved a Crewe North

Royal Scot going to Birmingham and one set of carriages going to, or coming from, Llandudno. You may wonder, as I do, why only 10000/1 had worked a 450 mile/day diagram involving the 8.50 Euston-Wolverhampton, 2/25 Wolverhampton-Euston, 6/50 Euston-Birmingham and 10/40 Birmingham-Euston parcels while the new type 4s worked far fewer hours in traffic.

To assist the civil engineers working between Manchester and Crewe, two diversions via Uttoxeter, Sheet Stores Junction and the Midland line were put in place for the 11/58 and noon trains from Manchester and with balanced return workings from St Pancras at 1.0 and 1/55. The 1.0 was interesting as it followed the Midland line throughout and was due into Manchester (Central) at 5.16 having run non-stop from Derby. On Sundays two additional services were on offer from St Pancras (10.20 and 5/30) and at least avoided the diversions through the West Midlands.

Watching the events of the year from the lineside was a wonderful experience. From the perspective of those watching from the distance of Whitehall, it was a concern, particularly as to the rate of expenditure and allotment to projects. The BTC review of 1956 was used to justify an acceleration of aspects of the Modernisation Plan in a BTC expectation of a net revenue surplus by 1961/62. The capital that was provided in the 1956-58 period was £221m and, in addition, there were short-term borrowing powers to relieve interest payments. Shortly after the 1956 review, the cost of the Plan was put at £1,500m and added £160m for new projects. Deficits on revenue account of a total of £216m (1956-58) were moved to a Special Account, which increased to £308m. Matters had deteriorated during 1958 and, in return for agreeing to extend the Commission's borrowing powers, the Minister for Transport required the Chairman of the BTC to undertake a re-assessment of the Plan. That review was undertaken in the first half of 1959 and was published as a White Paper, *Re-appraisal of the Plan for the Modernisation and Re-equipment of British Railways*. As with the National Coal Board's *Revised Plan for Coal* also in 1959, the re-assessment dealt with progress with modernisation, a forecast of its business prospects and estimates of demands for its production (NCB) and services (BTC). In the buoyant economy of the time it would have been far more difficult to see that railway traffics and demand for all but coal for power stations were in a state of secular decline. Harold Macmillan had been Chancellor of the Exchequer and knew very well the growing concerns about the railways. His hand to effect change was strengthened when the Conservative Party was returned in the General Election of 8 October 1959 with an increased majority of 100 seats. As part of his new Cabinet, Ernest Marples (formerly a Private Secretary to Macmillan, and Postmaster General in the previous administration) was appointed Minister for Transport. As a former director of a civil engineering company with contracts from the transport department, Marples found it difficult to avoid charges of conflict of interest (and eventually fled the country for a tax-free life in exile). 1960 would see far more scrutiny of the plans of the BTC.

In 1959, all but two of the six Regions of British Railways managed to improve their financial performance in terms of net receipts (i.e. gross receipts, less working expenses). The two which did not manage any improvements were the London Midland and the Scottish.

Chapter 7

1960: The Politicians Stride Forward

1960 was a year during which a great deal of the government's time was devoted to examining the planning and work of the BTC and particularly the railway activities. The outputs from that work shaped the political direction towards a Transport Act to replace both the outdated Act of 1953 and the Commission itself. The schemes to electrify the main lines south of Crewe to Euston and north to Liverpool were re-examined and the whole basis challenged. In parallel, physical progress continued to be made between Manchester and Crewe, with the introduction of more main line diesels. Levels of interest at the lineside were maintained at a high level.

Shortly after the General Election of October 1959, Ernest Marples established a Select Committee of thirteen MPs to examine the railway activities of the BTC. That Committee received evidence between January and May 1960 and reported in the July. When the Committee had just started its work, members of the Cabinet received from the Treasury and Ministry of Transport a memorandum which raised serious doubts about aspects of the BTC's 1959 re-appraisal of the Plan for the Modernisation and Re-equipment of British Railways; its optimistic forecasts of traffic, its underestimate of future labour costs and exaggerated estimate of net revenue improvement by 1962/63. Since the 1955 strike over pay by most enginemen, the position of railway workers in relation to those engaged in similar activities had again slipped back and was expected to be corrected during 1960. The memorandum also raised concerns about the methods of calculation of rates of return on capital investment and, in any event, the Commission would need further financial assistance. Marples decided that rather than await the results of the work of the Select Committee he would establish a Special Advisory Group consisting of a few leading businessmen with a remit to examine the 'structure, finance and working' of the BTC.

The Group was chaired by Sir Ivan Stedeford, head of Tube Investments, with Dr Richard Beeching, Technical Director of ICI Ltd (a nominee of the first choice, Sir Frank Smith who had recently retired from ICI Ltd), Frank Kearton of Courtaulds, Henry Benson of Cooper Brothers Accountants and a civil servant from each of the Treasury and Ministry for Transport.

Both the Select Committee and the Special Advisory Group spent time examining the Manchester/Liverpool-Birmingham-London electrification scheme. In the former case it emerged that the scheme had been costed in the original Plan at £75m, by 1959 it had reached £161m and the expected yield, or return, at £8m net represented a rate lower than the then current interest rate. There was considerable debate around the varying bases of financial calculation. The Committee's principal concern was that in accepting that the route should be electrified upon the basis of traffic density, no-one in Whitehall had requested from the BTC a comparison with diesels as an alternative. The Select Committee did not recommend that the project should be abandoned despite the low rate of return that would – based upon the interpretation of the financial bases of calculation – apply.

The Special Advisory Group covered much of the same ground as the Select Committee but in its recommendations went further in concluding that the Modernisation Plan was unsound, based upon technical merit rather than commercial justification and without due regard to capital costs. The initial conclusion of the Group in June pre-dated those of the Select

Committee and was that those parts of the Modernisation Plan that had been started, but not reached a point of no return, should be delayed pending a further examination. While Marples deliberated, the Group examined schemes in progress; the BTC submitting 120 projects with a total capital cost of £227m. The schemes were divided into:

a) too far advanced to be sensibly stopped
b) self-evidently justified
c) unavoidable replacement
d) started, but not passed the point of no return.

The Group recommended that a) – c) should, in the main, be allowed to proceed; those in d) should be halted and the Crewe-Liverpool electrification should be transferred from a) to d). Beeching was convinced that diesels would be more cost effective than a full-scale electrification, but Stedeford was less convinced.

In spite of Beeching's opposition to the electrification scheme, it survived and, following a further examination by a Ministerial Group on modernisation set up by Marples, was endorsed to proceed in January 1961. Out of the wreckage of a bruising process of reviews, the BTC had at least saved the electrification scheme and submitted a revised programme of reduced modernisation for 1961-64. One casualty of this was the timescale of the completion of the building works at Manchester London Road station, actually completed in 1963.

The diesel v electric traction debate is worth a few more words. The electrification proposals had consistently included locomotives that could produce 3,300hp whereas, in the original submission, the diesel alternative had included locomotives with a maximum output power of 2,500hp. When the original submission reached the BTC for review, the differences in costs were quantified; use of 2,000hp electric locomotives would reduce the cost of the scheme by £2.2m or, alternatively, the use of 3,300hp Deltic diesel locomotives would increase it by £16.5m, thus favouring the case for electrification but not recommending it. By the time that the Special Advisory Group came to review the scheme in detail, the average cost for suitable main line diesel locomotives had risen to £138k (from £100k in 1959) due to the inclusion of Deltic locomotives at £150k each. The number of Deltic locomotives within the total expected to be needed was 207 (of 538) which seems very high when set against the east coast route's 22 of a total of 218. Just contemplate that: 207 Deltics!

At the time of the deliberations in 1959/60, the appeal to the travelling public of cleaner, faster electrically heated carriages with improved journey times was not fully appreciated and the only route available for comparison was that between Sheffield and Manchester over and through the Pennines, electrified (though not to 25kv a.c.) from 1954. By reference to continental Europe, more support could have been found for the 'sparks effect' on travel.

While the politicians and others debated and either agreed or disagreed, the task of progressing the Manchester-Crewe electrification continued. Despite the headlines of 1959 in the local press warning of total shutdown of London Road station for part of 1960, the station continued to be operated throughout. The necessary work was undertaken in phases that closed sections of the station in sequences that started on 4 January and lasted until 28 August 1960. The planning was influenced by the layout as used by the former Great Central/LNER electrified route from/to Sheffield via the Pennines and Guide Bridge (into platforms 1-3) and the LNWR/LMS route from Wilmslow and Stockport (into platforms 4-7 which were re-modelled to form six platform faces 5-10). The trackwork and re-signalling work for the

LNER side was undertaken between 4 January and 23 April during which time electric traction on trains from/to Sheffield (fourteen weekday passenger trains plus one overnight service to London Marylebone) was changed to steam between Guide Bridge and either Victoria, Central or Mayfield stations in Manchester. When that work was completed, attention turned to that affecting the former LMS side of London Road station and caused diversions between 25 April and 12 September; most London Euston and Birmingham passenger services using Victoria station and gaining Stockport via Droylsden although the businessmen's favoured morning service to London, *The Mancunian*, left from Exchange station (essentially a platform extension from Victoria). Manchester to Crewe trains were re-arranged until 12 June during which time they used Victoria station. The final section to be dealt with was that allowing access above street level the short distance to Oxford Road station (from where the Manchester South Junction and Altrincham electrified services ran). The terminus station at Mayfield (on the Down side approach to London Road station) was not electrified.

The work could be categorised into civil engineering for trackwork and footbridges, signalling and communications and overhead line structures catenary and power sourcing. One single power signal box was built to replace thirteen mechanical signal boxes and controlled all fourteen platform faces at London Road and the entrance to Mayfield station. The geographical limits of the new signal box were between Oxford Road and Heaton Chapel (Stockport line), to Gatley on the Styal line (both then forming an interface with Wilmslow box), to Ashburys (Glossop and Sheffield lines) and to Midland Junction (at Philips Park, Victoria station access line). The information held in the signalling display available to the signalmen included four character train descriptions which enabled better planning and regulation. The final stage to complete the preparatory works at Manchester London Road was the installation of the overhead catenary between Ardwick and Oxford Road.

The effect on the travelling public was significant. Due to the exchange between electric and steam traction up to 25 April, journey times were extended by up to 25 minutes while the general disturbance to London and Birmingham services did not go down well with the business community. The favoured businessmen's trains were all re-timed to depart from Victoria up to 19 minutes earlier and, as an added irritant, most services were reduced in length due to platform restrictions there; *The Mancunian* (9.33 which became 9.27 for the duration) escaped that latter indignity by using Exchange station. Diesel hauled *The Mancunian* and *The Comet* passed through Crewe non-stop. That arrangement continued even after the introduction of electric traction on most trains between Manchester and Crewe with a consequential saving of time while traction types were changed. In the Down direction adjustments to journey times were limited to a very few minutes, but the 20 plus minutes of recovery times en route were very unwelcome. The Regional planning to mitigate the effect of change and protect the expectations of business travellers between Manchester and London included the introduction from 4 January 1960 of a first-class only diesel Pullman service titled *Midland Pullman*. The introduction was delayed by a dispute over the potential employment of staff of the Pullman Car Company working to different conditions of employment to those of the National Union of Railwaymen. Trial running of the six-car set offering at seat dining and refreshments at all 132 seats commenced in February 1960 and included a demonstration run for the Minister for Transport in March. Introduction into public service was from 4 July with a departure time from Manchester (Central) at 8.50 (later revised by request to 7.45) with a well-received call at Cheadle Heath and a non-stop run (14 minutes recovery time) to St Pancras due at 12/03 (following revision 11.0). The return service left St Pancras at 6/10, due into Manchester

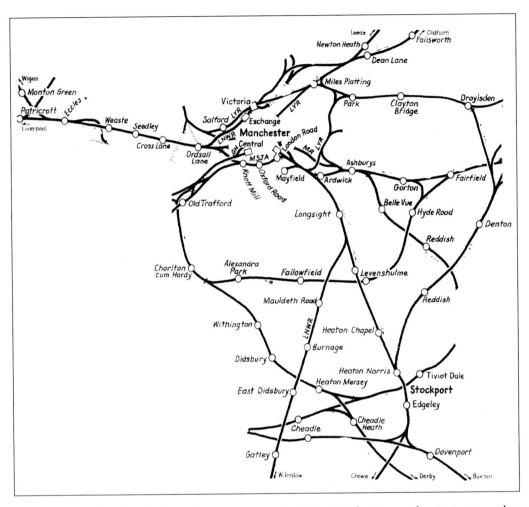

This map (18) identifies the diversionary route used whilst electrification work was progressed at London Road station. Some passenger trains used Exchange and Victoria stations and then went via Miles Platting, Clayton Bridge, Droylesden, Denton and Heaton Norris to reach the main line.

(Central) at 9/21. Despite some hard riding characteristics, the new service proved popular and loaded well. The Western Region introduced similar diesel units for services between Paddington and Bristol and also to Birmingham (Snow Hill); the units being of eight cars and accommodating both first and second-class ticket holders.

With the physical work on the infrastructure and stations well under way, the focus of attention of senior management turned to the availability of electric traction (locomotives and multiple unit trains) and the heating of trains formed of carriages fitted for heating by steam, but planned to be hauled by electric locomotives with no steam heat facility. The functionality and human operation of boilers providing steam from diesel locomotives was a problem for all the Regions involved with the pilot and production builds of main line diesels. The EE type 4 locomotives for the Western Division of the LM Region were introduced during the summer and early autumn and, therefore, before the start of the steam heat season on 1 October. As autumn turned to winter, the incidence of steam substitution or insertion as a pilot or train locomotive purely to provide expensive steam increased.

Of the main contractors for the pilot orders of electric locomotives, Metropolitan-Vickers and British Thomson-Houston, (MV and BTH) retained their separate workshops (Manchester and Rugby) but merged to form a single contracting entity, Associated Electrical Industries Ltd (AEI). Despite mounting problems, NBL Co continued for some time as a supplier of mechanical parts to GEC.

The progressive development of the five separate builds into 1960 was impressive in that recent experience from France and Germany was taken into account, two of the builds featured Alsthom drives (French development) and aspects of the design were standardised. The cabs at each end of each build were to be standard, the driving technique to be the same, the driving console desks were to be identical and major components including the pantographs and circuit breakers were purchased by the BTC and free issued to the contractors. A review of the array of controls available (or to become available) to the driver included electric train and cab heat (foot warmer for driver), automatic warning system and standard indicators, vacuum and air brakes and a windscreen demister. The Longsight men had never seen or known anything like it. The locomotives were to be turned out in a light blue livery for the body with white cab roofs and surrounds; as such they were very similar to the new diesel Pullman sets.

The Civil Engineer expressed the same concerns over axle loads as had applied to the pilot orders for diesel locomotives. All of the a.c. electric locomotives for the LM Region would be of the Bo-Bo configuration (i.e. four powered axles) with a weight expected to be between 75 and 80 tons. The Civil Engineer required a wheel diameter of a minimum of four feet and that is what was provided. The actual weights varied between 73 tons (EE) and 79.6 tons (AEI Rugby/BTH built by BRCW at Smethwick).

The first of the new locomotives emerged in autumn 1959 and was accepted during the period ended 5 December. E3001 was the first of the AEI (Rugby), BRCW build of what had been identified in 1957 as type A. Early in 1960 E3002/3 followed and were used together with E3001 on crew training along the Styal line from the home depot base of Longsight. The first locomotives of the GEC, AEI (Manchester M-V) and EE batches were accepted in periods ended 21 March, 21 May and 16 July respectively (E3036, E3046, E3024) leaving the AEI, Rugby/BR Doncaster works build series of forty to follow from June 1961. The build-up of the fleet in readiness for the planned start of electrified services between Manchester and Crewe on 12 September 1960 was:

Builder	Locomotive numbers and period accepted			
AEI (Rugby)/BRCW	E3001	5 Dec 59	E3002	30 Jan 60
	E3003	27 Feb 60	E3004	23 Apr 60
	E3005	21 May 60	E3006	16 Jul 60
	E3007	13 Aug 60	E3008-9	8 Oct 60
GEC/NBL	E3036	21 Mar 60	E3037	21 May 60
	E3038	18 Jun 60	E3039	16 Jul 60
	E3040	13 Aug 60	E3041-2	8 Oct 60
AEI (Manchester) BP	E3046	21 May 60	E3047	10 Jul 60
	E3048	13 Aug 60	E3049-50	8 Oct 60
EE	E3024-5	16 Jul 60	E3026	13 Aug 60
	E3027-9	8 Aug 60		

While the build programmes and physical progress between Manchester and Crewe were being progressed, the deliberations 200 miles away in London were drawing to their conclusions. It was those conclusions that cast doubts about whether the AEI (Rugby)/BR Doncaster build would proceed and whether the balance of the orders in progress from the other producers would be completed. After the Minister for Transport endorsed the continuation of the electrification scheme (January 1961) the picture became clearer. Full details of deliveries and what happened to the envisaged type B locomotives is as follows:

Builder	Number series	Type	BR identity	Note
AEI (Rugby)	E3001 – 23 11/59 – 2/62	A	AL1 C181	
	E3301 – 2 8/61 and 7/64	B		1
EE	E3024 – 35 7/60 – 7/61	A	AL3 C183	
	E3303 – 5 2/61 – 6/62	B		2, 3
GEC	E3036 – 45 3/60 – 3/61	A	AL4 C184	4
AEI (Manchester)	E3046 – 55 5/60 – 8/61	A	AL2 C182	4
AEI (Rugby)	E3056 – 95 6/61 – 12/64	A	AL5 C185	

Notes
1. Three of originally intended type B became type A; doubt as to completion date for E3302
2. Two of originally intended type B became type A
3. £3301-5 were later allocated numbers E3096-100
4. All five of originally intended type B became type A

The conclusion as far as main line electric locomotives were concerned, therefore, was that there would be a more than adequate supply for the start of services from 12 September 1960. A similar situation was desirable for the fifteen four-carriage multiple unit trains to provide stopping services. That build formed a small part of a total of 207 unit trains for use on Modernisation Plan schemes for the LM, Eastern (GE lines) and Scottish (Glasgow) Region. The units for Manchester (and 20 four-carriage sets intended for Crewe-Liverpool stopping services) were to be built in BR workshops (Wolverton) with AEI as electrical contractors. Each unit had a cab at each end and used Westinghouse air braking. Seating was predominantly for second-class ticket holders in an open saloon arrangement with three compartments with a side corridor for a total of nineteen first-class ticket holders. Passenger access was via traditional side swing doors of which there was a draughty total of sixty-four. Heating of the compartments and open saloons was by electric heaters. Power was sourced via a single pantograph and, like the electric locomotives, the cab roofs were equipped with a manually worked, four-character train description panel (as featured in the power signal boxes) to assist identification by operating staff. The bodies were mounted on Gresley (LNER) style bogies with axles fitted with roller bearings. The body sides of the units were turned out in a dark green livery relieved at waist level by a single yellow line and with grey roofs.

As had applied for the new locomotives, the early arrivals of the unit trains were used for crew training and then held in the Manchester area, particularly at East Didsbury.

Although the distance and travelling time between Manchester and Crewe for express trains was relatively short, the fact that the locomotive hauled rolling stock was equipped for heating by steam presented a problem. The medium-term solution would involve some carriages being equipped for dual heating (steam or electric), new by electric only and countless headaches as sets of carriages were formed and operators found motive power that was suitably equipped; add into that the later policy decision to adopt air braking systems rather than vacuum and any combination of heating and braking of locomotives and stock became a daily problem. In the short-term, diesel locomotive 10203 was used to trial an electrical train heating system and later in 1960 EE type 4 D255 was used on the LM Region on further trials. The short-term solution was in the form of a small number of boiler vans (converted carriages) from BR Derby works. The extent of the use of the vans (in the number series DM444XX) beyond preheating sets of carriages at Manchester is a topic of which I have to admit little knowledge.

At the lineside, motive power changes during 1960 offered great interest while, for those trying to manage operational change, it produced plenty of headaches. The total fleet of main line diesel locomotives was increased by deliveries of further EE type 4s, the availability

The a.c. electric locomotives were not fitted with steam heat boilers. The heating of trains by electricity was some way off and the LM Region resorted to the use of vehicles converted to be boiler vans from Manchester initially as far as Crewe. (67)

to the Western Division of the first batch of ten Derby-built BR/Sulzer type 4s - and late in the year the first few of the follow on production from both Derby and Crewe Works – and an increase in the number of BR/Sulzer type 2s (D50XX series) both new and re-allocations. The commencement from September of electric locomotive hauled passenger trains between Manchester and Crewe, the demands of the engineers for track possessions and consequential use of diversionary routes meant that all three forms of motive power were in use and in need of maintenance facilities and suitably trained and adaptable manpower. As the year progressed, the demands placed upon the steam power classes 6 and 7 were reduced and allowed the re-allocation of such locomotives to depots that had not previously had use of them. In other cases, the higher power class becoming available was used on vacuum fitted goods trains more usually worked by class 5 power and, in some cases, for goods trains diverted due to the electrification work.

For steam the front-line passenger fleet as at the principal depots at the start of 1960 and 1961 was:

Depot	Power Class	1960	1961
Camden	6	-	1
	7	11	4
	8	9	10
Willesden	6	9	12
	7	-	4
Bushbury	6	3	-
	7	6	2
Aston, Birmingham	6	-	3
Crewe North	6	17	15
	7	20	24
	8	18	15
Longsight	6	9	5
	7	13	2
Edge Hill	6	18	16
	7	8	5
	8	4	4
Holyhead	7	2	4
Carlisle Upperby	6	17	22
	7	3	5
	8	11	13
Carlisle Kingmoor	6	20	17
	7	-	5
Polmadie	6	5	2
	7	8	3
	8	9	9

The additional EE type 4s came now in small batches mainly at the end of the year and between batches produced by EE for other Regions. D267-9 and D287-96 arrived in the spring and summer respectively and D297-314 and D325-7 in late autumn/early winter.

The delivery sequence was disturbed by the production being from the works of both EE and the works of Robert Stephenson & Hawthorn, Darlington (which EE had acquired). The EE type 4s had already established a good reputation and other Regions were keen to have examples for crew training; D301/2 going to the North Eastern Region for that purpose. The BR/Sulzer type 4s D8-10 were allocated new to Camden but probably spent time running in from Derby and those three plus the other seven were re-allocated as follows:

2 April	D4 to Camden
9 April	D1 to Camden
23 April	D3/5/7 to Camden
30 April	D5/6 to Carlisle Upperby
	D8/10 to Crewe North
7 May	D2 to Carlisle Upperby
14 May	D3 to Crewe North
21 May	D1/2/9 to Longsight
16 July	D2/5 to Camden

The ten locomotives were turned out in a green livery (Sherwood green) relieved by a broad white line a few inches above the bottom edge of the body, the larger of the main grill coverings on the body side were also white and the roof a light grey. All ten carried small, rectangular aluminium nameplates:

D1	*Scafell Pike*	D6	*Whernside*
D2	*Helvellyn*	D7	*Ingleborough*
D3	*Skiddaw*	D8	*Penyghent*
D4	*Great Gable*	D9	*Snowdon*
D5	*Cross Fell*	D10	*Tryfan*

D11, the first of the Derby follow-on production batch of 2,500hp and fitted with split, four character train describer boxes on the front of each nose, was allocated to Camden in early October. D68-77 appeared new from Crewe and, while initially allocated to Crewe North, were soon on their way to the beleaguered Midland Division. It had been decided that Crewe would build the locomotives to be fitted with Crompton Parkinson electrical equipment (D68-137 and then D50 to 67) while Derby built those with Brush electrical equipment (D11-49 and D138-165).

Also appearing in greater numbers along the Western Division were BR/Sulzer type 2s (D50XX series) either new or re-allocated as part of a wider inter-Regional effort on standardisation in place of the projected pilot order extended trial periods. Longsight was a major beneficiary and received in October new D5133-42 and intended for vacuum fitted goods workings to London, where Willesden received new and re-allocated examples for similar northbound workings. Willesden would probably have received up to half a dozen more but, as the Metrovick diesels equipped with Crossley engines were proving increasingly troublesome and affecting availability for *Condor* workings, the default position was to allocate BR/Sulzer 2s to Cricklewood. The non-availability of the Metrovicks and the use of the BR/Sulzer type 4s D1-10 on the Western Division had left the important St Pancras-Manchester Central passenger services in the hands of the Britannias based at Trafford Park. As part of a re-organisation of class 7 steam power that followed the introduction of electric locomotive worked services from Manchester in September 1960, the Midland Division received more Royal Scots and rebuilt Patriots and saw its Britannias re-allocated to Willesden (70004/17/42), Newton Heath, Manchester (70014/5) and one to Longsight (from whence it had come earlier, 70031).

For completeness of record, the deliveries of electric locomotives in the latter part of 1960 were:

To	Number
5 Nov	E3010/30/51
3 Dec	E3011–3/31/2/43/52
31 Dec	E3014/5/33/44

The official allocation of the fleet was changed to LMW (Western A.C. Lines).

Taking 1 January as the guide date, the total steam locomotives in the front-line fleet of the Western Division (classes 6, 7 and 8) had fallen from 249 in 1959, 220 in 1960 to 202 in 1961. An adjustment for 1960 and 1961 needs to be made as the rebuilt Patriot and a handful of Jubilee Class 6 locomotives were re-deployed onto vacuum fitted goods work. During the same period, the number of main line type 4 diesel locomotives delivered new had been twenty-seven in 1959, increased by a further fourty-four in 1960 (all EE except ten BR/Sulzer) to give a total at 1 January 1961 of seventy-one. Add to that the availability for Manchester-Crewe of the new electric locomotives and with the pattern of passenger services in the Winter and Summer Timetables being largely unchanged, an opportunity existed to reduce the front-line steam fleet, particularly for class 7, and to re-deploy some locomotives to new work. The way in which the EE main line diesel locomotives were first introduced into traffic was to substitute them for steam into existing steam locomotive and enginemen lodging turns and, when judged against the mileages accumulated by their contemporaries on the Great Eastern lines, could be defended by reference to the route distances, pattern of services and journey times. A more radical approach would have been to dieselise all the publicly timetabled express passenger train services for a complete section, say Euston to Crewe, and to change locomotives and men there with out and home, single shift arrangements. Additional services could have been worked by steam or, at summer weekends, by pairs of type 1 or 2 diesels from Willesden depot and timed for steam.

A further point for discussion is whether there was a need for the 2,300hp BR/Sulzer type 4 locomotives to be used and required training of crews/maintainers on a small fleet? The policy would seem to reflect the earlier plan of the BTC to use the pilot orders to compare types and find those best applicable to the differing needs of the Regions. Given the state of things on the Midland Division in 1960 the deployment of D1-10 between St Pancras and Manchester (Central) would have been far more beneficial.

With regard to steam, the first significant change affected the Britannias at Holyhead with four of the five headed to Manchester (70046/9 to Longsight and 70045/8 to Newton Heath with all but 70046 being re-allocated via a short holiday season spell helping out from

Camden). All five (70045-9) had been re-allocated in November 1959 to Chester (45/9) and Crewe North but only 70047 remained for more than a few weeks. A little later in the winter, Holyhead received two Royal Scots and – for the period including the Easter traffic – three Jubilees. The three Jubilees went to Camden in June and, of the two Royal Scots (46163/70) that went to Holyhead 46170 did not stay long (to 5A). 46163 was joined for the peak summer season by three more Royal Scots (46138/50/6). The one former Holyhead Britannia that had not found eventual employment from Manchester (70047) was re-allocated to Llandudno Junction for the summer. In return for 70046/9, Longsight saw their smaller capacity tender version 70031/2 go to nearby Trafford Park to help out on the Midland Division trains to St Pancras. The big step forward was that, at long last, Newton Heath had class 7 power to use on the Manchester-Glasgow lodging turn and thus relieve Jubilees of that arduous duty. In the West Midlands withdrawal of most of the Wolverhampton/Birmingham-Euston express services saw a distribution of most of its Jubilees with some going to the quiet shed of Aston, Birmingham which, over the next couple of years, would see the arrival of class 7 power. In the short-term Aston deployed a Jubilee – usually 45647 – on the thrice weekly, seasonal Sutton Coldfield-Stirling car sleeper overnight service, usually returning with the balancing working from Carlisle.

For Easter class 8s 46220/33 went to Carlisle and, for shipping services, 46233/56 went to Camden at the end of April. For the start of the Summer Timetable 46243/6/8 went to Camden and 46252 to Carlisle Upperby and, as the summer progressed 46209/48 also worked from Upperby. At the end of the Summer Timetable 46233 went to Edge Hill and to Crewe (North). As at mid-August 1960, the allocation of the class 8 Princess Royals and Princess Coronations was:

Depot	Princess Royal	Princess Coronation
Camden	46207	46221/9/33/9/40/2/3/5/6/7/54
Crewe North	46200/3/5/6/12	46220/8/35/41/9/51/3
Carlisle Upperby	46209	46225/6/34/6-8/44/8/50/2/5-7
Polmadie	46201/10	46222-4/7/30-2
Edge Hill	46204/8/11	-

In Crewe Works at that time were 46203/5/6/8/11 and 46229/32/4/6/7/9/40/2/51/5 but, with the increased number of type 4 diesels, the total fleet was less exposed than in 1959.

With the balance of the distribution across the principal depots, LM Region depots allowed flexibility in use with the type 4s. The average miles accumulated by LM examples during 1960 was only marginally less then than in previous years while those home based in Scotland saw a welcome increase:

Year	Average Miles *Princess Coronation*	
	LMR	ScR
1957	73,159	49,912
1958	72,131	54,715
1959	71,187	50,894
1960	69,884	53,634

Those statistics support a theory that the EE type 4 diesels were considered to be the successor for class 7 steam power and were deployed accordingly.

From the summer, Longsight received three Royal Scots which ventured further south-west than had previously been the case. For passenger services to Cardiff and Plymouth, Shrewsbury had been the usual engine change point, sometimes Crewe, but Hereford and even Pontypool Road became new outposts for out and home workings.

Through all of this, Crewe North remained the great centre of change and from the spring was regularly able to turn out a class 8 for the 9.20 to Holyhead; perhaps a sign of the end of the period during which carriages required heating and an inability of the diesels to provide such, or usual seasonal surfeit of power.

Edge Hill retained its stud and the arrival of the diesel type 4s allowed the cross-Pennine passenger and parcels traffic to feel the benefit of greater availability of steam class 7.

The Midland Division of the LM Region received further transfers; Sheffield (Millhouses) received seven class 7 locomotives in the period ended 6 February for express services to and from St Pancras. By mid-July the Midland Division (including Leeds Holbeck and Millhouses which were North Eastern and Eastern Region depots, but provided power for the routes to St Pancras) boasted thirty-seven class 7 locomotives, of which thirty had been progressively re-allocated from the Western Division.

To complete a summary for the year up to the end of the Summer Timetable, efforts to find work for the Clans continued with all five of those at Polmadie (72000-4) heading east to Edinburgh Haymarket for the seed potato and sugar beet seasons and the five at Carlisle (Kingmoor) being used more frequently on the Midland route to Leeds (Settle and Carlisle). Once at Leeds (Holbeck) they were on occasions used to head south on cross country services to Derby/Birmingham (and beyond Birmingham to Bristol on one weekend).

For observers at the lineside it was another year full of interest. The specials for the springtime sporting events at Wembley brought forth the usual varied selection of power. For the women's hockey match on 14 March the Southern Region sent five Bulleid pacifics and a Schools, although the efforts of the Region's sales team were less well rewarded for the schoolboys' football international on 30 April which produced just one pacific and a named BR Standard 5. For that latter match, two Longsight Patriot Class (45509/15) brought specials from their area. The FA Cup Final on 7 May featured Blackburn Rovers and Wolverhampton Wanderers. For trains for the former club, four Royal Scots and two Britannias were provided to work from Rose Grove and, with both teams bringing trainloads up the same route south from Rugby, some ran through to Euston from where a shuttle service to Wembley was arranged. The Rugby League Challenge Final on 14 May was an all Yorkshire match featuring Wakefield Trinity and Hull and did not 'produce'. That year it was the turn of Scotland to host the international football fixture with England.

On 12 May D210 was named *Empress of Britain*, the name of one of the ships of the Canadian Pacific shipping line that used Liverpool for its weekly sailings to and from Montreal.

The Summer Timetable included the usual seasonal extras and these were predominantly steam hauled. For the three daytime titled Anglo-Scottish services (*Royal Scot*, *The Caledonian* and *The Mid-Day Scot*) a standard timing of seven and a quarter-hours, limited to eight carriages and with class 8 steam power throughout. The recovery time allowance between Euston and Crewe had increased to at least 32 minutes, 42 minutes to Liverpool and by a further 20 minutes to Manchester (including diversions to Victoria) compared to winter 59/60. It was, therefore, far better to observe than to travel. Major station works at Stafford and Coventry added to the disruption.

Living close to the railway and with a natural interest in its local operation, much of my summer holidays were spent with friends watching trains. Each summer our slim ranks were swelled for a couple of weeks by a visitor from Scotland who had relatives living locally. His note book was full of numbers and names which would never be entered into our own books, but in contrast he was very keen to see many of the locomotives that to us were common. Towards the end of his visit in August 1960, he said that on the Saturday he was returning home by train, via a change and pause at Crewe, had a permit for two people to visit Crewe North shed and wondered whether any of us would like to join him as far as Crewe. As luck, parental permissions, pocket money and privilege rate (son of a railwayman) travel would have it, I was the only one able to say yes.

Although the Derby-Crewe passenger service was provided by diesel railcars, summer Saturdays included two steam hauled services to Llandudno, one of which was Burton Crab 2-6-0 and enginemen worked. We joined that lightly loaded service and had ample time as the train made the most of the 51 miles before arriving at Crewe. With his luggage safely lodged, we took up a position at the North Junction end of the station and joined many others who needed little persuasion to tell us what we had missed earlier that busy morning. The collective vantage point was opposite the wall of the long, straight shed with a more open yard and half roundhouse beyond out of sight and the imposing coaling and ash plants to the right. With multiple running lines between the platforms and the shed, access had always been out of the question and, in the parlance of the time, Crewe North was considered 'unbunkable'. Some tried, of course, and would be apprehended and just for good measure the British Transport Police had a presence. Dashing around engine sheds was part of the fun of the time, but was far more dangerous than any of us realised. Earlier that summer, two of my friends had been caught at Edge Hill and, in the ensuing chat with the police, had been asked to give their names and address. 'Are you worried?' I asked. 'Not at all' said one … 'I gave him your name and address!'

Having watched a Princess Coronation head north with the Birmingham-Edinburgh, I let it be clearly heard that it was then time to visit the shed. 'You'll never get beyond the footbridge/office/end of the building,' summarised the Brummie, Scouse and Cheshire dialects of advice. Sure enough and with much pointing and laughing from the gallery we were actually stopped three times and each time managed to show the relevant piece of paper without it being apparent to other than the challenger. We were in … and without a guide shedman. I could hardly await the sight of the interior of the long shed and was certainly surprised when I saw it … except for 71000 it was empty! I had never contemplated exploring what was beyond the long shed, but it was a sight to behold with a range of powerful locomotives either at rest, or being shunted into order of examination, preparation and release to traffic. Beyond were the coaling and disposal activities. It was wonderful and the very definition of a dangerous, industrial environment. Two Polmadie Princess Coronations had me in raptures, but left my friend somewhat unimpressed, particularly when he was told that one was to work his train north. Upon our return to the platform we never mentioned the fact that we had a permit and, for all I know, there are memories elsewhere of the Crewe two who bunked Crewe North.

No summer was complete without a visit to Crewe Works and for most weeks it was easy to obtain a permit and congregate just before 2pm at the Deviation entrance, a ten-minute walk from the station. Walking from the station and taking a route using the terrace housed streets, it was always the case that at least half the properties had curtains drawn and passers- by would ask us to be quiet as people were sleeping … the 24-hour railway at rest.

The visit to the Works started with a longish walk to the paint shop and yard, followed by another long walk along the main yard and into the vast erecting shop (15,000 square yards). Along the way, the guides would advise what new locomotives were in the course of production and discussion then centred upon at what stage of construction it could reasonably be claimed that the 'locomotive' had been seen. The walk up and down the lines of engines (no tenders) was the highlight, line or belt six being the one where the pacifics were repaired, with a total of seventeen overhead cranes at two levels in constant action lifting this, placing that and a 100 foot traverser moving engines from one belt to another. It was always, even in summer, cool. The local story had it that a man employed during the war to paint over the panes of glass (to hinder air raid bombing accuracy) had never been challenged as he continued his paid task throughout the 1950s.

On days when visits to Crewe did not include a visit to the Works, a final hope was to see the 'drag out' from the works that occurred on Monday to Fridays at around 5pm. Locomotives that were released were coupled together and taken to Crewe South shed by one of the works' shunting engines. The first evidence of the move was sound rather than sight as the pistons of several dead locomotives drew and expelled air, never synchronised. It was always worth seeing and a shame that, with the sun behind it, photographic records of it are lacking. If it worked out, a quick dash along the platform would allow a sight of a GW Manor on the stopper to Shrewsbury in the west bay platform, then over the footbridge for the train home.

The highlight days were always Summer Saturdays and in Appendix 6 I have included some detailed 'interludes' at Preston, Chester and Tamworth Low Level. Observing at such locations was a wonderful experience; for railway operators a continuum of being ready for the next move … locomotives, rolling stock and train crews all working to the book.

Beattock Summit from the north and the first carriage gives away the fact that Princess Royal Duchess of Kent has the Glasgow-Birmingham. The leading carriage will be detached at Crewe and taken forward to Plymouth. (68)

Kensal Rise in north west London provided an excellent and popular location for photography. Here, Jubilee Mysore is heading north on the Down east line. To enjoy more of this location see pages 194/195 (69).

On 12 September, the Minister of Transport formally opened the electrified Manchester-Crewe line and locomotive E3040 worked the first public passenger train; the 12/15 Manchester Piccadilly (having been renamed from London Road) to Plymouth. The local diversions came to an end and, for travel between intermediate stations and improved, standard 'clock face' departure times applied to the electric multiple unit service. Timings to Crewe reflected the end of the period of diversions but did not immediately deliver the benefits of the acceleration capabilities of the 3,000hp locomotives. E3003 was damaged by a fire within the body, but otherwise the service settled in well.

For passenger trains from Euston to Preston and beyond, additional recovery time was included in the timetables and then totalled an unpalatable 48 minutes, with adjustments made to departure times to allow minimal disruption at Crewe. As work was progressed in connection with the electrification of the Crewe-Weaver Junction-Liverpool section, it was necessary to divert trains between Crewe and Warrington. That involved the working through Manchester Piccadilly of class 8 pacifics which, up to that time, was a fairly rare event confined to out and home running in turns from Crewe and use on Fridays on the 4/45 express to Euston. Similarly, and very unusually, an 8P (46224) was routed via Stoke-on-Trent and allowed through the Harecastle tunnels only within special provisions. There were, though, some improvements and the overnight sleeper from Glasgow (10/25) was due into Euston at 7.43 and the 12/15 from Perth was due at 10/05. The start of the Winter Timetable also saw more Blackpool services handed over to EE type 4 diesels and both types (EE and BR/Sulzer) were used on the overnight Crewe-Perth and return lodging turns. On the steam front, one Wolverhampton round trip was worked by a Camden class 8, Down with the 4/35 and back with either the 6.48 or 9.48 the following morning and routed via Dudley Port.

Two more EE type 4s received stylish nameplates as for D210; D211/2 became *Mauretania* and *Aureol* respectively, both vessels of Cunard White Star Line.

As further evidence that the use of steam power class 7 was the one most disturbed by the use of the EE type 4s, 16 Royal Scots found new home depots (all but two internal to the Western Division and the other pair to Newton Heath) in September while the usual reshuffle of some class 8s was much reduced. In that latter regard and, with steam heat problems likely, it made sense to have big steam power spread along the main route.

At the northern end of the route to Scotland access on Sundays to Glasgow Central became limited and trains using the former Caledonian Railway route were diverted to Buchanan Street station. The reason was the replacement of the 374 lever, electro-pneumatic signal box which itself had replaced three mechanical signal boxes in 1906 and was, at that time, the largest electro-pneumatic type box in the country. The engineers were finalising the works and signalling arrangements for the start of electric suburban (Cathcart circle) services which, having made a good start and had use by the local population increasing, fell upon technical difficulties and the embarrassment of a hasty reintroduction of steam while matters were resolved. Such was the short-term demand for suitable steam locomotives for suburban passenger services that, on at least one day, the station pilots at Central Station were Austerity 2-10-0s.

The main focus of attention for Regional senior management was what the Minister of Transport would conclude from the advice and recommendations of the committees and Special Advisory Group he had established. What was clear was that much of the basis for the Modernisation Plan and its re-appraisal by the BTC had become heavily criticised, confidence in the Commission's ability to meet changing economic, social and political requirements was low and that the provisions of the Transport Act 1953 needed to be reviewed. While the Minister considered the advice and recommendations, he imposed upon the BTC a limit of £250k for new schemes; any above that amount required his authorisation.

The trading (revenue) position of the Commission worsened in 1960 and, while gross revenue increased by £8.4m, costs rose by a greater extent (£28m in part due to a wage award) to leave a deficit of £67.7m. The London Midland Region returned a deficit of £26m, up from £15.2m in 1959, but was not alone as all five other Regions returned worsening net positions. The overall trend of market share within the total by various modes of transport showed a decline from 19.9 per cent in 1954 to 15.4 per cent in 1960 (passenger miles) and 42.3 per cent to 32 per cent (freight ton miles). It was time for a change.

This chapter marks the half-way point in the period of interest to this book. It is appropriate to pause and reflect from different perspectives upon the position in which the route found itself; operationally, financially, commercially, managerially and politically.

Operational change had become visually apparent in the form of an increasing number of main line diesel locomotives and latterly a few electric locomotives for initial services between Manchester and Crewe. The main line diesels had been allocated across the principal passenger work depots as far as Carlisle and the number of footplate crews able to use them increased by training. Steam traction continued to dominate the total mileage operated. The programme of maintenance continued to support a high level of reliability in traffic with the Working Timetable established around a figure of 70% availability of the front-line fleet. The main line diesels had been found wanting during the winter of 1959/60 and their usage generally was confined to steam class 7 duties. Maintenance schedules for the diesels were lacking and they were required to share steam depots while the London Midland Region lagged behind the Eastern and Western Regions in that regard. North of Carlisle matters changed little with Polmadie providing class 8 power for the principal expresses.

Financial consideration is perhaps best divided into the revenue account – essentially the income generated from the sale of services and the costs of providing those services – and the capital account – investment and upkeep of new equipment and infrastructure as underwritten by the BTC/government under the terms of the Modernisation Plan and being required to be spent prudently. Both the revenue and capital accounts were under stress. The revenue account for the LM Region had slipped into deficit in 1957 and by end 1960 the cumulative losses over four years totalled £57m with gross working expenses (labour, materials) increasing by some £9m while gross income fell by some £16m. The Modernisation Plan as proposed by the BTC and accepted rather too easily by the government made the LM Region a major beneficiary of new capital traction equipment and the electrification of the London-Manchester/Liverpool route. Based upon the early success in revenue terms from the introduction of diesel multiple units some similar early returns from the deployment of main line diesels were expected though for the LM Region difficult to identify when compared to the Eastern Region where they were single route specific. Beyond diesels and electrification plans for marshalling yards had high planning costs and the siting of such was incorrectly based upon long-standing operating arrangements rather than speed of transit between point of production and point of consumption.

From a commercial perspective there had been a success in the form of *Condor* with the concept of a fast transit time between centres of population 400 miles apart using demountable containers on flat bed wagons equipped with roller bearing axleboxes; a concept that was capable of rapid expansion for perishable traffic (meat and fish, where freezing of the products was increasingly applied). The introduction of the high-speed *Caledonian* express passenger service was of marginal benefit to the route and very marginal when extended; at a time when the real competition was from road and air it seemed that the activities at and from King's Cross were the limit of the understanding. The balloon like nature of inflated demand for seasonal services continued to be catered for and as required by the 1953 Act; the Starlight Special and car sleeper trains catered for a new market and were successful. Goods agents selling services were hampered by an overly hierarchical organisation structure and a (national) lack of a grasp of actual costs and therefore margins of profitability. Under the terms of the 1953 Act the railways continued to be obliged to act as a common carrier and accept whatever was offered. The route was not a hostage to economic fortunes to the same extent as the North Eastern Region, but its reliance upon merchandise traffic was crucial.

From its formation the LM Region was a huge managerial undertaking and challenge. The General Manager knew very well the history of the dilemma of operating and geographically based organisations and had lost the argument favouring the latter. He also knew well the provisions of the Transport Act, the workings of BTC with government and the fact that the government had not conceded justifiable requests for price increases for services based upon identifiable increases in labour and material costs. Finally, he knew very well how the Modernisation Plan had been assembled. Therefore, the General Manager was well informed and able to defend the financial performance of his Region, deflect criticism of deployment of the mainline diesels and impose a Euston headquarters-based executive. With a Regional Board Chairman who was seemingly supine, the BTC was somewhat frustrated by the LM Region.

In the same way that the BTC was becoming frustrated with the performance of the LM Region, so too was the government with the performance of the BTC and its Chairman. With a healthy majority of seats in the House of Commons the new Conservative government had a Prime Minister who had been Chancellor of the Exchequer and was well aware of the need to shape change for the railways. It was clear that the provisions of the Transport Act 1953 had been overtaken by socio-economic changes and that as the needs of the nation were changing, so too would the railways need to change.

Chapter 8

1961: No-one Said It Would Be This Difficult

Although the scrutiny under which the electrification scheme had been placed by the Select Committee and two groups of advisers had prompted various concerns and criticisms it had survived. During 1961, further physical progress was made to the north and south of Crewe. The disturbance to normal operating arrangements continued to slow some passenger services and necessitated the diversion and working of many freight trains. As more main line diesel and electric locomotives were received, the hold of the front-line steam passenger fleet was further weakened and the cascade of power reached depots that had previously not maintained such classes in any quantity. While it was not apparent at the lineside, the future shape of Britain's railways and their organisation was being considered in Whitehall.

The BTC emerged somewhat discredited from the scrutiny by the Select Committee and Special Advisory Group in 1960. The Minister of Transport had an abundance of evidence of the weaknesses inherent within the organisation of the Commission and how aspects of the Modernisation Plan had been mismanaged. His third review body – the group of Ministers – would also have noted that the review process in Whitehall departments had not achieved the essential levels of challenge and check. Much of the work of the Select Committee and the Special Advisory Group was an attempt to reconcile several objectives. Firstly, the Transport Act 1953 had provided the terms under which the BTC was to provide railway services for the nation; a national service throughout the year with its daily and seasonal peaks and troughs of demand. Secondly, the BTC wanted to modernise the railways after years of neglect and a lag between changing needs and response time from the government. Thirdly, the public wanted a modern railway network of about the same size as that at 1955. Fourthly, the government wanted the BTC to break even in terms of financial performance. It was clearly impossible to reconcile these objectives and change was inevitable. In addition, the Minister knew full well about the planned growth of roadway improvements, the network of motorways and the increasing demand for private ownership of family cars.

For 1961 and 1962 there were three main activities to be pursued in parallel; to support the railways with the modernisation schemes that had survived the scrutiny, to plan and introduce a new organisation structure and, thirdly, to put in place the necessary legislation to replace the Transport Act 1953 with something the government considered to be more appropriate for the age … something closer to that of a business rather than a service. Of the four businessmen who formed the Special Advisory Group, Dr Beeching was the one who looked beyond organisational outlines and argued that recommendations on organisation could be made only after the Group had acquired a closer understanding of basic economics of railway operation in order to assess the future place of the railways in the country's transport system. For that logical reason, the Group first concentrated upon establishing an understanding of the size and pattern of the railway system, the general soundness of the modernisation proposals and the changes necessary in the Commission's financial structure.

In parallel, the Minister placed a restriction on the amount for capital investment in 1961, £125m plus a reserve of £15m for electrification; a figure that was 30 per cent less than that the Commission was working to less than 12 months prior to that decision. In a more rigorous environment of analyses of investment proposals, the Commission submitted a four-year modernisation programme for 1961-4. It is unsurprising that the overall fall in gross railway investment in real terms from 1959 to 1962 was 38 per cent. Examples of why there was a need for greater scrutiny were plentiful and included the risks taken to secure quick returns with, for example, manufacturers new to the production of diesel locomotives, weak negotiating over contract pricing, lengthy deliberations over marshalling yard plans, a lack of data about changing patterns of wagon load traffic, the plan to fit vacuum brakes and screw couplings to fleets of mineral wagons and the debate over vacuum or the widely accepted continental practice of air braking.

Along our routes of interest, a flyover built at Bletchley became a white elephant, the proposed yard at Swanbourne had no future, Carlisle Kingmoor yard was wrong, but too far advanced and, with the pilot orders overtaken by production orders before any realistic comparative testing for Regional suitability was possible, the decisions to train staff for EE and BR/Sulzer type 4 diesels and then deploy a small number of the latter could have seemed misguided. The London Midland Region was not alone in this sorry tale of waste and could claim a hollow victory in that the electrification scheme had survived. The government's White Paper of December 1960, *Re-organisation of the National Transport Undertakings*, took no more account of railway opinion than had been the case for the Transport Act 1953. Beyond the pure railway activities there was an intention to place the other 'Undertakings' – British Road Services, the bus companies, docks, inland waterways, railway workshops, property and hotels – within a separate holding company. The White Paper also included an intention to create a National Transport Advisory Group with a role to co-ordinate transport services. The Paper then rather ran out of steam in that it proposed to give both the Ministry and British Railways Board (the replacement for the Commission) control over finance and investment. Its race run, the discredited Commission had no medium or long-term future, though in the short-term it would be required to act as a 'bridge' to the new organisation. From February 1961, two informal governmental bodies (Treasury and Transport) sat, with representatives from the Commission; one worked on the transitional arrangements and the other formed a Steering Group to prepare the provisions of what would become the Transport Act 1962 to sweep away the outdated act of 1953. In the interim period of nearly two years the Regions were expected to get on with it. At least for a while, the railwaymen had lost overall control of their industry.

Liverpool provides an excellent example of a centre that provided commercial opportunities within the parameters of its railway origins. Much though the operators and planners of the late 1950s may have wished they could change many aspects, they were constrained by railway history and the decisions taken by the Railway Executive/BTC since nationalisation.

As a growing port, centre of production, industry and commerce in the late 19th century, Liverpool naturally attracted railway company interest with each competing for a share of burgeoning trade. The predecessor to the LNWR had established at Edge Hill a large-scale goods yard and depot which in turn served the centre of the city (Lime Street terminus) and docks via tunnels. The yards were developed in 1899/1900 using a then novel gravity system for distributing wagons.

Map 19: Edge Hill Sorting Sidings

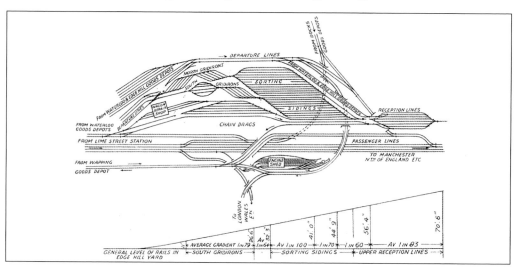

Map 20: Liverpool Area

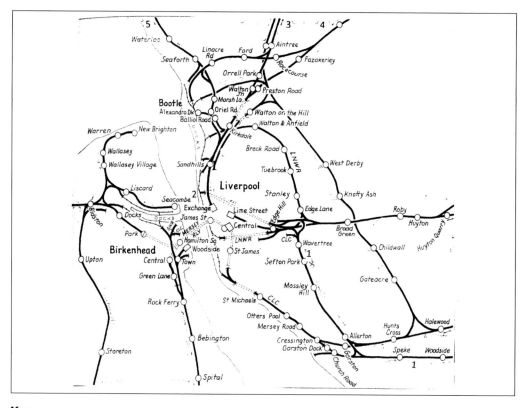

Key

1 Main line Liverpool Lime Street, Runcorn,
  Weaver Junction
2 Liverpool Riverside

3 To Preston
4 To Preston
5 To Southport

Map 21: Edge Hill Area

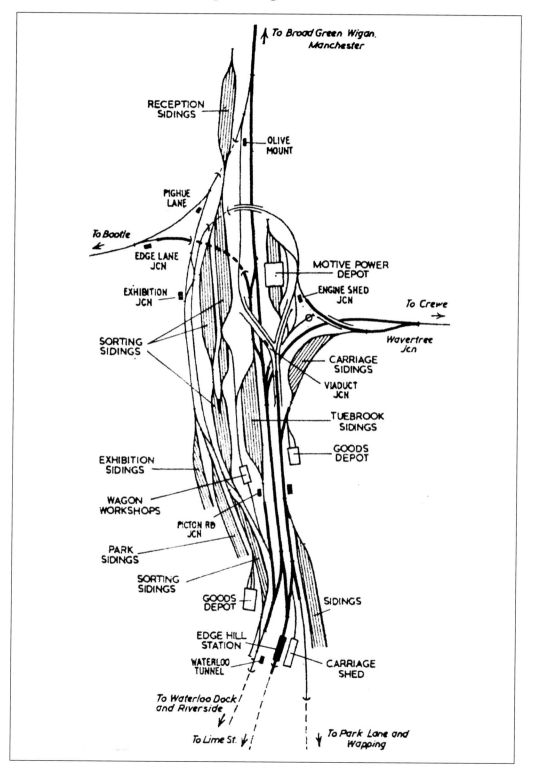

Other railway companies were attracted to the honey pot; principally the L&Y and CLC (the joint initiative of the GN, GC and MR) both of which found ways to open new facilities. On the far side of the River Mersey the GWR and GC were soon accessing trade at Birkenhead. The geology allowed ease of new construction east at least as far as Manchester and two new routes became established with each generating new business in the areas of Wigan and Warrington while the LNWR had access to St Helens and the main line to the north. The barrier of the Mersey protected the LNWR dominance of a direct route south to Crewe, Birmingham and London.

By the time of prime interest to this book Liverpool and its network of railways were beginning to feel the wind of change; international passenger shipping in decline, labour disputes in the docks, a need for new investment in clean industries, a rapid growth in competition for transport services particularly for merchandise, old railway facilities and arrangements largely unchanged since the end of the second world war.

The planners of the main line electrification at least as far as Crewe did not have the luxury of a new route and had to make the best they could within the existing tunnels and arrangements around Edge Hill. What was needed was something for more radical and forward thinking, but the reality was 'make do and mend'!

The challenge of future organisation is of relevance because it was the position taken by Dr Beeching (and Henry Benson) within the Group that eventually persuaded the Minister and paved the way for Dr Beeching to replace Sir Brian Robertson as Chairman of the doomed Commission (1 June 1961) and as Chairman designate of the replacement, the British Railways Board. Dr Beeching was by training a scientist and, like all scientists, he sought data and then information upon which to form conclusions. His approach to the work of the Special Advisory Group had found favour with the Minister and the latter sought his services on a five-year secondment from his employer, Imperial Chemical Industries Ltd, where he was Technical Director. At high cost – a salary very nearly twice that of the Chairman of the National Coal Board and nearly five times that of the Minister – a deal was arranged and Beeching commenced work from 1 March 1961. His initial requests for traffic and commercial data demonstrated the paucity of such and, while a number of studies were conducted to produce data, he turned his attention to the development of the functional Board of management he had argued for. The developments from this and the implications for the London Midland Region are in chapter 9.

The LM Region had taken some steps to reorganise itself at senior management level. Each Region had a Board separate to the day-to-day activity of the Region as under the control of the General Manager. The Chairmen of the LM and the Eastern Boards were also full-time members of the BTC and they could bring authority and influence matters such as policy and organisation. The Chairman of the LM Board, throughout the time of Blee's tenure as General Manager, had been Lord Rusholme, a political appointee to the BTC upon its formation (1947/48) and previously General Secretary of the Co-operative Union. In the early stages of the nationalised industry, he was heavily engaged in establishing the working arrangements with the five major trade unions that represented the transport undertakings. He became Chairman of the LM (Area) Board upon its inception in 1955 and would have been involved in the appointment of Blee as General Manager (a Chief Officer at the BTC) in 1956 and may well have retained the ear of the trade unions in matters such as lodging turns. In 1960 Lord Rusholme reached 70 years of age, retired and was replaced as Board Chairman by Sir Reginald Wilson, another full-time member of the BTC who had been Chairman of the Eastern Region Board. His background was accountancy and, as a much younger man than Lord Rusholme, who was 55, perhaps had more appetite for change than had his predecessor or Blee. Having seen how the Eastern Region had benefited from a Line organisation and, notwithstanding the railway geography of the northern parts of the LM Region, something similar was introduced. The Director of Traffic Services, working from headquarters at Euston, was replaced by three Line Traffic Managers (LTM) at Manchester, Derby and Crewe who reported directly to the General Manager. The step forward was that the six Divisional Traffic Managers reported to their Line Manager who had a greater appreciation of local conditions and opportunities; Liverpool, Manchester and Barrow-in-Furness to the LTM at Manchester, Nottingham and part of the former London to the LTM at Derby and Birmingham plus the other part of the London to the LTM at Crewe.

The biggest decision arising out of scrutiny of the electrification scheme was that the West Midlands loop (Stafford-Wolverhampton-Birmingham-Coventry-Rugby) would be the final section to be completed and work would be progressed on the Trent Valley route from Crewe to Stafford, Nuneaton and on to London with a projected completion date of 1964. With work being progressed between Crewe and Liverpool that would allow electrically worked services to progress south and, with a change of traction at Crewe and, later (for London services) at Nuneaton. For planning purposes, the Crewe-London (including the West Midlands loop) was divided into eleven major sections and forty-four smaller sections. Within that overall plan, there was to be four aspect electric colour light signalling throughout. The availability of four aspect signalling allowed two yellow aspects to be displayed simultaneously and, if showing, was an indication to the driver that the next but one signal was at danger. A single yellow aspect was the equivalent of the semaphore distant signal placed at danger which indicated that the next home signal was at danger. Having four aspects would allow the planning of the headways between trains to be five minutes.

As previously described, the Manchester-Crewe section was controlled from three signal boxes that used the four-digit train description system displayed on illuminated track diagrams. The original plan for the entire scheme had envisaged a total of forty-five new power operated signal boxes but later revised to retain and upgrade some of the existing as electro-mechanical. New cabins were planned for Weaver Junction and Edge Hill (Crewe-Liverpool section), Norton Bridge (Crewe-Stafford), Nuneaton, Rugby, Watford and Euston (Stafford-Trent Valley-Euston), Stoke (Cheadle Hulme-Colwich-Stafford), Wolverhampton, Birmingham New Street and Coventry (West Midlands loop).

The civil engineering works involved stations, tunnels, bridges (over and under) and re-modelling of major junctions. The work around Manchester London Road had involved considerable disruption. Rebuilding at Macclesfield, Stafford, Tamworth, Northampton, Birmingham and Coventry would be progressed by a combination of weekend diversions and progressive use of only certain areas. The rebuilding of Birmingham New Street and Euston stations were major projects by any measure and included new overhead decking and use of land for extensive property development. Alterations rather than rebuilding were arranged for Liverpool Lime Street, Crewe, Wolverhampton, Rugby, Lichfield, Nuneaton, Bletchley and smaller, intermediate stations using prefabricated buildings. Along the route were nineteen tunnels, the longest of which was Kilsby (7,362 feet), the most challenging of which were near Stoke-on-Trent (the Harecastle tunnels) which required a track diversion, a new road bridge, three over bridges, two footbridges and new track connections, the ones with limited clearance for electrification were at Linslade, Northchurch and Watford requiring either lowering of the track and/or slewing of the track. On the final approach to Euston, the 2,865 foot tunnel used for getting empty stock into the station required the roof to be raised by 15in. At Crewe, the usual option of either lowering the tracks or raising the height of the roofs was not available; because of the cut and cover approach adopted for the 1890s remodelling and the complexity of track work above ground the only available option was lowering the tracks. Liverpool, and particularly the approach from Edge Hill, occupied the civil engineers between January and May 1961. The Crewe-Liverpool section involved 94 bridges, a figure that pales against the 478 requiring some alterations on the Crewe-London section (including the West Midlands, Northampton route between Rugby and Roade, and the Cheadle Hulme-Stoke-on-Trent-Norton Bridge sections) of 318 route miles.

Along the route starting from Liverpool were several important junctions – Weaver, Crewe, Norton Bridge, Colwich, Stafford, Rugby – where conflicting movements of trains could be reduced by remodelling the track geometry and direction of travel over four track sections. At Weaver Junction, a flyover carried the Up line over the Warrington-Crewe main line and then joined it, a similar arrangement was applied at Rugby for the West Midlands while at Norton Bridge and Colwich the working arrangements were revised to allow, for example, for better regulation of traffic for/from Stoke-on-Trent/Wolverhampton in the section from/to Stafford. Crewe was a complex exception as well as an exceptional complex where the independent lines and goods lines were helpful but offered no panacea. Just when the engineers within a section were content to have completed their tasks, the last thing anyone wanted was a derailment. On 14 February 1961, the driver of E3025 with a stock train of various vehicles within a total of eighteen exceeded the maximum permitted speed of 60mph with the result that a short wheelbase van became derailed on plain track just south of Holmes Chapel. The vehicle remained upright and in line but ran for 3½ miles with one wheelset running along the sleepers and the other wheelset running over the chairs supporting the rails until it encountered a set of points which caused it and other vehicles to completely derail. One of the derailed vans then struck and carried away one of the masts supporting the overhead wires and, having thus also damaged the next mast, the catenary collapsed. Because the steel bodied vehicles forming the train had been bonded to their underframes, no arcing occurred and put to rest many concerns about exactly what would happen in such an eventuality.

The operators also had their frustrations. Short-term problems elsewhere on the network caused the transfer of several electric multiple units and substitution of locomotive hauled suburban stock between Manchester and Crewe. Against this background of intensive activity, the Region had to continue to provide a service that met the expectations of its customers.

The pattern of goods traffic along the routes of interest had not changed very much throughout the 1950s but the end of the decade saw an increase in the proportion of goods trains that were at least partially fitted with vacuum brakes and a slow reduction of tonnage of coal for industrial and domestic markets. While economic downturns always damaged the minerals sector for which the railways were well suited, the road haulage industry was able to continue to attack the market for merchandise traffic. Keeping the vacuum fitted goods trains and particularly the perishable traffic on the move was, therefore, important even though much of it was running when the engineers wanted possessions of sections of track at night. A similar set of needs applied to time sensitive postal, newspaper and parcels trains.

For summer 1961, the vacuum fitted goods train services heading north out of London (and Northampton) on weekdays were as follows. The section of the WTT is for Camden to Lichfield, including Northampton and trains leaving/joining at Willesden and Bletchley. Because of routing, attaching, detaching and working either on the fast or slow lines, it is not possible to list them strictly in order of time of departure.

Time	Day(s) run	Class	Train
12/47	MSX	C	Camden – Carlisle (Note a)
12/47	SO	C	Camden – Bamfurlong
12.30	MX	C	Brent Sidings – Tile Hill (Cov) (ex-Ripple Lane, fuel oil)
2.25	MSX	D	Northampton – Edge Hill
10/20	MSX	E	Somers Town – Crewe
1.25	MO	E	Brent Sidings – Curzon Street (B'ham)
2.0	MSX	D	Brent Sidings – Crewe
4.0	MO	E	Northampton – Stoke-on-Trent
4.25	MO	E	Northampton – Warrington
2.56	MX	C	Brent Sidings – Hawkesbury Lane (Cov)
3.20	MO	C	Brent Sidings – Tile Hill (as 12.30 MX) (Note b)
3.40	MO	D	Brent Sidings – Carlisle Viaduct
7.18	MSX	E	Nuneaton – Northwood
7.18	MO	E	Nuneaton – Middlewich
4.30	MO	D	Brent Sidings – Crewe
5.20		E	Brent Sidings – Northampton
8.45	SX	E	Brent Sidings – Crewe
10.0		D	Broad Street – Northampton
10.50		D	Brent Sidings – Stockport
12/35	SX	C	Brent Sidings – Northampton
1/0		C	Broad Street – Carlisle Dentonholme
3/35	SX	C	Northampton – Carlisle
2/18	SX	C	Camden – Glasgow Buchanan Street
2/45	SX	C	Brent Sidings – Crewe
3/05	TthSO	D	Stonebridge Park – Toton (coal hopper empties)
3/15	SO	C	Brent Sidings – Crewe
4/25	SO	D	Camden – Walsall
4/55	SO	C	Camden – Manchester
9/10	SX	D	Brent Sidings – Hooton (Wirral)
9/20	SX	D	Camden – Manchester
9/25	SO	D	Camden – Carlisle Kingmoor
9/28	SX	D	Camden – Crewe
9/45	SXQ	D	Camden – Hillhouse (Huddersfield)
9/55	SX	D	Camden – Warrington
10/20	SX	C	Broad Street – Stockport
10/15	SX	C	Brent Sidings – Carlisle Viaduct
10/15	SO	C	Brent Sidings – Crewe
10/25	SX	D	Camden – Nuneaton
10/50	SX	D	Camden – Curzon Street
11/20	SX	E	Camden – Northampton
Postal			
8/30		A	Euston – Glasgow/Aberdeen

Time	Day(s) run	Class	Train
newspapers			
1.37		A	Euston – Wolverhampton
2.15		A	Euston – Northampton
7/30	SO	A	Euston – Lairg
10/15	SO	A	Euston – Manchester
Parcels (ex-Marylebone Goods joined route at Bletchley)			
1.10	MX	C	Crewe (Rep 237)
3.0		C	Crewe (Rep 459)
9/05	FO	C	Preston
9/45	FSX	C	Preston

Notes
a. diverted at Nuneaton to take Midland Division route to Carlisle
b. worked by Eastern Region type 2 diesels in pairs with LM pilotman

The early planning for goods services between London and Manchester/Liverpool had envisaged the use of the former Great Central route via Bletchley, Calvert, Nottingham, Sheffield and Guide Bridge or Mottram where a change of locomotive (electric traction over the Pennines) would be necessary, alternatively or additionally via the Midland main line particularly south of Nuneaton via Wigston to Cricklewood thence to Willesden/Brent Sidings/

Below and opposite: *At the same location as in photograph 69 on page 183 early prototype diesel 10001 has passed Stonebridge Park power station, Willesden. Opposite are two more pictures; one Euston bound with Princess Arthur of Connaught and the other is City of Coventry on the northbound Shamrock (70-72).*

Camden and between Nuneaton and Stockport via Wigston, Burton, Tutbury and the Churnet Valley line. Use of alternative routes would inevitably disturb long-standing arrangements at motive power depots and, for that reason, were something of an anathema to trade unions at local and Regional level. Use of the former Great Central line would require co-operation of the Eastern Region for the partial use of capacity on the heavily used electrified section and naturally that Region sought to protect its own revenue earning, originating traffic. South of Heath (near Chesterfield) the former GC route was the responsibility of the LM Region. For protectionist reasons when the GC line was built it had no connections of potential use for north-west to London flows except at Calvert. The solution that was arrived at was possible because of the phasing of the electrification work and used the same diversionary routes as

for passenger trains (the North Staffordshire route via Stoke-on-Trent, the West Midlands loop and the Northampton loop) plus some diversions via the Midland main line and Churnet Valley using either pilotmen or route learning. Nuneaton men, for example, learned the route via the Churnet Valley. Rearrangements for motive power are covered later in this chapter. Some of the workings were unbalanced with train crews going 'home' on the next available service. For one Nuneaton turn there was no convenient passenger service, but a parcels train was unofficially available even though not booked to stop at Nuneaton; by arrangement the driver of the train would slow just sufficiently to allow train crew to jump/step off. The former Great Central route did see some later use for sleeping car trains diverted either throughout via Sheffield (Manchester service) or in part south of Bletchley to and from Marylebone.

During the course of the Winter Timetable the increasing dominance of the EE type 4 diesels on express passenger trains was strengthened marginally by use of new BR/Sulzer type 4s of 2,500hp then emerging new from Crewe Works. The level of consistent dominance was, however, challenged firstly by erratic levels of availability due to failures of, in particular, train heating boilers and secondly by some adherence to multi day locomotive diagrams. If, for example, a locomotive failed on day two of its four-day cyclic working it may have been the case that its substitute would complete the diagram. For those two reasons, planned and actual utilisation differed from week to week and steam classes 7P, 7MT and 8P Princess Coronations could appear. Although Edge Hill Princess Royal Class locomotives were used on occasions in late 1960 on Liverpool-Glasgow trains, they were not favoured for the wider diagram involving Manchester as they were banned between Euxton Junction and Bolton. No such restriction applied to the Britannias and, when Newton Heath received a pair on loan (70014/5), they soon found themselves taking the air of the Clyde Valley. The lightweight (eight carriages) *Royal Scot* and *The Caledonian* services continued with 8P haulage until 30 January 1961 when the latter changed to EE type 4 haulage in each direction. The Polmadie based locomotive that worked through on the Up *Royal Scot* went north the following morning with the 9.50 Euston-Perth. The third of the three daytime London-Glasgow services (at or over seven hours, twenty-five minutes they could hardly be described as flyers), *The Mid-Day Scot*, was strengthened and had a stop inserted at Crewe. With a carriage off the 8.0 from Plymouth attached, this regularly also had a change of locomotive for a 420-ton train timed to complete the journey in seven and three-quarter hours. With such weights came an opportunity to evaluate in service conditions the relative merits of the two builds of type 4 diesels and the effect of the extra 500hp of the BR/Sulzer type. In fact, the duration of any comparisons was limited by increasing demands from the Midland Division for replacements for pairs of Metrovick 1,200hp locomotives that were awaiting modifications and an emerging Regional concern that investigation of faults of EE type 4s and BR/Sulzer type 4s could lead to two varying solutions for the same type of fault. Locomotive drivers on top link duties tended to be the older men who received basic training, but whom even with the best will in the world were not electrical technicians and not equipped for maintenance 'on the road'. Failures in traffic with steam were straightforward, with the crew of the failed locomotive taking forward the replacement; with a diesel failure the odds were that the nearest depot to the failure would have no-one trained and available to remove and stable the failed locomotive, causing more delay.

The Birmingham-Manchester passenger services were also increasingly given over to the EE type 4s and the same type began to appear on the Birmingham-Glasgow services.

As the winter months and therefore the steam heating season was drawing to a close, eleven of the dozen Princess Royal Class locomotives were placed into storage, serviceable and the final one (46204) followed in May, someone presumably having noticed that a dozen new EE type 4s had been accepted into traffic thus far during 1961 (D315 – 7/9/20/8/9/30/4-7) and the Ministry may be watching. If it was not, the accountants certainly were.

The commercial policy of the LM Region, with its daytime London-Glasgow trains, was difficult to understand. It could not compete with the Eastern and North Eastern Region services along the east coast route with the soon to be introduced 3,300hp Deltics, but seemed unwilling to place a higher seating capacity above the timings for lightweight and still steam hauled trains. It would seem to provide further evidence of a lack of faith in 2,000hp diesels to work heavy trains and a position that changed only as experience was gained. The operating authorities had no such crisis of faith in placing class 8Ps on trains such as the important perishable goods and milk traffic.

The sporting fixtures of the spring failed to produce much excitement except for the then expected parade of Bulleid pacifics between Wembley and Watford. The FA Cup Final was between Leicester City and Tottenham Hotspur with some specials from Leicester taking the Market Harborough and Northampton route to join the main line at Roade. A Rugby League Challenge Cup Final involving St Helens and Wigan brought a succession of trains but, with nothing exceptional hauling them. Perhaps sensing that their team was a relatively weak one, there were fewer supporters of Scotland to witness the 9-3 defeat by a very strong England football team.

The Summer Timetable brought the benefits of work completed and from experience gained over the recent years of operating. The sacrosanct timing position of Crewe meant that the changes were mainly reversions to former departure times and closer to former arrival times; 10 minutes for departures and between 10 and 20 minutes for arrivals. The *Royal Scot* and *The Caledonian* each benefited with improved timings of seven hours northbound and an extra five minutes southbound. Both Manchester and Liverpool also benefited with the morning trains aimed at businessmen re-timed to give arrivals at 11.51 and noon respectively and southbound arrival into Euston at 11.49. The boat train services to both Heysham and Holyhead also showed similar savings in time and made connections a little more comfortable. The seasonal services followed a pattern very similar to that for 1959 and 1960.

New words were appearing in the press and increasingly in family conversations; Ford Anglia, Mini, Vauxhall Viva, Hillman Minx and, particularly, Morris Minor, of which one million had been produced by the end of 1961. For the businessmen, Rover offered a range of alternatives to what had been a deteriorating level of service on the railways and, for the time conscious, British European Airways had developed a London-Glasgow service with Vanguard aircraft that saved long distance railway travel. Well-heeled travellers with alternatives available were being lost to the LM and Scottish Regions; between January and May 1961 the number of journeys in first-class was 11.7 per cent and 20.9 per cent less than for the equivalent period in 1960. The number of families that owned a car was increasing and, at that time, represented some 22 per cent of all families. Ownership of a car brought more choice and freedom, the development of a new network of roads encouraged greater use. For the main railway line from Euston to Carlisle, the threat to patronage (both passenger and merchandise) was visible from glimpses of the M1 opened to Rugby near Watford Gap. The extension of the M1 and the new M6 would reach Preston in 1963 and Lancaster in 1965. The Ministry of Transport was, of course, well aware of these threats to the position of the railways and the need to reshape the industry for a future role.

In terms of motive power, it was a year full of interest and considerable change. New diesel and electric locomotives were received; twenty-six EE type 4s (twenty-three of which arrived before the end of May) and twenty-three electric locomotives. New electric multiple units were received in readiness for the public opening of the electrified Liverpool-Crewe section on 1 January 1962, with new maintenance facilities at Allerton (Liverpool) and Crewe. Twenty-two of the new diesel locomotives were delivered mainly before the start of the Summer Timetable, while the electric locomotives from the various builders were spread through the year – a dozen prior to the start of the Summer Timetable.

As already noted, all of the *Princess Royal* Class locomotives had been placed into store and it was a surprise when, in June and July, nine of them were returned to traffic for at least the summer seasonal traffic. The three that remained in store were 46201/10/2 with the final two listed condemned in the October together with 46204/5/7/11. To withdraw half of the Class with the other half to follow in 1962 seemed an arbitrary decision and the reasons why the particular half was selected were unclear.

Number	Built	Last boiler change	Last Heavy General	Last overhaul
46200	1933	Jan 60	Jan 60	Jan 60
46201	1933	Apr 60	Apr 60	Apr 60
46203	1935	1958	Aug 58	HI Feb 61
46204	1935	1955	Jy 55	HC Nov 60
46205	1935	1958	Oct 58	LC Oct 60
46206	1935	1958	Mar 58	LC Jan 61
46207	1935	1958	May 58	LC Feb 61
46208	1935	1960	Jan 60	LC Dec 60
46209	1935	1958	Dec 58	LI Feb 61
46210	1935	1958	Mar 58	HI Nov 60
46211	1935	1958	Sep 58	LC Oct 60
46212	1935	1960	Jan 60	Jan 60

Notes

HI Heavy intermediate repair HC Heavy casual repair
LI Light intermediate repair LC Light casual repair

The mileages recorded for each locomotive as at 31 Dec 1960 showed no great variation; 46204 was the lowest and 46209 the highest. 46208 was placed back into store on 30 August and was followed in the first few days of September by 46200/3/6/9. 46201 was the subject of a potential private purchase and remained in store until late January 1962 when the other five were also returned to revenue earning service.

Based on the table, the only clear case for early withdrawal was 46204 with 46200/1/8/12 having a reasonable chance of another two years on reduced annual mileages before becoming due for another heavy repair. The reason why 46204/10-12 were condemned may have been due to them being the four fitted with boilers not having combustion chambers. 46205/7 may have been selected upon the basis that they were allocated to work from Willesden depot/yard where their wheelbase was not at all well suited to the track geometry.

The way in which the operations and mechanical engineering departments were working is evident from the granting of only 'light' repairs in response to Shopping Proposals and the same approach was adopted later for the Princess Coronation Class. In 1959 and 1960, a total of eleven Heavy General or General Repairs were granted; for 1961 it was nine and five in

1962 (the final year in which such levels of repairs were undertaken). For mid-August 1961 the number of Princess Coronation Class locomotives in Crewe Works was six (46221/5/33/8/9/41) and, therefore, a total of forty-one class 8Ps was potentially available for service (plus 71000 if available), 74 EE type 4 diesels and a handful of BR/Sulzer type 4s. The Division was persisting with a policy of either steam or diesel and, consequently, the average mileages achieved by the latter frequently were equivalent to a Manchester-Euston or Liverpool-Euston round trip in 24 hours with long, steam-era layovers at depots; 380-400 miles a day was not what modernisation and capital investment was intended to deliver. Two years following introduction, Edge Hill had an allocation of fifteen EE type 4s (plus one BR/Sulzer) for which it had ten diagrams in the Western Division; two three-day diagrams, (three locomotives) and one four-day diagram (four locomotives). A typical three-day diagram involved (day one) Liverpool-Euston, Euston-Manchester, (day two) Manchester-Euston, Euston-Birmingham, Birmingham-Crewe and (day three) Crewe-Euston and Euston-Liverpool. The total mileage was some 1,100 and hours in traffic twenty-three. That was a very poor advert for modernisation and investment; it was also repeated elsewhere. Two more diesels were assigned to work on diagrams taking them to Newcastle to give work for twelve of the sixteen diesels, or 75 per cent available. There was no single major problem with the newly introduced total fleet of BTC diesel electric locomotives. The causes of poor availability were mechanical (75 per cent of failures) and electrical (25 per cent). Within the mechanical percentage were steam heating equipment (27 per cent), power units, superchargers and fuel systems (22 per cent) and pipework (15 per cent) and brake and air systems (10 per cent) while, for electrical faults, it was predominantly generators, traction motors, auxiliaries, cables, batteries, fire protection and the aws. During the spring, 10000/1 and 10201/2 were still around and working from Willesden but, by early summer, all but 10001 had been transferred away to Derby Works where they languished. The increasing complexities of railway operation resulted in restrictions being placed on various types being coupled together. That 10000/1 could be coupled was denoted by a red diamond marking on the nose, but neither nor both could be coupled to 10201/2 (red/white rectangle). Similar restrictions were placed on locomotives with either electro-pneumatic control (blue star) or electro-magnetic control (red circle). 10203 had, by that time, become captive to the Research Department for electric train heating, but that involvement was curtailed when early widespread introduction of electric train heating became a casualty of the investment cut backs. The number of steam class 7 4-6-0s available for front-line passenger services had been reduced by further re-allocations to the Midland Division and also to depots on the Western Lines that handled vacuum brake fitted goods traffic. A similar situation of internal re-allocations applied to some Jubilee Class 6 locomotives and, as the cascade effect continued, several Patriot class locomotives, which had not been rebuilt (45500-3/8/9/11/6/39/44) and one that had been rebuilt (45514) were condemned. Preston depot (damaged by fire in 1960) was closed in September.

During a year when the use of the various steam classes started to become blurred between express passenger and express goods, the most significant changes occurred in the spring and autumn. In March, Carlisle Kingmoor received nine class 8Ps, two of which were the Princess Royals latterly at Polmadie (46201/10), for which Princess Coronations 46242/9 were replacements; the other 8Ps to Kingmoor were 46221/6/37/44/52/5/7. The arrival of these locomotives further reduced the call upon the Clans also allocated and they then saw less of Perth and more of Dumfries and Kilmarnock. At the same time 46229/41/3 went to Edge Hill partly to replace the stored 46203/8/11 and the soon to be stored 46204 and because two of the Edge Hill EE type 4 diesels were working Liverpool-Newcastle passenger trains. The big move in the autumn involved the transfer in to the Western Division of the Britannias that had gravitated to Cardiff as part of the Western Region's diesel and King Class changes. The re-allocation of the Western Region examples saw 70016/8 at Carlisle Canal depot, 70019/20/2/3 at Carlisle Kingmoor and 70024-9 at Aston, Birmingham. Other Britannias involved in this change were 70014/5/45/8/9 to Neasden and 70047 to Carlisle Kingmoor. Of these depots Aston had assumed a higher profile and its Britannias joined others of the Class that had arrived in summer (70017/31/42) and made available for vacuum fitted goods trains work plus the seasonal Sutton Coldfield – Stirling car sleeper train. If Britannias were a novelty, an ex-LNER A3 (60088) turning up having worked the car sleeper from Carlisle or Leeds to Sutton Coldfield and then the empty sleeping cars for servicing was another. Banned from the route it had taken from Wichnor Junction (near Burton), the locomotive was sent to Crewe and worked a northbound goods from there.

The cascade of 1961 had also allowed class 7 and 6 locomotives to be allocated to the depots where the principal work was goods; Willesden, Rugby, Nuneaton, Crewe South, Llandudno Junction, Warrington and Springs Branch Wigan each benefiting. Nuneaton featured strongly in the programme of diversions and for the duration had four Patriots (45533/7/41/8) and several of the very useful Stanier 2-6-0s. The Patriots gave service during the summer months, but were placed into store in October and replaced by Jubilees from Rugby.

By the end of the year, Longsight had just two class 7 locomotives and regularly used them on the middle of the day (diverted) service to St Pancras. The BR/Sulzer type 2s allocated there found employment in pairs on goods workings to London balanced by pairs working from Willesden. For unfathomable reasons, eleven Black 5s went to Holyhead and, for fathomable reasons, three Royal Scots went to Bushbury (to cover the skeletal Wolverhampton-Euston passenger and parcels jobs). However, they did not stay very long, went to Willesden and then to the Midland Division at Trafford Park and releasing two Britannias for the Western Division.

The following summary illustrates the transition of steam power allocations at principal depots as at the beginning of 1957, 1961 and 1962.

Depot	Power class	At start of		
		1957	1961	1962
Camden	6	7	1	-
	7	15	4	-
	8	15	10	4
Willesden	6	6	12	13
	7	-	4	-
Bushbury	6	10	-	-
	7	-	2	-
Aston	6	-	3	4
	7	-	-	9
Crewe North	6	20	15	21
	7	21	24	11
	8	17	15	9

Depot	Power class	At start of		
		1957	**1961**	**1962**
Longsight	6	17	5	-
	7	22	2	2
Edge Hill	6	15	16	8
	7	14	5	7
	8	6	4	5
Holyhead	6	-	-	-
	7	7	4	6
Carlisle Upperby	6	16	22	22
	7	8	5	5
	8	4	13	6
Carlisle Kingmoor	6	23	17	9
	7	-	5	5
	8	-	-	9
Polmadie	6	5	2	-
	7	10	13	8
	8	9	9	9

Names were bestowed upon D214/5/8/21/3/30/2/3; *Antonia, Aquitania, Carmania, Ivernia, Lancastria, Scythia, Empress of Canada* and *Empress of England* respectively.

Starting from D325, the EE type 4s were fitted with display panels on either side of each nose end (later, after a decision to dispense with a ladder and connecting doors) placed centrally on each nose end. The display panel(s) enabled the train crew to indicate (by use of blinds) the four-character train description as also used in the modern signal cabins. The London Midland Region adopted the following. When looking at the front of a locomotive the first display was numeric and the second was alphabetic:

0	Light engine(s) with not more than two brake vans	A	Euston	
		B	Euston Rugby	
1	Express passenger, newspaper, or breakdown crane, snow plough, engine to assist disabled train	C	St Pancras Marylebone Manchester Central	
		D	Chester Nottingham	
2	Ordinary passenger train, breakdown crane not on duty	F	Leicester	
		G	Birmingham	
		H	Manchester South Stoke-on-Trent	
3	Parcels, fish, fruit, livestock, milk, empty coaching stock	J	Manchester North	
		K	Crewe Liverpool Lime St Liverpool Central	

4	Express goods 90 per cent vacuum brake fitted	L	Preston (excluding Fylde)
			Barrow
5	As 4, not less than 50 per cent vacuum brake fitted		Carlisle
		P	Blackpool and Fylde
			Derby
6	As 4/5, 20 per cent vacuum brake fitted and next to locomotive	*Inter-Regional trains were denoted:*	
		E	to Eastern Region
7	Express goods not brake fitted	M	to London Midland Region
		N	to North Eastern Region
8	Through goods not as 4-7	O	to Southern Region
		S	to Scottish Region
9	Pick up goods, mineral or ballast train	V	to Western Region
		Excursion and Special passenger or goods trains:	
		T	local to London Midland Region
		Z	local to London Midland Region
		X	inter-Regional

By this system, *The Mid-Day Scot* Euston-Glasgow became 1S57 and was helpful to station staff. Most depots continued with the long-standing practise of steam locomotives carrying boards on the front of the smokebox, but gradually changed from the W …. method to the four-character descriptions, particularly as new signalling displays came into use.

When the Winter Timetable was published, it became clear that many of the timing improvements of the summer could not be maintained; the engineers were re-organising locations for the start, continuation or completion of individual schemes, particularly south of Crewe. For the business communities needing to travel between London and Manchester the King's Cross-Sheffield-Pennine route again found favour and between London and Rugby there were those who made their way to and from Marylebone. The commercial policy of the day-time Anglo-Scottish expresses proved to be variable with stops at Carlisle and Preston re-inserted and *The Mid-Day Scot* in each direction remaining a 420-ton train and calling at Crewe. In mid-December a replacement ship for the Stranraer-Larne service began sailings. The *Caledonian Princess* replaced the *Princess Victoria* which had been damaged during a storm in 1953 and eventually sank with the loss of 128 lives. In the interim, the *Hampton Ferry* was redeployed from its normal route of Dover-Dunkerque. The new vessel was able to make two return sailings each day and an enhanced rail service was arranged accordingly.

A sign of increased confidence in the EE type 4s was evident in the Working Timetable of the Scottish Region. Ten weekday southbound expresses were shown as being worked by a diesel locomotive between 11 September 1961 and 17 June 1962.

Each service had a balancing Northbound working, some within cyclic diagrams and as lodging turns for the London Midland footplate crews as for steam.

During the course of the year drafting of the Transport Bill and, in parallel, Dr Beeching progressed moves and recruitment of individuals for the incoming British Railways Board. The Bill gave the Minister control over the future direction of the transport undertakings and particularly the railways. As part of the move towards more competition between forms of transport, the railways would cease to be common carriers; in other words, no longer obliged to accept and transport whatever was presented to them. A large amount of capital debt would be written off.

Acting upon Beeching's recommendations, the Minister appointed Philip Shirley (seconded from Unilever) to be the Member of the British Railways Board for Finance, Sir Steuart Mitchell (a former colleague of Dr Beeching) to oversee a re-organisation of the railway workshops and place them under central, rather than Regional, control and Leslie Williams, recently retired from Shell Chemicals. Sir Philip Warter – a part-time member of the BTC – was to be the first Deputy Chairman and would act as a 'bridge' between the old and new organisation. Beeching was sufficiently astute to recognise the need for professional railway knowledge and guidance. Initially he appointed Stanley Raymond, later Gerard Fiennes and finally Fred Margetts and it was the latter who, having adapted to the fact that the railways were becoming more of a business than a service industry, implemented the far-ranging provisions of what became known as the Beeching Plan.

For 1961 the working losses of the London Midland Region were £34.7m, an increase of £8.7m over that for the previous year. The awful combination of lower revenue (by £3.1m) and higher costs (by £5.6m) applied and was replicated by the Western and Scottish Regions. The total deficit for British Railways was £86.9m. The Minister had most of the ammunition he needed.

Chapter 9

1962: Service at a High Cost

While the London Midland Region was continuing with its electrification scheme and struggling with the transition from steam, other bodies were concentrating on the future for the entire railway network. The politicians had little difficulty in having the provisions of The Transport Act 1962 accepted by Parliament and some of those paved an easier pathway to be followed when Dr Beeching's report and recommendations became available in 1963. Dr Beeching spent much of the year on recruitment of his functional Board and in parallel others were building traffic and economic data upon which a report could be soundly based.

1962 involved Dr Beeching furthering two particular aspects of his work; raising data upon which to take decisions and make recommendations and, secondly, to recruit additional, talented management into the railway industry. Being a trained scientist, it was natural for Beeching to set out to raise empirical data, particularly so after briefing meetings with the Directors of Costings and Statistics, when he would have been made fully aware that the Annual Reports of the Commission provided the best available information. The paucity of information about the detail of the workings of the industry may have surprised him, but Beeching was not fettered by the emotionalism that seemed to characterise so much railway work and managers; rather it was a case of a cold, rational approach applied in a consistent manner as was the norm in his profession. A national traffic census pre-arranged for the April was authorised to proceed and, while the analysis of the data would be a mammoth clerical task, it would provide information which extended beyond the Regional boundaries that pervaded the accounting. Beeching was more interested in flows of traffic along routes, not why trains were shunted and locomotives and men changed at odd places along the routes. In 1955, the Railway Clearing House had largely ceased its main role of allocating costs for transits that passed through Regional or long dated boundaries; the 'originating traffic' basis from the early days of railways still irritated Regions through which trains were worked, but did not produce any income.

Beeching was content to set the menu of questions and allow time for others to respond in time with the answers; his skill was in asking the right questions. When his report was published in March 1963, the majority of the traffic information was based on 1961 and the layout of what was available followed the same approach to categories of traffic as had been stipulated by the Board of Trade in 1911. For goods traffic there the three categories; coal, coke and patent fuel, minerals (Beeching later merged these for reporting purposes), merchandise and livestock. Passenger traffic was classified as either fast and semi-fast, stopping and suburban. Similarly, track costs followed the approach as applied in the accounts. In summary the approach to that aspect of his wider brief was:

- define the nature of the railway problem
- analyse the problem
- examine the present state of the railway in terms of organisational responsibility, types
- of traffic and how the physical network was used

- analyse by types of traffic to identify their contribution to the revenue account
- having established a base of information, conduct deeper analyses to provide a basis for making rational decisions.

All of the foregoing would take much of 1962 and, in the interim, Beeching turned his attention to people and to organisation. Between October 1961 and April 1963, nearly forty senior officers were recruited from leading companies including Shell, ICI, General Electric, English Electric, Lever Brothers, Jaguar Cars and Beaverbrook Newspapers. Beeching recognised the need for, and value of, a good public relations and publicity department at headquarters to present the corporate view. An executive with experience of working for BOAC (later British Airways) and the Metal Industries Group was recruited as General Manager of BR Workshops which would involve the Regional Chief Mechanical Engineers being customers of the workshops rather than having total control of them. Unsurprisingly, cost accountancy was strengthened, as was research and marketing development; a major success of the latter being the growth of oil traffic using privately owned tanker wagons hauled by BR locomotives. That there was talent within the railway was not doubted, but it was largely confined to safe operation of a complex network within a still heavily centralised organisation working to the provisions of the Transport Act 1953. Beeching recognised the need for professional railway expertise and, for operating and rolling stock, selected Fred Margetts (who had impressed him at a conference in 1961) and John Ratter for the technical departments (mechanical and electrical engineering, civil and signal/telecoms engineering, the architects, research, new works, work study) and the Design Panel.

During the course of the year there was a significant change in the ranks of senior management and a re-organisation of Regional boundaries affecting the London Midland Region.

At the turn of the New Year Henry 'Bill' Johnson – a future Chairman of the British Railways Board – General Manager of the Eastern Region – succeeded David Blee as General Manager of the LM Region. In the gentlemanly ways of the Commission, Blee was 'asked to retire', his tenure since 1956 having been undistinguished. Many would say that he had something of a fortunate career. When the Railway Executive was formed as part of nationalisation it was natural that the former railway companies should be represented. Sir James Milne, General Manager of the Great Western Railway, declined the leadership due to closeness of retirement and two senior subordinates also declined the opportunities. That resulted in Blee becoming the youngest member of the Executive as the Member responsible for commercial matters. He had joined the Great Western Railway immediately after leaving school in 1913. Following the Transport Act 1953 the RE was abolished, but he found his way to the British Transport Commission as a member of the central staff. He was, therefore, very well placed to know the workings of the Commission and as a headquarters man involved with policy making by committees, found a sharper Regional role and a need for delegation of decision-making more difficult than perhaps would have a man who had progressed through the Regional operating hierarchy. It showed in his dislike of the line management organisation adopted by the Eastern Region and with which the Chairman of the LM Board (Sir Reginald Wilson) and Henry Johnson were well familiar and, importantly, had seen the benefits from making it work while the latter was General Manager (from 1958) and previously Assistant General Manager responsible for all (railway) traffic matters.

The decentralisation under the BTC plans was organised by the Regional Board, though with limitations placed upon the extent of the power and finance levels delegated. The opportunity to improve matters by responding to local conditions could be within the control of the Region by improving the operating and commercial management. That was what the Eastern Region became very good at unlike the London Midland. From 1956, the Eastern Region placed control over operating, commercial and motive power matters with three Line Managers, responsible in turn for the former Great Northern (King's Cross), Great Eastern (Liverpool Street) and the newly acquired London, Tilbury and Southend self-contained route. The chain of command was clear; Assistant General Manager (Traffic) to the Line Managers and in turn to Traffic Managers at District level. The Eastern Region had at that time some talented and keen managers who responded to the new-found greater freedom to make things happen. Blee had by far the largest Region, with three potential Lines similar to the Eastern (the London and North Western, the Midland and the Lancashire & Yorkshire, plus part of the Great Central) and could have adopted something very similar, but had chosen to place responsibility within headquarters with a Director of Traffic Services, making decision-making hierarchical and time-consuming. Only when Sir Reginald Wilson became Chairman of the LM Board did a change start to materialise and Line Managers were appointed. Henry Johnson supported the approach and his appointment of W. G. Thorpe (formerly Line Manager, Great Eastern lines) as Assistant General Manager (Traffic) was a demonstration of intent. However, the work of Dr Beeching and his functional Board (from 1963) limited the opportunity for much needed change to be implemented. 1956-61 was, for the LM Region, an era of lost opportunities.

From the time of nationalisation there had been a lingering dilemma over the duplication of routes; for examples London to Plymouth from both Paddington and Waterloo (Western Region/Southern Region) and London to Birmingham and Wolverhampton from both Euston and Paddington (LM Region/Western Region). The dilemma revolved around old, operational boundaries and motive power arrangements as opposed to purely geographical boundaries. The modernisation provided opportunities for change; the Southern Region lost two chunks of its previous territory including Devon and Cornwall and Dorset while the London Midland Region gained the Western Region main line (from Paddington) north of (near) Banbury through Birmingham, Wolverhampton to Shrewsbury, Aberystwyth, Pwllheli and Barmouth. After the completion of the electrification scheme linking Euston with Birmingham and Wolverhampton, there would be no need for a competing through service from Paddington and similarly north of Derby through the Peak District to Manchester. That latter route had been identified by the BTC as having only a short-term role after the completion of electrification and similar thinking was also being applied to the southern half of the former Great Central Railway main line.

When the railways were taken into public ownership in 1948, the Government established an organisation of Transport Users Consultative Committees (TUCC). These area TUCCs, of which there were eleven, each had an independent chairman and unpaid representatives (appointed by the Minister) to represent all users of public transport, including, from 1953, bus services. The functions of the Committees were wide and could 'make recommendations in regard to any matter affecting the services and facilities provided … to which consideration ought to be given …' The Committees made recommendations to the Central Transport Consultative Committee (CTCC) and the main role of that body was to receive, consider and confirm or reject the recommendations as received, and also produce an annual report.

In the first decade of service, the TUCCs investigated and agreed to the closure of just over 3,000 route miles of track and over 700 stations; the CTCC was generally supportive of the BTC and towards the end of the 1950s there were indications of a better co-ordination between rail and road services, particularly where railway services were pruned.

The Minister recognised that the administration of the anticipated recommendation of wide-scale closure of railway lines and services would sorely test the capabilities of the voluntary membership of the TUCCs and would cause delays while objections were heard and recommendations made. In recognition that a lack of good, accurate corporate traffic and route costing data was something that neither he, Dr Beeching nor anyone else had or would have, the Minister made provision in the Transport Act 1962 for a change to the basis upon which objections to a closure could be considered. There would be no question of objections on the basis of profitability of individual lines or sections of routes; the only basis for an objection would be 'hardship'.

The dovetailing of the Act of 1962 and the (Beeching) Report of 1963 was a masterpiece; a perfect 'stitch up'. In the latter document was stated:

'It would be folly to suggest that widespread closure of stopping train services will cause no hardship anywhere or to anybody and the Transport Act 1962 makes the consideration of hardship the special responsibility of the TUCC where objections to closures are lodged. For the purposes of judging the closure proposals as a whole, however, it is necessary to have some idea of the scale and degree of hardship which they are likely to cause'.

The paragraph then referred to bus services and concluded that 'in most of the country, therefore, it appears that hardship will arise on only a very limited scale'. The well briefed Public Relations and Publicity Department then prepared 'standard' letters of reply stating that what mattered was the 'overall position'. As an exercise in emasculation it was exceptionally good.

The Transport Act 1962 received Royal Assent on 1 August 1962. The political and statutory machinery for change was in place, the organisation was being put in place; the missing piece was the report (of March 1963) of the findings of the studies undertaken, the consideration of the data and the recommendations made.

The introduction of electrically worked passenger services along the 36 route miles section between Liverpool Lime Street and Crewe was in two stages; from 1 January 1962 for some locomotive hauled trains and from 18 June a full service involving new electric multiple units on stopping services. Although, like the Manchester-Crewe section (30 route miles) it was short in terms of route miles, the number of track miles involved was 154 and included the replacement of twenty-seven signal boxes by sixteen and the use of colour light signalling. New and/or improved stations better served the urban population of greater Liverpool (Mossley Hill, Allerton, Ditton, West Allerton and Runcorn) and communities on the main line south of Weaver Junction (near milepost 176) at Acton Bridge, Hartford and Winsford. From 18 June there were timing improvements of up to 15 minutes. With the exception of expresses not booked to stop at Crewe, all Liverpool services had a change of traction at that station.

In the vicinity of Crewe, attention had been more directed towards the task of electrifying the 22 track miles of Basford Hall sidings and the installation of a new chord line to allow easier access for traffic from Stoke-on-Trent. The smaller concentration of sidings and facilities around Gresty Lane had been dealt with during 1961 and, by use of the tunnel under the main line at the north end of the station, had enabled goods traffic from/to Manchester to be worked by electric locomotives.

From Crewe to Euston via the Trent Valley route (Stafford-Tamworth-Rugby) it is 158 miles and, as previously described, the essential, preparatory engineering tasks of drainage, digging out through tunnels, raising or eliminating overbridges, track remodelling, signalling, catenary support structures, wiring and testing were conducted as resources and timetable planning dictated. There were, therefore, sections where progress was physically more advanced than others to one or both ends of them. Colour light signalling between Lichfield and Nuneaton was put into use over the weekend of 3-5 November.

The next big target was to enable electrically worked services to reach Stafford (milepost 133) at the year-end (services started 7 January 1963), 25 miles south of Crewe. That section included the complex Basford Hall sidings, major alterations at Norton Bridge (milepost 139) and other track improvements at Betley Road (156), Madeley (149), Badnall Wharf (141¼) and Great Bridgeford (136¾) with closure of six signal boxes. The section between Betley Road and Milford & Brocton (on the Trent Valley route south of Stafford, milepost 131¾) was energised from 26 November. Significantly for certain classes of steam locomotives, the maximum clearance between track and overhead wires was 13ft 1in.

While that work was being progressed, teams were able to complete the signalling and overhead wiring (though not operational) for sections of the Trent Valley including also the rebuilding of the Down side station facilities at Tamworth. The rather depressing, corporate style of station was by then evident at intermediate stations between Liverpool, Manchester and Tamworth (and remains so today). Although seemingly well advanced, the 51-mile Stafford-Rugby section was not at that time expected to be energised before December 1964.

Just as track remodelling had been undertaken at Basford Hall and Norton Bridge to reduce conflicting movements of trains across multiple tracks, a similar, though greater in scale, requirement existed just north of Rugby (milepost 83½). At that point traffic from or to Coventry, Birmingham and Wolverhampton (the West Midlands loop) joined or left and southbound traffic had to cross the main line. The solution was a flyover bridge which eliminated the flat junction and significantly increased track capacity on the main lines north to south. The flyover was available from 17 September 1962. It would seem that Nuneaton – where conflicting movements were also prevalent – was a casualty of the cost cutting exercise of 1960/61 – this was not corrected until some 30 years later.

Planning for the final 82 miles from Rugby to Euston involved a revision of plans for the signalling to be in five control sections (Rugby-Castlethorpe/Wolverton, Wolverton-Cheddington/Tring, Tring-Watford-Kenton, Kenton-Willesden-Mitre Bridge Junction, Mitre Bridge Junction-Euston) and for the reconstruction of Euston station.

As consequences of electrification, there would be no possibility of a continuation of high-speed collection of mail by the Travelling Post Office (leading to an enhancement of the role of Tamworth) and little need for water troughs (which were progressively removed).

High speed collection of mail was one thing, high speed collection of electricity by locomotive pantographs was another. On 27 October, train IV98 (the 3/05 Manchester Piccadilly-Plymouth) was worked between Manchester and Crewe by two electric locomotives, both of which were drawing energy. A fault with the pantograph of the pilot locomotive caused part of it to break free, bounce along the roof, dislodge part of the pantograph of the train locomotive, bring down the overhead wires for three quarters of a mile and, with the components of the pantographs breaking several windows in the leading three carriages.

In such circumstances, the availability of the alternative route (for Birmingham and London services) via Macclesfield and Stoke-on-Trent to Norton Bridge and Colwich was extremely valuable. A long-term engineering problem along that route (and which inhibited the use of ex LMS pacific locomotives) were the tunnels at Harecastle. Although the North Staffordshire route was not to be electrified until later in the overall scheme, the planning involved a closure of the tunnels and a new replacement deviation.

The most interesting sports related matter was over the weekend of 30 March-1 April. Involved were the Grand National steeplechase at Aintree, Liverpool and, on the same day, the semi-final matches of the FA Cup competition at Villa Park, Birmingham and Hillsborough, Sheffield. Adding to the interest was a dock strike at Liverpool that disturbed arrangements for shipping and connecting services.

Grand National day formed the Saturday highlight of the annual spring meeting at Aintree and attracted tens of thousands of spectators from far and wide. Special trains were run from both St Pancras and Euston; from the latter, five specials with full catering were advertised and marshalled ready during the Friday. The on-off nature of the dock strike was such that the trains from Euston on the Friday for the *Caledonia* (sailing to Bombay) and *Ivernia* (sailing to Montreal) had run on the basis that passengers could take up their cabins and the trainsets could await the arrival of the *Sylvania* (inbound from New York early on the Saturday) and bring to London any passengers. During the Friday it became clear that the *Sylvania* was unlikely to be able to dock at Liverpool and Cunard Line diverted it to Tilbury, London where the tide dictated a very early arrival. Cunard Line requested connecting train services for passengers and crew to reach Liverpool. Tilbury Docks were served from St Pancras and the sets of carriages were suitable only for journeys of short duration and also lacked catering facilities. It was a problem for the Midland Division to sort out during the night and, with the Western Division unwilling to disturb its five specials for Aintree traffic, did so by utilisation of specials, marshalled with catering, to take supporters of Tottenham Hotspur to Sheffield. So, during the early hours, Midland Division trainsets were routed from Tilbury to gain the Euston main line at Willesden and the Eastern Region prepared sets and locomotives for football trains from King's Cross. At least on night shift things got done far more efficiently than when tiers of 'management' had to be consulted.

On the Saturday morning, five class 7 hauled specials left for Aintree (45529, 46126/7/46/59) and, later that morning, three more class 7s (70021/32/3) took supporters of Fulham to Witton (for Aston Villa's ground nearby). Tottenham Hotspur and Burnley triumphed in the semi-final matches and, for the final itself on 6 May 1962, the small town of Burnley became deserted and nine specials were run to Wembley. Motive power was provided by the Midland and Central Divisions in the form of Royal Scots 46100/12/30/42, plus Jubilees 45552/615/705 and two pairs of Black 5s.

The Rugby League Challenge Final was on 13 May 1962 and involved Huddersfield and Wakefield Trinity and, as such, did not unduly trouble the operators along our lines of interest. There were two special trains of note. Each year the Creative Travel Agents Conference was held and involved the running of a special train for delegates. Two carriages were taken from Walsall to Preston for attachment and, up to 1961, it had been a job for a 4-4-0, latterly 40646. In 1962 the 'train' was worked by a Royal Scot. The second special was to commemorate the passing of steam locomotives from Anglo-Scottish services. The train ran from King's Cross to

Aberdeen and returned from there on day two to Euston. The locomotives used for the return leg included Princess Royal 46200 (3 June 1962).

The Summer Timetable included the benefits that accrued from the completion of electrification work between Manchester/Liverpool and Crewe, but the allowances to the south thereof remained and at times proved to be excessive. The length of individual allowances varied due to the planned work within a section for the period of each timetable with, for example, large margins for say Norton Bridge to Colwich Junction including Stafford which would be needed and several allowances for speed restrictions between Stafford and Tamworth which may have proven to be temporary. For long distance trains, Crewe remained the fulcrum for timing. Any lingering Regional thoughts of competing with the East Coast route for journey times to Scotland were lost as up to 155 minutes were allowed for the 141 miles between Crewe and Carlisle. The long-distance, non-stopping England-Scotland services were becoming very rare; stops were inserted at Preston and Stafford for *The Caledonian* and at Wigan North Western for *The Mid-Day Scot* in the Up direction. Bigger changes were, though, planned for the Winter Timetable as more possessions of track were planned for nights and due to the start of preparatory works for the reconstruction of Euston Station. For many travellers the unpalatable result was that, from 10 September, some Manchester services would be cancelled and some others diverted to start/terminate at Marylebone or St Pancras. Services cancelled included *The Comet* business train in each direction, *The Lancastrian* in the Up direction and the (latterly diverted via the North Staffordshire/Midland Lines routes) 12/10 from Manchester and 1.0 and 1/55 St Pancras-Manchester services. Services to be diverted (actually started from November, not September) were the sleeping car services from/to Manchester and Liverpool plus two from Glasgow (all used Marylebone and the Calvert/Bletchley route into and from London), while the Workington/Barrow service was routed from Nuneaton to Wigston (south of Leicester) and the Midland main line to St Pancras. Of the London services that remained from Manchester Piccadilly the 8.0, with calls at Stockport and Alderley Edge, was due into Euston at 11.45 and provided an alternative to the *Midland Pullman* (7.45 called at Cheadle Heath and was due into St Pancras at 10.55). The corresponding morning business train from Euston (*The Lancastrian*) did not fare so well and took just under four hours (via Crewe where the Liverpool portion was detached). Benefiting from a higher availability of 2,500hp diesels, the Midland Lines route offered ten Down direction and eleven Up direction Manchester services (an increase of three/four respectively) at an average journey time of three hours and forty-eight minutes, the fastest taking 13 minutes less by a combination of train weight, XL timings and avoidance of a stop at Derby (six trains including the *Midland Pullman* using the Chaddesden-Spondon cut off).

More parcels work was transferred from Euston to Marylebone and, with the increasing restrictions on fast, overnight services to Scotland, the LM Region saw its market share damaged as British European Airways used more of the load capacity of its Vanguard aircraft to offer a parcels service between London and Glasgow overnight.

Motive power continued to provide a great amount of interest, partly due to the Line Managers seeking access to the most appropriate power for the services for which they then carried additional responsibility. Of the six Princess Royals that survived 1961 (46200/1/3/6/8/9), all were in store at the turn of the new year; 46201 having been in store since March 1961 and the subject of potential interest to a private buyer and the other five since the end of August/early September. However, all six re-emerged into revenue earning traffic from January 1962 at a time when the EE type 4s were achieving low levels of availability and, despite greater attention being paid to maintenance of steam heat boilers, reliability in regularly completing diagrams.

Whatever the reasons, the fact remains that early in the new year 1962, class 8P power was in demand to maintain express passenger services and to find return workings on either passenger, parcels or perishable traffic. Extracts from the control log at Preston for 21-31 January show 30 trains with either Princess Royals, Princess Coronations or *Duke of Gloucester* (71000). I have included the list here rather than as an appendix to highlight the regularity of certain trains being steam and also the use of Polmadie locomotives south of Carlisle.

Date (January)	Locomotive	Depot	Train
21	46232	66A	3L09 Willesden – Clsle (pcls)
22	46220	12B	1A33 8.40 Clsle – Eus
	46238	12B	1S81 1/05 Eus – Perth
	46239	1B	1L22 10.25 Eus – Clsle
23	46251	5A	3 ... Down, banana spl
	46234	12B	1581 1/05 Eus – Perth
24	46225	12B	1581 1/05 Eus – Perth
25	46251	5A	2K12 6/45 Crewe – Clsle
26	46227	66A	1M24 10.15 Glgw – B'ham
27	46223	66A	3L06 10.23 Mon L – Clsle
	46220	12B	3207 9.55 Willes – Clsle
28	46203	12B	3L09 10.20 Crewe – Clsle
29	46224	66A	1L98 Willes – Clsle (milk)
	46250	12B	1561 11.15 B'ham – Glgw
	46253	5A	1M24 10.15 Glgw – B'ham
	46227	66A	1M37 9.0 Perth – Eus
	(45632)	12B	1581 1/05 Eus – Perth
30	46201	12B	3L09 10.20 Crewe – Clsle
	46209	1B	4 ... 3/30 Clsle – Crewe
	46232	66A	1M24 10.15 Glgw – B'ham
	46227	66A	1S63 9.50 Eus – Perth
	46240	1B	1L98 Willes – Clsle
	46244	12A	3L14 Crewe – Clsle
31	71000	5A	3L06 10.23 Mon L – Clsle
	46230	66A	3L09 10.20 Crewe – Clsle
	46227	66A	1M24 10.15 Glgw – B'ham
	46203	12B	1A ... 3/30 Clsle – Willes (milk)
	46250	12B	1581 1/05 Eus - Perth

Note
Mon L Monument Lane, Birmingham
(45632) class 6 *Jubilee*

In January 1962 misfortune befell 46238 in the form of a dangerous situation that arose with the low level of water in the boiler. When the level of water failed to cover the crown sheet (as the roof of the inner firebox) it was ripped away from the crown stays that 'bridged' the space to the outer firebox wrapper. It was only the third such incident with the Class (the other two both involved 46224 and one occurred during war-time) and, as a result of the first two, an additional fusible plug had been placed at a high level on the backhead to give the footplate staff some warning of a fast developing, dangerous situation. After lengthy deliberations, 46238 was granted a Heavy Casual repair during which it received a replacement boiler and was returned to traffic in mid-June.

For the major part of 1962, the route had available forty-five class 8 passenger locomotives (still, but only just, including 71000) plus sixty-six class 7s. Given that a further 13 EE type 4s were delivered prior to 21 April (and six electrics during the same spell) and took the Region's total of that type to 100, that gave a front-line fleet of 211 steam and diesel locomotives (excluding 10001). A reflective look at the position at the start of 1957 shows a total of 148 class 8s and 7s plus the five BR diesels and the on-trial *Deltics*. As the volume of passenger traffic to be worked was largely unaltered (electrification and reduction of Wolverhampton/ Birmingham as against increase in Anglo-Scottish services) some serious questions needed to be asked in regard to the 'return' on the capital investment of £9m worth of diesel power (purchase plus maintenance facilities).

On the surface, it was difficult to understand why the working of the diesels was so erratic, particularly as other Regions seemed to be making a better job of it in similar operational circumstances. Just beneath the surface was a combination of factors that probably answered most of the questions; the lack of a standard MP11 type approach to maintenance, the temperamental nature of steam heating boilers, a tendency to return diesels with faults to their home shed for attention, the difficulty at a time of high economic activity to attract and retain technicians in what was still a dirty, working environment with unsocial hours, failures occurring within steam era cyclic diagrams leading to the remaining legs of the diagram being lost, the wrangling with English Electric as the end of the 12 month period of contractor responsibility for manufacturing/construction faults leading to formal assessments and, finally, the position of the Scottish Region.

For Anglo-Scottish workings, most trains changed locomotives at the Regional boundary station of Carlisle; the power from north of the border being predominantly Polmadie and Perth. There were exceptions; the long-standing through workings of Crewe locomotives to Perth and also to Glasgow, a Newton Heath locomotive to Glasgow, the more recent through workings between Glasgow and London and the balancing working with Newton Heath. When the EE type 4s were introduced as a production batch (D210-36) they went to the London Midland Region. The first of the type delivered to the Scottish Region arrived in early 1960 (D256-64) then followed by two more in the spring (D265/6) and all allocated to Edinburgh Haymarket. Training of enginemen and maintenance staff was then concentrated on Haymarket and other principal depots on the eastern side of Scotland which the locomotive would visit. *The Royal Highlander* was worked by a Crewe North locomotive through to either Perth (steam) or Inverness (diesel). The Scottish Region changed the arrangement to apply with a diesel and, instead of working through to Inverness and standing idle for nine hours, substituted the following:

Perth arrive 4.33 to depot
Perth depart 9.0 to Carlisle, arrive 12/49
Carlisle depart 1/41 to Perth, arrive 5/20 to depot
Perth depart 9/50 to Crewe, arrive 4.50
Round trip Crewe to Crewe 672 miles over 31 hours

Weight of train ex-Crewe and back to Crewe 300 tons tare
(270 from Motherwell northbound, 270 to Motherwell southbound)
Weight of 9.0 Perth – Carlisle 330 tons tare
Weight of 1/41 Carlisle – Perth 180 tons tare

Unlike the London Midland Region Western Division, the Scottish Region had a wide
variety of pilot and production order diesels to accept and for which to arrange training;
the problematic North British units and the Birmingham Railway Carriage & Wagon (both
type 2s) as well as diesel hydraulic and diesel mechanical shunting locomotives. The
Scottish Region was more interested in training staff for the BR/Sulzer type 4s as they could
see advantages from through workings from Edinburgh to Leeds via the Waverley route
(Hawick) to Carlisle and from Glasgow to Leeds via the Glasgow and South Western route
(Kilmarnock/Dumfries) to Carlisle. In the case of the latter, it was the men of Corkerhill
depot who were trained. With the production build of the Deltic Class approaching and
involving six hour expresses to London crossing three Regional boundaries, the needs
of Polmadie were not paramount. Some Polmadie men had received training on diesels,
but only the Metrovick class for the *Condor* fast goods service as far as Carlisle via the
Caledonian Railway route (Beattock).

Having London Midland Region EE type 4s 'sit down' north of the border caused problems
of crewing and the use of a pilotman for diesel trained, but not route trained, Carlisle men sent
to recover a disgraced machine. When the Scottish Region became more involved with the
use of diesels north of Carlisle, they did something with a lot more intent and conviction than
had been the case south of Carlisle; they conducted tests involving examples of the 2,000hp
EE type and the 2,500hp BR/Sulzer type with varying weights of trains between 400 and 500
tons. The route selected was the demanding one via Hawick, southbound, involving lengthy
adverse gradients of 1 in 70 for 7½ miles (Hardengreen Junction to Falahill) and 1 in 75-123
for 11 miles (Hawick to Whitrope). EE D264 took trains of 400 tons and 420 tons (12/13
carriages) and D153 took 450/500 tons (14/15 carriages). On the two trains worked by D264,
the first arrived eight minutes early, the second one minute late; D153 right time and four
minutes early.

Quite what was the basis of the London Midland Region's fixation that an EE type 4 was
the equivalent of a class 7 and its lack of conviction to work the locomotives more intensively
is an unknown to me. What does seem clear to me is that any consideration of route planning
foundered somewhere along Hadrian's Wall and the two Regions went about their business in
their own different ways.

All thirty-eight of the Princess Coronations had started the year as being available for traffic.
Three casualties were 46227/31/2, all of Polmadie and, following periods in store, withdrawn
at the end of 1962. Other locomotives in the Class were placed into store as follows:

	From	To		From	To
46221	29 Oct	26 Jan 63	46241	5 Nov	26 Jan 63
46230	3 Dec	29 Dec 62	46243	5 Nov	26 Jan 63
46233	6 Oct	26 Jan 63	46246	5 Nov	26 Jan 63
46234	8 Oct	26 Jan 63	46248	6 Nov	7 Dec 62
46235	6 Nov	3 Jan 63	46251	6 Nov	6 Dec 62

	From	**To**		**From**	**To**
46237	29 Oct	26 Jan 63	46253	3 Oct	26 Jan 63
46239	11 Nov	8 Dec 62	46254	3 Oct	3 Jan 63
46240	18 Nov	8 Dec 62	46256	21 Oct	20 Jan 63

Of the locomotives stored, 46230 had received a General repair in 1962 (with no replacement boiler fitted) and 46221/35/43/54 had replacement boilers fitted during 1961.

1960	**1961**	**1962**	**1963**
46220	46221	46220	Nil
46223	46225	46224	
46226	46227	46236	
46230	46235		
46232	46243		
46251	46250		
46252	46254		
46253			

Note: six other members of the Class had Heavy repairs in 160, nine in 1961 and 5/6 in 1962. 46238 had a replacement boiler fitted in 1962 as part of a Heavy Casual repair.

Following an unfortunate failure of a diesel locomotive while hauling the Royal Train on the Eastern Region, the London Midland Region took no such chances for the Queen's visit to Liverpool in mid-December. 46248 was taken out of store at Crewe and given the attention it deserved before taking the train to and from Liverpool. Following the overnight stop, 46220 was used for the short journey into Lime Street station on the 15th and 46248 worked the train back to Watford Junction where the royal party alighted.

Four of the Princess Royal Class (46201/3/6/9) had worked through the year until the September and one until November (46200), at which times all five were placed back into store prior to final withdrawal in October/November respectively. The final one (46208) was available for traffic until withdrawal in the October. All were shown as nearly fully depreciated in the accounting records, having given a quarter of a century of service.

There were three other areas of interest involving diesels. The pilot order of ten BR/Sulzer type 4s, 2,300hp was returned in the spring to the Midland Lines and, following removal of the train heating boilers, all were concentrated upon Toton (between Nottingham and Derby) for working coal and mineral trains. All but one of the 20 Metrovick 1,200hp diesels – another pilot – were transferred to Barrow with the final one (D5719) expected to follow. Finally, English Electric had responded to the noises coming out of Euston that 2,000hp was insufficient and 2,700hp would be better. The result was *DP2*, a 107-ton Co-Co which followed in the commercial footsteps of *Deltic* and remained in private ownership, but was made available as a demonstration of a type that could be produced. *DP2* was an outstanding success and was run on 600 miles/day diagrams for each weekday (Euston-Carlisle and return) and was made available for maintenance on Sundays (at Camden). Confidence in the machine was so high

Ex-works Royal Scot British Legion *and apart perhaps from one or two boiler washout plugs needing tightening is ready for duty. Modellers, note the style of steam pipes unique to this locomotive, the different arrangement of the aws battery box and air reservoir tank as compared to picture 70. The placement of the electrification flashes complies with the BR drawing. (73)*

Below and overleaf: *Hatch End also afforded late afternoon opportunities and here are three photographs to enjoy. Recalled to traffic* **Princess Marie Louise** *in a very unregal external condition has the 4/35 to Wolverhampton (74). Royal Scot 46165* **The Ranger (12th London Regiment)** *(75) has an unidentifiable service, but welcome nevertheless and Edge Hill's* **Duchess of Sutherland** *has the 6/0* **The Merseyside Express** *(76).*

that a technical representative of EE rode with it only on its run to Euston on the Saturday and, after overseeing the maintenance, rode with it as far as Crewe on the Monday morning. In its final few weeks with the LM Region it was used on a Euston-Blackpool and return service, to give a weekly mileage of 3,000. Over a period of 13 months, *DP2* accumulated 164,580 miles with one failure in traffic due to arctic conditions, start-stop journeys and a freezing up of radiator pipework. EE was not alone in developing a Co-Co that was lighter than the D200s and D1-193 and Brush Traction was well advanced with D1500, a Co-Co weighing in at 114 tons and negating the need for two extra weight bearing axles. The D1500s were extremely successful and, over a long period, a total of 512 were built. *DP2* came to an unfortunate and early end as the result of a blameless involvement in a high-speed accident on the North Eastern Region, but its design paved the way for the later build of 50 D400 class that were hired by the British Railways Board and paid for based upon the number declared available for traffic at 3.0 each weekday morning. Evidently, some lessons were learned.

Allocation details for the Princess Royals and Princess Coronations as at mid-August 1962 were:

Camden 1B	46206/9	46239/40/5/6
Crewe North 5A		46228/35/48/51/3/4/6
Edge Hill 8A	46208	46229/33/41/3
Carlisle Upperby 12B	46201	46220/1/5/6/34/6-8/50
Carlisle Kingmoor 12A	46200/3	46244/7/52/5/7
Polmadie 66A		46222-4/7/30-2/42/9

Reflecting the improving availability of the by then complete allocation to the Region of its EE type 4s, the need for use of 8P steam power reduced from the start of the Winter Timetable. Extracts from the Preston control log for November showed:

Date (November)	Locomotive	Depot	Train
3	46238	12B	IM26 9.0 Perth – Eus
7	46238	12B	IM35 Glgw – Eus
9	(45373)		IS75 Eus – Glgw
22	46236	12A	IM23 Glgw – Man
	(46162)		IM26 9.0 Perth – Eus
36	46220	12B	3/30 Clsle – Broad St
27	46220	12B	4.45 Crewe – Clsle
	46238	12B	3/30 Clsle – Broad St
28	46238	12B	4.45 Crewe – Clsle
	46220	12B	3/30 Clsle – Broad St
30	46220	12B	4.45 Crewe – Clsle
	46220	12B	IM26 9.0 Perth – Eus

Notes
IM35/1S75 *The Mid-Day Scot*
(45373) Black 5
(46162) Royal Scot
Clsle – Broad St (milk)

Princess Coronation Class locomotives available for traffic at the turn of the year 1963 and for the most severe winter since early 1947 were:

Number	Depot	Number	Depot
46220	12B	46240	1B
46222	66A	46242	66A
46223	66A	46244	12A
46224	66A	46245	1B
46225	12B	46247	12A
46226	12B	46248	5A
46228	5A	46249	66A
46229	8A	46250	12B
46230	66A	46251	5A
46236	12A	46252	1B
46238	12B	46255	5A
46239	1B	46257	12A

Therefore, Edge Hill had just one as a reserve for the Glasgow services (joint with Manchester during the winter), four at both Crewe North and Camden.

During the year, Longsight had been left with very few steam passenger turns; two to Birmingham (8.30 and 7/0) and one to London (middle of the day Euston, but St Pancras for the Summer Timetable) all via Stoke-on-Trent. While the Birmingham trains were irregularly steam worked, the London turn was almost consistently steam (anything from a Black 5 to a Jubilee, Royal Scot or Britannia) and, with a return working overnight, could produce mileages to shame many an EE type 4 diesel. It was not unusual for the same locomotive to work the round trip on three consecutive days (70028, 44911, 44681, 45256) to produce some 1,200 revenue earning miles while being continuously in steam. The middle of the day London service ceased to run from the start of the Winter Timetable and, during its final week, had a pair of Black 5s. Other steam turns into Manchester were mainly those using Mayfield station which had not been electrified. Mayfield station continued mainly as a parcels receiving and despatch point as part of a wider Regional plan to concentrate such activities on only a small number of centres, including Marylebone, Nottingham, Leicester, Birmingham, Manchester, Liverpool and (short term) Oldham.

Also during the course of the year, withdrawals of the Patriot class locomotives in un-rebuilt form had progressed and by year end all had gone; all but three finished on the London Midland Region and the others (45504/6/19) had upset quite a few at Gloucester and Bristol while helping out on cross-country services. Also withdrawn was the disappointing single class 8 BR pacific 71000, all remaining 4-4-0s (on all Regions) and all the Stanier designed 2-6-2 tank locomotives. In the final accounting period of the year, 18 class 7P and 17 class 6P ex-LMS design 4-6-0s (Royal Scot, rebuilt Patriot and Jubilees) were withdrawn. The Scottish Region had faced up to the reality that their five Clans (72000-4) had no future other than in the form of motor cars or washing machines.

For the Britannias it had been a quieter year, but involved Longsight, Aston in particular, Rugby received four in October (70017/22-4) and the motive power situation along the North Wales Coast was strengthened at year end by 70014-6/33 going to Llandudno Junction and

70045/6/8/9 (old friends there) and 50/1 to Holyhead. Also of note was a major upheaval of class 6 power (Jubilee) power at Carlisle Upperby; a total of sixteen finding new homes, at least for a while.

Leighton Buzzard sub-shed was closed.

The first year of electrification between Liverpool and Crewe had been largely uneventful, but sadly that changed during the early evening of Boxing Day. Despite the investment in the automatic warning system, four aspect colour light signalling and track circuits, no amount of additional money could override human error.

The rapidly falling temperature caused points in the Crewe area to freeze and, at Coppenhall Junction, the need for trains to be routed into any one of several platforms at Crewe caused congestion. The 4/45 Liverpool-Birmingham express followed by the 1/30 Glasgow-Euston were approaching from the north and the former was brought to a halt at signal 114, just south of Winsford. After some delay, the red aspect of signal 114 was replaced by a single yellow aspect indicating to the driver that he may proceed at caution towards the next signal, number 110. The driver of the 1/30 from Glasgow then brought his train to a halt at signal 114, showing a red aspect due to the presence in that section of the Liverpool-Birmingham train. Both signals 114 and 110 were automatic, while those at Coppenhall Junction were controlled manually. Train crews waiting time in the automatically signalled section were required to telephone Coppenhall Junction and it was unfortunate that an electrical circuit failure had rendered the telephones at signals 114 and 110 inoperable. Although he was aware of an instruction to use any signalpost telephone in such circumstances (the Down line in this case) the driver of the Glasgow train decided to proceed cautiously towards the next signal ahead (110) which he could see brightly displaying red. At about the half way point between the signals, 110 changed to display a single yellow aspect, allowing the Liverpool-Birmingham train to proceed at caution. The driver of the Glasgow train, however, thought the yellow was for his train and, not until too late, did his fireman spot the paraffin red tail lamp on the rear carriage of the Liverpool-Birmingham train. The rear end collision caused telescoping of two carriages, eighteen passengers dead and thirty-three others seriously injured. The Glasgow train was hauled on that day by an EE type 4 diesel.

In 1962 the working loss for the London Midland Region increased by £6m to £40.7m (£34.7m in 1961).

Chapter 10

1963: All Change for the New Order

1963 was eventful in that it ushered in the British Railways Board intent upon applying the provisions of the Transport Act 1962. The content of the Report and supporting maps of the work of Dr Beeching (*The Reshaping of British Railways*) revealed the detailed data that had been produced from the traffic studies and which formed the basis for recommending widespread changes affecting much of the network. Our routes of interest emerged well from the scrutiny, but not so the sections between Chester and Holyhead and Carlisle and Glasgow. The general management of the London Midland Region was consumed by internal re-organisation while, at an operational level, matters started to improve with the main line diesel fleet.

As at the end of 1962, the transition in traction and rolling stock for British Railways was clear.

Year end	Steam locomotives	Diesel		Electric locomotives
		shunting	other	
1955	17,960	447	9	71
1956	17,527	600	9	71
1957	16,959	775	28	71
1958	16,108	1,091	110	72
1959	14,457	1,373	427	85
1960	13,276	1,708	842	135
1961	11,691	1,894	1,285	158
1962	8,796	2,010	1,673	178

Year end	Multiple unit stock			Hauled stock	
	diesel	electric	total	passenger	non-passenger
1955	179	4,675	4,854	36,861	15,687
1956	453	4,939	5,392	36,130	15,163
1957	1,349	5,004	6,353	35,474	14,994
1958	2,417	5,261	7,678	34,325	14,926
1959	3,244	5,843	9,087	31,450	14,271
1960	3,820	6,430	10,250	29,841	14,871
1961	3,998	6,890	10,888	26,961	14,551
1962	4,074	6,958	11,032	22,575	12,482

1962	Wagons 848,591	Containers 46,585

Within a few weeks of joining the BTC, Dr Beeching had decided the bases upon which much more information than that previously available should be sought. A number of traffic studies were organised to enable him and others to better understand the working of the railway and its future prospects. There were five traffic studies:

- to determine the contribution each station, depot and section of line made to the system as a whole in both the passenger and freight fields
- to establish the characteristics of all wagon load freight traffic and to determine which traffics were profitable to the railway and under what conditions
- to ascertain the pattern and characteristics of all wagon load mineral and merchandise traffic not passing by rail, and the volume, direction, distance and terminal requirements of that part of it judged to be favourable to rail
- as immediately preceding, but in respect of coal class traffic
- to establish the volume and characteristics of less than wagon load traffic with the object of deciding upon the practicability of devising a plan for remunerative handling of this type of traffic.

Route mileage open to traffic was 17,830. Arising from the first study it was clear that one-third of the route mileage (approx 6,000) carried only 1 per cent of the total passenger miles and, similarly, one-third of the route mileage carried 1 per cent of the total freight ton miles. Half of the total route mileage carried only 7½ per cent of the total passenger and freight traffic. As would have been expected, the main routes were between the key centres of population, industry, sources of raw materials and the major ports; the majority of the little used lines were away from these centres.

Stations open for passengers numbered 4,300. One-third of stations (approx 1,400) contributed only 1 per cent to passenger revenue and half of the total contributed only 2 per cent. 57 per cent of the stations contributed only 1 per cent of total parcels receipts, but 100 of the stations contributed 69 per cent of the total receipts.

Stations and sidings available for freight numbered 5,031, 4,000 of which dealt with less than 2,500 tons of freight in the year and 57 handled 50,000 tons and over.

From these traffic studies, Dr Beeching had more and better-quality information than had been available to the Railway Executive and the BTC. His studies went further and identified the level of utilisation of passenger rolling stock, the types of products that formed the total tonnage of mineral and merchandise traffic, considered the threat to passenger travel from air transport and the tonnage of traffic that was suitable for rail, though not then carried by rail.

Chapter 2 identified the main traffic carried along the lines of interest to this book and the expectations of the various users/customers. Chapter 6 made reference to the growing threat of air services between England and Scotland and within England. Although most of *The Reshaping of British Railways, part 1, Report* dealt with the matter at a national system level, there were references therein of particular relevance to this book. With the scheme to electrify the main line linking the major centres of London-Birmingham-Manchester/Liverpool having been sanctioned upon the basis of traffic density and having survived the scrutiny of multiple bodies of enquiry, the main lines of interest to this book should have caused fewer fears than many others. That said, there were sections that were exposed to, and by, the analyses of the various traffic studies; for examples Chester to Holyhead and Carlisle to Glasgow as being one of three routes. Chapter 2 also identified how the demands placed upon our main lines of interest changed at weekends in the summer season and to meet the needs of the shipping companies.

The *Report* made reference firstly to competition for passenger traffic. The conclusion for road competition for the business traveller was that, as long as 'continuing attention is given to speed, reliability and comfort of trains' they would 'remain preferable to road transport'. It was felt that air transport was not competitive in terms of speed for inter-city distances of less than about 200 miles, nor was it competitive in terms of cost except by cross subsidisation. The routes over which air could compete seriously with rail included London-Manchester and London-Scotland. The expectation of a post-electrification centre to centre journey time by rail of 2¾ hours was expected to strengthen the position of rail, as was the level of comfort for the business traveller. On the Scottish routes, air had made inroads into the loadings of day-time trains and was expected to make further inroads. Sleeping car trains for overnight journeys were expected to maintain or increase their level of attraction. Seasonal passenger traffic during the months of June to September exceeded the average for the other eight months of the year by 18 per cent in June, 47 per cent in July, 43 per cent in August and 21 per cent in September. Ten years earlier, the percentages were much higher: 48 per cent in June, 96 per cent in July, 87 per cent in August and 44 per cent in September. The reason for the decline – despite workers winning the right to have holidays with pay, greater general affluence and the fact that taking a holiday was a family expectation – was the increase in the growth of family motoring which was expected to continue. The *Report* identified that to meet the regular summer service, some 2,000 gangwayed carriages were retained beyond the total in use all year and a further 8,900 carriages were available for the high peaks of demand services. Some 2,000 carriages were used on only ten occasions during the year, 2,000 on fourteen and a further 2,000 on eighteen occasions. The total fleet was being progressively reduced and the *Report* identified that, by the end of 1965, rolling stock would not be available for use solely at times of peak demand. Chapter 2 also identified the raw materials of production found or brought to centres of production along our lines of interest. The main mineral classification traffic was in the form of iron ore, lime and limestone, iron and steel scrap, iron and steel bars, strips and billets; of these much of the traffic originated (and therefore where the revenue was credited) away from our main lines of interest. For general merchandise, iron and steel products, fuel and petrol, cement, animal feed and chemicals, were the largest in terms of tonnage; here the route did directly benefit from cement and (from Stoke-on-Trent and Furness) steel production. Although the route conveyed much perishable traffic (e.g. meat, fish and vegetables, it was not 'originating') in train loads and in containers it was a generator of low individual tonnages of merchandise that were conveyed in covered vans that provided the opportunity for much traffic. That latter traffic was, of course, also of interest to the road haulage industry. The opportunity of more traffic being drawn to rail was particularly strong in the north-west of England: Liverpool six and a half million tons, Warrington two and three-quarters million, Manchester three million and Bolton one and three-quarter million tons. Quite how much such tonnages could have been lost in the schemes put forward by the Region for the Modernisation Plan is a valid topic for debate; Liverpool struggled to concentrate its Cheshire and Lancashire traffic and Manchester was left with a legacy of small yards from the days of the LNWR, Great Central, Midland, Cheshire

Lines Committee and Great Northern. Finally, coal traffic flowed in large tonnages, but gradually decreasing tonnages, to London and the other centres of population/production for domestic and industrial markets.

Examples of BR publicity

The *Report's* recommendations included the closure of many stations. As expected, the route to be electrified escaped such a fate, but others felt the full force of the exposure from the traffic studies and would have to make a case based upon 'hardship'.

Euston to Crewe (including loops):
  Mow Cop and Scholar Green
  Norton Bridge
  Roade
  Trentham

Crewe to Chester line:
  Beeston Castle and Tarporley
  Calveley and Rodley
  Tattenhall Road

Chester to Holyhead:
  Abergele
  Bagillt
  Caernarvon (also branch to Afonwen)
  Connah's Quay
  Conway
  Deganwy
  Flint
  Gaerwen
  Holywell Junction
  Llanfairfechan
  Llanfair pg
  Mostyn
  Penmaenmawr
  Rhosneigr
  Shotton
  Talacre
  Ty Croes
  Valley

Crewe to Preston:
  Balshaw Lane & Euxton
  Coppull

Preston to Carlisle:
  Garstang & Catterall
  Milnthorpe
  Scorton
  Shap

Carlisle to Glasgow Central:
  Abington
  Cleghorn
  Crawford
  Elvanfoot
  Flemington
  Gretna Green
  Lamington
  Symington
  Thankerton

Others of interest:
  Blackpool North
  Fleetwood
  Morecambe Euston Road
  Stranraer Harbour

The future organisation of the main workshops had been decided in 1962 and did not form part of the *Report*. The workshops would no longer be under the control of the Regional Chief Mechanical Engineer and would be a separate cost centre to undertake work for the Regions and possibly others. Along our main lines of interest there were three works: Wolverton (carriages), Crewe (locomotives) and Earlestown (wagons). Wolverton had a workforce of 3,094 and would continue as a carriage works with a small reduction in the workforce to 2,800 by 1965. Crewe, with a workforce of 5,842, would continue as a locomotive works with an increase in staff in 1963 and 1964. Earlestown was not so fortunate and was to close in mid-1964 with the loss of some 1,350 jobs, though with special provisions for apprentices wishing to stay with the industry. Overall, twelve of the twenty-nine workshops were to be closed with a reduction of staff from 56,000 to 38,000.

The winter of 1962/63 was by far the worst since 1947 and affected the whole country. All forms of transport suffered while arctic conditions endured particularly severely through January and much of February. In anticipation of the probability of a high incidence of problems with train heating by the EE type 4 diesels, four Princess Coronation pacifics had been taken out of store early in December (46239/40/8/51) and they were joined by ten more in January (46221/30/33-5/7/41/3/54/6). 46234/46/53 were not so fortunate and all three were withdrawn from future service. Some of the Royal Scots stored at Carlisle Kingmoor were also returned to traffic and one (46106) withdrawn from capital stock found itself returned to service off the scrap line.

In the prevailing weather conditions, most depots resorted to forming a line of steam locomotives kept permanently in steam to form a wind break and on the lee side to have braziers to protect injector pipework, water cranes and tenders. Once on the move, the movement of the locomotives would prevent water in the tender and tanks from freezing. Exposed pipework, radiators and steam heat boilers were of concern for the diesels and any lengthy delay in severely low temperatures or wind chill when in motion could cause failures.

As an insurance, many depots were equipped with snow plough equipment that varied from a device fitted between the lower edge of the buffer beam and close to rail height of locomotives, to large, arrow-shaped constructions that were attached to the front of the locomotives. With the large ploughs, two or more locomotives would be coupled with the outer pair enabling 'ploughing' in either direction. Every section along our route of interest suffered on a daily basis, but the one for which I have most information is the area covered by Preston Control. To give a flavour of the difficulty faced, I have selected the following:

23 January 1963

Reporting number	Train	Incident
IS19	10/45 B'ham – Glasgow	D328 stopped out of course. Requested steam heat provisions. 45258 attached at Carnforth.
IS21	11/45 Lpl – Glasgow	D343 held at Lancaster 3.20 – 3.58 whilst IS19 attended to.
IS14	2.5 Carnforth – Glasgow	70025 at Carnforth, short of coal.
IM48	9/25 Glasgow – Euston	D300 stopped out of course Carnforth to request steam heat provision. 46240 forward from Preston (off 6/50 22 Jan, Euston – Preston parcels).
1A …	10.0 Blackpool C – Euston	D322 failed at Blackpool, train cancelled.
IS83	3/45 Euston – Glasgow C	D325 failed at Preston, 46136 forward.
IM35	1/15 Glasgow – Euston	46223 failed at Preston. 46251 (previously worked 9.30 Glasgow – Manchester. IM27 to Preston, taken off 6/50 Preston – Morecambe) forward.

Also that day:
46106 (withdrawn) on 5.13 Carlisle – Sudbury Junction returned with 3L07 6/50 Crewe – Glasgow
46221 3/30 Carlisle – Willesden – milk
46222 4.45 Crewe – Carlisle
46225 8.17 Warrington – Carlisle
D5133 7/30 Aston – Glasgow Gushetfaulds *Condor*

In the severe weather, extremely low ambient temperatures and wind chill, the diesels were particularly vulnerable. The engines would shut down through water starvation resulting from very little warm water initially circulating through the radiator. Any combination of a lengthy stand in section awaiting clearance to proceed or slow running between a series of signals at caution or danger – such as occurred on every day of early 1963 – was likely to produce a failure.

Further evidence of the level of disturbance was that the Up *Royal Scot* was hauled by a Black 5 on 24 January and by 46221/4 on 26 and 29 January. Having had its fault rectified the day before, D325 failed again on the 24th with the same boiler problem. The same locomotive was in trouble again on 13 February when working the IM16 Glasgow-Birmingham. In his wisdom, the fireman elected to pick up water from the troughs at Dillicar, overdid it and coated the sides of the locomotive with excess water that promptly froze. Removed at Preston the locomotive later took a following service forward to Crewe with a Black 5 providing steam heat.

5 February 1963

Reporting number	Train	Incident
3L04Q	1.05 Crewe – Carlisle	60089 (previously worked 1X80 Edinburgh Wav – Treherbert rugby supporters' special)
IS21	9.30 Man Vic – Glasgow	46256 forward from Preston (42701 Man Vic – Preston

6 February 1963

Reporting number	Train	Incident
		Settle & Carlisle route blocked by snow. Down *Condor* stuck in snowdrift at Mallerstang. All Midland Division trains diverted via Ingleton and Low Gill.
Time/train		
9.0		Main line blocked by snow between Shap station and Shap Summit
9.26		Glasgow – Oxley goods stuck in snowdrift (Shap), Tebay banking locomotive sent to assist also stuck in Snowdrift.
11.0		Carnforth depot snowplough sent to assist and clear drift, then to Ingleton to keep line open. Five trains, including Carlisle Upperby snowplough, in Carlisle – Shap section awaiting clearance.
IM22		Up *Royal Scot* diverted from Carlisle to Newcastle via Hexham (D300 throughout).
-		Skipton and Hellifield snowploughs deployed on Settle and Carlisle route. S&C did not re-open until week ended 23 February 63.

The use of A3 60089 on the special to Treherbert was doubtless because it had arrived at Carlisle from Edinburgh as one of five such specials for returning supporters of Welsh rugby and was able to continue to Crewe. The specials had been worked north by 46157/67, 46251 and 70053; in all probability one had been requisitioned by the Scottish Region and the A3 was sent with a reasonable expectation that it would be changed at Carlisle and sent home. During what was an exceptionally difficult time, an overnight service on 24 January from Euston due into Glasgow Central at 9.30 actually arrived nearly ten hours late, headed by A2 60532 of Dundee, driven and fired from Carlisle by a Perth footplate crew.

With the withdrawals of 1962, the front-line steam passenger fleet as at 1 January 1963 totalled 125 of which 35 were class 8, 60 class 7 and 30 were class 6 (1962, 172). With thirteen class 7 at Holyhead and eighteen class 6 at Crewe North there would seem to have been scope for further reductions. In fact, at the start of 1964 the front-line steam passenger fleet had grown to 137 (22 class 8, 85 class 7 and 30 class 6) and with additional class 6 locomotives at depots handling fitted goods trains. The increase in class 7 was influenced by an influx of Britannia Class locomotives finally released by the Eastern Region. At the London end of the routes there was far more steam in evidence at Willesden than Camden; the latter, as a steam depot, had only a limited time left and was closed to steam from 9 September 1963. A visit to both Camden and Willesden on 31 March confirmed the intent with fewer than fifteen steam locomotives at the former while seventy-two (including eleven Britannias, three Princess Coronations and five 7P 4-6-0s) were at the latter. Morale also seemed high at Willesden where 10001 looked cared for and 45530, *Sir Frank Ree*, was a sight to behold. It was suggested to me that 45530 was 'bulled up' for a Grand National excursion to show the Liverpool lads that their 45527 *Southport* was never really clean by comparison.

As winter finally relented and the steam heat season came to an end, the availability of the EE type 4 diesels improved with consequential reduced demand upon steam power. However, such was the level of concern that the Princess Coronations were not returned into store and, apart from 46247/52/3 (withdrawn) those that were in service remained so until the September/October when 46228/33/5/9/40/1/3/8/51/4/6 were placed back into store, serviceable as may be required. 46228/35/9/40/3/51/4/6 resumed service in the December and by that date Camden had none, but five were at nearby Willesden. No Princess Coronation received a classified repair in 1963. A class 8 found a very unusual new home depot in May 1963 when withdrawn Princess Royal 46203 – painted in LMS maroon livery – was taken by rail to the holiday camp at Pwllheli where it formed an attraction for its new owner, Billy Butlin Ltd.

The winter period had not been the ideal time to launch the second *Condor* freight service. Diesel hauled by a single type 2, the train was a similar formation to that operated from Hendon and linked Birmingham (Aston) and Gushetfaulds, Glasgow via Stafford and the route via Preston and Carlisle. (Note: the other *Condor* service used the west coast main line from 1964.)

A real gem for eagle eyed carriage spotters. On summer Saturdays a train for North Wales was composed of vehicles that included surviving examples from the trainset that toured parts of the USA. An articulated pair can be seen to the left of the second telegraph pole, itself worthy of note for the extent of its loading. **City of Leeds has just passed Stonebridge Park. (77)**

The aftermath of the winter of 1962/63 included the postponement of fixtures at Wembley Stadium. The schoolboys' international football match on 27 April produced specials including this one with Jubilee Seychelles and Black 5 45349. (78)

Despite the advance of electrification south from Crewe and the improving availability/reliability of the EE type 4 diesels, north of Crewe the Princess Coronations continued to 'do the business'. City of Lichfield is near Broughton with a Euston-Glasgow summer relief. (79)

*Crewe Works continued with Classified Heavy repairs on BR Britannia Class locomotives and Black 5s and one of the former – **Firth of Clyde** – is seen from the unusual location of a coaling plant at Crewe North depot. (80)*

The sport fixtures of the spring were in an unusual sequence with the FA Cup Final not played until 25 May and preceded by England v Scotland on 4 May and the Rugby League Challenge Final on 11 May. The round ball was contested by Leicester City and Manchester United with little to excite the observers of railway specials along our routes of interest and the oval ball was contested by Wakefield Trinity and Wigan, again with little interest at the lineside. It was left to the Grand National at Aintree to lift spirits somewhat on 30 March with four specials from Euston producing 45530, 46125/50/6/67 and the Schoolboys' Football international at Wembley producing Bulleid 34102.

Having given some 13 months service on the main line, *DP2* was withdrawn for an overhaul followed by reintroduction on the Eastern Region. Working six-day passenger train diagrams for 3,600/2,800 miles per week and one day each week for maintenance at Camden, the locomotive had suffered one failure in traffic. The support afforded by English Electric to its locomotive provided a template for the wider application by the BRB; the timescale for establishing a structured maintenance regime having suffered during the 'bridging' between the BTC and the new organisation.

Until the formation of the British Railways Board and the separation of the workshops from the Regional Chief Mechanical and Electrical Engineers, the necessary organisational responsibility for the running and maintenance of traction had been lacking. Each Region in receipt of diesel locomotives (whether diesel electric or diesel hydraulic) developed its arrangements in isolation of the others and, while the London Midland Region put in place plans and physical works for diesel multiple units and planned a major diesel maintenance facility at Toton, it lagged behind the Eastern and Western Regions in terms of bespoke facilities for main line diesels, for training of staff and a detailed maintenance structure based upon time in service/engine hours. The BRB moved to establish standard examination schedules for each of the principal makes of production types; one covered the English Electric types 1, 2, 3 and 4 locomotives. The schedules were in two sections; the first an alphabetic list of items requiring attention showing the period to apply in engine hours between examinations and the second itemised groups of items to be checked during the same examination. For examples, at the 125-150 engine hour examination, the engine was to be run to full speed, the turbo charger checked for free running, the specific gravity of the batteries was to be tested and levels topped up, lights were checked, the voltage regulator tested, parts lubricated, the running gear including bogies and wheels checked and the engine room and engine cleaned. Further examinations of an increasingly comprehensive nature were to take place after 5-600 hours, 1,500 hours and 3-3,600 hours. The expectation was that the 1,500-hour examination could be completed in sixteen hours utilising up to five technical staff. The 3-3,600-hour examination would also take sixteen hours, but utilise six members of staff throughout. While the Eastern Region had developed Colchester, Stratford and Finsbury Park and the North Eastern Region Holbeck and the Western Region at Laira (Plymouth), the London Midland Region lagged behind and used motive power depots still servicing steam locomotives. For electric traction, the London Midland Region was better placed with new facilities at Longsight, Crewe and Allerton. Longsight was responsible for accepting electric locomotives having equipment from, or built by, GEC/EE, and Crewe for those locomotives having equipment from, or built by AEI, but for maintenance purposes either depot could deal with any locomotive. Maintenance schedules were based upon 7, 35, 70, 140, 280 and 560-day periods. Casualty rates in the first three years of operation had improved from one every 3,000 miles (1961) to one every 13,000 miles (1963) but, surprisingly, at that time the projected annual mileage per locomotive was put at 100,000, only 10 per cent more than a steam class 8P. The three depots mentioned also maintained the fleet of forty-five multiple units.

The British Railways Board consisted of a Chairman (Dr Beeching), a Vice-Chairman (Sir Steuart Mitchell, with responsibility for the workshops), six full-time Members and five part-time Members. The six full-time Members each had a functional responsibility:

- A.R. Dunbar – manpower adviser
- P.H. Shirley – finance

- L.H. Williams – commercial
- Maj. Gen. G.N. Russell – co-ordination with Regions
- F.C. Margetts – railway operating and planning
- J. Ratter – railway technical and productivity.

The five part-time Members included H.P. Barker who had been a 'shining light' in a very dull BTC since 1951 and who had single-handedly at times encouraged approaches to at least try to keep pace with the changing world of commerce and socio-economic conditions.

The early indications of change affecting passenger traffic included the decision to no longer offer the *Starlight Specials*, an internal policy to not run many of the summer seasonal relief services and to encourage pre-booking of seats on those services that were to run. The consequences were, of course, the withdrawal of the older stock that formed much of the 'reserve' fleet identified in the Beeching Report and with those withdrawals or reduction in need for repairs.

Throughout 1963, the senior management of the London Midland Region were consumed by matters of internal reorganisation. In what seemed a strange move, the General Manager became Chairman of his Regional Board, as did his colleagues in the other Regions and, in the process, changed the flow of communication from upwards to downwards. Far more demanding was the decision to eliminate a tier of management (the District level within the traffic organisation) and place those responsibilities with the various Divisional Managers who, in turn, still reported to the three Line Managers. To try to give the new arrangements a greater impetus, the former Line Manager for the Eastern Region (J. Bonham-Carter) was appointed as an Assistant General Manager. The revised arrangements were aimed at improving commercial, operating and (through Divisional Maintenance Engineers) rolling stock matters within particular railway boundaries. What was lacking – and by then Beeching and Margetts had recognised it and were addressing it – was a strategy for the entire routes across Regional and Divisional boundaries. The economics of freight transport of merchandise and some classifications of minerals favoured rail only over distances of more than 250 miles, while coal traffic needed the co-operation of the National Coal Board.

The Summer Timetable included a few changes for the better, but not to the extent that should have been possible between Crewe and both Manchester and Liverpool. South of Crewe, the total journey times to London remained very similar, although the times between intermediate stations could vary due to the movable feast of engineering work. North of Crewe an additional stop at Wigan North Western for *The Caledonian* enabled afternoon travellers from Manchester and Liverpool to reach Glasgow at 11 pm with a similar arrangement possible with the stop at Preston with the southbound morning train. The reconstruction work at Euston necessitated further diversions of sleeping car and other services into Marylebone, St Pancras or Kensington Olympia; the range of stations being influenced by platform face capacity at Marylebone. For those interested in coaching stock, the summer of 1963 allowed a further and perhaps last opportunity to see or travel in vehicles that had been built by the LMS for the tour of parts of North America by the *Coronation Scot* trainset. The vehicles were easily identified by being articulated pairs and were regularly used on a summer Saturday train from Euston to North Wales. Of the forty-six vehicles (counted singly for the thirteen articulated pairs) built in 1937 (twenty-seven) and 1940, thirty-seven were available for service at the start of 1963 and twenty-nine at the end of the year. (Note: the final four were withdrawn in 1967, the last articulated pair in the previous year.) 1963 also saw a reduction in the number of boat train services for international sailings from and to Liverpool as the new jetliners attracted the regular rather than emigrant or immigrant clientele. In an effort to attract or re-attract Mancunians to rail travel at weekends, the Divisional Manager launched a combined train ticket plus hotel in London package that (years later) would become known as the *Merrymaker*, not that Sunday return travel in the early 1960s was anything approaching a merry experience.

As the year progressed, so too did the electrification work. From 7 January most passenger trains linking Manchester via Crewe and Liverpool with Birmingham were worked by electric locomotives. Main line passenger trains between Crewe and Euston via the Trent Valley remained either diesel or steam hauled as before, as did goods trains. There was at that time just one Euston service in each direction that travelled from Stockport via Macclesfield and Stoke-on-Trent and anyone using the through carriages between Birkenhead and Euston via Chester was required to change trains at Chester or use the services from/to Paddington. A brighter note was apparent for business travellers living around Wilmslow with a stop added to the 9.40 from Manchester Piccadilly to Euston and (diesel hauled) non-stop thereafter.

Work was progressed from Stafford both up the Trent Valley line and towards Wolverhampton; it being possible to energise the overhead catenary to a point between Lichfield and Tamworth on

The north end of the shed yard at Camden provides a very adequate perspective on the transition of types of motive power used. Five EE type 4s are dominating the steam era running shed, an EE type 1 is depot pilot and two Princess Coronations are in steam and ready for service. The angle of light suggests one Princess Coronation is to work **The Ulster Express**, *a round trip of 17½ hours for some 450 miles including stabling overnight at Carnforth. (81)*

31 August and use the Crewe-Lichfield section for crew training. The next section to be energised would be to Nuneaton, expected in spring 1964. Work also continued in sections south of Rugby with an intention to use the 13-mile Tring to Watford section for crew training purposes.

There were three accidents; one related to the electrification work, another to a wagon in the process of becoming derailed and both of those occurred during April. The third accident occurred on the evening of 1 August. On 1 April, a van forming the fifth vehicle of the 2/18 Camden-Sighthill fully-fitted goods became derailed on plain track and then turned from the vertical into the path of any train approaching from the opposite direction. The up *Royal Scot* was approaching, but at slow speed and caused damage to the EE type 4 diesel and several carriages while three other vans on the goods train became derailed. The accident on 21 April involved the slewing of a crane engaged on electrification work. Although the engineers had possession of the two slow tracks, the necessary slewing of the crane brought it over the next of the four tracks. In such circumstances there were rules involving signals to be placed at danger and additionally the use of hand signalmen with detonators to warn the driver of any train approaching the encroachment. On the day of the accident, the communication between the traffic inspector, signalmen and the placement of one of the hand signalmen was incorrect and the EE type 4 diesel and four carriages of the Holyhead-Euston passenger train were derailed with injuries sustained by the crane driver and a member of railway staff on the derailed train. The third accident involved two passenger trains at Norton Bridge near Stafford on a four-track section equipped with four aspect colour light signalling, track circuits and the automatic warning system from signalling to the locomotive in question, an EE type 4. The 6/17 Euston-Liverpool passenger train passed a signal at danger and collided at low speed with the electric locomotive hauled 7/20 Liverpool-Birmingham passenger train which was crossing the path of the northbound train. The accident was found to have been caused by human error on the part of the driver of the diesel who received little assistance from his colleague in the cab. Four of the six carriages of the Birmingham bound train were damaged or derailed and twenty-nine passengers and the train guard required hospital treatment. Three accidents in the space of four months were, of course, three too many and the two involving human error would have been of particular concern to the senior management.

Another incident occurred early on the morning of 8 August and made national news for several days thereafter. The 6/50, 7 August, Aberdeen/Glasgow-Euston Travelling Post Office train hauled by EE type 4 D328 was progressing normally until halted by a colour light signal at danger near Sears Crossing, north of Cheddington. The signal had been tampered with, the colour light showing green being taped over and the red powered by batteries. As far as the signalmen were concerned the train had halted for reasons not associated with signalling and, in such circumstances, they would expect to receive advice from the footplate crew. It being quite usual for a track gang to be working in the area, the footplate crew opened the cab door to allow access and receive advice. However, in this instance they were overpowered and, following this, the thieves uncoupling the first two carriages – containing registered mail, banknotes and jewellery estimated to be worth £2.5m – they were forced to drive the locomotive plus the two carriages to a road underbridge known as Bridego where the sacks were thrown down to accomplices. The alarm was eventually raised when Post Office staff on the train became suspicious of the lack of information about the delay. Such a daring raid was marred by the coshing of driver Jack Mills of Crewe North who, although he did eventually resume footplate duties, was never able to work again on main line turns. The later lauding of the likes of Ronnie Biggs and their lifestyles on the run was never appreciated by railwaymen.

During the spring and summer, confidence in the EE type 4 diesels increased in line with a more rigorous approach to formalised methods of recorded maintenance. A measure of that confidence was the use of truly immaculately turned out D308 for the Royal Train on 4 July.

1963 also saw the consecration of the new cathedral at Coventry bringing to that city (and nearby Nuneaton) special trains from far and wide including several from the north-east of England hauled by V2 2-6-2s, two Clans on trains from Barrow and two BRCW type 2s from Margate and Portsmouth. The passenger train marketeers had also shown initiative in continuing holiday week specials with a different destination each day; *The City of Coventry, The City of Birmingham, The City of Nottingham* and *The City of Leicester* trains could turn up almost anywhere but mainly at the coastal resorts. The loss of the *Starlight Specials* was replaced, to some extent, by making available a limited number of special, low cost *Dayrider* and *Nightrider* tickets.

My own summer activity included another marketing initiative; the weekly rover which gave remarkable value for travel on seven consecutive days within a wide geographical zone. The Midlands Rover had border stations at Malvern, Shrewsbury, Rugby, Grantham, Matlock and Leamington Spa. Each day our small party set off for Birmingham and, if the Wolverhampton-Euston was steam hauled with a Princess Coronation, we would go with it to Coventry, otherwise head for Snow Hill and enjoy the Leamington Spa-Shrewsbury section. The final day of travel coincided with the Bank Holiday weekend and no-one could possibly have been more frustrated than was I at Shrewsbury as 46256 backed on to the Plymouth-Manchester; the ticket not allowing travel over the section to Crewe and my half-crown reserve for dire emergencies only being insufficient to buy another ticket.

The Winter Timetable for the routes followed a developing trend of being published and then being followed a few weeks later by a sheaf of amendments. The express services to the West Midlands started and terminated at Birmingham New Street with connections available for Wolverhampton. Initially there were improvements of between ten and twenty minutes, but from 4 November all Up main line services had ten minutes added to allow for engineering work between Watford and Euston. The Down *Royal Scot* was restored to its traditional departure time of 10.0, ran non-stop to Carlisle with a total journey time to Glasgow of seven hours and five minutes. The 10.0 did not convey a portion for Perth and a separate train for that destination was timed to leave at 10.10, call at Crewe and Preston before Carlisle and reach Perth at 7/20. The Down *Caledonian* made four stops (Stafford, Crewe, Wigan and Carlisle), but was timed to complete the run in only ten minutes more than the *Royal Scot*.

During the year, sixteen new electric locomotives were delivered including the originally intended type B E3301 which was re-numbered E3096, type A.

For steam, the main interest lay in the continuing turnover of members of different classes, particularly Britannias and Royal Scots. As previously noted, six Britannias were transferred from the Eastern Region in early spring (70000/1/5/10/2/34) to work from Willesden and later in the year the rest of the Eastern Region's fleet of that Class was transferred to work from Carlisle (70002/3/6-9/11/3/35 at Kingmoor and 70036-41 at Upperby). Having two cylinders rather than the three of the Royal Scots and rebuilt Patriots, roller bearings and finger bars in rocker firegrates were all helpful to the maintenance teams and reduced the calls made upon the older 4-6-0s. As at the end of 1963, all fifty-five of the Britannias were on the LM Region.

For the summer services, Longsight had welcomed a pair of Royal Scots (46140/2) and Willesden also had a handful added for seasonal work (46114/25/50/6/67). Further down the power chain both Speke (for Garston docks traffic) and Warrington received three and two Jubilees respectively. From 9 September, Aston depot became code 2J within a reorganised

West Midlands area which had depots formerly of the Western Region transferred as part of boundary and management responsibility changes.

October and November saw big changes affecting Polmadie. Of its long-standing allocations of nine Princess Coronation Class locomotives, three (46227/31/2) had been withdrawn at the end of 1962. In October 1963 three more were withdrawn (46222-4) and the final one on 9 November (46230). The balance of two more of the Class had been 46220/1, but they had been transferred in 1958 to the London Region and replaced by Princess Royals (46201/10). The two Princess Royals worked from Polmadie until March 1961 when a further swap took place; Princess Coronations 46242/9 were withdrawn in October and November respectively, thus ending a continuous association of the Class with Polmadie over a period of 24 years. It ended a long association with the Class which started from when the locomotives were new and 46223/4/30-2 had been allocated to the depot since 1939/40. In all, the nine locomotives as allocated at the end had (recorded) mileages totalling some 13 million. Probably with the forthcoming winter in mind, the Scottish Region arranged to re-allocate six ex-LNER A2 Class pacifics from the eastern side of the country to Glasgow. They were able to do that largely due to an influx of A4 pacifics for the Glasgow-Aberdeen service for which the new North British type 2 diesel had been intended, but failed to reach fruition. The six A2s were from a more recent build programme (1946/47) than were the Princess Coronations, but were classified by BR as class 7MT; that was the same as a Britannia. Finding six locomotives suitable for the work involved three from the North Eastern Region (60512/22/4) which had recently received classified repairs being 'swapped' with three Scottish Region examples which were then promptly condemned and transferred only on paper. The three locomotives re-allocated within the Scottish Region were 60527/30/5 and were moved from Edinburgh Haymarket. For top link Polmadie men, there was no substitute for an ex-LMS 8P and the A2s proved to be unpopular. All lasted until 1965 (60530 until November 1966) and as the height of the locomotive exceeded 13ft 1in 60512/22 were denoted (by a yellow stripe on the cab side) that they were not to be allowed to work south of Crewe.

While Carlisle was in the process of becoming a depository for class 7 steam power and with a pragmatic reserve of class 8P for the winter months, the availability and reliability of the EE type 4s had improved considerably during the year. That improvement was achieved by a combination of a more rigorous approach to scheduled maintenance, attention being given to component histories for the fleet and some acknowledgement of the need for facilities better suited to diesels than steam. As part of the Region's policy of allocations on a home depot basis and cyclic diagrams, Carlisle Upperby had an allocation of EE type 4s for passenger goods and parcels works. They had started to earn a better reputation with heavier (14/15 carriage) trains and being able to better the point to point 'standard load' timings for Preston – Carlisle and return over Shap. The higher availability allowed deployment on parcels and fitted goods trains which were of good value to BR.

The north-west of England was a centre for marketing and distributing ranges of clothing, homeware and general merchandise marketed to families by means of attractive colour catalogues. From the comfort of their homes, families could select and order goods and pay on the 'never, never'; a method of easy credit whereby monthly payments including finance charges were collected locally by agents for the sellers such as John Moores. Each weekday afternoon, consignments were collected by BR and conveyed from Wavertree (Liverpool) and Oldham (Clegg Street). Scotland had become attracted to this method of purchasing and, as part of the distribution, a train from each of Wavertree and Oldham was despatched to Carnforth where they were re-formed to become the 2.05 Carnforth-Glasgow and afforded class 1 status (1S14).

The 2.05 1S14 was identified as being high priority traffic and its working from Carnforth to Carlisle formed part of a three locomotive, three-day cyclic diagram for Carlisle Upperby. The full diagrams with their starting positions on each day were:

Loco A	Loco B	Loco C

6.20 Carlisle – Crewe
11.20 Euston – Workington
    Crewe to Preston
4/03 Manchester – Barrow
    Preston to Barrow
6/28 Workington – St Pancras
    Barrow to Preston
 	
END ➡		

	1.10 Preston – Crewe
	6.55 Crewe – Carlisle
	3/55 Carlisle – Broad St
	    to Crewe
	8/32 Monument Lane –
	    Carnforth from
	    Crewe
	
	END ➡
		2.05 Carlisle – Glasgow
		    to Carlisle
		8.15 Carlisle – Crewe
		2/18 Camden – Sighthill
		    from Crewe to
		    Carlisle
		END ➡

By the conservative standards of the London Midland Region, daily mileages of 284, 401 and 372 were good, particularly as the diagrams included parcels and goods workings.

1S14 and its trains of origin would have made a fine study for Dr Beeching's team trying to identify the costs of, and contribution made by, different classifications of traffic. On the one hand it was at least part trainload to Carnforth and trainload at least to Carlisle where vehicles may have been attached or detached. As such, good business for BR. However, if the commercial arrangements with John Moores Ltd, etc included delivery to the customer, the traffic became individual packages for multiple addresses over a wide geographical area. Small consignments to wayside stations for collection or for delivery by BR road services made the calculation of actual costs far more relevant. Up until 1963 BR did not have a good grip on its costs.

During 1963 four of the six Regions of British Railways were able to show improved financial performance in terms of net receipts and one of the four (the Eastern Region) moved into profit. The Southern Region deficit increased by £0.1m to £1.4m. The London Midland Region was obliged to declare an increase in the deficit from £44.5m in 1962 to £46.8m in 1963. During the span of seven years of interest to this book the aggregate losses of the London Midland Region totalled some £232m.

Chapter 11

You'll Never Believe What's Been Through

This chapter is for the lineside enthusiasts and modellers of railway scenes prototypical to the late 1950s/early 1960s.

The characteristics and pattern of services along the routes of interest offered daily a rich variety of traction types and rolling stock. For many, that richness was sufficient to sustain a level of personal fascination; they would happily watch the same Princess Royals, Princess Coronations and Royal Scots pass by day in, day out, year in, year out. For others, there was a constant search to see locomotives that would not normally pass a particular location; they wished to see each and every member of a class of locomotive, to underline the number in books made available to meet the considerable demand and, as opportunities allowed, may have travelled in search of their quarry.

Within our lines of route of interest, the principal main line ran some 400 miles south from Glasgow to Euston with the flow of traffic swelled by tonnages of goods and numbers of passengers from north-west England, Preston, Manchester, Liverpool, Holyhead, Wolverhampton and Birmingham. In addition to this core route, there were flows of goods traffic running east to west and vice versa; primary materials for production and consumption, merchandise for use at home and overseas, while for passenger traffic the coastal resorts of Lancashire and north Wales welcomed the seasonal traffic, as did the short-haul ferry routes from Holyhead, Liverpool, Fleetwood, Heysham and Stranraer. Perishable traffic in the form of fish, meat, fruit, vegetables and milk was in constant demand while coal for industrial and domestic markets flowed from the high output coalfields of the north Midlands and Yorkshire.

The national sports stadium at Wembley, north London catered for hockey, soccer and rugby football matches and generated, from mid-March to mid-May, a succession of 'final' and international matches attended by crowds of up to 100,000 people. Elsewhere, the horticultural shows at Southport, the pleasure gardens at Belle Vue and the popular resorts of Llandudno, Rhyl and Blackpool/Lytham provided destinations for day or longer visits.

As explained in other chapters of this book, the development of railways over time resulted in complex operational arrangements involving 'railway' boundaries for locomotives, rolling stock and men. Each motive power depot had a number of locomotives and men with knowledge of particular routes who worked shifts which resulted in many cases of the men 'lodging' away from their 'home' depot before returning later. It was unusual for any steam locomotive to work more than 400 miles in a day and for each to be expected to be available for more than 72 per cent of the time. The main line passenger trains ran within timing 'bands' dictated by the weight of the train and the power classification of the locomotives expected to be able to haul the train. This combination of operational boundaries, working arrangements for enginemen and maintenance staff, the expectation of safe, comfortable and quick journeys resulted in the principal passenger depots having allocations of locomotives that changed little in the 1950s. The enhanced demand for passenger trains in the months of the railway summer (mid-June-mid-September) resulted in some re-allocations of power (typically involving class 8s at Edge Hill, Crewe North and Carlisle Upperby plus class 7s at Camden and, with additional services worked from depots which, on Mondays-Fridays, were more fully occupied by goods working.

Within these overall arrangements many locomotives worked from 'home' depots to which they were allocated over periods up to 20 years; Polmadie depot at Glasgow being home to some Princess Coronations and using them predominantly on heavy Anglo-Scottish services as far as Carlisle. For observers north of the border the likes of *Duchess of Buccleuch* were 'common' while the sight of such south of Crewe would produce much excitement. What to one set of spotters was 'common' was 'rare' to others but, through the 1950s the LNW main lines were fairly predictable, particularly for the regulars at particular locations. Another reason for predictability was restrictions placed upon locomotives of certain classes. The LMS 8Ps were banned from main line workings over the North Staffordshire Railway route through Stoke-on-Trent (Harecastle tunnels) and, as the turntable at Longsight could not accommodate their length, they had to be turned by use of triangular junctions. Therefore, the Manchester-Euston trains were the preserve of Britannias and Royal Scots with the exception that on Fridays the heavy evening express was worked (via Crewe) by a Crewe North Princess Coronation and returned on the Saturday morning to Crewe. Those 'in the know' north of Wigan knew their best chance of a Clan was at the weekend. After 1956 the use of class 9F 2-10-0 locomotives on holiday trains from the Midlands and Sheffield became common and a gradual increase in the level of encroachment by Eastern Region types for the same purposes (particularly Blackpool) was apparent.

The maintenance regime for the 51 class 8Ps was such that all found their way to Crewe for attention at the Works; that was one reason why Crewe was something of a mecca.

The period covered by this book includes the final three good years of main line steam services unsullied by the production of batches of main line diesels. As that transition made its uncertain steps forwards and backwards, the level of predictability was reduced and the level of interest increased. As time moved on, the sports sections of newspapers took on a greater level of meaning as an indicator of enhanced flows of traffic. An FA Cup Final involving Blackburn Rovers or Burnley and/or a Rugby League Challenge Final involving Barrow was of far greater interest than, say, Aston Villa versus Tottenham Hotspur.

For a keen spotter, the last thing you would want to hear upon arrival at a location was … 'you'll never believe what's just been through'. Usually accompanied by looks of delight, the enjoinder would be particularly difficult … it was the 'just' that hurt the most. The following is a non-comprehensive listing of the unusual and the remarkable.

Date	Loco number	Loco class	Shed	Detail
1957				
2 Jan	61638	B17	30A	at Willesden
16 Jan	10201	SR	1A }	introduced to route; initially
	10202	SR	1A }	Euston – Carlisle then through to Glasgow, worked in pairs
Jan	10000	LMS	1A }	worked in pairs Euston to
	10001	LMS	1A }	Glasgow and vice versa
19 Jan	46134}	Scot		10.40 Euston – Carlisle double
	46244}	Coro	5A	headed at least to Crewe
2 Feb	10001	LMS	1A	fire at Roade
Feb	10203	SR	1A	introduced to route; 8.50 Eus – Wolv, 1/55 Wolv – Eus, 5/50 Eus – Wolv, Up night parcels

Date	Loco number	Loco class	Shed	Detail
1957 Cont				
Feb	70044	BR7	9A	named *Earl Haig*
9 Mar	46163}	Scot		double-headed Down express
	46247}	Coro	1B	
Mar	DELTIC	-	-	temporarily withdrawn for modification
9 Mar		Bull		at Wembley (specials for women's hockey match) 34046/66/87/90/1
16 Mar	40631}	2P	10B	10.40 Euston – Carlisle, double
	46229}	Coro		headed
Mar		J35	66A	two allocated to Polmadie
30 Mar	34048	Bull		at Willesden
May	70043	BR7	9A	named *Earl Kitchener*
May	48202	8F	55E	Whitsun weekend specials to and from
	61011	B1	40B	Blackpool ex North Eastern Region
	61053	B1	50A	
	61224	B1	51A	
	61274	B1	51A	
	61276	B1	51A	
3 Jun	DELTIC	-	-	weekdays 700-mile diagram 0.37 Crewe – Eus 7.55 Eus – Lpl 2/10 Lpl – Eus 7/20 Eus – Crewe
11 Jun	64833	J39	56B	at Fleetwood
18 Jun	46236	Coro	1B	down *Mid-Day Scot* derailed at Uddingston (carriage defect)
Jun	601	WD(1)	-	on loan to Polmadie, later Carlisle Kingmoor. Conversion to oil burning?
21 Jun	5071	Castle	83A	8.05 Kingwear – Manchester to Crewe
Jun	D8000	EE1	1A/D	first EE type 1 delivered to Willesden
13 Jul	61309	B1	56C	4/37 Leeds – Llandudno relief
13 Jul	4916	Hall	86A	6.45 Treherbert – Blackpool Spl at Crewe
14 Jul		Dmu		two x three car on Tunstall – Euston Spl
16 Jul	70045	BR7	6J	named *Lord Rowallan*
20 Jul	61966	K3		Hadfield – Llandudno
25 Jul	72000	Clan	66A	at Stoke-on-Trent
27 Jul	34046	Bull		at Willesden
	34063	Bull		at Willesden
29 Jul				to 14 August. 187 specials run in connection with International Scouting Jamboree
1 Aug	92141	9F		5/15 Carlisle – Crewe goods passenger trains
10 Aug		9F		to and from Blackpool 92050/5/107/77
17 Aug	92022	9F	15A	Blackpool
17 Aug	61824	K3		Nottingham – Blackpool via Stoke-on-Trent and Stockport
14 Sep		B1		Seven of class at Blackpool

Date	Loco number	Loco class	Shed	Detail
1957 Cont				
Oct		Scot		transfer of six of class to Midland Division
6 Oct	61306	B1		cyclists' excursion, Hull – Windermere to Carnforth
18 Oct		Coro		dislocation of workings in area of Preston 46236/41/2/6/54 on Carnforth shed
Nov		Clan	66A	four of class re-allocated to St Margaret's, Edinburgh for seasonal goods traffic
19 Dec	46245	Coro	1B	repainted maroon, white cab interior (first of 16)
1958				
16 Jan		WD		derailment in Preston station
25 Jan	40694} 45599}	2P Jub	24K	10/25 Glasgow – Euston double headed
3 Feb		dmu		postponement of new service B'ham – Stafford – Stoke – Man
24 Feb				diversions via Blackburn – Hellifield due to blockage by snow of main line
8 Mar		Bull		34046/89/91/2 at Wembley (spls for women's hockey match)
10 May				Rugby League Final at Wembley refer to main chapter text
May	46207	Prin	8A	repainted maroon (first of four)
Jun		Scot		transfer back of Royal Scots from Midland Division; refer to main chapter text
Jun		Brit		Britannias to Midland Division 73041/2 from Holyhead to Stewarts Lane as part of wider moves
Summer		4P	2A	used on passenger trains Rugby – Euston
Summer		9F		in use to Blackpool/n. Wales/Fleetwood
20 Jun		B1		61020/49 Sowerby Bridge – Llandudno
28 Jun	61061	B1		Bradford Exchange – Llandudno
7 Jul				derailment at Oxenholme; diversion via Hellifield – Blackburn. 46124 on Down *Caledonian*
Jul	70048	BR7	6J	named *The Territorial Army 1908-1958*
25 Jul	90764	WD	66A	at Rugby
6 Aug	49508	7F		at Watford
6 Aug	46238	Coro	12B	at Bescot (tender wheelset)
19 Aug	46231	Coro	66A	failed at Stafford on Up *Caledonian*; forward with crab to Rugby, then Black 5
Aug				turntable at Longsight disposed to Heaton Mersey
Aug	47517	3F	1D	last steam loco at Devons Road; refer to main chapter text
2 Sep	46105	Scot	66A	4/10 Manchester Vic – Blackpool
6 Sep	123	Cal		at Beattock
11 Nov				derailment between Stafford and Crewe; diversion via Wellington and Shrewsbury with usual motive power

Date	Loco number	Loco class	Shed	Detail
1958 cont				
12 Nov	46224	Coro	66A	at Stoke-on-Trent; spl arrangements for safe passage through Harecastle tunnels
Nov	58926	Coal	-	last LNWR 0-6-2T withdrawn for preservation
17 Dec	2279	22XX		at Blisworth
1959				
2 Jan	*DELTIC*			failed at Rugby while working 7.55 Euston – Liverpool; forward with two *Crabs*
17 Feb	60920	V2		Carlisle – Warrington goods. At Springs Branch 1 March
17 Feb	61838	K3	2F	at Leighton Buzzard, iron ore
19 Mar		Bull		34008/19/67/77/101/5 Wembley
		Schools		30937
				at Wembley, women's hockey match
24 Apr	45374}	B5	1A	1.00 Euston – Glasgow; double
	45669}	Jub	1B	headed to Carlisle
May				short-term power crisis at London end resulted in double heading of 4-6-0s 45064/324, 44763/45324, 45706/22
28 Jun	7920	Hall		B'ham (Snow Hill) – Manchester (Central) excursion to Crewe
4 Jul	61306	B1		excursion to Rhyl
Aug		K1		62005/9/47 at Blackpool 1st – 4th
Aug	70046	BR7	6J	Named *Anzac*
5 Aug	62064	K1		Hull – Llandudno special
6 Aug		B5		Royal Train 45032/184 ex Euston
27 Aug	D226	EE4		failed at Watford on Up *Lancastrian*; fwd with 80035
30 Sep		Jub		45606/32 double headed
				10.0 Euston – Glasgow
3 Nov		Scot		launch of new vessel at Barrow shipyard. 46111/44
15 Nov				diversions away from main line due to engineering works between Garstang and Carnforth. Also on 22 Nov
5 Dec	E3001	Elec	9A	first of type accepted
1960				
8 Feb				derailment of York – Swansea at Sandbach
spring				sporting fixtures at Wembley, refer to main chapter text 34008/39/68/87/9/99/100, 30921, D5000/4, 19 March 34010, 30921/2, 73112, 30 April
12 Mar				engineering work diversions Runcorn – Warrington
15 Mar	61077	B1	14D	down goods
22 Mar	76080	BR3	24D	down goods at Watford
Apr		BR/Sul		pilot order of BR/Sulzer locos introduced onto route

Date	Loco number	Loco class	Shed	Detail
<u>1960</u> <u>cont</u>				
9 May	46121	Scot	66A	11.42 Man Vic – St Pancras
12 May	72001	Clan	66A	11.42 Man Vic – St Pancras
21 Jun	61113	B1		at Tamworth Low Level
26 Jun	D5346	BRCW	64B	5/15 Inverness – Euston to Crewe
Jun				at Southport B1s 61053 (50A), 61337 (50A) and 9F (18A)
1 Jul	61010	B1	50B	at Windermere
summer		9F		Leicester allocated examples used on seasonal trains to Eastbourne (part way only)
30 Jul	61856}	K3	56B	Blackpool – Sheffield relief,
	61932}	K3	50B	double headed
17 Aug	60011	A4	64B	12/20 Perth – Euston to Carlisle
31 Aug	64789	J39	40E	at Shilton
1 Sep	60530	A2	64B	12/20 Perth – Euston to Carlisle
12 Sep	E3040	Elec	LMNW	first public departure from electrified Manchester London Road 12/15 to Plymouth
17 Sep		WR		specials to Blackpool ex WR Castles 5042 (81A), 7007 (85A) and Hall 5980 (87A) to Crewe
24 Sep	60842	V2	50A	at Stockport Edgeley shed
14 Dec	D5519	Brush	ER	on Up *Ulster Express* at Tring following failure of EE type 4
22 Dec	2257	22XX	84E	Northampton – Wolverton goods and return
30 Dec	61323	B1	31B	coal empties at Wolverton
<u>1961</u>				
7 Jan	61048	B1	32A	Footex Portsmouth v Peterborough Utd
	61052	B1	31B	(via Northampton – Bletchley)
11 Feb				return specials ex Edinburgh following Scotland v Wales rugby Castle 5048 (to Cardiff), Halls 6944, 7925 (to Treherbert) ex-Crewe
2 Mar	61171	B1	31A	Bletchley – Northampton goods
11 Mar		Bull		34038/46/86/90 at Wembley for women's hockey match
16 Mar	76052	BR3	12D	at Wolverton
5 Apr	92122	9F	18A	8.0 Blackpool – Euston failed at Tring with D7
19 Apr	72003	Clan	66A	Footex Wolverhampton Wanderers v Glasgow Rangers
29 Apr				30923, 34007/45 at Wembley for boys' football match
6 May	60103	A3	34A	Lincoln – Keswick spl. Worked return from Penrith and via Preston
24 May				Royal Train to Belle Vue 44734/44927. Forward with 46137
27 May				specials to Blackpool D5687/90/2, 61846/99 (from Hull), 61922 (Bradford)
28 May	61033	B1		Sheffield – Blackpool

Date	Loco number	Loco class	Shed	Detail
1961 cont				
May	E2001	MetV		insulator cleaning on Helensburgh line (ex gas turbine 18100)
20 Jun	72000	Clan	66A	5/05 Blackpool – Euston
22 Jun	61954		31B	ecs to Wolverton works
24 Jun		Brush	41A	D5684/8 Chesterfield – Blackpool
1 Jul	60088	A3	55A	at Aston off Inverness – Sutton Coldfield. Return via Crewe
10 Jul	1005	Coun		at Crewe
29 Jul	30911	Schools		at Camden shed
summer		9F		in use Sheffield – Blackpool and N. Wales
Aug		Pann		3739/47/86/9661 at Stockport en route to Beyer, Peacock/ Gorton
5 Aug	61047	B1		at Watford
6 Aug		Prin		at Windermere
14 Aug	61066	B1		at Watford
23 Aug	53801	S&D		at Crewe Works
24 Aug	61204		31B	at Leighton Buzzard
25 Aug	45165	B5	63A	Oldham – Carnforth parcels
30 Sep	60022	A4	34A	Retford – Blackpool spl. Assisted by Compound 1000 on return
Oct		22XX		2201/10 at Northampton
Oct	GT3			Crewe – Carlisle ecs test runs
21 Nov				derailment at Watford Junction. Diversions to St Pancras and Marylebone. 46240 on *Merseyside Express* into Paddington
21 Dec	61053	B1		Stourton – Heysham tank wagons
21 Dec	61198	B1		Liverpool – Blackpool special
1962				
1 Jan	D132	BR/Sul		up *Caledonian*
6 Jan	D6706	EE3	30A	Footex Broxbourne – B'ham
Jan		B1		61062/61198/61370 at Nuneaton shed
17 Feb	D5695	Brush		Footex Broxbourne – B'ham
27 Feb	64727	J39	9G	ex-works Cowlairs, to home depot via Newcastle, Carlisle
27 Feb	D860	War	83A	fill in turns Shrewsbury – Crewe for later through workings of Class
15 Mar	46200	Prin	12B	up *Comet*
23 Mar	46233	Coro	8A	up *Comet*
28 Mar	D153	BR/Sul		tests on ScR
31 Mar				Aintree horse race meeting, refer to main chapter text

Date	Loco number	Loco class	Shed	Detail
1962				
cont				
6 Apr	75038	BR4		up *Caledonian* failed with EE type 4
7 Apr	61252	B1	31B	Bletchley – Northampton
11 Apr	61325	B1	40B	ecs for Wolverton works
May	DP2			introduced to route for trial running
May	63948	O2	34F	Northampton – Blisworth – Roade – Market Harborough
22 May	63686	O4	9G	at Rhyl
26 May	61389	B1	34F	Newark – Blackpool special
27 May		Brush	41B	D5805/25 Grimesthorpe – Blackpool special
23 Jun		War		D850/67 on through workings Bristol – Crewe
23 Jun	46255	Coro	12B	on Windermere branch
29 Jun	46252	Coro	12A	on Windermere branch
11 Jul	61418	B16	50A	at Northampton
14 Jul	30856	LN		at Willesden off Portsmouth – Colne special
25 Jul	46250	Coro	12B	up *Comet*
18 Aug	60529	A2	64A	at Beattock shed
31 Aug	63837	O4		Immingham – Heysham tanks
3 Nov	34087	Bull		at Nuneaton on Bournemouth – Coventry footex via Leamington
3 Nov	34006	Bull	70A	At Watford J. footex
1963				
winter				refer to main chapter text
3 Feb	60089	A3	64A	Scotland v Wales rugby special, refer to main chapter text
Feb	D1047	Wes		Oxley – Crewe fitted goods working
7 Feb	61402	B1		6.30 Crewe – Shrewsbury parcels
Feb	34094	Bull		crankex, Marylebone – Crewe
Feb				1A Royal Scots in store at Devons Road
11 Mar	61454	B16	50A	at Stockport shed
25 Mar	60856	V2	50A	at Nuneaton on special for Coventry Cathedral. Others up to 16 Sep worked by 60810/28/969, 61018/49, D6755 and D398
30 Mar				Aintree horse race meeting specials. Refer to main chapter text
27 Apr	34102	Bull		at Wembley
3 May	70027	BR7	21D	on Aston – Gushetfaulds *Condor*
13 May	34089	Bull		at Willesden on Sutton – Coventry special
21 May	61026	B1		Lincoln – Windermere special
4 Jun	46100	Scot		ex Crewe dead. Sold to B. Butlin Ltd
9 Jun	D5824	Brush	41A	Chesterfield – Llandudno special
18 Jun	62005	K1		at Stockport Edgeley shed
15 Jul	60871	V2	36A	Northampton – Euston and Euston – Rugby passenger services

Date	Loco number	Loco class	Shed	Detail
1963 cont				
Aug	46201	Prin		sold. Worked in steam Carlisle to Ashchurch via Leeds/ Derby
1 Aug	61285	B1	40E	at Watford on coal empties
19 Aug	D8041	EE1		at Aston for crew training
1 Sep	60802	V2		9/50 Perth – Euston to Carnforth
Sep	46239	Coro	6J	on loan to Holyhead shed
28 Sep	D7022	Hy		footex Northampton versus Swindon Town
28 Sep	60114	A1	36A	Lincoln – Blackpool special
Nov		Brush 4		crew training Crewe – Shrewsbury
11 Dec	7012	Castle		Wellington – Crewe parcels
12 Dec	D1072	Wes		on ecs test run at Preston
14 Dec				ex Western Region at Stockport Edgeley en route to Wigan (Ince) for scrapping Castle 5015 County 1017/22/26 2-6-0 7309/7326

Notes to listings

Locomotive class:

Western Region
Castle   Castle 4-6-0
County   County 4-6-0
Hall   Hall 4-6-0
22XX   0-6-0

Southern Region
Bull   Bulleid pacific 4-6-2
LN   Lord Nelson 4-6-0
Schools   Schools 4-4-0

London Midland Region
B5   Black 5 4-6-0
Coro   Princess Coronation 4-6-2
Jub   Jubilee 4-6-0
S&D   7F 2-8-0
Scot   Royal Scot 4-6-0
2P/4P   4-4-0
3F   0-6-0T
7F   0-8-0
8F   2-8-0

Eastern Region

A1	4-6-2
A2	4-6-2
A3	4-6-2
A4	4-6-2
B1	4-6-0
B16	4-6-0
B17	4-6-0
J35	0-6-0
J39	0-6-0
K1	2-6-0
K3	2-6-0
O2	2-8-0
O4	2-8-0
V2	2-6-2

British Railways

BR3	2-6-0
BR4	4-6-0
BR7	4-6-2
Clan	4-6-2
9F	2-10-0

Other

Cal	Caledonian 4-2-2
Coal	LNW 0-6-2T
WD	Austerity 2-8-0
WD(1)	Longmoor 2-10-0

Western Region
Diesels

BRCW	type 2
BR/Sul	type 4
Brush	type 2
Brush 4	type 4

DELTIC

dmu	diesel multiple unit
EE1	English Electric type 1
EE3	English Electric type 3
EE4	English Electric type 4
Hy	Hymek, hydraulic
LMS	prototype
SR	prototypes
War	Warship, hydraulic
Wes	Western, hydraulic

Electric:

Elec	production builds for Man/Lpl – London
MetV	conversion from 18100 gas turbine

Crankex	enthusiast excursion
down	away from London
ecs	empty coaching stock
Eus	Euston
Footex	football excursion
spl	special
up	towards London

Sheds:

1A	Willesden	14D	Neasden	51A	Darlington
1B	Camden	15A	Wellingborough	55A	Leeds Holbeck
1D	Devons Road	18A	Toton	55E	Normanton
2A	Rugby	24K	Preston	56B	Ardsley
2F	Woodford Halse	30A	Stratford	56C	Copley Hill
6J	Holyhead	31B	March	63A	Perth
8A	Edge Hill	32A	Norwich	64A	St Margaret's
9A	Longsight	34A	King's Cross	64B	Haymarket
9G	Gorton	40B	Immingham	83A	Newton Abbot
10B	Preston	40E	Colwick	84A	Plymouth Laira
12A	Carlisle Kingmoor	41A	Darnall	84E	Tyseley
12B	Carlisle Upperby	50A	York	86A	Newport
12D	Kirkby Stephen	50B	Hull		

Appendices

1. Example extracts from working timetables

2. Listing of main line departures from London (Euston) in 1898 and 1908 (weekdays)

3. Listing of main line passenger train departures from London (Euston) in 1935 and 1956 (weekdays, winter)

4. Listing of locomotives designed for the LMS by Sir William Stanier

5. Listing of visits to, and times in, Crewe Works by Princess Coronation and Princess Royal Class locomotives between 1957 and 1959

6. Listing of main line passenger trains passing Preston North Union, Chester (General) and Tamworth Low Level on summer Saturdays in 1960

Appendix 1

Example Extracts from Working Timetables

Extracts have been included to list the abbreviations as generally applicable and for:

Euston to Crewe passenger, early evening
Crewe to Liverpool and Preston passenger, night
Camden to Nuneaton, evening.

Appendix 1/2

EXPLANATION OF REFERENCES

M	...	Monday	**Th**	...	Thursday
T	...	Tuesday	**F**	...	Friday
W	...	Wednesday	**S**	...	Saturday

The addition of the letter " **O** " indicates that the train will run on that day or those days only. The letter " **X** " indicates that the train will not run on that day or those days.

CL — Carriage Line   **GL** — Goods Line
FL — Fast Line   **SL** — Slow Line

AE — Stops only to attach or detach assisting engine.
D — Stops only to set down.
DI
D2 } Diesel Multiple Unit Trains—for formation see Loads of
D3 } Passenger Trains Booklet.
E — Stops only for examination.
ECS — Empty coaching stock train (Class **C**).
† — Empty coaching stock train (Class **C**), or empty diesel train (Class **C**).
L — Stops only to change engine or trainmen.
M — Mails delivered or received at line side apparatus.
‡ — Advertised time in public time table.
Q — Runs when required.
R — Stops when required.
U — Stops only to take up.
W — Stops only for water.
X — Indicates points (a) at which train is booked to run from one running line to another, (b) at which trains are booked to cross each other on a single line at a crossing place.
* — Stops or shunts for other trains to pass, or for staff or token purposes only.
♠ — 4-wheeled vehicles with a wheelbase of less than 15 ft. must not be conveyed on this train.
‖ — Light engine (Class **G**).
§ — Indicates that head code is changed en route.
→ — For continuation of train timings see subsequent column.
← — Train timings continued from previous column.

a	—	arrives 1 minute earlier.		
b	—	,,	1½ minutes	,,
c	—	,,	2	,,
d	—	,,	2½	,,
e	—	,,	3	,,
f	—	,,	3½	,,
g	—	,,	4	,,
h	—	,,	4½	,,
j	—	,,	5	,,

P — Motive Power Depot.
▣ — Indicates the number of minutes allowed for recovery time between the points named.

Appendix 1/4

EUSTON TO CREWE

DOWN

		A	A	A	C	A	B	A	A	A	B	B	B	A	A	B	B
		To Holyhead	2.55 pm Yarmouth V. to Walsall		Empty Diesel			To Holyhead	6.50 pm Birmingham to Heysham	5.22 pm from Broad St.	To Bletchley	To Northampton	To Wolverhampton	To Wolverhampton		To Bletchley
		145	317	413		413	411	145	371		415	417	135	135	409	415
		SO	SO	SX	SO	SO	SX	SX	FO	SX	SX	SO	SX	SO	SX	FO
		PM	PM	PM	PM	PM	PM	PM	PM	PM	PM	PM	PM	PM	PM	PM
EUSTON .. .. .. dep	1	5 20	..	5 20	..	5 27	5 25	5 35	..	5X35	5 43	5 46	5 50	5 50	5 48	5 48
Camden	2	FL	....	FL	SL	FL	SL	FL	..	SL	SL	SL	FL	FL	SL	SL
Kilburn High Road	3	..	....	..	..	..	..	..	..	..	..	..	..	..	..	..
Willesden Jn........... arr	4										5 53				5 58	5 58
.. .. dep	5	5 30	..	5 30	..	5 37	5 34	5 45	..	5 41	5 54	5 55	5 59	6 0	5 59	5 59
Wembley Central	6															
Harrow and Wealdstone arr	7						5 42			5 49		6 3			6 8	6 8
.. .. dep	8				5†35		5 43			5 50		6 6			6 10	6 10
Hatch End	9														6 14	6 14
Bushey and Oxhey	10									5 57					6 19	6 19
WATFORD JN. .. arr	11	..	..	5 45	5†50	5 52	5 51			6 1	6 8	6 14			6 23	6 23
.. .. dep	12	5 44		5 47		5 54	5 53	5 58		6 3	6 11	6 16	6 11	6 14		6 26
King's Langley and A.L. ..	13						6b 0			6b10						
Apsley	14		From 12th July to 30th August inclusive		After working 5.20 pm from Belmont		6c 6			6a15	Will not run 1st and 8th August		XL Limit	Special Limit	Will not run 1st and 8th August	Runs 1st and 8th August only
Hemel Hempstead and arr	15						6 9			6 18						
Boxmoor .... dep	16					Limited Load	6 10			6 19						
Bourne End	17															
Berkhamsted .... arr	18						6 16			6 25						
.. .. dep	19						6 17			6 26						
TRING .. .. arr	20						6 23			6 32						
.. .. dep	21	6 1		6 6		6 13	6 25	6 14		..	C		6 25	6 30		
Cheddington .... arr	22						6 31									
.. .. .. dep	23		Limited Load				6 32	Special Limit			ECS					
Leighton Buzzard .. .. arr	24			6 15		6 22	6 38									
.. .. dep	25			6X17 SL		6X24 SL	6 41									
BLETCHLEY .... arr	26			6 26		6 33	6 50			B						
.. .. dep	27	6 15		6 28	B	6 35	6 53	6 27			6†40 SL	6 37	6 43		
Wolverton .. .. .. arr	28			6 36		6 43	7 1				6†N46				
.. .. .. dep	29			6 37		6 46	7 4		6.14 pm Rail Motor Northampton to Leamington Spa						
Castlethorpe	30				6.14 pm Rail Motor Northampton to Leamington Spa	6d53	7d11								
ROADE .. .. arr	31					7 1	7 19								
.. .. .. dep	32	6 28		6 48		7 3	7 21	6 39			After working 5.6 pm from Euston	6 48	6 55		
Middleton	33			6 52		7 8	7 26		Limited Load						
Blisworth .. .. .. arr	34			SX						SO		6 51	6 58		
.. .. .. dep	35	6 31		6 30				6 42		6‡35		6 57	7 5		
Weedon	36	6 38		6a41				6 49		6a46					
Welton	37														
Duston Jn. North	38														
NORTHAMPTON C arr	39			6 57		7 13	7 31				Z Loughton Goods Siding				
dep	40			7 2		7 18				B1§					
Althorp Park	41														
Long Buckby	42			7a19		7a34		‡7.58 pm	‡ 6.30 pm						
Kilsby and Crick	43														
RUGBY MIDLAND arr	44	6 53	7 0	7 32		7 47									
dep	45	6 57	7 3	..		..		7 2		7.45 pm Diesel Wolverhampton to Stoke-on-Trent.		7 9	7 18		
Midland Jn.	46														
NUNEATON T.V... arr	47														B5
.. dep	48	7 14						7 17		D2					
Atherstone	49									§ B4 from Stafford					
Polesworth..	50					C			‡ 8.37 pm					6.40 pm Diesel from Birmingham	
Tamworth L.L. .. .. arr	51									A					
.. .. dep	52	7 28						7 30							
Lichfield T.V. .. .. arr	53									4.40 pm from Cardiff	§ B4 from Stafford			SX	
.. .. dep	54	7 35						7 36						D1	
Armitage	55				7.15 pm FSX, 7.5 pm FO Dudley Port to Stoke-on-Trent										
Rugeley T.V........... arr	56													7 56	
.. .. dep	57	7 43						7 44		257					
Colwich	58									FO Runs SL Stafford to Norton Bridge					
Milford and Brocton	59	7 48				SX X SL		7 49		SX Q					
Stafford No. 1	60										FL				
STAFFORD.. .. .. arr	61	7 54				7 45		7 55	7 54		8 6				
.. .. dep	62	7 58				7 52		7‡59	8X4 FL	When run forms 9.0 pm SX Crewe to Liverpool	8 7				
Norton Bridge	63	8 6				8 1		8 7	8 12		8 14½				
Whitmore	64	8 17						8 16	8 23						
CREWE.. .. .. .. arr	65	8 28						8 27	8‡34	8 30					
.. .. dep	66	8 36						8 36	8 41						

Appendix 1/3 EUSTON TO CREWE WEEKDAYS A35

	C	A	A	B	B	A	B	B	B	B	A	B		A	A	B	C	B	A
ECS		To Manchester	To Manchester	6.36 pm Rail Motor from Buckingham	7.18 pm Rail Motor from 'Wellingboro' Mid.Rd.	To Manchester	Rail Motor to Bedford	5.43 pm from Euston	5.46 pm from Euston	5.48 pm from Euston	To Manchester			To Liverpool	To Liverpool	To Stafford	Pcls to Carlisle	To Heysham	
		133	139			139		415	417	415	133	417		137	137	179	3	429	247
	SO	FO	SO		SX	SX	SX	SX	SO	FO	SO	SX		SX	SO	SX	SO	SX	FO
1	PM	PM	PM	PM	PM	PM	PM	PM	PM	PM	PM	PM		PM	PM	PM	PM	PM	PM
2	..	5 55	6 0	..	..	6 0	..	SL	SL	SL	6 5	6 6	..	6 10	6 10	..	6 10	6 12	6 15
3	..	FL	FL	..	..	FL	..	SL	SL	SL	FL	SL	..	FL	FL	..	SL	SL	FL
4	..	..	..	..	..	..	..	..	..	..	..	..		..	..		..	..	..
5	..	6 5	6 10	..	..	6 10					6 15			6 20	6 20		6 29	6 21	6 26
6	..																7X52 FL		
7	..	Is FSX	FSX	..													→	..	..
8	..					Euston and Rugby		Will not run 1st and 8th August	Euston and Rugby		Will not run 1st and 8th August								
9	..																		
10	..					[2]		6 8	6 14	6 23	[2]						Willesden No.1 pass 6.27 pm	6b35	6 39
11																			
12		6 18	6 23			6 25		6 11	6 16	6 26	6 30	6 29		6 33	6 37			6 41	6 40
13								6b18	6b23	6b33								6b48	
14		Special Limit	Special Limit		Special Limit			6a23	6a28	6a38		6 40						6a53	
15								6 26	6 31	6 41		6 42					Will not run 1st and 8th August		Special Limit
16								6 28	6 33	6 43	Is regular 28th June to 23rd August inclusive, Q other Saturdays			Special Limit	Special Limit			
17																			
18								6 34	6 39	6 49		6 48							
19	After working 5.3 pm from Euston							6 39	6 41	6 51		6 50							
20								6 45	6 47	6 57									
21		6 33	6 38			6 40		6 47	6 49	6 59	6 45	6 55		6 48	6 52			7 7	6 55
22							Will not run 1st and 8th August	6 55	6 57	7 5		7 0				Euston and Rugby		7 13	Euston and Rugby
23	Not advertised							6 58	7 3	7 13		7 1						7 14	
24									7 7	7 14		7 7						7 20	
25								6 59				7 13				[4]		7 23	[2]
26				7 7				7 8	7 16	7 23		7 23						7 32	
27	6†45	6 46	6 51			6 53	7 17		7 30		6 58	7 27		7 1	7 5				7 8
28	SL 6†53								7 38		Not advertised	7 35							Not advertised
29									7 40	Runs 1st and 8th August only		7 37				B			
30				B			B		7 45			7 42							
31									7 53			7 50							
32		6 58	7 3			7 5		7 55		7 10	7 52		7 13	7 17				7 20	
33							B	8 0			7 57					6.12 pm from Peterboro' East		
34							4.50 pm from Ely											
35		7 1	7 6	Rail Motor from Leamington Spa Avenue		7 8	7 33			7 13			7 16	7 20			7 23	
36		7 8	7 13			7 15				7 20			7 23	7 27			7 30	
37							7 41								A		
38							7 43	7 57	8 5		8 2						
39	B					7 46					Special Limit						
40								B									
41	To Leicester		Rugby and Crewe							7 10		Leighton Buzzard and Bletchley				7.40 pm from Birmingham	
42			[2]									[1]					
43					N 7.44 SO		A		To Stafford					7†47			
44																	
45	7 24	7 21	7 26			7 28			179		7 33		7 36	7 40		463	7 43
46				7N41		To Llandudno											
47								SO								SO	
48		7 36	7 41	A		7 43		7 49		7 48		7 51	7 55	7 55	G	7 58
49								SL						SL	Limited Load	
50				10.5 am Penzance to Manchester	A		455	8g 1						8g 7		
51								8 8		8 1		8 4	8 8	8 14		
52		7 49	7 54		A	7 56	FO	8 14						8 20	7.50 pm from Oxley Shed	8 11
53								8 16						8 29		
54		7 55	8 0	285	4.40 pm Cardiff Liverpool	8 2		8 26		8 7		8 10	8 14	8 39		8 17
55				SX				8 44						8 41		
56					257	Applies only Chester to Llandudno Jn.			B				SX		
57	B6	8 3	8 6			8 10					8 18	8 22		Stafford and Crewe	8 25
58				SO			To Liverpool							[2]	
59		8 8	8 13		8 15		257		To Wellington	8 20		8 23	8 27	To work 10.4 pm to Bristol	X.	8 30
60							SX			594					SL	
61			Applies only Crewe to Liverpool						SO						8 31	
62	7.15 pm Diesel from Derby Midland	8 13	8 18			8 20	Formed at 4.40 pm SX from Cardiff when that train runs	8 22	8 25	12.30 pm Paignton to Manchester		8 28	8 32	7.50 pm to work 10.4 pm	8X36 FL	8 35
63		8 20	8 25			8 27			8 32	‡9.0 pm		8 35	8 39		8 45	8 42
64	D2	8 29	8 34	8 41	8†2	8 36	8.40	8 41				8 44	8 48		8 56	8 51
65	8 41						‡9 0		8 48					N— North Jn.	9N7	9 2
66		8 39	8 46	8 57	9‡2	8 46	8†45	FL	9‡10			8 54	8 58		9 7	9 7

Appendix 1/5 — CREWE TO LIVERPOOL AND PRESTON

DOWN

Column descriptions (left to right):

- **291** (A) — To Glasgow C.
- **291** (A) — 10.10 pm Coventry to Glasgow C.
- **293** (A) — 10.54 pm Sun from Leeds City S.orth. 12.11 am MX from Stalybridge
- **177** (A) — 11.10 pm Birmingham New Street to Glasgow C.
- **299** (A) — 1.10 am from Chester Gen.
- **60** (A) — 9.25 pm Euston to Glasgow C.
- **171** (A)
- **385** (C) — 12.15 am Pcls from Crewe
- **448** (A) — 11.15 am Holyhead to Manchester Ex.
- **301** (C) — 9.42 pm Euston to Glasgow C.
- **23** (A) — Pcls to Perth
- **1** (C) — 1.50 am News from Manchester Ex.
- **45** (A) — To Whitehaven B.
- **45** (A) — 10.45 pm Euston to Whitehaven B.

		291	291	293	177	299	60	171	385	448	301	23	1	45	45
Condition		MSX Q	SO				SO	↑		MX	SO ↑	SO Q		MX ↑	MO ↑
		am	am	am	am	am	am	am	am	am	am	am	am	am	am
CREWE ... dep	1	12 40 FL	12 40 FL	12 45 FL			1 0 FL	1 15 FL			1 20 FL	1 25 FL		1 50 FL	1 50 FL
Crewe Coal Yard	2														
Coppenhall Jn.	3	12 45	12 45	12 50			1 5	1 20			1 25	1 30		1 55	1 55
Winsford	4														
Winsford Jn. arr	5	12 51	12 51	12 56	1 11			1 26			1 32	1 37		2 1	2 1
Hartford ... dep	6/7		*Not advertised*	*Crewe and Edge Hill*		*Commences 26th July*			*Commences 26th July*						
Hartford Jn.	8														
Acton Bridge arr	9														
... dep	10										[14]	[13]			
WEAVER JN.	11	12 59	12 59	1 4			1 19	1 33			1 42	1 50		2 8	2 8
Frodsham Jn.	12			1 12		1 26		1 29							
Halton Jn.	13														
Runcorn ... arr	14														
... dep	15														
DITTON JN. arr	16					1 35									
... dep	17			1 18		1 35									
Halebank	18														
Speke Jn.	19			1 25		1 42									
Allerton arr/dep	20/21														
West Allerton	22		*Commences 28th June*	*Edge Hill and Liverpool L. St.*		*Chester Gen. and Liverpool L. St.*		*Limited Load*	*Limited Load*	*Limited Load*	*Not advertised*	*Limited Load*		*Limited Load*	*Limited Load*
Mossley Hill	23														
Sefton Park	24														
Wavertree	25														
Wavertree Jn.	26														
Edge Hill arr	27			[2] 1 34		1 51									
... dep	28			1 40		[5] 1 51									
LIVERPOOL LIME STREET arr	29			1 47		1 57									
Norton	30														
Acton Grange Jn.	31	1 7	1 7				1 27	1 40			1X42 SL	1 54	2 4	2 15	2 15
Walton New Jn.	32										1X43				
Walton Old Jn.	33										FL				
WARRINGTON arr	34								12 55	1 45					
BANK QUAY dep	35	1 9	1 9	A			1 29	1 42	1X48 FL	1 52	1 56	2 6		2 17	2 17
Winwick Jn.	36	1 13	1 13				1 33	1 46	1 53	1 57	2 1	2 10		2 21	2 21
Vulcan Halt	37							A							
Earlestown arr/dep	38/39														
Newton-le-Willows arr/dep	40/41			12.46 am Liverpool L.St. to Glasgow C.		12.46 am Liverpool L.St. to Glasgow C.			Warrington B.Q. and Wigan N.W.	2 1					
Lowton Jn.	42														
Golborne Jn.	43							[7]							
Golborne	44			[7]											
Bamfurlong Jn.	45							7							
Springs Branch	46	1 22	1 22	1X33 SL / 1 36	1 36 FL / 1 39	1 42		1 59	2 3		2 10	2 20	2 25 FL	2 29	2 29
WIGAN N.W. arr	47			1 36	1 39		1 36		2 6				2 28 FL	2 32	2 32
... dep	48	1 24	1 24	1 55 →		1 44	1 55	2 1	2 30		2 12	2 22		2 43	2 43
Boar's Head Jn.	49			→											
White Bear	50														
Adlington Jn.	51			*Mails to Wigan N.W.*	*Mails*										
Amberswood Jn. East	52														
De Trafford Jn.	53														
Whelley Jn.	54														
Standish Jn.	55	1 31	1 31			1 51		2 4	2 9	2 39	2 19	2 29		2 52	2 52
Coppull	56														
Balshaw Lane and Euxton	57														
EUXTON JN.	58	1 39	1 39			1 59	2 12	2 18	2 47		2 27	2X38 SL		3 0	3 0
Leyland	59														
Farington Jn.	60														
Farington	61														
Ribble Sidings	62														
PRESTON N.U. arr	63	1 46	1 46			2 6	2 20	2 25	2 55		2 40	2 46		3 8	3 8

Column notes:
- **448 (C9):** From 28th June to 30th August inclusive. Limited Load.
- **45 (C13):** Applies only Crewe to Lancaster C. Limited Load.
- **45 (C14):** Applies only Euston to Lancaster C. Limited Load.
- **60 (C6):** Applies only Euston to Penrith and Carlisle to Glasgow C.
- **301 (C10):** Crewe and Preston N.U.
- **23 (C11):** Crewe and Preston N.U.

Appendix 1/6

CREWE TO LIVERPOOL AND PRESTON — WEEKDAYS — F7

	C	A	A	A	C	C	A	A	A		C	A	A	A	A	A	A	C	C	C
	1.40 am Perishable Chester Gen.	10.52 pm Euston Manchester Ex.	10.52 pm Euston to Perth	10.52 pm Euston to Perth	8.42 pm Eastbourne to Glasgow St. Enoch	1.40 am Perishable Chester Gen. to Manchester Ex.	1.40 am Perishable Chester Gen. to Manchester Ex.	11.5 pm Euston to Windermere	11.5 pm Euston to Windermere	News	Pcls to Carnforth	11.15 pm Euston to Blackpool North	News	11.40 pm Euston to Glasgow St. Enoch	11.40 pm Euston to Glasgow St. Enoch	11.50 pm Euston to Glasgow St. Enoch	Pcls to Blackburn	Pcls to Carlisle	Pcls to Carlisle	Pcls to Preston N.U.
	78	195	195	105	78	78	193	193	231		387	183	231	21	21	173	35	35	167
	MX	MX	MO	TThO	WF SO	TThO	TThX	TThO	MX		MX	SO	MO	MO	MX		MSX Q	SO	MO
1	am	am 2U5 FL	am 2‡7 FL	am 2L10	am	am	am 2 18 FL	am 2 20 FL	am 2 25 FL	..	am	am 2 30 FL	am 2 35 FL	am 2 50 FL	am 2 56 FL	am	am 3 0 FL	am 3 0 FL	am 3 5 FL
2																			
3	...	2 10	2 12	2 15	..	..	2 23	2 25	2 30	..	..	2 35	2 40	2 55	3 1	..	3 6	3 6	3 10
4 5	...	2 16	2 18	2 21	..	..	2 29	2 31	2 37	..	..	2 42	2 47	3 1	3 7	..	3 13	3 13	3 17
6 7 8 9 10		Mails	Mails						Mails				Mails						
11	...	2 23	2 25	2 29			2 36	2 38	2 45			2 50	2 55	3 9	3 15		3 21	3 21	3 25
12 13 14 15 16		Applies only Euston to Carlisle	Applies only Euston to Carlisle						2 53		From 21st June to 6th September inclusive	3 3							
17									2 59			3 9							
18 19				Will not run on 5th August					3 6			3 16							
20 21 22 23 24 25 26 27 28		Limited Load	Limited Load				Limited Load	Limited Load	Crewe and Liverpool L. St. 3X15 SL 3 21		Crewe and Warrington B.Q. [2]	Crewe and Liverpool L. St. 3X25 SL 3 31	Applies only Euston to Preston N.U.	Applies only Carlisle to Glasgow St. Enoch	Applies only Carlisle to Glasgow St. Enoch				
29																			
30 31	2 3 2X8 SL	.. 2 30	2 32	2 37	....	..	2 43	2 45			2 57		3 17	3 23		3 29	3 29	3 33
32 33 34	2 9 2 12				2 12	2 12	2 46	2‡48			3 0							3X35 SL 3 37
35 36	2X739 FL →	2 32 2 36	2 34 2 38	2 39 2 43	2X39 FL SL 2 44	2 44 SL 2 49	2 54 2 59	2 54 2 59			3 8 3 13		3 19 3 23	3 25 3 29		3 31 3 35	3 31 3 35	4X5 FL →
37 38 39 40 41 42 43	Departs 2X44 pm SL TThO	Crewe and Wigan N.W. [3]	Crewe and Wigan N.W. [1]	Crewe and Wigan N.W. [6]	2 48	2 53		‡2.46 pm			Not advertised Euston to Crewe	Crewe and Preston N.U. [10]				Crewe and Ribble Sidings [8]	Crewe and Ribble Sidings [8]	
44 45																		
46	..	2 47	2 47	2 58	..	..	3 7	3 7			3 21		3 35	3 38		3 52	3 52	
47		2U50	2U50	3L 1			3 10	3 10			3 24							
48 49 50 51 52 53 54 55		2U56 3 5	2U‡58 ‡ Crewe dep. 2.5 am Wigan N.W. dep. 2U56 am	3L10 3 16 3 23 Not advertised	3 16	3 16	3 25	3 25		3 21 3 30	3 31 Limited Load 3 40		3 37 4 2 3 45	3 40 3 47	Mails	3 50 3 55 4 1	3 54 4 1	3 54
56 57 58		3 13	3 15				3 33	3 33			3 38	3 48	3 57	3 57		4 9	4 9	
59 60 61 62														Crewe and Preston N.U. [4]		4aL17	4aL17	
63		3U21	3U23				3 41	3 41			3 46	3 56	4 6	4 6		4 19	4 19	

Appendix 1/7

CAMDEN TO LICHFIELD   *1757-1726*

DOWN

Station		#	To Edge Hill (D) SO	To Toton (D) TTh SO	D§ SX	K SO [117]	L E (G) SX [31]	To Colwick (F)	9.25 pm empties Bletchley Flettons Loop to Toton (F) SO	L E to Northampton Bridge Street (G) ThO	To Walsall (D) SX	Watford Yard dep 8.45 pm (D) ThSX	7.20 pm from Banbury (F) ThO	Watford Yard dep 8.45 pm (D) ThO	To Walsall (E) SO	E B V (G) SX [154]	D SX
CAMDEN .. dep	1		PM 7 35 SL	PM	PM	PM 7 43 SL	PM 7|50 SL	PM	PM	PM	PM 7 55 SL	PM	PM	PM	PM 8 15 SL	PM	PM 8 23 SL
Kilburn High Road	2																
Queen's Park	3																
Willesden Junction .. arr	4																
.. dep	5		7 45			7 58	8 0				8 8				8 27		8 33
BRENT SIDINGS .. arr	6					8 10											8 40
.. dep	7			7N45													
Sudbury Junction	8			8X5 SL													
North Wembley	9																
Harrow and Wealdstone	10					F											
Hatch End	11		8X6												SL		
Bushey and Oxhey	12		FL												8 53		
Watford Junction .. arr	13														8 59		
.. dep	14		8 14	8 24						8 32		8 50 8X52 SL		8 50 8X52	8 49		
King's Langley	15																
Hemel Hempstead and B.	16																
Bourne End	17																
Berkhamsted	18																
Tring	19		8 36	8 50								9 8	9 18	9 18	9 16		
Cheddington	20					WO Q										G	
Leighton Buzzard .. arr	21																
.. dep	22																
BLETCHLEY .. arr	23					8 56 GL							8 56				
.. dep	24		8 57	9 13		GL			9X30 SL	9 28	9 38	9X34 SL	9 44		9 41		
Wolverton	25																
Castlethorpe	26																
ROADE .. arr	27																
.. dep	28		9 21	9Y33		K			10 0	9 49	9 59	10 3	10 13	10 13	10 10	ThX	
Middleton	29		9 27	9Y39					10 7	9 57	10 7		10 19	10 19	10 17		
Blisworth .. arr	30																
.. dep	31									9|52		10R12			10 10		
Gayton	32																
Weedon	33																
Hillmorton	34					85											
NORTHAMPTON Carr	35					SO											
.. dep	36		9 33	9Y45		10 5 GL			10X15 GL	10 4	10X15 GL	10 20	10X43 GL	10X25 GL	10X24 GL		
NORTHAMPTON arr	37			9|Y50		10 10 GL						10 48	10 30	10 29			
DOWN SDGS. .. dep	38			9*59		10L20								11 9			
Althorp Park	39					11*15		10 45									
Long Buckby	40		9 55											11 35			
Kilsby and Crick	41									10 26							
Hillmorton	42		10 8											11 49			
RUGBY MIDLAND .. arr	43		10E15							10 37				11 54			
.. dep	44		GL 10X*54 FL							GL 11 2				GL 12 24			
Brinklow	45																
Midland Junction	46			Y—3 minutes later SO													
NUNEATON T.V. .. arr	47					9 5											

Station	#	L E (G) SX	K SX Q	L E (G) SO	To Carnforth (C) SX	8.37 pm, Broad St. to Stockport (C) SO	10.5 pm L E from Seaton (G) SO	To Brewery Sidings (C) SX	To Hooton (D) SX	To Manchester London Road (D) SX	To Carlisle Kingmoor (D) SO	To Crewe (D) SX	To Hillhouse (D) SX Q	To Warrington (D) SX	10.2 pm, Broad Street to Stockport (C) SX
	[20]		[20]	[90]											
	1	PM 8|28 SL	PM 8 28 SL	PM 8||28 SL	PM 8 50 SL	PM 8X55 SL	PM	PM 8 55 SL	PM	PM 9 20 SL	PM 9 25 SL	PM 9 28 SL	PM 9 45 SL	PM 9 55 SL	PM 10X20 SL
	2														
	3		8 43												
	4														10L30
	5	8 43		8 43	8 59	9 9		9 9		9 35	9 35	9 43	9 55	10 10	10X32 FL
	6														

Appendix 2

Listing of Main Line Departures from London (Euston) in 1898 and 1908 (Weekdays)

1898

Time	Destination(s)
5.15	Newspapers express, Crewe. Connection at Crewe for Carlisle due 1/03
7.15	Irish and North Mail, Crewe. Via Birmingham. Portions added for Holyhead Manchester, Liverpool, Carlisle
7.30	Manchester (12/05) via Stoke-on-Trent
8.05	Birmingham, Manchester, Liverpool (attach at Birmingham for Carlisle)
9.20	Birmingham express (11.40)
9.30	Irish day express, Holyhead
10.0	Scotch express (Carlisle at 4/25). 15-minute refreshment break at Preston
10.10	Liverpool and Manchester express, divided at Crewe
Noon	Special express, Liverpool Riverside. Vestibuled train. Runs on 4 days in May only
Noon	Birmingham, Stoke and Manchester express
12/10	Liverpool express
12/30	Special express, Liverpool. Vestibuled train including luncheon carriages. Runs 4 days in May
1/30	Birmingham, Shrewsbury, Welshpool and North Wales express
2/0	Corridor and dining saloon express, Preston and Carlisle
2/10	Manchester, Liverpool, Southport and Windermere express
4/0	Stoke-on-Trent and Manchester express
4/10	Dining cars. Liverpool/Shrewsbury, Welshpool and Bangor*
4.10	SO Special American mail to Chester
4/30	Birmingham express
5/30	Dining cars. Liverpool and Manchester. Divided at Crewe
5/35	Birmingham and Manchester express. Slip carriage for Blisworth SX
6/30	Greenore (Ireland) Boat Express. Dining car to Holyhead
8/0	SX Scotch Express. (Carlisle 2.12) Glasgow sleeping carriages
8/45	Irish Mail, Holyhead
8/50	Birmingham, Preston, Carlisle
10/0	Manchester, Liverpool (to Crewe), Carlisle
10/15	Irish Night Express
11/50	Sleeping saloon express, Glasgow, Edinburgh
Midnight	Sleeping saloon express, Liverpool, Manchester, Preston, Chester, Carlisle Sux

---

* Slip carriage for Nuneaton. Slip carriage for Aylesbury conveyed on 6/0 Bletchley service

1908

Time	Destination(s)
5.0	Birmingham, Manchester, Liverpool, Chester, Preston, Carlisle (12/33)
7.10	Birmingham, Stoke-on-Trent, Manchester, Chester
8.0	Birmingham, Breakfast Car Express
8.30	Irish Mail, Holyhead
9.20	Birmingham. Carriage for Northampton slipped at Blisworth. Through carriage for Leamington Spa
10.0	Luncheon and dining car express. Glasgow, Edinburgh, Dundee, Aberdeen
10.10	Birmingham, Manchester, Liverpool, Carlisle
10.30	Liverpool, Manchester, East Lancashire. Luncheon car express. Through carriages for Blackburn, Accrington, Burnley, Colne
10.37	Crewe. Carriage for Buxton slipped at Nuneaton, then via Burton and Ashbourne
11.50	Birmingham. Luncheon car express
12/10	Liverpool, Manchester, Birkenhead. Luncheon car express
12/15	Stoke-on-Trent, Manchester (4/45)
12/25	Liverpool. Through carriages to Southport
1/20	Irish Boat Express. Holyhead, Kingstown Pier
2/0	Glasgow, Edinburgh, Aberdeen. Corridor luncheon and dining car express
2/20	Pass Willesden Junction. Eastbourne, Brighton. Luncheon and tea corridor express
2/40	Liverpool, Southport, Manchester, East Lancashire, Windermere, Shrewsbury. Through carriage for Shrewsbury slipped at Rugeley. Through carriage for Colne
4/5	Stoke-on-Trent, Manchester, East Lancashire express. Carriage for Banbury slipped at Bletchley
4/10	Birmingham, Preston. Through carriages for Bangor, Blackpool North
4/30	Rugby. Through carriage for Melton Mowbray
4/45	Birmingham tea car express. Carriage for Leamington Spa slipped
5/30	Belfast Dining Car Express. Through carriages for Fleetwood, Birkenhead. Carriage for Buxton slipped at Nuneaton
5/35	Manchester, Liverpool, Chester, Preston
5/55	Liverpool Dining Car Express
6/5	Manchester and East Lancashire Dining Car Express. Carriage for Northampton slipped at Blisworth
6/55	Birmingham, Wolverhampton (B'ham 8/55)
7/0	Birmingham, Wolverhampton
7/30	SX Belfast and North of Ireland Dining Car Express via Holyhead
8/0	SX Belfast and North of Ireland Dining Car Express via Carlisle, Stranraer
8/45	Irish Mail, Holyhead
8/50	Glasgow sleeping car express
10/0	Manchester, Liverpool, Chester, Preston, Carlisle. Divided at Crewe
10/15	Irish Night Express, Holyhead
11/50	Glasgow, Edinburgh, sleeping car express
Midnight	Birmingham, Manchester, Liverpool, Chester. Also Sux Preston, Carlisle
0.10	Birmingham, Liverpool, Manchester sleeping saloon express

Appendix 3

Listing of Main Line Passenger Train Departures from London (Euston) in 1935 and 1956 (Weekdays, Winter)

1935

Time	Destination(s)
0.30	Glasgow St E, Manchester
0.35	Liverpool, TC Blackpool C, TC Preston
7.0	Windermere, Barrow, Whitehaven
8.30	Birmingham, Manchester
8.40	Holyhead
9.0	Wolverhampton
9.10	Wolverhampton (fast)
10.0	Glasgow, Edinburgh, Stranraer, Aberdeen
10.30	Manchester, TC Colne, TC Halifax, TC Pwllheli, TC Bangor, TC Birkenhead
10.40	Liverpool, TC Southport, TC Swansea
10.40	Carlisle, TC Llandudno, TC Windermere, TC Whitehaven, TC Blackpool N
11.20	Wolverhampton
11.50	Manchester, Liverpool, TC Birkenhead
12/05	Crewe, Birmingham
1/30	Glasgow C, Edinburgh, Aberdeen, TC Whitehaven
2/20	Wolverhampton
2/40	Liverpool, TC Southport, TC Birkenhead
2/50	Manchester, TC Blackburn
4/0	Liverpool, Carlisle
4/10	Manchester, Birmingham, TC Melton Mowbray
4/35	Stafford via Wolverhampton, TC Walsall
5/20	Preston, TC Barrow, TC Blackpool C, TC Birkenhead, TC New Brighton, TC Holyhead
5/50	Wolverhampton
6/0	Manchester
6/05	Liverpool
6/10	Heysham, TC Colne, TC Heysham
6/55	Wolverhampton
7/0	Birmingham (slow)
7/30	Inverness, Aberdeen (restaurant car to Crewe)
7/40	Stranraer (Note 1)

Time	Destination(s)
8/30	Glasgow, Aberdeen (Note 2)
8/50	Holyhead
9/25	Glasgow C
9/35	Birmingham
10/50	Aberdeen, Edinburgh, Dundee
11/45	Glasgow C
11/55	Crewe

Notes
1. also conveyed milk tank wagons for Dumfries
2. Royal Mail travelling post office train

1956

Time	Destination(s)
0.02	Crewe
0.20	Glasgow, TC Preston
0.30	Liverpool
0.40	Manchester
6.40	Windermere, Barrow, Workington
7.55	Liverpool, Manchester
8.30	Liverpool, Manchester
8.50	Wolverhampton
9.0	Wolverhampton
9.45	Manchester, TC Colne (forward from Stockport)
10.0	Glasgow, Perth (forward from Crewe to Carlisle)
10.40	Carlisle, TC Lancaster (Barrow), TC Windermere
10.50	Blackpool N, TC Holyhead (forward from Crewe)
11.45	Manchester, TC Barrow, TC Workington (both forward from Crewe)
Noon	Crewe, TC Birmingham (forward from Rugby)
12/30	Liverpool
12/50	Wolverhampton
1/30	Glasgow
1/35	Perth, TC Blackpool N (forward from Crewe)
2/20	Wolverhampton
2/30	Liverpool, TC Southport, TC Birkenhead (Notes 1, 2)
2/45	Manchester, TC Colne (forward from Stockport)
3/45	Manchester
4/30	Manchester, TC Heysham (forward from Crewe)
4/37	Wolverhampton
4/55	Liverpool
5/05	Blackpool C
5/35	Holyhead, TC Llandudno, TC Birkenhead (each forward from Chester)
5/50	Wolverhampton

Time	Destination(s)
6/0	Manchester
6/10	Liverpool, TC Southport (forward from Edge Hill)
6/20	Heysham
6/30	Preston, TC Colne, TC Manchester (each forward from Crewe)
6/55	Wolverhampton
7/0	Birmingham
7/20	Inverness (restaurant car to Crewe)
7/30	Perth, TC Stranraer (forward from Carlisle)
8/30	Glasgow, Aberdeen (Note 3)
8/50	Holyhead
9/10	Glasgow
9/25	Glasgow (TC ex Penzance forward from Crewe)
9/35	Birmingham
10/45	Manchester
10/52	Perth
11/05	Windermere, TC Blackpool N (forward from Crewe)
11/50	Glasgow St E

Notes
1. carriages for Southport detached at Edge Hill
2. carriages for Birkenhead forward from Crewe
3. Royal Mail travelling post office train

Titled trains (winter)

Time	Destination(s)
7.55	*The Lancastrian* (from 1957)
9.45	*The Comet*
10.0	*Royal Scot*
12/30	*The Red Rose*
1/30	*The Mid-Day Scot*
4/55	*The Shamrock*
5/35	*The Emerald Isle Express*
5/50	*The Midlander*
6/0	*The Mancunian*
6/10	*The Merseyside Express*
6/30	*The Ulster Express*
7/20	*The Royal Highlander* (from 1957)
8/50	*The Irish Mail*

Note: *The Caledonian* (added from summer 1957)

Listing of Locomotives Designed for the LMS by Sir William Stanier

Class	Wheel arrangement	Date of build	Total	Note
Princess Royal	4-6-2	1933	2	
Princess Royal	4-6-2	1935	10	
Princess Royal	4-6-2	1935	1	1
Mixed traffic 5	2-6-0	1933/4	40	
Tank 4P	2-6-4	1934	37	
Jubilee	4-6-0	1934-36	191	2
Jubilee	4-6-0	1942	2	
8F	2-8-0	1935-46	852	3
Mixed traffic 5	4-6-0	1935-51	842	4
Tank 3P	2-6-2	1935	139	
Royal Scot	4-6-0	1935	1	5
Royal Scot conversion	4-6-0	1943-55	70	6
Princess Coronation	4-6-2	1937-48	38	
Tank 4P	2-6-4	1945-51	277	7
Patriot conversion	4-6-0	1945-49	18	

Notes
1. Turbomotive, rebuilt, destroyed in accident at Harrow and Wealdstone 8 Oct 1952
2. Total includes 45637 destroyed 8 Oct 1952 and 45735/6 built as Class 7
3. Total includes locomotives for war-time service overseas
4. Total includes developments following retirement of Stanier
5. Components from scrapped loco 6399 used
6. Total includes as note 5
7. Development by C. Fairburn

The mixed traffic 2-6-0 type is shown here represented by 42968 and hauling a fine set of LMS/ BR design carriages at the Severn Valley Railway. (82)

Black 5 4-6-0 45428 'purchased in running condition from BR' is seen at work at the North Yorkshire Moors Rialway. (83)

Steam on main line excursions can still be enjoyed. Here Jubilee 45699 (as 45562) is with Royal Scot Class 46115 at Bessy Gill. (84)

46100 Royal Scot is seen here in preservation during a visit to the Severn Valley Railway. (85)

Duchess of Sutherland *on its old stamping ground at Linslade. (86)*

Listing of Visits to, and Times in, Crewe Works by Princess Coronation and Princess Royal Class Locomotives Between 1957 and 1959

Notes

A   Classified repair work only
B   Does not include visits purely for fitment of automatic warning system and fitment of speedometers
C   On a few occasions, locomotives had to be returned for rectification work
D   *Princess Coronation* 46231 was taken in to St Rollox works at Glasgow in December 1957 for a Light Casual repair over four days, including 25/26 December.

Princess Coronation Class – Works Visits

Year and month	Loco	Dates			
		1 – 8	9 – 17	18 – 24	25 – 31
1956 Dec	46228	IN 1			
	46231		IN 12		
	46252		IN 15		
1957 Jan	46228		OUT 17 HI 38		
	46229			IN 21	
	46230	IN 7			
	46231			OUT 26 LI 37	
	46232	IN 5			
	46238	IN 4			OUT 31 LI 23
	46248	IN 7			
	46252				OUT 26 HG 34
	46256	IN 7			
	46257	IN 5			
Feb	46220		IN 12		
	46230		OUT 16 HI 35		

Year and month	Loco	Dates 1 – 8	9 – 17	18 – 24	25 – 31
1957 cont					
	46232				OUT 26 G 41
	46239	IN 8			
	46248			OUT 19 HG 37	
	46256	OUT 2 LC 23			
	46257			OUT 19 HI 30	
Mar	46220			OUT 22 LI 33	
	46226				IN 28
	46229	OUT 2 HI 38			
	46239		OUT 15 HC 30		
	46240				IN 25
	46242				IN 27
	46246				IN 25
	46254		IN 11		
Apr	46222			IN 19	
	46223	IN 8			
	46242		OUT 17 HG 22		
	46254		OUT 17 HG 32		
May	46223		OUT 17 HI 34		
	46226		OUT 10 HG 36		
	46234		IN 15		
	46236		IN 10		
	46240		OUT 10 LI 39		
	46244				IN 25
	46246	OUT 2 HG 32			
June	46220	OUT 1 HI 37			
	46227			IN 24	
	46236		OUT 15 LI 31		
July	46224				IN 27
	46234	OUT 5 HG 44			
	46244		OUT 11 HG 40		
	46249				IN 26
August	46225		IN 15		
	46227		OUT 17 LC 47		
	46234		IN 13		
	46249	OUT 3 HG 31			
	46251	IN 3			
	46255			IN 20	
	46221				IN 28
Sept	46224			OUT 24 HG 50	
	46225				OUT 28 HI 38
	46234		OUT 14 HC 28		

Year and month	Loco	Dates 1 – 8	9 – 17	18 – 24	25 – 31
1957 cont					
	46237		IN 9		
	46251			OUT 21 HG 42	
Oct	46237			OUT 19 HG 35	
	46243	IN 8			
	46250			IN 21	
Nov	46221		OUT 9 LI 35		
	46223		IN 9		
	46227		IN 17		
	46243		OUT 16 HG 34		
	46245		IN 12		
	46250				OUT 30 HG 50
Dec	46223		OUT 14 LC 31		
	46245				OUT 28 LI 38
	46253	IN 4			
	46255	OUT 2 HG 64			
	46257	IN 3			
1958 Jan	46235		IN 14		
	46239			IN 21	
	46241	IN 1			
	46242			IN 18	
	46250			IN 21	
	46253				OUT 25 HG 43
	46257				OUT 24 LI 43
Feb	46227	OUT 8 LI 73			
	46233			IN 24	
	46235				OUT 26 HG 37
	46241		OUT 11 HG 35		
	46250			OUT 20 LC 26	
	46252				IN 28
Mar	46231				IN 51
	46232	IN 3			
	46234			IN 19	
	46239	OUT 1 HI 34			
	46242	OUT 1 HI 36			
	46256				IN 25
Apr	46232		OUT 12 HI 34		
	46233		OUT 12 HI 40		
	46234				OUT 25 LC 31

Year and month	Loco	Dates			
		1 – 8	**9 – 17**	**18 – 24**	**25 – 31**
1958 cont					
	46247		IN 10		
	46248				IN 25
	46252		OUT 11 HI 41		
May	46220			IN 19	
	46228		IN 9		
	46231			OUT 23 G 46	
	46236				IN 26
	46238	IN 6			
	46247			OUT 24 LI 38	
	46256				OUT 27 LI 53
June	46220				OUT 26 HI 35
	46225		IN 13		
	46228			OUT 21 HI 37	
	46238			OUT 20 HI 39	
	46240	IN 3			
	46248	OUT 6 LI 36			
July	46229		IN 14		
	46236		OUT 11 HG 40		
	46240		OUT 17 HG 38		
	46254			IN 22	
	46255	IN 8			
Aug	46225	OUT 7 HG 47			
	46230	IN 4			
	46255			OUT 23 LC 40	
Sep	46223				IN 30
	46229		OUT 10 HI 50		
	46230		OUT 17 HI 35		
	46243	IN 7			
	46244		IN 13		
	46246	IN 2			
	46254	OUT 5 LI 39			
Oct	46226		IN 15		
	46243		OUT 11 HI 33		
	46244			OUT 24 HI 35	
	46246		OUT 9 LI 32		
	46251	IN 18			
Nov	46221		IN 17		
	46223		OUT 15 HI 40		
	46226				OUT 28 HI 38
	46237	IN 5			

Year and month	Loco	Dates			
		1 – 8	9 – 17	18 – 24	25 – 31
1958 cont	46249		IN 13		
	46251			OUT 22 HI 30	
Dec	46222	IN 5			
	46237		OUT 11 LI 31		
	46254	IN 5			
1959 Jan	46221	OUT 1 HI 37			
	46222				OUT 27 G 43
	46232				OUT 26 LI 41
	46234				IN 25
	46237		IN 1G		
	46241				IN 27
	46249		OUT 17 LI 54		
	46252	IN 7			
	46254		OUT 10 LC 29		
Feb	46227		IN 16		
	46234				OUT 28 LI 29
	46237	IN 2			
	46239			OUT 18 HC 28	
	46245	IN 9			
	46252		OUT 13 HI 32		
Mar	46232		OUT 14 LI 41		
	46239		OUT 13 HG 34		
	46241	OUT 7 HI 34			
	46245			OUT 20 HI 34	
	46252		IN 16		
	46253				IN 31
Apr	46220	IN 2			
	46224	IN 3			
	46227	OUT 4 LI 40			
	46240			IN 21	
	46242	IN 2			
	46252	OUT 2 LC 18			
	46255		IN 12		
May	46220		OUT 9 HI 35		
	46224			OUT 20 LI 40	
	46235			IN 20	
	46240				OUT 30 HI 34
	46250	IN 2			

Year and month	Loco	Dates			
		1 – 8	**9 – 17**	**18 – 24**	**25 – 31**
<u>1959</u> <u>cont</u>					
	46253	OUT 8 LI 33			
	46255				OUT 25 LI 35
June	46235				OUT 27 HI 33
	46242		OUT 9 HG 67		
	46247	IN 2			
	46248				IN 28
	46250		OUT 17 LI 35		
	46256	IN 8			
July	46228	IN 3			
	46231			IN 22	
	46247				OUT 25 HG 46
	46257		IN 13		
Aug	46229		IN 17		
	46230		IN 17		
	46233	IN 1			
	46236				IN 28
	46248			OUT 22 HG 47	
	46251		IN 14		
	46254		IN 15		
	46256		OUT 15 HG 60		
Sep	46221		IN 10		
	46222		IN 9		
	46228	OUT 2 HG 52			
	46231		OUT 12 HI 45		
	46233				OUT 26 HG 48
	46246			IN 20	
	46251				OUT 25 LI 36
	46257	IN 4			
Oct	46221				OUT 30 LC 43
	46224	IN 5			
	46229	OUT 8 HG 45			
	46232			IN 19	
	46243			IN 19	
	46254		OUT 16 HI 53		
	46257			OUT 24 HC 43	
Nov	46222		OCT 13 LC 56		
	46225	IN 6			
	46230	OUT 6 HC 70			
	46236	OUT 5 LI 59			
	46250	IN 5			

Year and month	Loco	Dates			
		1 – 8	**9 – 17**	**18 – 24**	**25 – 31**
1959 cont Dec	46224	OUT 4 LC 52			
	46232	OUT 5 LC 41			
	46238		IN 12		
	46243			OUT 18 HG 52	
	46250	OUT 4 LC 25			
1960 Jan	46225	OUT 1 LI 46			
Feb	46238		OUT 12 HI 51		

Princess Royal Class – Works Visits

Year and month	Loco	Dates			
		1 – 8	**9 – 17**	**18 – 24**	**25 – 31**
1956 Nov	46210				IN 26
Dec	46209	IN 3			
1957 Jan	46200				IN 29
	46201	IN 1			
	46204				IN 26
	46209		OUT 11 LC 32		
	46210	OUT 4 LC 32			
Feb	46201	OUT 2 HC 28			
	46208			IN 20	
Mar	46200	OUT 2 HC 28			
	46204	OUT 2 HI 29			
	46205			IN 20	
	46207				IN 29
	46212	IN 4			
Apr	46208	OUT 3 HG 36			
	46210		IN 16		
	46212	OUT 6 HI 29			
May	46201	IN 6			
	46205	OUT 4 HI 38			
	46207		OUT 15 LI 39		
	46210				OUT 25 HC 33

Year and month	Loco	Dates			
		1 – 8	9 – 17	18 – 24	25 – 31
1957 cont					
June	46201		OUT 11 LC 31		
	46203	IN 1			
	46211		IN 12		
July					
Aug	46203	OUT 3 LC 34			
	46204	IN 2			
	46211		OUT 10 HI 51		
Sep	46208			IN 18	
Oct	46203			IN 18	
	46204		OUT 10 LC 43		
	46208			OUT 22 LC 29	
	46209				IN 28
	46212	IN 6			
Nov	46201			IN 19	
	46212		OUT 9 LC 29		
Dec	46203	OUT 7 LC 43			
	46205			IN 23	
	46209		OUT 11 LI 38		
1958					
Jan	46201		OUT 11 LI 44		
	46206			IN 21	
Feb	46205		OUT 13 LC 43		
	46208			IN 20	
	46210		IN 13		
	46212	IN 5			
Mar	46200		IN 9		
	46206	OUT 7 HG 39			
	46207	IN 8			
	46210				OUT 29 HG 38
	46212		OUT 15 HG 33		
Apr	46208	OUT 2 LC 35			
May	46207		OUT 9 HC 52		
June	46200	OUT 6 HI 67			
	46203		IN 13		
July	46204	IN 4			
	46211	IN 5			
Aug	46203		OUT 14 HG 53		
	46204				OUT 29 LI 48
	46205		IN 14		
	46208		IN 13		

Year and month	Loco	Dates			
		1 – 8	**9 – 17**	**18 – 24**	**25 – 31**
<u>1958</u> <u>cont</u>					
Sep	46200			IN 22	
	46207			IN 24	
	46208			OUT 24 LI 36	
	46211		OUT 12 HG 59		
	46212	IN 1			
Oct	46200			OUT 22 LC 27	
	46201	IN 6			
	46205	OUT 2 HG 42			
	46207			OUT 24 LC 26	
	46209	IN 8			
Nov	46200	IN 6			
	46204		IN 15		
	46207		IN 17		
	46212		OUT 12 HG 62		
Dec	46200	OUT 6 HC 27			
	46201			OUT 23 HI 67	
	46207	OUT 5 LC 16			
	46208	IN 8			
	46209		OUT 10 HG 54		
<u>1959</u>					
Jan	46204		OUT 10 HC 46		
	46207		IN 17		
	46208			OUT 20 LC 35	
Feb	46206	IN 4			
	46209	IN 4			
	46211	IN 2			
Mar	46207		OUT 14 LC 48		
	46211		OUT 14 LC 35		
Apr	46200				IN 29
	46201		IN17		
	46204				IN 29
	46206	OUT 4 HI 50			
	46212	IN 5			
May	46201		OUT 14 LC 23		
	46207		IN 14		
	46209			OUT 22 LC 91	
June	46200			OUT 18 LC 43	
	46204		OUT 17 LC 38		
	46212	OUT 3 LC 50			
July	46207	OUT 8 LI 47			

Year and month	Loco	Dates			
		1 – 8	9 – 17	18 – 24	25 – 31
1959 cont Aug	46209				IN 26
	46210				IN 24
Sep	46203		IN 9		
	46204				IN 29
Oct	46209	OUT 3 LC 35			
	46210			OUT 24 HI 53	
Nov	46203	OUT 6 HI 50			
	46204				OUT 27 LI 51
	46208		IN 12		
	46212		IN 12		
Dec	46200		IN 14		
1960 Jan	46200				OUT 30 HG 39
	46208		OUT 13 HG 51		
	46212			OUT 19 HG 56	

Appendix 6

Listing of Main Line Passenger Trains Passing Through Preston North Union, Chester (General) and Tamworth Low Level on Summer Saturdays in 1960

Time	Arrive, depart or pass	Direction	Train	Reporting Number
Preston North Union 10.15 – 1/0				
10.17	a	d	6.15 Coventry – Blackpool N	439
10.19	d	u	9.26 Morecambe E Rd – B'ham	286
10.28	d	u	9.35 Morecambe E Rd – Man V	336
10.32	p	u	9.45 Blackpool C – Euston	330
10.43	p	d	5.45 Desford N – Blackpool N	M3
10.43	p	d	8.14 Eccles – Blackpool N	C299
10.47	p	u	10.0 Blackpool C – Bletchley	324
10.50	d	u	8.20 Carlisle – B'ham	456
10.51	a	d	9.15 Crewe – Glasgow C	241
10.52	p	u	10.25 Blackpool N – L'str L Rd	M336
11.0	a	d	9.25 Crewe – Aberdeen	27
11.02	d	u	7.13 Workington M – Euston	70
11.03	p	d	9.0 Stoke-on-Trent – B'pl N	351
11.08	p	d	9.40 Crewe – Blackpool N	389
11.16	d	u	8.40 Carlisle – Euston	74
11.23	p	u	10.55 Blackpool N – Coventry	412
11.27	p	d	8.50 Sheffield M – B'pl C	M5
11.34	p	d	8.34 Walsall – Blackpool N	257
11.40	p	u	11.15 Blackpool N – Crewe	384
11.43	p	d	7.25 Nottingham M – B'pl N	M7
11.55	a	d	8.25 Coventry – Blackpool N	443
11.56	p	d	9.43 Stoke-on-Trent – B'pl N	123
Noon	a	d	10.55 Man V – Blackpool N	C174
12/07	a	d	7.50 Northampton – M'cbe E Rd	373
12/13	p	u	11.45 Blackpool N – Coventry	262
12/15	p	d	6.35 L'str C - Blackpool N	C326
12/20	d	u	12/20 Preston – Wigan N W	-
12/22	p	u	8.22 Workington M – Crewe	76

Map 22: Preston Area

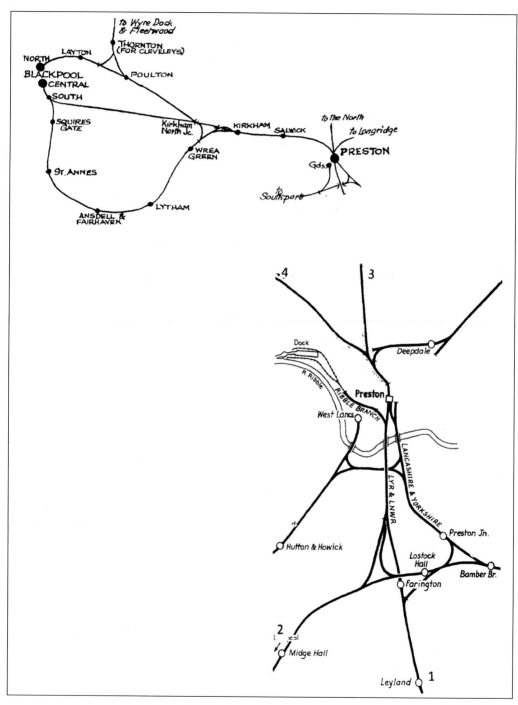

Key

1 Main line to Wigan and Warrington
2 To Liverpool

3 Main line to Lancaster and Carlisle
4 To Blackpool

Time	Arrive, depart or pass	Direction	Train	Reporting Number
Preston North Union 10.15 – 1/0 (cont/...)				
12/28	a	d	11.0 Crewe – Workington M	273
12/29	p	u	Noon B'pl N – Warrington BQ	200
12/34	p	d	7.36 Bletchley – Blackpool N	441
12/43	d	u	10.50 Windermere – Euston	86
12/46	a	d	9.15 B'ham – Morecambe E Rd	295
12/49	p	d	7.25 Cleethorpes – B'pl N	C452
12/52	p	u	12/25 Blackpool C – Euston	396
12/56	a	d	6.30 Euston – Windermere	33
12/58	d	u	12/15 Blackpool N – B'ham	264
1/01	a	d	7.35 Cardiff – Blackpool N	297
Chester General 10.0 – 1/0				
10.0	a	u	7.30 Holyhead – Euston	48
10.05	a	u	9.20 Rhyl – Birmingham	244
10.17	a	d	7.47 B'ham – Llandudno	345
10.20	a	u	8.45 Llandudno – Leicester	218
10.23	a	d	9.15 Lpl – Llandudno	403
10.25	d		Chester – Ruabon	WR
10.32	p	d	9.25 Man – Llandudno	C369
10.34	a	u	9.05 Llandudno – Euston	56
10.36	a	u	9.15 Llandudno – Newcastle	236
10.36	p	d	Birkh'd – Llandudno	439
10.40	p	d	9.33 Stoke-on-Trent – Lldno	173
10.44	p	d	10.15 Q Wolvhpton – Bangor	355
10.47	a	u	9.22 Lldno – Leamington Spa Ave	226
10.50	a	u	10.10 Rhyl – Manchester	486
10.50	p	d	8.35 B'ham – Llandudno	329
10.54	a	d	8.10 B'ham – Birkenhead	WR
10.55	a	d	9.36 Liverpool – Penychain	399
10.59	p	d	Smethwick – Lldno	D
11.03	p	d	9.45 Manchester – Lldno	C401
11.04	a	u	9.45 Lldno – Manchester	242
11.10	a	u	8.10 Holyhead – Liverpool	238
11.12	a	d	7.45 Leamington Spa – B'head	WR
11.15	a	u	10.30 Prestatyn – Man	234
11.17	a	d	10.06 Manchester – Holyhead	C421
11.20	a	d	9.06 B'ham – Holyhead	185
11.22	a	u	10.23 Abergele – Man	210
11.23	a	u	B'head – Chester	WR
11.25	p	d	10.30 Lpl – Llandudno	405
11.27	p	u	8.10 Afonwen – Man	460
11.28	a	d	10.44 Crewe – Rhyl	87
11.30	p	d	10.20 Man – Llandudno	C375

Map 23: Chester Area

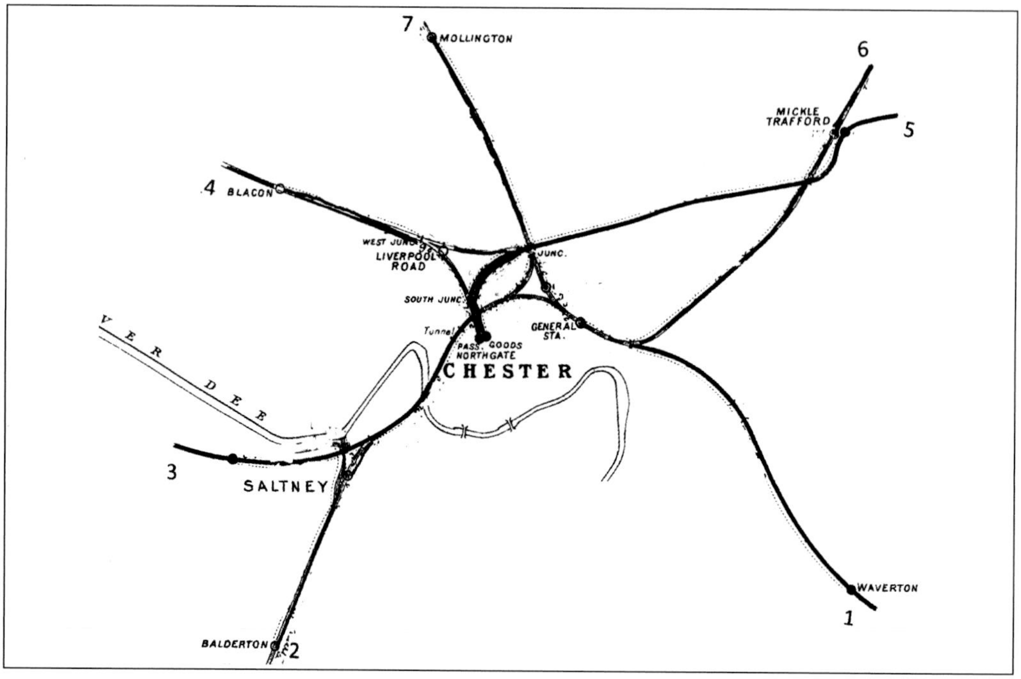

Key

1 To Crewe
2 To Shrewsbury
3 To Llandudno and Holyhead
4 To Birkenhead

5 To Northwich (Cheshire Lines Committee)
6 To Warrington
7 To Birkenhead

Time	Arrive, depart or pass	Direction	Train	Reporting Number
Chester General 10.0 – 1/0 (cont/...)				
11.31	a	u	10.0 Llandudno – Euston	66
11.37	p	d	8.45 Leeds City S – Lldno	444
11.38	a	u	10.15 Llandudno – Derby M	22
11.41	a	d	8.04 Leicester – Lldno	M32
11.48	a	d	9.27 Derby M – Llandudno	135
11.48	a	u	11.07 Llandudno - Lpl	490
11.55	a	d	10.25 Manchester – Valley	C457
11.55	a	u	10.30 Llandudno – Man	648
11.57	a	u	11.05 Rhyl – Stoke-on-Trent	108
12/05	d	d	Birkenhead	WR
12/07	a	d	7.35 Euston – Holyhead	49
12/07	a	u	9.20 Holyhead – Manchester	480
12/10	a	u	11.28 Birkenhead – Paddington	WR
12/14	a	u	8.45 Penychain – Stoke-on-Trent	164

Time	Arrive, depart or pass	Direction	Train	Reporting Number
Chester General 10.0 – 1/0 (cont/...)				
12/19	a	u	10.42 Llandudno – Cardiff	118
12/19	p	u	9.10 Q Penychain – Manchester	252
12/20	p	d	9.12 Leeds City S – Lldno	448
12/22	a	u	11.40 Birkenhead – Padgton	WR
12/25	d	u	Chester – Crewe	-
12/27	a	d	8.0 Euston – Holyhead	37
12/28	a	u	10.35 Caernarvon – Man	206
12/30	a	d	11.10 Man – Llandudno	C319
12/32	a	d	10.15 Wellington – B'head	WR
12/34	a	d	9.45 Bradford Ex – Lldno	C446
12/38	a	u	11.0 Llandudno – Liverpool	102
12/39	p	d	10.10 Sheffield Mid – Lldno	M66
12/40	d	d	Chester – Rhyl	-
12/42	a	d	8.23 Cardiff – Llandudno	227
12/43	a	u	9.45 Penychain – Manchester	138
12/45	d	d	Chester – Denbigh	-
12/50	a	u	11.15 Lldno – Sheffield Mid	496
1/0	a	d	11.25 Manchester - Lldno	C459
Tamworth Low Level 10.30 – 1/30				
10.28	p	u	8.0 Manchester V – Euston	1120
10.40	p	d	8.0 Euston – Holyhead	37
10.41	d	u	10.0 Stafford – Nuneaton	D6
10.53	d	u	8.08 Manchester V – Euston	1126
10.55	p	d	8.15 Euston – Liverpool	39

Map 24: Tamworth Station

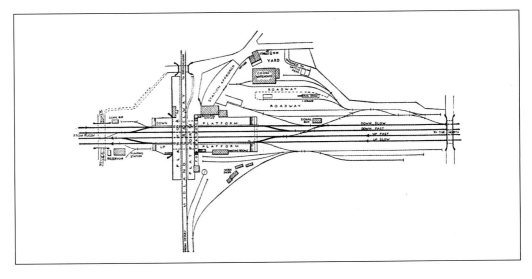

Time	Arrive, depart or pass	Direction	Train		Reporting Number
Tamworth Low Level 10.30 – 1/30(cont/...)					
11.12	p	u	8.0	Blackpool N – Euston	296
11.13	p	d	8.30	Euston – Manchester V	1501
11.17	p	u	9.22	Manchester V – Euston	1111
11.22	a	d	11.0	Nuneaton – Stafford	D6
11.33	p	d	9.05	Euston – Glasgow C	63
11.37	p	u	7.30	Holyhead – Euston	48
11.46	p	d	9.10	Euston – Liverpool	51
11.46	p	u	9.20	Q Lpl Riverside – Euston	476
11.52	p	d	9.25	Euston – Manchester V	1502
11.53	p	u	9.50	Liverpool – Euston	222
Noon	p	u	10.0	Liverpool – Euston	54
12/01	p	d	9.35	Euston – Manchester V	1502
12/07	p	u	8.0	Colne – Euston	C180
12/14	p	u	10.0	Man Ldn Rd – Euston	1121
12/16	p	d	9.50	Euston – Aberdeen	65
12/28	p	u	8.45	Llandudno – Leicester	218
12/32	p	d	10.0	Euston – Glasgow	57
12/41	p	d	10.15	Euston – Liverpool	71
12/46	d	u	9.05	Llandudno – Euston	56
12/54	d	u	12/17	Stafford – Nuneaton	D6
12/59	p	d	10.25	Euston – Carlisle	251
1/06	p	d	10.33	Euston – Blackpool	127
1/08	p	u	11.0	Liverpool – Euston	112
1/11	p	u	9.45	Blackpool C – Euston	330
1/19	p	u	10.0	Llandudno – Euston	66
1/21	p	d	11.45	Bletchley – Blackpool C	337
1/31	p	d	10.40	Euston – Blackpool N	77

Notes

Time 10.17 before noon 12/17 after noon

Arrive a Depart d Pass (non-stop) p

Direction d down, away from London or as defined locally

U up, towards London or as defined locally

Reporting numbers C Central Division (LM Region), M Midland Division, W Western Division, D6 Diesel multiple unit code, WR Western Region 11XX Manchester diversion

Q train ran as required

B'ham Birmingham New Street

B'head Birkenhead

Blackpool C Blackpool Central

Blackpool N Blackpool North

Reporting number W unless shown otherwise

Derby M Derby Midland

Glasgow C Glasgow Central

Leamington Spa Ave Leamington Spa Avenue (LM)

Lldno Llandudno

Lpl Liverpool Lime Street

Lstr C Leicester Central

Lstr Ldn Rd Leicester London Road

Man Ldn Road Manchester London Road

Man V Manchester Victoria

Morecambe E Rd, Morecambe Euston Road

Nottm M Nottingham Midland

Sheffield M Sheffield Midland

Workington M, Workington Main

Bibliography

Acworth, W.M., *Railways in 1843*
Allen, C.J., *British Express Trains*
Allison, J.E., *Mersey Docks and Harbour Board: Business in Great Waters*
Ashworth, W., *History of the British Coal Industry, volume 5*
Baker, A.C., *The Book of the Coronation Pacifics*
Barman, C., *Introduction to Railway Architecture*
Barman, C., *The Architecture of Railways*
Betjeman, J., *The Railheads of London*
Biddle, G., *The Oxford Companion to British Railways History*
Board of Trade Annual Railway Returns
Bonavia, M.R., *The Four Great Railways*
Bonavia, M.R., *The Organisation of British Railways*
Bourne, J.C., *Drawings of the London and Birmingham Railway*
Bradshaw's. Railway Manual, Shareholders Guide and Directory 1869, 1877, 1901
British Newspaper Library
British Rail Main Line Gradient Profiles
BTC, *Refreshment Car Circuits: Royal Journey*
Burtt, P., *The Principal Factors in Freight Train Operating*
Carter, C.S., *LMS-LMR Passenger Train Formations: 1923-89*
Chambers, J.G., *The Rise of Industrial Society in England 1815-85*
Cole, G., Arnot, R.P., *Trade Unionism on the Railways*
Conolly, W.P., *British Railways Pre-grouping Atlas and Gazetteer*
Dow, J.G., *The Management of the British Economy 1945-60*
Dyos, H., Aldcroft, D., *British Transport*
Elliot, Sir John, *Modern Railways On and Off the Rails*
Ellis, C.H., *The Golden Years*
Ellis, C.H., *The Midland Railway*
Empty Coaching Stock arrangements: Euston – Willesden
Engine Record Cards
Eyre Todd. G., *The London & North Western Railway*
Gourvish, T.R., *British Railways 1948-75*
Greaves, J.N., *Sir Edward Watkin*
Greville, M.D., Holt, G.O., *Railway Development in Liverpool*
Hansard
Haresnape, B., *Stanier Locomotives*
Hodgkins, D., *George Carr Glyn – Railwayman and Banker*
Institute of Locomotive Engineers *Journal*
Institute of Mechanical Engineers *Journal*
Johnson, J., Long, R.A., *British Railways Engineering 1948-80*

Journal of Transport History:1957 The Furness Railway
Journal of Transport History:1966 Northampton
Karmel, D., Potter, K., *The Transport Act 1953*
Lamb, D.R., *Modern Railway Operations 1926*
Lee, C.F., *Passenger Class Distinction*
Lloyd, R., *Racing to Scotland*
LMS Route books 3 and 4
Macaulay, J., Hall, C., *Modern Railway Works 1926*
McKillop, N., *The Lighted Flame*
Milne, D., Laing, H., *The Obligation to Carry*
Nock, O.S., *A History of the LMS*
Ottley, G., *A Bibliography of British Railway History*
Passenger timetables
Pearson, *Man of the Rails*
Radford, J.B., *History of Derby Carriage & Wagon Works*
Railway Magazine
Railway Observer
Reed, M.C., *Railways in the Victorian Economy*
Rogers. H.C., *Transition from Steam*
Rolt, L.T.C., *Red for Danger*
Rose, R.E., *The LMS & LNER in Manchester*
Sectional Appendices LMS/BR
Staff magazines LMR/Sc Region
Steel, W.L., *The History of the LNW Railway*
Stevens, W.J., *Home Railways as Investments 1897*
Talbot, E., *The Coronation Scot*
The Re-shaping of British Railways 1963
The Transport Act 1962
Trains Illustrated
Transport (Railway Freight Charges) *Journal*
Working Timetables

Photographs of Princess Coronation Class locomotives grace the cover of this book. Both 46229 and 46233 survived due to the fact they were purchased by Billy Butlin Ltd for display at holiday camps and later overhauled by new owners, the National Railway Museum and a Trust. Both locomotives have seen action on the main line network and, from time to time, at heritage railways. On the cover 46229 is shown at the Great Central Railway and 46233 at the East Lancashire Railway. (88)

Index